PRAISE FOR *DESTINED FOR*

Destined for Joy ranges over theological, biblical, and church-historical questions, providing accessible essays on each issue, building, step by step, to a broad, coherent, and powerfully persuasive account of the universal reach of the gospel. Throughout Father Kimel weaves together intellectual rigor, pastoral practicality, and sheer spiritual depth, along with a vulnerability that unfolds within some of the darkest places to which life can take us. The result is that as we read we are gently but persistently challenged to go deeper into God, and to know "a divine love that exceeds our capacity . . . to grasp it" (Eph 3:18-19). A wonderful book that proclaims a wonderful God.
— Douglas Campbell, Ph.D., Professor of New Testament at the Duke Divinity School and author of *Pauline Dogmatics: The Triumph of God's Love*

The God of Love cannot be a punitive deity. If everything is not restored, then our joy is incomplete and we are all lost. Al Kimel puts brilliantly the argument for full Christianity that has too rarely been made in the past. No other apologetic can now convince anyone in the future.
— John Milbank, Ph.D., Professor Emeritus of Theology and Religious Studies, University of Nottingham, and author of numerous books and essays, including *Theology and Social Theory, Being Reconciled*, and *The Suspended Middle*

An extensive and considered collection of essays, written and reworked over many years, on the topic of universal salvation, touching upon all aspects from the proclamation of the gospel to the historical controversies it provoked (and provokes) as well as the pastoral compassion it entails. This is an excellent entry point into the ancient topic of 'apokatastais' and the claim that God will be 'all in all.'
— Fr. John Behr, Ph.D., Regius Professor of Humanity, University of Aberdeen, and author of books including *John the Theologian and his Paschal Gospel, The Way to Nicaea* and *The Mystery of Christ*

This is a book that many of us have been waiting for for a long time—a collection of Alvin Kimel's mature theological musings on divine love, human freedom, hell, and universal restoration. Father Kimel is deeply orthodox (concerned to be true to biblical revelation, orthodox tradition, and rational reflection) and eclectic (attending to Orthodox, Catholic, and Protestant theological voices, past and present). The result is a set of reflections that are both theologically stimulating and pastorally sensitive. Heck!—the essay on whether the Fifth Ecumenical Council denounced universalism as heretical is worth the price of the book, even before one factors in the wealth of wisdom in the other essays. Enthusiastically recommended!
  — Robin A. Parry, Ph.D., Anglican priest, editor, and author of
    The Evangelical Universalist

Much of religion, but especially Christianity, is caricatured in the following way: do good and go to heaven; do bad and go to hell. After years of careful study of the Christian sources, Fr. Aidan shows convincingly that there is another way to think of what awaits us across the threshold of finitude and death. Grounded in a trinitarian, incarnational, and theotic logic, this book argues convincingly that, in the end, "nothing shall be able to separate us from the love of God which is in Christ Jesus our Lord" (Rom. 8:39).
  — Aristotle Papanikolaou, Ph.D., Professor of Theology, Archbishop
    Demetrios Chair in Orthodox Theology and Culture, Co-founding
    director, Orthodox Christian Studies Center

Every knee shall bow and every tongue confess that Jesus Christ is Lord." Militant threat or promise of indefatigable Love? Be prepared to be challenged. Buy a copy for your friends. This book should be on everyone's coffee table!
  — Robert F. Fortuin, Adjunct Professor of Orthodox
    Theology at St Katherine College

This is book that needs to be read back-to-front, starting with the homily at the end. Although labeled an appendix, it is not in fact back-matter; indeed, it lays bare the *heart* of the matter. First, foremost, it makes unmistakably clear what is at stake in these pages, which is everything,

really. And, second, it makes even more abundantly clear *who* it is that has written these words: not only a bereaved father and a wise and discerning priest, but also a God-wrought preacher spirited enough to say, in spite of everything, even Hemingway's nothing, the 'something more' that makes the Gospel truly glorious.
— Chris E. W. Green, Ph.D., Professor of Public Theology, Southeastern University, and author of *Surprised by God* and *All Things Beautiful*

Some worry that faith in Christ would wane and evangelical fervor would cool if universal salvation were believed to be true. Far less often noticed is what I encounter on a regular basis: not only do people lose faith before the prospect of unending conscious torment, but they regain it before the beauty of Christ's victory over Hell. And when these people experience the profound spiritual healing that comes by beholding the beauty of Christ's infinite love, they tend to ask for a single volume to read and recommend to others in their newfound desire for God. From now on I will unhesitatingly recommend Alvin Kimel's *Destined for Joy*.
— Jordan Daniel Wood, Ph.D., Catholic theologian and author of *The Whole Mystery of Christ: Creation as Incarnation in Maximus Confessor*

This book is typical Fr Aidan Kimel. Drawing together the fruits of many years' pastoral practice and theological thought, it expresses the cosmic hope he has learned by hard experience must rest at the heart of the Gospel. He happily and confidently trawls through the contributions to the deposit of faith made by figures across the Christian tradition, on the assumption that orthodoxy revels in the encounter with itself. In this respect, and in many others, the book is a joy to read - as names as diverse as George MacDonald and St Gregory of Nyssa meet in dialogue. If this was all Fr Kimel contributed to our contemporary apprehension of the Christian life (and it most certainly is not!), it would be enough; as an outstanding treatise on the God's limitless love, though, it is a work not to be missed.
— Fr. James Siemens, Ph.D., Orthodox priest and author of *The Christology of Theodore of Tarsus*

Long ago and astride a dung-beetle, Trygaeus stormed heaven and demanded to know why the gods had abandoned Athens. They absconded with their retinue, Hermes explains, because they wearied of their charges preferring war to peace. If war without end is what the Athenians wanted, receive it they shall. In our time Fr Kimel too braves the question of divine justice only now emboldened by God's revelation in Christ. Will he, too—like the gods of old—tire of us and permit struggle to reign as his regent? *Destined for Joy* risks scandalizing us anew with the Gospel's disclosure of a God whose mercy is profligate and deathless and terrible. Readers of all eschatological pieties will benefit from Fr Kimel's near-patristic gift for translating the idiom of theological abstraction into the homiletical style of kerygma.
— Justin Shaun Coyle, PhD., Associate Professor of Theology, Church History, & Philosophy at Mount Angel Seminary

Love is one of those fundamental words that gathers to itself both vagueness and too easy genuflection. And God defeats all human attempts at conceptual capture. So, it is with careful and dogged persistence that Fr. Kimel meditates upon the mystery of God's love. Meditations inspired by modern theologians like Bulgakov, Jenson and Hart are joined with patristic witness, close examination of the Fifth Ecumenical Council, appreciation for the mystical revelations of Julian of Norwich and poets such as George MacDonald to convey robust wrestling with the ardor of grace amidst the times. Ultimately, one is gifted a compelling vision of apokatastasis as the only fully convincing and just announcement of the good news of divine care for Creation.
— Brian C. Moore, Ph.D., author of *Beneath the Silent Heavens*

ALVIN F. KIMEL, JR.

DESTINED *for* JOY

THE GOSPEL OF
UNIVERSAL SALVATION

Destined for Joy is a production of
The Works of George MacDonald
worksofmacdonald.com

Copyright ©2022 by Alvin F. Kimel, Jr.
Cover art and design by Alexander von Ness, nessgraphica.com
Cover image: Resurrection of Christ and the Harrowing of Hell, 1500s. Egg tempera on wood, unknown Russian Icon painter. Ikonen-Museum, Recklinghausen
All rights reserved.
ISBN: 9798841664772

For My Beloved Son

Aaron Edward Kimel

1980 - 2012

"Renewed shall be blade that was broken"

Destined for Joy: The Gospel of Universal Salvation

CONTENTS

Foreword by Bradley Jersak	xi
Introduction	xiv

Part One: The Greater Hope and the Absolute Love of God   1

1.	The Astonishing Love of God	1
2.	The Wondrous Prodigality of God's Love for Sinners	7
3.	The Scandalous Injustice of Grace	20
4.	The God of Wrath and the Father of Jesus Christ	30
5.	The Radical Gospel of Unconditional Love	45
6.	The Gospel as Story and Promise	56
7.	The Explosive Nothing of Grace	82
8.	Preaching Very Good News: The Grammar of Apokatastasis	94
9.	Redemption Eternal: The Caponian Vision of Grace	106
10.	Sometimes Eternity Ain't Forever: *Aiónios* and the Universalist Hope	127

Part Two: The Greater Hope in History   152

11.	St Augustine and the Misericordes	153
12.	The Scourge of Love	168
13.	The Triumph of the Kingdom Over Gehenna	178

14. Will Satan Be Saved?	190
15. The Shewings of Julian of Norwich: How Well is Hell?	202
16. Did the Fifth Ecumenical Council Condemn Universal Salvation?	223

Part Three: The Gospel of Universal Salvation	**276**
17. Freedom for Hell?	277
18. Revealing the God Behind the Curtain	298
19. Doomed to Happiness	310
20. The Secret of the Greater Hope	332
21. Eternal Damnation and the Solidarity of Love	350
22. The Roar of Aslan and Afterlife Possibilities	362
23. Gehenna as Universal Purgatory	378
24. The Apokatastasis of Judas Iscariot	389
25. The Irresistible Truth of Final Judgment	399
Afterword by David Bentley Hart	406

Appendix

The Salvation of Lilith	412
Funeral Homily for Aaron Edward Kimel	420
Index	427

Foreword

Bradley Jersak, Ph.D.

With great joy, I have for a decade followed Fr. Aidan Kimel as he forged a path of inquiry that unveiled answers, of exploration that yielded discovery, of hope that became deep conviction—for me and many others. His biblical, historical, and philosophical posts have completely convinced me that the *apokatastasis panton* (the restoration of all things) is not merely a doctrinally tolerable idea—it is, as Fr Aidan says, "the gospel of Christ's absolute and unconditional love sung in an eschatological key."

As he has faithfully shared his treasury of findings, I have come to believe without reserve in Christ's bold claim that through his Passion he will indeed draw all of humanity and the entire cosmos to himself. For that reason, I now see *apokatastasis* as intrinsic and indispensable to proclaiming the ancient gospel in this fraught and faltering century.

In *Destined for Joy*, Fr Aidan has gathered a "best-of" collection of his insights that paint a vista I cannot now unsee, and wouldn't ever want to!

Even for those who follow Fr. Aidan's blog regularly, *Destined for Joy* is well worth reviewing and having on hand as a definitive resource. The book faithfully and creatively reflects the faith of those great saints of the past (Origen, Macrina, Gregory of Nyssa, Isaac of Nineveh, Maximos the Confessor, Silouan the Athonite, and yes, George MacDonald) and the boldest minds of our era (Sergius Bulgakov, Robert W. Jenson, Thomas Talbott, Ilaria

Ramelli, David Bentley Hart, John Behr). It also offers essential and sometimes startling corrections, revealing, for example, how the fifth-century anathemas against Origenism—long thought to have decisively condemned universal salvation—were *never* conciliar or even synodal. Fr Aidan demonstrates that they amount to nothing but an imperial edict that has no doctrinal authority. He has at last firmly closed the door on centuries of misconception, divorced the anathemas from the Fifth Ecumenical Council and removed them from the Infernalist arsenal.

But by far his most powerful contribution to me personally (by accumulated 'convincement') was guiding me to this very simple question: *Does the New Testament foresee the salvation of all?* Clearly it does. Repeatedly. Unequivocally. And all the "But what about . . . ?" counterpoints fail to address these Scriptures directly. Regardless of the difficulties we have interpreting judgment texts or harmonizing them with ultimate redemption, Christ and his apostles tell us how it all ends: "*God will be all and in all.*" But nothing. Full stop. Amen and hallelujah!

The issue of 'the End' now boils down to these questions for me:

- Do the Scriptures require a free and willing faith response to Jesus Christ? Yes! Many times.
- Do the Scriptures forecast a final judgment? Yes! Many times.
- Do the Scriptures foresee the salvation of all? Yes! Dozens of times.

How can all three of these statements be true without marginalizing any of the pertinent biblical texts? They can only all work if:

Foreword

- Death has been defeated so that a free and willing post-mortem response is possible.
It has been.
- The judgements of God are restorative and penultimate rather than retributive and ultimate.
They are.
- The human will is healed and freed from its delusions so we can freely respond to perfect Love when we see Christ face to face. I call this a 'freed will' response.
It will be.

While we can pile Scripture upon Scripture to verify these truths, I repeat, we have Jesus Christ's overt claim in John's Gospel: "If I am lifted up from the earth, I *will* draw all people to myself."

And we have the End described in expressly inclusive ways . . . *every eye shall see him, every knee shall bow, every tongue will confess, God shall be all and in all.* What others regard as exclusive conditions to this outcome, *apokatastasis* enfolds as the necessary means. The Incarnation, the Cross and Resurrection, faith in Christ, restorative judgment according to the first Christians—these are the means by which the foretold glorious, all-inclusive End will surely come about.

I can make these audacious assertions without presumption because whatever warrant our faith needs to embrace them, *Destined for Joy* offers in abundance. Over to you, Fr. Aidan.

Dr. Bradley Jersak is Dean of Theology & Culture and Professor of Religious Studies at St. Stephen's University (New Brunswick). He is the author of several books, including *Her Gates Will Never Be Shut, A More Christlike God, A More Christlike Word,* and *A More Christlike Way.*

Introduction

Ten years ago, on 15 June 2012, my second son Aaron died by suicide at the age of 32. He was brilliant and funny, articulate and eccentric. When he died, I was destroyed, as were my wife Christine and my other three children, Alvin, Bredon, and Taryn. Aaron was beloved and cherished by each of us. I was swallowed up in a fire of sorrow and grief that consumed everything inside of me. I mean that quite literally. I quickly became an empty shell. I wept uncontrollably day after day for over a year.

Four months after Aaron's death, I decided to start a blog, which I named *Eclectic Orthodoxy*. My goal was simple—to hold onto that sliver of sanity I had left. I determined to begin reading the Church Fathers and to summarize their thoughts on the blog. And so, I began. I first immersed myself in the orations of St Gregory of Nazianzus. He is venerated in both the Orthodox and Catholic Churches as one of the great theologians of the patristic period. Along with St Athanasius of Alexandria, he was instrumental in the victory of the Nicene confession that Jesus Christ is *homoousios* ("of one substance") with the Father. My articles on Gregory continued for several months. They did not draw many visitors, but that was fine. I wasn't writing for anyone but myself.

In March 2013, I began a series of posts on the 7th century ascetic St Isaac the Syrian, a beloved figure in Eastern Orthodoxy. What drew me to St Isaac was his profound conviction that God is absolute love:

> In love did He bring the world into existence; in love does He guide it during this its temporal existence; in love is He going to bring it to that wondrous transformed state, and in love will the world be swallowed up

Introduction

in the great mystery of Him who has performed all things; in love will the whole course of the governance of creation be finally comprised.

The series concluded with two articles devoted to St Isaac's confident belief that God will save all, human and angelic beings alike, no matter the depth of their wickedness. Suddenly the blog traffic exploded. Apparently not many were aware that Isaac was a universalist. A good God, the Syrian saint declares, would never condemn his children to everlasting torment:

> It is not the way of the compassionate Maker to create rational beings in order to deliver them over mercilessly to unending affliction in punishment for things of which He knew even before they were fashioned, aware how they would turn out when He created them—and whom nonetheless He created.

I was surprised by the interest the series generated. It was extensively discussed and debated on social media, as well as the comment box. Apparently, hell is a popular topic. Two months later I published a series on the eschatology of the great 20th century Orthodox theologian Sergius Bulgakov. Like Isaac, he too was a convinced universalist. And like my series on Isaac, the series on Bulgakov generated a goodly amount of traffic. The blog developed a following. A year later I followed up with articles on the writings of Thomas Talbott, an analytic philosopher and evangelical universalist. I had read Talbott two years before Aaron's death and found his arguments sufficiently persuasive to move me from the hopeful universalism I had held for over fifteen years to a confident universalism. While I continued to write on the Church Fathers, *Eclectic Orthodoxy* became known as a universalist blog, drawing visitors from a wide ecumenical spectrum. And so it has remained to the present.

Destined for Joy contains what I judge to be the best of my articles written on God's unwavering commitment to reconcile all human beings to himself in Jesus Christ. As the Apostle Paul declares: God "desires everyone to be saved and to come to the knowledge of the truth" (1 Tim 2:4). What God desires, he wills, and what he wills must come to pass. This is a controversial claim, I know, yet it logically flows from the LORD's self-revelation in the Nazarene and is well attested in the Scriptures. Jesus is the Good Shepherd who abandons his flock to search for the one lost sheep. He is the woman who turns her house upside-down to find a mislaid coin. He is the father who joyfully runs down the road to welcome home his prodigal son. He is the God who dies on the cross and rises into indestructible life. The Savior's love for humanity knows no bounds. For this reason, Christian universalists have long insisted that the everlasting damnation of sinners would be unworthy of the Father of Jesus Christ. In the words of the 19th century Anglican theologian Thomas Allin:

> And this brings us face to face with a blunder of our traditional creed, which is radical. It talks of God's love as though that stood merely on a par with his justice, as though it were something belonging to him which he puts on or off. It is hardly possible to open a religious book in which this fatal error is not found; fatal, because it virtually strikes out of the gospel its fundamental truth—that GOD IS LOVE. The terms are equivalent. They can be interchanged. God is not anger, though he can be angry; God is not vengeance, though he does avenge. These are attributes; love is essence. Therefore, God is unchangeably love. Therefore, in judgment he is love, in wrath he is love, in vengeance he is love—"love first, and last, and midst, and without end."

God is love, and his love will triumph. He will never rest until he has realized his salvific will throughout the cosmos and in the heart of every sinner. He will be "all in all," as the Apostle teaches (1 Cor 15:28).

The articles in this volume have been revised and expanded for this volume. While I have tried to avoid redundant overlap, this has not always been possible. In some cases, I have combined two or more articles into one. I have also given some new titles. All retain the colloquial-academic style of writing that I adopted for my blog, a mixture of preaching and theological reflection. "I'm a blogger, dammit, not a theologian!" is my byline. But of course, every preacher is a theologian, for good or ill.

I have divided the book into three sections:

The first section, "The Greater Hope and the Absolute Love of God," contains those articles devoted to the elaboration of the unconditional love and grace of God as revealed in Jesus Christ. Here you will find the theologians who have most informed my understanding of the gospel over the decades—James and Thomas Torrance, Robert W. Jenson, Gerhard Forde, George MacDonald, and Robert Farrar Capon. It closes with a lexical analysis of the Greek word *aionios*, which is often translated in our English Bibles as "eternal." When Jesus speaks of *aionios* punishment, must he be understood as declaring "eternal" damnation? Not necessarily! In these articles, you will often hear me speaking in my evangelical voice as a preacher of the gospel.

The second section, "The Greater Hope in History," contains my articles on important universalist figures from the premodern period. The great Syrian mystic Saint Isaac of Nineveh dominates. His argument for universal salvation is simple and, in my judgment, utterly compelling. Here also you will find my article on the wonderful mystic Dame Julian of Norwich. Her famous book *Shewings*, in which she shares her visionary revelations of the risen "Jhesu crist," is one of the great works of the theological and spiritual tradition. "All shall be well," Jesus promises her. Yet if all shall be well, how then can there be hell? The section concludes with a long article on the Fifth Ecumenical Council, which is commonly reported to have condemned the doctrine of universal salvation. As you will see, this claim is not historically well-founded. I am particularly proud of this article. I have worked on it over a period of seven years, and it has undergone numerous revisions. It's been read by three patristic scholars, including an expert in the Ecumenical Councils.

The third section, "The Gospel of Universal Salvation," presents the theological case for apokatastasis as advanced by modern theologians—Thomas Talbott, David Bentley Hart, Sergius Bulgakov, and Eric Reitan. In these articles my own *theological* voice makes a periodic appearance. How could it not, given my firm conviction that the gospel of Christ's atoning love entails universal salvation?

In these articles I often use the word *apokatastasis*. This Greek term refers to the cosmic consummation of all things in the Kingdom of the Incarnate Son. In my usage, it serves as a synonym for universal salvation, which I also term "the greater hope." Apokatastasis is but the gospel of Christ's absolute and unconditional love sung in an eschatological key.

First and foremost, I am a preacher of the gospel. I was ordained a priest in the Episcopal Church in 1980. I served as Curate in one congregation and pastored three others as Rector. Since 2011, I have been a priest (now retired) in the Eastern Orthodox Church and am addressed by my fellow Orthodox as "Fr Aidan." Please don't let that deter you from reading my articles. My blog has always been intended for an ecumenical audience. The gospel I proclaim is the gospel shared by most (alas, not all) Christians through the ages: God is absolute love, and his love intends the salvation of every human being.

Introduction

I wish to thank the many readers of *Eclectic Orthodoxy* for their enthusiastic support over the past decade. I also wish to thank Tom Belt, Robert Fortuin, and Brian Moore, with whom I have enjoyed long conversations on universal salvation and other theological topics. They have taught me so much. I wish to thank Jess Lederman, who has helped to bring this book to fruition. But most of all, I wish to thank my beautiful companion of 46 years, Christine. We have travelled a hard road together. In the love of Christ, we are still together, husband and wife.

Please pray for the soul of my beloved Aaron. To him this book is dedicated. He is present on every page, in every sentence, every word. May his memory be eternal!

PART ONE

The Greater Hope and the Absolute Love of God

Chapter One

The Astonishing Love of God

Who among the Eastern Fathers has written more eloquently, more profoundly about the astonishing love of God Almighty than St Isaac the Syrian? "In Isaac's understanding," writes Hilarion Alfeyev, "God is above all immeasurable love. This conviction dominates Isaac's thought: it is the source of his theological opinions, ascetical recommendations and mystical thought."[1] Sadly this great doctor of divine love remains relatively unknown in English-speaking Christendom. Only in recent decades have his discourses become available in translation.[2] Yet despite Isaac's relative obscurity, I believe that his writings might prove salutary reading for many Christians.

For Isaac the world is a gift of the divine love. It begins in love and will be consummated in love. This love is unconquerable and irresistible, not because it coerces—God forbid!—but because it woos us into the Trinitarian life through its intrinsic beauty, truth, and goodness:

> What profundity of richness, what mind and exalted wisdom is God's! What compassionate kindness and abundant goodness belongs to the Creator! With what purpose and with what love did He create this world and bring it into existence! What a mystery does the coming into being of this creation look towards! To what a state is our common nature invited! What love served to initiate the creation of the world! This same love which initiated the act of creation prepared beforehand

---

[1] Hilarion Alfeyev, *The Spiritual World of Isaac the Syrian*, pp. 35-36.
[2] Isaac's discourses are divided into two parts. The first part is published under the title *The Ascetical Homilies of Saint Isaac the Syrian*, 2nd ed. (2007); the second under the startling title *The Second Part* (1995).

by another dispensation the things appropriate to adorn the world's majesty which sprung forth as a result of the might of His love.

In love did He bring the world into existence; in love does He guide it during this its temporal existence; in love is He going to bring it to that wondrous transformed state, and in love will the world be swallowed up in the great mystery of Him who has performed all these things; in love will the whole course of the governance of creation be finally comprised. And since in the New World the Creator's love rules over all rational nature, the wonder at His mysteries that will be revealed then will captivate to itself the intellect of all rational beings whom He has created so that they might have delight in Him, whether they be evil or whether they be just. (II.38.1-2)

God has created the world in love and for love. Angels and human beings alike have been brought into existence to delight in the divine mercy and to enjoy eternal communion with the God who is love. Everything that God has done, everything that he does in the present and will do in the future, is an expression of love. "Among all his actions," the Syrian declares, "there is none which is not entirely a matter of mercy, love, and compassion: this constitutes the beginning and the end of his dealings with us" (II.39.22). Here is the purpose of creation and the Incarnation, "to reveal his boundless love to the world."[3]

The love of God is indiscriminate, promiscuous, prodigal. It intends every rational creature, angels and human beings alike. As Jesus teaches, the Father who is in heaven "makes his sun rise on the evil and on the good, and sends rain on the just and on the unjust" (Matt 5:45). There is no one "who is to the front of or to the back of God's love. Rather, He has a single equal love which covers the whole extent of rational creation, all things whether visible or invisible: there is no first or last place with Him in this love for any

---

[3] *Gnostic* Chapters IV.79; quoted in Alfeyev, p. 36.

single one of them" (II.38.2). The divine love addresses and upholds all equally. Isaac firmly rejects the thesis that God has predestined some human beings for damnation. Such a thesis is unthinkable, indeed blasphemous. Every being created by God is loved by God. Our disobedience does not change the character of the Father; our sin does not diminish his love for us. "There is no hatred or resentment in His nature," Isaac explains, "no greater or lesser place in His love, no before or after in His knowledge" (II.38.5). No matter how much disorder we cause in the world, no matter how grievous our sin, no matter how horrific the evil we commit, God's salvific will for us does not change. He eternally wills our good, and in his wise providence will accomplish this good. "There exists with Him a single love and compassion which is spread out over all creation, a love which is without alteration, timeless, and everlasting" (II.40.1).

The providence of love encompasses all material and spiritual dimensions:

> Let us consider then how rich in its wealth is the ocean of His creative act, and how many created things belong to God, and how in His compassion He carries everything, acting providentially as He guides creation; and how with a love that cannot be measured He arrived at the establishment of the world and the beginning of creation; and how compassionate God is, and how patient; and how He loves creation, and how He carries it, gently enduring its importunity, the various sins and wickednesses, the terrible blasphemies of demons and evil men. Then, once someone has stood amazed, and filled his intellect with the majesty of God, amazed at all these things He has done and is doing, then he wonders in astonishment at His mercifulness, how, after all these things, God has prepared for them another world that has no end, whose glory is not even revealed to the angels, even though they are involved in His activities insofar as is possible in the life of the spirit, in accordance with the gift with which their nature has been

endowed. That person wonders too at how excelling is that glory, and how exalted is the manner of existence at that time; and how insignificant is the present life compared to what is reserved for creation in the New Life; and how, in order that the soul's life will not be deprived of that blessed state because of misusing the freewill it has received, He has devised in His mercifulness a second gift, which is repentance, so that by it the soul's life might acquire renewal every day and thereby every time be put aright. (II.10.19)

The merciful God has provided a way for sinful creatures to avail themselves of the mercy of God—repentance. Nor is repentance something beyond our capabilities, says Isaac. God understands our weaknesses and limits. Repentance involves the whole person, mind, will, conscience, heart, "so that it might be easy for everyone to acquire benefit from it, both quickly and at any time" (II.10.19).

The infinite love of the Creator is dramatically displayed in the Incarnation of the Son. Why did God become man? Why did Jesus die on the cross? Certainly not to propitiate an angry deity. If God's sole purpose were to achieve the remission of sins, he could have accomplished this end by another means. The cross is the perfect and compelling revelation of the divine mercy. Isaac understood that sinners could not believe in the possibility of their reconciliation with their Maker without a revelation embodied in the terrible suffering and bloody death of God himself:

> If zeal had been appropriate for putting humanity right, why did God the Word clothe himself in the body, using gentleness and humility in order to bring the world back to his Father? And why was he stretched out on the cross for the sake of sinners, handing over his sacred body to suffering on behalf of the world? I myself say that God did all this for no other reason than to make known to the world the love that he has, his aim being that we, as a result of our greater love arising from an awareness of this, might be captivated by his love when he provided the

occasion of this manifestation of the kingdom of heaven's mighty power—which consists in love—by means of the death of his Son.[1]

God himself must die on the cross. Only thus can human hearts be pierced and turned away from self and sin; only thus can mankind apprehend the true identity and nature of their Creator and be converted to the path of salvation. It is the divine love, manifested in the humility and death of the Son, which converts sinners. The divine charity is cruciform:

> But the sum of all is that God the Lord surrendered His own Son to death on the Cross for the fervent love of creation. 'For God so loved the world, that He gave His only-begotten Son over to death for its sake.' This was not, however, because He could not have redeemed us in another way, but so that His surpassing love, manifested hereby, might be a teacher unto us. And by the death of His only-begotten Son He made us near to Himself. Yea, if He had had anything more precious, He would have given it to us, so that by it our race might be His own. (I.71)

Why do we not hear this message of the astonishing love of God every Sunday, Sunday after Sunday, in our Churches? This is the gospel. There is no other gospel worth preaching, no other gospel worth hearing. In a world filled with wickedness, suffering, despair, and death, we desperately need to hear the proclamation of the omnipotent power of God's love and mercy. We need to know that he treasures us, that he has a plan for us, that his saving will for the world will triumph. Only thus does it become possible for us to cooperate with him in prayer and good works. In the words of the great Catholic theologian Hans Urs von Balthasar:

---

[1] Quoted in Alfeyev, p. 52.

> Love alone is credible; nothing else can be believed, and nothing else ought to be believed. This is the achievement, the 'work' of faith: to recognize this absolute *prius*, which nothing else can surpass; to believe that there is such a thing as love, absolute love, and that there is nothing higher or greater than it; to believe against all the evidence of experience . . . against every 'rational' concept of God, which thinks of him in terms of impassibility or, at best, totally pure goodness, but not in terms of this inconceivable and senseless act of love.[5]

Without the preaching of the boundless love of God enfleshed in Jesus Christ, crucified and risen, the Church has no reason to exist; indeed, it is this word of love that creates the new life that is the Church. Without love, there is no *theosis*, no repentance, no sanctification, only Pharisaic zeal and deadly dogmatism.

---

[5] Hans Urs von Balthasar, *Love Alone is Credible* (2005), pp. 101-102.

Chapter Two

The Wondrous Prodigality of God's Love for Sinners

"It is very odd," remarks Herbert McCabe, "that people should think that when we do good God will reward us and when we do evil he will punish us."[1] It's not surprising, of course, that those outside the Church might think of the Deity that way. After all, that's what deities do—reward and punish. Yet Christians should know better. There is so much in the gospels that tells us that the living God does not easily fit into the retributive model. Orthodox readers will immediately think of the surprising words of St Isaac the Syrian:

> Be a herald of God's goodness, for God rules over you, unworthy though you are. Although your debt to Him is so very great, He is not seen exacting payment from you; and from the small works you do, He bestows great rewards upon you. Do not call God just, for His justice is not manifest in the things concerning you. And if David calls him just and upright, His Son revealed to us that He is good and kind. 'He is good,' He says, 'to the evil and to the impious.'
>
> How can you call God just when you come across the Scriptural passage on the wage given to the workers? 'Friend, I do thee no wrong: I choose to give unto this last even as unto thee. Or is thine eye evil because I am good?' How can a man call God just when he comes across the passage on the prodigal son who wasted his wealth with riotous living, how for the compunction alone which he showed the father ran and fell upon his neck and gave him authority over his wealth? None other but His very Son said these things concerning Him, lest we doubt it, and thus bore witness concerning Him. Where,

---

[1] Herbert McCabe, "Forgiveness," *Faith Within Reason* (2007), p. 155.

then, is God's justice? —for while we are sinners Christ died for us! But if here He is merciful, we may believe that He will not change.[2]

Justice has been so drastically redefined by the gospel that it may even be best to delete the word from our vocabulary. "Do not call God just!" Isaac clearly sees that Jesus has turned upside down our inherited notions of equity and redress. The divine Creator has no interest in who deserves what. His justice simply is his unmerited love and prodigal mercy.

The Death of the Prodigal Son

Consider the parable of the prodigal son. After squandering his inheritance and being forced to feed pigs for pauper's wages, he finally arrives at a recognition of his desperate situation: "I will arise and go to my father, and I will say to him, 'Father, I have sinned against heaven and before you; I am no longer worthy to be called your son; treat me as one of your hired servants'" (Luke 15:18-19). There are two things that need to be seen here, says McCabe: (1) the consequences of the young man's sins upon himself and his relationship with his father and (2) his recognition of these consequences:

> The vital thing is that the son has recognized his sin for what it is: something that changes God into a paymaster, or a judge. Sin is something that changes God into a projection of our guilt, so that we don't see the real God at all; all we see is some kind of judge. God (the whole meaning and purpose and point of our existence) has become a condemnation of us. God has been turned into Satan, the accuser of man, the paymaster, the one who weighs our deeds and condemns us.[3]

---

[2] Isaac, *The Ascetical Homilies of Saint Isaac the Syrian* (2011), Hom. 51, p. 387.
[3] McCabe, pp. 155-156.

The Wondrous Prodigality of God's Love for Sinners

The problem is with the son, not with the father. The father is who he has always been. Day after day he has prayed for his son's return, and when he finally espies him coming down the road, he puts aside his dignity and rushes to embrace him. He cuts short the prodigal's carefully worded confession and orders the insignia of sonship to be restored to him. The father never was the paymaster and stern judge the prodigal presumed him to be, nor was he ever in danger of losing his status as son, despite his selfishness and debauchery:

> The younger son in the story has escaped hell because he has seen his sin for what it is. He has recognized what it does to his vision of God: 'I am no longer worthy to be called your son; treat me like one of your hired servants' (Lk. 15.21). And, of course, as soon as he really accepts that he is a sinner, he ceases to be one; knowing that you have sinned *is* contrition or forgiveness, or whatever you like to call it. The rest of the story is not about the father *forgiving* his son, it is about the father *celebrating*, welcoming his son with joy and feasting. This is all the real God ever does, because God, the real God, is just helplessly and hopelessly in love with us. He is unconditionally in love with us.[1]

Robert Farrar Capon offers a similar interpretation of the parable. He proposes a two-step process of death for the younger son. The first occurs in the far country, when "the prodigal finally wakes up dead. Reduced to the indignity of slopping hogs for a local farmer, he comes to himself one dismal morning and realizes that whatever life he had is over."[2] He cannot conceive of reconciliation with his father ("I am no longer worthy to be called your son"), and so he concocts a new plan for his future ("treat me as one of your hired servants"). He acknowledges that his sin has forever abolished his status as beloved son. The filial relationship is irreparably broken. He will instead become a paid worker on his father's estate. So he

---

[1] Ibid., p. 156.
[2] Robert Farrar Capon, *Kingdom, Grace, Judgment* (1985), p. 294.

begins the journey home, intending to enter into a contractual relationship with the man who raised him as his heir. "But what he does not yet see," comments Capon, "is that, as far as his relationship with his father is concerned, his lost sonship is the only life he had: there is no way now for him to be anything but a dead son."[6]

It is only when the prodigal arrives home that the second step in the death-process occurs. Though Jesus does not tell us what the son was thinking when he saw his Father come rushing toward him in love and joy, we do see the result: the prodigal deletes from his scripted confession his plea for employment. His father's munificent welcome has demonstrated the impossibility of that request:

> The father simply sees this corpse of a son coming down the road and, because raising dead sons to life and throwing fabulous parties for them is his favorite way of spending an afternoon, he proceeds straight to hugs, kisses, and resurrection. . . . In the clarity of his resurrection, the boy suddenly sees that he is a dead son, that he will always be a dead son, and that he cannot, by any efforts of his own or even by any gift of his father's become a live anything else. And he understands too that if now, in his embrace, he is a dead son who is alive again, it is all because his father was himself willing to be dead in order to raise him up.[7]

Salvation is not a new opportunity to put things right before likely damnation. We are dead in our sins. Reform is out of the question. "Jesus came to raise the dead," declares Capon. "Not to improve the improvable, not to perfect the perfectible, not to teach the teachable, but to raise the dead. He never met a corpse that didn't sit right up then and there. And he never meets us without bringing us out of nothing into the joy of his resurrection."[8]

---

[6] Ibid., p. 295.
[7] Ibid., pp. 295-296.
[8] Robert Farrar Capon, *Between Noon and Three* (1997), p. 129.

Repentance is not about becoming a better person. It is recognition that we are corpses in need of new life. Confession, therefore, is not a transactional event. It is a waiting upon our Easter:

> As far as Jesus is concerned, all real confession—all confession that is not just a fudging of our tattered books but a plain admission that our books are not worth even a damn—is *subsequent to forgiveness.* Only when, like the prodigal, we are finally confronted with the unqualified gift of someone who died, in advance, to forgive us no matter what, can we see that confession has nothing to do with getting ourselves forgiven. Confession is not a transaction, not a negotiation in order to secure forgiveness; it is the after-the-last gasp of a corpse that finally can afford to admit it's dead and accept resurrection. Forgiveness surrounds us, beats upon us all our lives; we confess only to wake ourselves up to what we already have.
>
> Every confession a Christian makes bears witness to this, because every confession, public or private, and every absolution, specific or general, is made and given subsequent to the one baptism we receive for the forgiveness of sins. We are forgiven in baptism not only for the sin committed before baptism but for a whole lifetime of sins yet to come. We are forgiven before, during, and after our sins. We are forgiven before, during, and after our confession of them. And we are forgiven for one reason only: because Jesus died for our sins and rose for our justification.[9]

This is what Jesus does: he raises the dead! All that is left to do is slaughter the fatted calf and get on with the feasting.

Divine Forgiveness is Our Repentance

Note the profound agreement between McCabe and Capon. If God loves us unconditionally, then we must rethink both our understanding of divine justice and the relationship between

---

[9] Capon, *Kingdom,* pp. 296-297.

repentance and forgiveness. It cannot be the case that our penitence secures the divine forgiveness, for God forever meets us in the Lamb slain before the foundation of the world. God loves the wicked—scandalously, prodigally, astonishingly. That he does so is our salvation:

> His love for us doesn't depend on what we do or what we are like. He doesn't care whether we are sinners or not. It makes no difference to him. He is just waiting to welcome us with joy and love. Sin doesn't alter God's attitude to us; it alters our attitude to him, so that we change him from the God who is simply love and nothing else, into this punitive ogre, this Satan. Sin matters enormously to us if we are sinners; it doesn't matter at all to God. In a fairly literal sense he doesn't give a damn about our sin. It is we who give the damns. We damn ourselves because we would rather justify and excuse ourselves, and look on our self-flattering images of ourselves, than be taken out of ourselves by the infinite love of God. Contrition or forgiveness (remember that it is we who forgive ourselves) is almost the exact opposite of excusing ourselves. It is a matter of accusing ourselves—for now the sons of man (people, human beings) have power on earth to forgive sins, power to recognize sin for what it is and so abolish it. Contrition, or forgiveness, is self-knowledge, the terribly painful business of seeing ourselves as what and who we are: how mean, selfish, cruel and indifferent and infantile we are.[10]

If God does not give a damn about our sins, if our transgressions do not diminish his love for us one whit, what then does his forgiveness mean? Clearly it does not mean what it means in our daily social intercourse. When we forgive someone in ordinary life, it's because they have hurt and insulted us; but in the infinite plenitude of his impassible and immutable Being, God cannot be wounded,

---

[10] McCabe, p. 157.

damaged, or offended by our sins. Hence when we speak of God forgiving us, we are speaking figuratively. McCabe explains:

> God, of course, is not injured or insulted or threatened by our sin. So, when we speak of him forgiving, we are using the word 'forgiving' in a rather stretched way, a rather far-fetched way. We speak of God forgiving not because he is really offended but accepts our apology or agrees to overlook the insult. What God is doing is like forgiveness not because of anything that happens in God, but because of what happens in us, because of the *recreative* and *redemptive* side of forgiveness. All the insult and injury we do in sinning is to ourselves alone, not to God. We speak of God forgiving us because he comes to us to save us from ourselves, to restore us after we have injured ourselves, to redeem and re-create us.[11]

To be forgiven is nothing less than rebirth in the Spirit and elevation into divine life of the Holy Trinity. McCabe and Capon have purged from traditional soteriology all hints of juridicism and retribution. There is no dark side in God, no antinomy between the God of love and the God of wrath, no *Deus absconditus* hiding behind the back of Jesus. There is only the radical and astonishing Love that is the Father, Son, and Holy Spirit.

And yet . . .

Consider the following scenario:

- We sin and God gets angry.
- We repent and plead for mercy.
- God forgives.

Crudely put, isn't this what we learned in Sunday School? Who can read the story of the golden calf in Exodus 32 and not come away

---

[11] Herbert McCabe, *God, Christ and Us* (2003), p. 122.

with the conviction that when we act immorally, God's attitude towards us changes? The scenario can be made less offensive to modern sensibilities, but the basic structure remains: sin brings upon us divine judgment and wrath. It is now up to us to do something to abate the divine anger. Strategies have historically included repentance, confession of faith in Jesus, almsgiving, reparations, pilgrimages. Inherent to this structure are two elements: (1) a change in God's attitude and (2) a penitential transaction that placates God and repairs the relationship.

Why do we think that the above scenario accurately reflects the way of things? Because this is how it works between human beings. I injure you—not incidentally, not accidentally, but deliberately, degradingly, maliciously, gravely. Your heart cries out for vengeance. What must happen for the relationship to be restored? I must accept responsibility for my actions, express genuine contrition, ask for forgiveness, and make restitution. By so doing I disown the evil I have done. But there is still one thing left. You must forgive me. Only then will my guilt be removed and relationship restored; only then do we cease to be enemies.

Note that it is possible for the injured party to forgive the offender before he has apologized and made atonement. Philosophers and moral theologians debate whether this is a good or bad thing to do. Richard Swinburne, for example, suggests that forgiveness before repentance and reparation trivializes the evil that has been committed: "It is both bad and ineffective for a victim of at any rate a serious hurt to disown the hurt when no atonement has been made."[12] In Swinburne's eyes, forgiving a wrongdoer before he has repented amounts to condonation of his crime. On the other hand, many victims have found that forgiveness of the wrongdoer,

---

[12] Richard Swinburne, *Responsibility and Atonement* (1989), p. 86.

The Wondrous Prodigality of God's Love for Sinners

even absent their repentance, can be spiritually and psychologically beneficial.

But what about God? Many biblical texts can be cited to support the belief that divine forgiveness is contingent upon the sinner's repentance and change of heart. David Konstan believes that a conditionalist interpretation is supported by both the Old and New Testaments:

> Consider King Solomon's prayer to God in 1 Kings 8:33-34: "When thy people Israel are defeated before the enemy because they have sinned against thee, if they turn again to thee, and acknowledge thy name, and pray and make supplication to thee in this house; then hear thou in heaven, and forgive [or be propitious toward: cf. the Greek ἵλεως] the sin of thy people Israel, and bring them again to the land which thou gavest to their fathers." In the hymn that concludes the book of Isaiah, we again find an emphasis on returning to the path of God (55:7) "let the wicked forsake his way, and the unrighteous man his thoughts; let him return to the Lord, that he may have mercy on him, and to our God, for he will abundantly pardon." So too in Jeremiah, the Lord will accept the just and honest man (5:1), and reject the wicked, above all, those who have forsaken him (5:7); but those who return will find redemption. This idea found deep resonance in the later scriptural interpretation. . . .
>
> This concern with confession and remorse as the conditions for God's forgiveness is continued in the New Testament. The Gospel of Mark reveals a particular interest in the role of repentance (μετάνοια). Thus John the Baptist is described as having appeared in the wilderness, κηρύσσων βάπτισμα μετανοίας εἰς ἄφεσιν ἁμαρτιῶν ("preaching a baptism of repentance for the forgiveness of sins," 1:4; cf. Luke 3:3). Luke too affirms that repentance is essential for forgiveness: ἐὰν ἁμάρτῃ ὁ ἀδελφός σου ἐπιτίμησον αὐτῷ, καὶ ἐὰν μετανοήσῃ ἄφες αὐτῷ ("if your brother sins, rebuke him, and if he repents, forgive him," 17:3). Repentance is a crucial condition for forgiveness: there is

no evidence in the New Testament that forgiveness is understood to be unconditional, although this is not always stated explicitly.[13]

Many preachers, biblical scholars, and theologians agree with Konstan, as do many of the Church Fathers. Thus St Mark the Ascetic: "No one is as good and merciful as the Lord. But even He does not forgive the unrepentant." One might also invoke the penitential practices of the Church to support a conditionalist interpretation of divine forgiveness. After all, absolution always comes after the confession of sin, not before.

And yet . . .

Let's return to the popular scenario with which I opened this article: we sin, God gets angry; we repent, God forgives. This is a perfectly acceptable image of God, says McCabe. Wickedness is serious business, and it is appropriate for us to think of God as becoming angry when we break his holy commandments. God does not condone evil. He opposes it with all of his might. His love is his wrath. But this is only one image and needs to be set alongside the equally biblical image of "the God who endlessly accepts us, the God who endures our sins and forgives us all the same."[14] But consider also the magnitude of God's forgiveness displayed in the Scriptures.

- God is the faithful husband who repeatedly forgives his promiscuous wife (Hosea).
- God is the good shepherd who abandons his flock to rescue the one lost lamb (Luke 15:3-7).
- God is the woman who turns her house upside down to find a lost coin (Luke 15:8-10).

---

[13] David Konstan, "Before Forgiveness," *New England Classical Journal* 38.2 (2011): 101-102.
[14] McCabe, *God, Christ and Us*, pp. 15-16.

The Wondrous Prodigality of God's Love for Sinners

- God is the Messiah who answers St Peter's query "Lord, how often shall my brother sin against me, and I forgive him? As many as seven times?" And God answers: "I do not say to you seven times, but seventy times seven" (Matt 18:21-22).
- God is the Crucified who cries out from the tree: "Father, forgive them, for they know not what they do" (Luke 23:34).

Yet even the image of the absolving God does not tell us the whole truth. "The fact is," explains McCabe, "that the God of wrath and the God who relents are both good but inadequate images, merely pictures of the unfathomable, incomprehensible love which is God."[15] Neither image, in other words, is *literally* true. Both portray God as anthropomorphically changing his mind about us: when we sin, God becomes angry and punishes; when we repent, God puts aside his wrath and re-friends us. But the reality is that God never changes his mind. He is always and eternally in love with us. Recall McCabe's blunt words: "In a fairly literal sense, God doesn't give a damn about our sin. It is we who give the damns." We do not need to win the Father's forgiveness; he has already embraced us in grace and mercy.

> If we are going to understand anything about the forgiveness of sin we cannot just be content with pictures; we have to *think* as clearly as we can. . . . The initiative is always literally with God. When God forgives our sin, he is not changing *his* mind about us; he is changing *our* mind about him. He does not change; his mind is never anything but loving; he *is* love. The forgiveness of sin is God's creative and re-creative love making the desert bloom again, bringing us back from dry sterility to the rich luxuriant life bursting out all over the place. When God changes your mind in this way, when he pours out on you his Spirit of new life, it is exhilarating, but it is also fairly painful. There is a trauma

---

[15] Ibid., p. 16.

of rebirth as perhaps there is of birth. The exhilaration and the pain that belong to being reborn is what we call contrition, and this is the forgiveness of sin. Contrition is not anxious guilt about sin; it is the continual recognition in hope that the Spirit has come to me *as healing my sin.*

So it is not literally true that because we are sorry God decides to forgive us. That is a perfectly good story, but it is only a story. The literal truth is that we are sorry because God forgives us. Our sorrow for sin just *is* the forgiveness of God working within us. Contrition and forgiveness are just two names for the same thing, they are the gift of the Holy Spirit; the re-creative transforming act of God in us. God does not forgive us because of anything he finds in us; he forgives us out of his sheer delight, his exuberant joy in making the desert bloom again.[16]

McCabe invites us to contextualize the interpersonal model of forgiveness within a proper construal of divine transcendence and the Creator/creature relationship. When we tell a story of two or more persons, we of course must present them as acting and reacting: I do something, and you respond; I respond to your response, and you do something. That is what happens between persons who live *in time.* Hence it is not surprising that when the biblical writers sought to tell the story of the God who had entered into covenant with Israel and the Church, they portrayed him as one person among a universe of persons, a someone who believes and feels and acts and reacts, who gets angry when his creatures rebel against his just rule and who puts aside his anger when they repent. But it cannot be literally true. God is eternal. He transcends the temporality of our lives. The literal, timeless truth is something infinitely more marvelous:

> God does not respond to his world. He does not adjust his reaction to suit good people or bad. You do not have to be good before God will

---

[16] Ibid., pp. 16-17.

The Wondrous Prodigality of God's Love for Sinners

love you; you do not have to try to be good before God will forgive you; you do not have to repent before you will be absolved by God. It is all the other way round. If you are good, it is because God's love has already made you so; if you want to try to be good, that is because God is loving you; if you want to be forgiven, that is because God is forgiving you. You do not have to do anything, or pay anything, in exchange for God's love. God does not demand anything of you. Nothing whatsoever.[17]

The literal, fundamental truth: God is love—absolute, unconditional, infinite, unrelenting love.

---

[17] Ibid., p. 27.

Chapter Three

The Scandalous Injustice of Grace

Back in 2008, *60 Minutes* interviewed the Boston button man John Martorano. The interview is unsettling. In a quiet, detached, matter-of-fact tone, Martorano describes the twenty confessed murders he committed during his years as an enforcer for the Winter Hill Gang. At the conclusion of the interview, Steve Kroft asks the key question: Do you regret what you did?

"In some cases, regret can take over a person's life. I don't get the sense that that's the case with you."

"Well, maybe that's just not my temperament or my personality. Maybe it is, but you can't see it. Or maybe I can't express it the way you want it, but I have my regrets."

"You seem cold. You killed 20 people and that's all you have to say about it?"

"I wish it wasn't that way. I mean, I wish there was none. You know, you can't change the past. I'm trying to do the best I can with the future and explain it as best I can. I regret it all, I can't change it."

"You still a Catholic?"

"Sure."

"I mean, you can burn in hell for killing one person."

"I don't believe that. At one point, maybe a couple years ago, I sent for a priest and gave him a confession. It was maybe 30 years since my last confession. But I went through the whole scenario with him, and went through my whole life with him, and confessed. And at the end of it, he says, 'Well, what do you think I should give you for penance?' I says, 'Father, you can justifiably crucify me.' He laughed and says, 'Nope. Ten Hail Marys, ten Our Fathers, and don't do it again.' So I listened to him."

The Scandalous Injustice of Grace

This interview has been remarked upon throughout the blogosphere and social media. Most are dissatisfied with Martorano's expression of contrition. He seems too cool, too detached. They do not believe he has truly repented and therefore do not believe that God has forgiven him. Many mock the penance assigned by the priest. What struck me most was Martorano's trust in the sacramental word of the priest: "I listened to him." Martorano believes that God has forgiven him. He trusts the divine word of absolution, and that word is sufficient. God has spoken.

Yet our instinctive reaction is "That is not enough." We want to see deeper sorrow and shame, tears, reparations, a dramatic change in the man's life before we will consider the possibility that God has forgiven this murderer. It's all too easy and unfair. Grace is not cheap, as we preachers are wont to say.

But then we remember a parable that Jesus once told about the Kingdom of God. The householder hires laborers to work in his vineyard—some he hires at the break of day, then others at the third, sixth, ninth, and finally the eleventh hour. At the end of the day, he pays the laborers the same wage, no matter how many hours they worked. Those who worked the entire day are understandably upset. "These last worked only one hour," they protest, "and you have made them equal to us who have borne the burden of the day and the scorching heat." A fair point. How can that be just? The vintner replies:

> Friend, I am doing you no wrong; did you not agree with me for a denarius? Take what belongs to you, and go; I choose to give to this last as I give to you. Am I not allowed to do what I choose with what belongs to me? Or do you begrudge my generosity? (Matt 20:13-15)

The grace of God exceeds the norms of justice. So why are we scandalized by the extravagant generosity of God toward a contract killer like Martorano? After all, do we not hope that God will be equally generous with us?

In his book *That Man is You,* Louis Evely describes a scene from a play by Jean Anouilh:

> The good are densely clustered at the gate of heaven, eager to march in, sure of their reserved seats, keyed up and bursting with impatience.
>
> All at once, a rumor starts spreading: "It seems He's going to forgive those others, too!"
>
> For a minute, everybody's dumbfounded. They look at one another in disbelief, gasping and sputtering, "After all the trouble I went through!" "If only I'd known this . . ." "I just cannot get over it!"
>
> Exasperated, they work themselves into a fury and start cursing God; and at that very instant they're damned. That was the final judgment.

Talk about a surprising turn of events, both for the audience but especially for the righteous-damned. Imagine their shock and terror. Surely, we would not respond as they did, we think to ourselves. Or would we? Do we? It's quite one thing for God to invite *me* into the vineyard at the eleventh hour; but I still want him to mete out justice to everyone else. We talk a lot about the unconditionality of the divine love. We say we believe it; we joyously celebrate it. God is love and mercy, we proclaim. Yet the law of just deserts lies deep in our hearts, waiting for the right moment to erupt in righteous indignation. "And at that very instant they're damned." As the reprobate in our Lord's parable of the Great Assize are surprised by their condemnation—"Lord, when did we see thee hungry or thirsty or a stranger or naked or sick or in prison, and did not minister to thee?" (Matt 25:44) —so the those expectantly waiting in line to enter into heaven will be horrified to discover in themselves their own hatred of God. The injustice of grace scandalizes one and all. "So the last will be first, and the first last" (Matt 20:16).

St Isaac the Syrian and the Injustice of Grace

God is infinitely just, indeed is justice. So the Bible teaches. Over the centuries theologians have elaborated upon this divine attribute in various ways. All are agreed that the God of the Bible always acts in perfect equity and fairness . . . all, that is, except one. "Mercy is opposed to justice!" declares St Isaac of Nineveh.

> Mercy and justice in one soul is like a man who worships God and the idols in one house. Mercy is opposed to justice. Justice is the equality of the even scale, for it gives to each as he deserves; and when it makes recompense, it does not incline to one side or show respect of persons. Mercy, on the other hand, is a sorrow and pity stirred up by goodness, and it compassionately inclines a man in the direction of all; it does not requite a man who is deserving of evil, and to him who is deserving of good it gives a double portion. If, therefore, it is evident that mercy belongs to the portion of righteousness, then justice belongs to the portion of wickedness. As grass and fire cannot co-exist in one place, so justice and mercy cannot abide in one soul. As a grain of sand cannot counterbalance a great quantity of gold, so in comparison God's use of justice cannot counterbalance His mercy.[1]

A little later in the same homily, Isaac provocatively states: "Justice does not belong to the Christian way of life, and there is no mention of it in Christ's teaching." The disciple of Christ seeks to emulate in his life the outrageous mercy of God, for it this mercy that God has so graciously showered upon us. The holy mystic instructs his readers:

> Do not hate the sinner; for we are all laden with guilt. If for the sake of God, you are moved to oppose him, weep over him. Why do you hate him? Hate his sins and pray for him, that you may imitate Christ Who

---

[1] All quotations from Isaac are from Homily 51 in *The Ascetical Homilies of Saint Isaac the Syrian* (2011), pp. 378-389.

Destined for Joy

was not wroth with sinners, but interceded for them. Do you not see how he wept over Jerusalem. We are mocked by the devil in many instances, so why should we hate the man who is mocked by him who mocks us also. Why, O man, do you hate the sinner? Could it be because he is not so righteous as you? But where is your righteousness when you have no love?

What do we know of the justice of God, when all we know is his unmerited grace and forgiveness? The disciples of Jesus seek to become like their Lord and thus to become like God. As a counselor of souls, Isaac knows that when a person turns his heart toward justice, he inevitably becomes consumed with pride, vengeance, and the desire for requital and retribution. Remember the righteous-damned.

St Isaac then makes his famous pronouncement:

> Be a herald of God's goodness, for God rules over you, unworthy though you are. Although your debt to him is so very great, He is not seen exacting payment from you; and from the small works you do, He bestows great reward upon you. Do not call God just, for His justice is not manifest in the things concerning you. And if David calls him just and upright, His Son revealed to us that He is good and kind. "He is good," He says, "to the evil and to the impious."

Surely this must be one of the most revolutionary statements in patristic literature. Are you tempted to dismiss it as hyperbole? Know that you are not alone. Upon hearing this statement, biblical scholars will compile all the verses that speak of God's covenantal justice, and moral theologians will lecture on good works and justifying merit. As far as parish pastors, they will feel uncomfortable and not know what to preach. But all will agree that Isaac has crossed over into rhetorical excess, if not theological error. But it is precisely at this point of excess, Isaac tells us, that the gospel begins:

How can you call God just when you come across the Scriptural passage on the wage given to the workers? "Friend, I do thee no wrong: I choose to give unto this last even as unto thee. Or is thine eye evil because I am good?" How can a man call God just when he comes across the passage on the prodigal son who wasted his wealth with riotous living, how for the compunction alone which he showed the father ran and fell upon his neck and gave him authority over his wealth? None other but His very Son said these things concerning Him, lest we doubt it, and thus bore witness concerning Him. Where, then, is God's justice, for while we are sinners Christ died for us! But if here He is merciful, we may believe that He will not change.

If you hear in these words echoes of Martin Luther, you would not be wrong; but Isaac is no *sola fide* Protestant. Luther would find the way that Isaac combines his understanding of the unconditionality of the divine love with a rigorous asceticism quite unacceptable. Yet, I think Luther would rejoice in this powerful proclamation of the gospel that triumphs over every legalism and every justice. The gospel dramatically turns upside down conventional, and even biblical, construals of divine justice. The Holy Trinity wills only the good of the sinner, even at the cost of justice.

Pope John Paul II and the Unity of Justice and Mercy

Latin theologians are loath to speak of a conflict between divine love and divine justice; ultimately, they cannot conflict. Yet, as Pope John Paul II acknowledges in his encyclical *Dives in misericordia*, justice must be reinterpreted through a hermeneutic of love.[2] Speaking of the revelation of God's loving kindness in the Old Testament, he writes:

---

[2] *Dives in misericordia* may be found at the Vatican website: https://www.vatican.va/content/john-paul-ii/en/encyclicals/documents/hf_jp-ii_enc_30111980_dives-in-misericordia.html.

> In this way, mercy is in a certain sense contrasted with God's justice, and in many cases is shown to be not only more powerful than that justice but also more profound. Even the Old Testament teaches that, although justice is an authentic virtue in man, and in God signifies transcendent perfection nevertheless love is "greater" than justice: greater in the sense that it is primary and fundamental. Love, so to speak, conditions justice and, in the final analysis, justice serves love. The primacy and superiority of love vis-a-vis justice—this is a mark of the whole of revelation—are revealed precisely through mercy. (III.4)

Like St Isaac, John Paul looks to the parable of the prodigal son as a revelation of the mystery of divine love. Neither *justice* nor *mercy* are mentioned in the parable, yet the relationship between the two is stated exactly. "It becomes more evident," John Paul writes, "that love is transformed into mercy when it is necessary to go beyond the precise norm of justice—precise and often too narrow" (IV.5). Within the order of justice, the son deserved the loss of sonship. He deserved to be hired as one of his father's servants and to live thenceforth on a modest income. But the father shows mercy, not justice. The graciousness of the father reveals his faithfulness to his love, which is the essence of his fatherhood:

> Going on, one can therefore say that the love for the son the love that springs from the very essence of fatherhood, in a way obliges the father to be concerned about his son's dignity. This concern is the measure of his love, the love of which Saint Paul was to write: "Love is patient and kind ... love does not insist on its own way; it is not irritable or resentful ... but rejoices in the right ... hopes all things, endures all things" and "love never ends." Mercy—as Christ has presented it in the parable of the prodigal son—has the interior form of the love that in the New Testament is called agape. This love is able to reach down to every prodigal son, to every human misery, and above all to every form of moral misery, to sin. (IV.6)

The Scandalous Injustice of Grace

But it is in the Paschal Mystery that the love and mercy of God is perfectly and fully revealed. The Son of God is arrested, abused, condemned, crowned with thorns, nailed to the cross, and dies in torment. He who had so beautifully communicated mercy is denied mercy. He is not spared from the injustice of man. "For our sake God made him to be sin who knew no sin," the Apostle declares, "so that in him we might become the righteousness of God" (2 Cor 5:21). These words succinctly summarize the work of divine redemption through the sufferings, death, and resurrection of Christ. The cross discloses the holiness of God:

> Indeed, this Redemption is the ultimate and definitive revelation of the holiness of God, who is the absolute fullness of perfection: fullness of justice and of love, since justice is based on love, flows from and tends towards it. In the passion and death of Christ—in the fact that the Father did not spare His own Son, but "for our sake made him sin"—absolute justice is expressed, for Christ undergoes the passion and cross because of the sins of humanity. This constitutes even a "superabundance" of justice, for the sins of man are "compensated for" by the sacrifice of the Man-God. Nevertheless, this justice, which is properly justice "to God's measure," springs completely from love: from the love of the Father and of the Son, and completely bears fruit in love. Precisely for this reason the divine justice revealed in the cross of Christ is "to God's measure," because it springs from love and is accomplished in love, producing fruits of salvation. The divine dimension of redemption is put into effect not only by bringing justice to bear upon sin, but also by restoring to love that creative power in man thanks also which he once more has access to the fullness of life and holiness that come from God. In this way, redemption involves the revelation of mercy in its fullness.
>
> The Paschal Mystery is the culmination of this revealing and effecting of mercy, which is able to justify man, to restore justice in the sense of that salvific order which God willed from the beginning in man and, through man, in the world. (V.7)

Divine justice flows from love, and through this love justice is restored to God's creation. The Pope avoids the rhetorical opposition of love and justice of which St Isaac is so fond. He will not speak of such an opposition because, in his eyes, to divorce love and justice would suggest an approval and indulgence of wickedness and injury. Christ commands us to forgive seventy-times-seven, but this command does not abolish the "objective requirements of justice," the need of those who have been forgiven to make compensation and reparation to those whom they have injured. In this sense we may say that justice is the goal of forgiveness. "Thus the fundamental structure of justice," John Paul explains, "always enters into the sphere of mercy. Mercy, however, has the power to confer on justice a new content, which is expressed most simply and fully in forgiveness. Forgiveness, in fact, shows that, over and above the process of 'compensation' and 'truce' which is specific to justice, love is necessary, so that man may affirm himself as man" (VII.14).

The mercy of God is infinite and inexhaustible. The Father always stands ready and eager to welcome home his prodigal children. Flowing from the sacrifice of Christ—"that 'kiss' given by mercy to justice"—the power of God's forgiveness breaks through all boundaries. "No human sin," proclaims the Pope, "can prevail over this power or even limit it. On the part of man only a lack of good will can limit it, a lack of readiness to be converted and to repent, in other words persistence in obstinacy, opposing grace and truth, especially in the face of the witness of the cross and resurrection of Christ" (VII.13). Conversion is not a precondition for God's mercy but the discovery of his mercy, a discovery of a love that is always patient and kind. Those who attain to this knowledge of the merciful love of God live in a state of perpetual repentance, constantly turning to God and re-experiencing the tender forgiveness of the Father.

The Scandalous Injustice of Grace

John Paul's encyclical reflects that careful precision and balance one expects from a theologian trained both in Thomism and modern philosophy. But as a preacher I have to admit that I miss the note of the "injustice of grace" that we hear in the Syrian: "Do not call God just, for His justice is not manifest in the things concerning you." Isaac delights in the scandal of Christ's extravagant forgiveness in a way that John Paul does not. Yet both share a deep faith in the God who justifies the ungodly.

Chapter Four

The God of Wrath and the Father of Jesus Christ

When we confess that God is just, what do we mean? Quite likely we mean that God rewards good deeds and punishes evil deeds, either in this life or the next, in the exact proportion they deserve. God is likened to a wise magistrate, knowing all motivations, particulars, contingencies, and consequences. He dispenses impartial justice, universally and comprehensively. The virtuous are rewarded with goods and blessings, and the wicked are punished by the infliction of privation and suffering. Each receives their due. No one can complain that they have been treated unfairly; no one can protest that God has not set things right. Yet if we define the divine justice as the rewarding of good and the punishing of evil, God would seem to be committed to punish *every* iniquitous and sinful act, without exception. To do otherwise would be an abdication of duty and a violation of justice. What then of the divine mercy? Has it been expunged from God? That cannot be correct. As the psalmist sings: "For you, O Lord, are good and forgiving, abounding in steadfast love to all who call upon you" (Ps 86:5). We thus appear to be presented with a contradiction in God himself. For the way forward, we turn to the prophet of Scotland, George MacDonald.[1]

The Injustice of Retribution

In his famous sermon "Justice," MacDonald rejects the popular identification of justice with retribution:

---

[1] George MacDonald's son Greville named his father "St George the Divine."

The God of Wrath and the Father of Jesus Christ

> If you ask any ordinary Sunday congregation in England, what is meant by the justice of God, would not nineteen out of twenty answer, that it means his punishing of sin? Think for a moment what degree of justice it would indicate in a man—that he punished every wrong. A Roman emperor, a Turkish cadi, might do that, and be the most unjust both of men and judges. Ahab might be just on the throne of punishment, and in his garden the murderer of Naboth. In God shall we imagine a distinction of office and character? God is one; and the depth of foolishness is reached by that theology which talks of God as if he held different offices, and differed in each. It sets a contradiction in the very nature of God himself. It represents him, for instance, as having to do that as a magistrate which as a father he would not do! The love of the father makes him desire to be unjust as a magistrate![2]

Instead of imagining God as a courtroom judge, imagine him as a perfect father. How does a good father treat his children? Is he principally concerned to punish according to the letter of the law? Absolutely not. All of his acts toward his children are motivated by love, by the desire to advance their long-term well-being. When they injure someone, he insists they make apology and restitution. He may even administer corporal punishment (my father typically used a yardstick), but always the good of the child is uppermost in his mind. His goal is to set his child on the right path. This is the *fair play* which constitutes genuine justice and best accords with the merciful character of the God and Father of Jesus Christ. God is just because he always acts in service to the good. Justice and love are one.

Is God bound to punish sin? George MacDonald's answer is an emphatic no. If the answer were yes, then forgiveness would be impossible. Justice and mercy would find themselves opposed to each other, generating a schism within the Godhead. But we know

---

[2] George MacDonald, "Justice," Unspoken Sermons, Series Three (1889).

that God does forgive sin; hence it must be just and right for him to forgive. But wickedness *deserves* punishment, the retributivist replies. The *lex talionis* enjoys a long history, and several texts in Scripture appear to support it. Yet how do we reconcile retribution with mercy? If justice demands the punishment of our sinful acts, then they must be punished to the full extent required by justice. It will not do to think of God as first punishing sin and then subsequently forgiving it. "If sin demands punishment, and the righteous punishment is given, then the man is free," comments MacDonald. "Why should he be forgiven?"[3] Clearly there is something odd about the idea of pardoning an offense *after* punishment has been dispensed. The jurist within us demands that wrongdoers endure the suffering they deserve. If one of my loved ones have been wounded, harmed, or murdered, I want the criminal to suffer. That's why we have prisons and executions. Vengeance must be exacted—"eye for eye, tooth for tooth, hand for hand, foot for foot, burning for burning, wound for wound, stripe for stripe" (Ex 21:24-25).

Yet the infliction of pain, declares MacDonald, cannot put the world to rights:

> Punishment, deserved suffering, is no equipoise to sin. It is no use laying it in the other scale. It will not move it a hair's breadth. Suffering weighs nothing at all against sin. It is not of the same kind, not under the same laws, any more than mind and matter. We say a man deserves punishment; but when we forgive and do not punish him, we do not always feel that we have done wrong; neither when we do punish him do we feel that any amends has been made for his wrongdoing. If it were an offset to wrong, then God would be bound to punish for the sake of the punishment; but he cannot be, for he forgives. Then it is not for the sake of the punishment, as a thing that in itself ought to be

---

[3] Ibid.

done, but for the sake of something else, as a means to an end, that God punishes. It is not directly for justice, else how could he show mercy, for that would involve injustice?[1]

God forgives! This liberating gospel truth alone should alone compel us to reevaluate our inherited notion of retributive justice. The infliction of suffering upon the wrongdoer does not provide redress; it does not rectify; it does not heal the disorder created by the crime. Retribution has no place in the divine heart. If God is just, he has but one duty: to destroy the sin that has entered into his good world:

> Primarily, God is not bound to punish sin; he is bound to destroy sin. If he were not the Maker, he might not be bound to destroy sin—I do not know; but seeing he has created creatures who have sinned, and therefore sin has, by the creating act of God, come into the world, God is, in his own righteousness, bound to destroy sin.[2]

The true justice of God is *restorative*, not punitive. The infliction of suffering, in and of itself, makes better neither the world nor the sinner.

The Hermeneutics of Love

MacDonald denounces every reading of Scripture, no matter how literal and plain, that attributes to God what, in our heart of hearts, we *know* to be evil:

> But you say he does so and so, and is just; I say, he does not do so and so, and is just. You say he does, for the Bible says so. I say, if the Bible said so, the Bible would lie; but the Bible does not say so. The lord of life complains of men for not judging right. To say on the authority of

---
[1] Ibid.
[2] Ibid.

the Bible that God does a thing no honourable man would do, is to lie against God; to say that it is therefore right, is to lie against the very spirit of God.[6]

MacDonald is not afraid to appeal to conscience in his interpretation of the Scriptures. "I acknowledge no authority calling upon me to believe a thing of God," he comments, "which I could not believe right in my fellow man."[7] This may sound like mere humanism, but that would misread the Scotsman's intent. He is appealing to a conscience that has been fully informed by God's self-revelation in Jesus. He reads the Scriptures *in Christ* and *through Christ*. Hence he will not entertain any construal of the Bible that contradicts the character of the Father made known in the teachings and example of the Incarnate Son. Against the literalism of a naive biblicism, MacDonald proposes a *hermeneutic of love*. When confronted with difficult Scriptural texts, we must strive to bring our interpretation in line with the dominical revelation that God is love—absolute, infinite, unconditional love. What we must not do is justify evil in the name of Jesus Christ:

> If you say, That may be right of God to do which it would not be right of man to do, I answer, Yes, because the relation of the maker to his creatures is very different from the relation of one of those creatures to another, and he has therefore duties toward his creatures requiring of him what no man would have the right to do to his fellow-man; but he can have no duty that is not both just and merciful. More is required of the maker, by his own act of creation, than can be required of men. More and higher justice and righteousness is required of him by himself, the Truth;—greater nobleness, more penetrating sympathy; and *nothing* but what, if an honest man understood it, he would say was right. If it be a thing man cannot understand, then man can say nothing

---

[6] Ibid.
[7] Ibid.

as to whether it is right or wrong. He cannot even know that God does *it*, when the *it* is unintelligible to him. What he calls *it* may be but the smallest facet of a composite action. His part is silence. If it be said by any that God does a thing, and the thing seems to me unjust, then either I do not know what the thing is, or God does not do it. The saying cannot mean what it seems to mean, or the saying is not true. If, for instance, it be said that God visits the sins of the fathers on the children, a man who takes *visits upon* to mean *punishes*, and *the children* to mean the innocent children, ought to say, 'Either I do not understand the statement, or the thing is not true, whoever says it.' God *may* do what seems to a man not right, but it must so seem to him because God works on higher, on divine, on perfect principles, too right for a selfish, unfair, or unloving man to understand. But least of all must we accept some low notion of justice in a man, and argue that God is just in doing after that notion.[8]

MacDonald is not proposing a novel way to read the Holy Scriptures. Many of the Church Fathers insist that we may not attribute to God words, actions, characteristics that would be *unworthy* of the Father made known in his Son Jesus Christ. St Isaac the Syrian, for example, is clear: the crucified and risen Christ is our hermeneutic; we read the Scriptures through the spectacles of cruciform love. We must not, therefore, remain at the surface of the text but must delve deeper until we find the divine Lover waiting for us:

> That we should imagine that anger, wrath, jealousy or the such like have anything to do with the divine Nature is utterly abhorrent for us: no one in their right mind, no one who has any understanding at all can possibly come to such madness as to think anything of the sort against God. Nor again can we possibly say that He acts thus out of retribution, even though the Scriptures may on the outer surface posit this. Even to

---

[8] Ibid.

think this of God and to suppose that retribution for evil acts is to be found with Him is abominable. By implying that He makes use of such a great and difficult thing out of retribution we are attributing a weakness to the divine Nature. We cannot even believe such a thing can be found in those human beings who live a virtuous and upright life and whose thoughts are entirely in accord with the divine will—let alone believe it of God, that He has done something out of retribution for anticipated evil acts in connection with those whose nature He had brought into being with honour and great love. Knowing them and all their conduct, the flow of His grace did not dry up from them: not even after they started living amid many evil deeds did He withhold His care for them, even for a moment. . . . For it would be most odious and utterly blasphemous to think that hate or resentment exists with God, even against demonic beings; or to imagine any other weakness, or passibility, or whatever else might be involved in the course of retribution of good or bad as applying, in a retributive way, to that glorious divine Nature.[9]

The Obligations of Love

Of particular interest is MacDonald's claim that by his creation of the world God has assumed moral obligations toward his creatures. MacDonald seems to be departing from the classical teaching that because the Creator is the transcendent source of morality, he has no obligations toward the world. In reply, MacDonald insists that the Father of Jesus always acts for the good of his children. What we call divine obligation is but an expression of his faithfulness and love:

> 'Ah, but,' says the partisan of God, 'the Almighty stands in a relation very different from that of an earthly father: there is no parallel.' I grant it: there is no parallel. The man did not create the child, he only yielded to an impulse created in himself: God is infinitely more bound

---

[9] Isaac of Nineveh, *The Second Part* (1995), II.39.2-3.

> to provide for his child than any man is to provide for his. The relation is infinitely, divinely closer. It is God to whom every hunger, every aspiration, every desire, every longing of our nature is to be referred; he made all our needs—made us the creatures of a thousand necessities—and have we no claim on him? Nay, we have claims innumerable, infinite; and his one great claim on us is that we should claim our claims of him.[10]

We are made by the Good for the Good. Will our heavenly Father be satisfied with anything less than our rectification and glorification in his Kingdom?

The Salvation of the Outer Darkness

If the justice of God is essentially restorative and redemptive, how then can the eternal condemnation of the wicked ever be just and right?

> Punishment, I repeat, is not the thing required of God, but the absolute destruction of sin. What better is the world, what better is the sinner, what better is God, what better is the truth, that the sinner should suffer—continue suffering to all eternity? Would there be less sin in the universe? Would there be any making-up for sin? Would it show God justified in doing what he knew would bring sin into the world, justified in making creatures who he knew would sin? What setting-right would come of the sinner's suffering? If justice demand it, if suffering be the equivalent for sin, then the sinner must suffer, then God is bound to exact his suffering, and not pardon; and so the making of man was a tyrannical deed, a creative cruelty.[11]

---

[10] George MacDonald, "The Voice of Job," *Unspoken Sermons*, Series Two (1885).
[11] "Justice."

The Scottish preacher speaks boldly, some might say blasphemously. If the LORD foreknew that human beings would sin, thus necessitating their just condemnation to everlasting torment, his creation of the world can only be understood as a tyrannical deed and act of cruelty. Whatever the number of the damned turns out to be, God decided to create them anyway, knowing full well their ultimate fate. The damned are the collateral damage of divine creation—the many (or few) must suffer so that the few (or many) may thrive. What is this but a deal conceived in the depths of Tartarus. The God and Father of Jesus Christ has become a monster. MacDonald's powerful objection is directed against the retributive model of hell (no doubt the only model he knew) but can easily be extended to contemporary free-will models as well. However we understand eternal perdition, if it lacks redemptive purpose, it is an unholy abomination. The preacher continues:

> The path across the gulf that divides right from wrong is not the fire, but repentance. If my friend has wronged me, will it console me to see him punished? Will that be a rendering to me of my due? Will his agony be a balm to my deep wound? Should I be fit for any friendship if that were possible even in regard to my enemy? But would not the shadow of repentant grief, the light of reviving love on his countenance, heal it at once however deep? Take any of those wicked people in Dante's hell, and ask wherein is justice served by their punishment. Mind, I am not saying it is not right to punish them; I am saying that justice is not, never can be, satisfied by suffering—nay, cannot have any satisfaction in or from suffering. Human resentment, human revenge, human hate may. Such justice as Dante's keeps wickedness alive in its most terrible forms. The life of God goes forth to inform, or at least give a home to victorious evil. Is he not defeated every time that one of those lost souls defies him? All hell cannot make Vanni Fucci say 'I was wrong.' God is triumphantly defeated, I say, throughout the hell of his vengeance. Although against evil, it is but the vain and wasted

cruelty of a tyrant. There is no destruction of evil thereby, but an enhancing of its horrible power in the midst of the most agonizing and disgusting tortures a *divine* imagination can invent. . . .

The one deepest, highest, truest, fittest, most wholesome suffering must be generated in the wicked by a vision, a true sight, more or less adequate, of the hideousness of their lives, of the horror of the wrongs they have done. . . . Not for its own sake, not as a make-up for sin, not for divine revenge—horrible word, not for any satisfaction to justice, can punishment exist. Punishment is for the sake of amendment and atonement. God is bound by his love to punish sin in order to deliver his creature; he is bound by his justice to destroy sin in his creation. Love is justice—is the fulfilling of the law, for God as well as for his children. This is the reason of punishment; this is why justice requires that the wicked shall not go unpunished—that they, through the eye-opening power of pain, may come to see and do justice, may be brought to desire and make all possible amends, and so become just. Such punishment concerns justice in the deepest degree. For Justice, that is God, is bound in himself to see justice done by his children—not in the mere outward act, but in their very being. He is bound in himself to make up for wrong done by his children, and he can do nothing to make up for wrong done but by bringing about the repentance of the wrong-doer. When the man says, 'I did wrong; I hate myself and my deed; I cannot endure to think that I did it!' then, I say, is atonement begun. Without that, all that the Lord did would be lost. He would have made no atonement. Repentance, restitution, confession, prayer for forgiveness, righteous dealing thereafter, is the sole possible, the only true make-up for sin. For nothing less than this did Christ die.[12]

Critics of the greater hope often accuse its proponents of abolishing hell. Nothing could be further from the truth. Note MacDonald's creative reimagining of hell as purgatory. While lecturing on Dante, he once quipped: "When the Church thought that three places for

---

[12] Ibid.

departed spirits was too many, she took away the wrong one."[13] In his semi-autobiographical novel *Robert Falconer*, the protagonist meets with his father and urges him to repent. His father despairingly replies there is no repentance in hell. The narrator comments:

> In those few words lay the germ of the preference for hell of poor souls, enfeebled by wickedness. They will not have to do anything there—only to moan and cry and suffer for ever, they think. It is effort, the out-going of the living will that they dread. The sorrow, the remorse of repentance, they do not so much regard: it is the action it involves; it is the having to turn, be different, and do differently, that they shrink from; and they have been taught to believe that this will not be required of them there—in that awful refuge of the will-less. I do not say they think thus: I only say their dim, vague, feeble feelings are such as, if they grew into thought, would take this form. But tell them that the fire of God without and within them will compel them to bethink themselves; that the vision of an open door beyond the smoke and the flames will ever urge them to call up the ice-bound will, that it may obey; that the torturing spirit of God in them will keep their consciences awake, not to remind them of what they ought to have done, but to tell them what they must do now, and hell will no longer fascinate them. Tell them that there is no refuge from the compelling Love of God, save that Love itself—that He is in hell too, and that if they make their bed in hell they shall not escape him, and then, perhaps, they will have some true presentiment of the worm that dieth not and the fire that is not quenched.[14]

In the depths of Gehenna, there we will find the Crucified waiting for us. He will never rest until every sinner has been restored to him through repentance and faith. We may not know how this will be

---

[13] Quoted by Barbara Amell, "George MacDonald on Purgatory," *Wingfold* 89 (Winter 2015): 39.
[14] George MacDonald, *Robert Falconer* (1868), chap. III.XV.

accomplished, but we may nonetheless be confident that in his abundant love God will find a way. "He is their Father," MacDonald exclaims; "he had power to make them out of himself, separate from himself, and capable of being one with him: surely he will somehow save and keep them! Not the power of sin itself can close all the channels between creating and created."[15] MacDonald may not be able to explain the mechanism of universal salvation; but he knows that Love has destroyed sin and death and risen into glory. The Scotsman cannot envisage the Father of Jesus ever abandoning the children he has brought into being. God has created human beings for union with him—not for death, not for annihilation, not for perdition. He will always and unrelentingly do his best for them, even if it means immersing them in the Gehennic fire of his love.

Yet how? we still ask. How might God convert those who have definitively set their wills against him? Here the author of fairy tales is willing to speculate.

Once upon a time . . .

Imagine a human being, any human being, perhaps you, perhaps me, digging in his or her heels and refusing to love God. "I will not repent," he declares. "I will not obey God. I will not love him. I would be rid of him once and for all." In this state of mortal sin, he dies and awakens in the outer darkness. God grants him the autonomy he desires. He is removed from all materiality, from all the goods of the world to which he so idolatrously enslaved himself during his earthly life. He is divorced from all creaturely intercourse. There is no up, no down, no left or right. There is no where, no passage of time, nothing to perceive, no sounds to hear, no presences to feel. Imagine the soul's bewilderment, disequilibrium, vertigo, terror. There is only the void—a sensory deprivation tank of total isolation:

---

[15] "Justice."

> It is the vast outside; the ghastly dark beyond the gates of the city of which God is the light—where the evil dogs go ranging, silent as the dark, for there is no sound any more than sight. The time of signs is over. Every sense has its signs, and they were all misused: there is no sense, no sign more—nothing now by means of which to believe. The man wakes from the final struggle of death, in absolute loneliness—such a loneliness as in the most miserable moment of deserted childhood he never knew. Not a hint, not a shadow of anything outside his consciousness reaches him. All is dark, dark and dumb; no motion—not the breath of a wind! never a dream of change! not a scent from far-off field! nothing to suggest being or thing besides the man himself, no sign of God anywhere. God has so far withdrawn from the man, that he is conscious only of that from which he has withdrawn. In the midst of the live world he cared for nothing but himself; now in the dead world he is in God's prison, his own separated self. He would not believe in God because he never saw God; now he doubts if there be such a thing as the face of a man—doubts if he ever really saw one, ever anything more than dreamed of such a thing:—he never came near enough to human being, to know what human being really was—so may well doubt if human beings ever were, if ever he was one of them.[16]

No matter how hard he tries, the lost soul cannot escape from the void nor will himself out of existence. There is nothing to satisfy his disordered desires, no one with whom to converse, no one to dominate or exploit—sheer nothingness and the misery of interminable solitude. The self is alone in the phantasmagoria of nightmare. Madness beckons.

Yet perhaps there may be a way to reality, to sanity, to love:

> The most frightful idea of what could, to his own consciousness, befall a man, is that he should have to lead an existence with which God had nothing to do. The thing could not be; for being that is caused, the

---

[16] George MacDonald, "The Last Farthing," *Unspoken Sermons*, Series Two (1885).

causation ceasing, must of necessity cease. It is always in, and never out of God, that we can live and do. But I suppose the man so left that he seems to himself utterly alone, yet, alas! with himself—smallest interchange of thought, feeblest contact of existence, dullest reflection from other being, impossible: in such evil case I believe the man would be glad to come in contact with the worst-loathed insect: it would be a shape of life, something beyond and besides his own huge, void, formless being! I imagine some such feeling in the prayer of the devils for leave to go into the swine. His worst enemy, could he but be aware of him, he would be ready to worship. For the misery would be not merely the absence of all being other than his own self, but the fearful, endless, unavoidable presence of that self. Without the correction, the reflection, the support of other presences, being is not merely unsafe, it is a horror—for anyone but God, who is his own being. For him whose idea is God's, and the image of God, his own being is far too fragmentary and imperfect to be anything like good company. It is the lovely creatures God has made all around us, in them giving us himself, that, until we know him, save us from the frenzy of aloneness—for that aloneness is Self, Self, Self. The man who minds only himself must at last go mad if God did not interfere.

Can there be any way out of the misery? Will the soul that could not believe in God, with all his lovely world around testifying of him, believe when shut in the prison of its own lonely, weary all-and-nothing? It would for a time try to believe that it was indeed nothing, a mere glow of the setting sun on a cloud of dust, a paltry dream that dreamed itself—then, ah, if only the dream might dream that it was no more! that would be the one thing to hope for. Self-loathing, and that for no sin, from no repentance, from no vision of better, would begin and grow and grow; and to what it might not come no soul can tell—of essential, original misery, uncompromising self disgust! Only, then, if a being be capable of self-disgust, is there not some room for hope—as much as a pinch of earth in the cleft of a rock might yield for the growth of a pine? Nay, there must be hope while there is existence; for where there is existence there must be God; and God is for ever good, nor can be other than good. But alas, the distance from the light! Such a soul is at the farthest verge of life's negation!—no, not the farthest! a man is nearer heaven when in deepest hell than just ere he begins to reap the reward of his doings—for he is in a condition to receive the smallest show of the life that is, as a boon unspeakable. All his years in the world he received the endless gifts of sun and air, earth and sea and human face divine, as things that came to him because that was their way, and there was no one to prevent them; now the poorest thinning of the darkness he would hail as men of old the glow of a descending angel; it would be as a messenger from God. Not that he would think of God! it takes long to think of God; but hope, not yet seeming hope, would begin to dawn in his bosom, and the thinner darkness would be as a cave of light, a refuge from the horrid self of which he used to be so proud.[17]

"Help me," the tortured soul whispers. "Help me." And then comes the word he is so desperate to hear:

"I am the resurrection and the life."

---

[17] Ibid.

Chapter Five

The Radical Gospel of Unconditional Love

What is at Stake?

What is at stake in the universalist/infernalist debate? Perhaps the best way to answer this is to first identify what is *not* at stake.

- What is *not* at stake is the Christological foundation of salvation. I wholeheartedly affirm that salvation is through and in Jesus Christ, the incarnate Son of God.
- What is *not* at stake is the freedom of the human being. I wholeheartedly affirm that God neither violates personal integrity nor coerces anyone into faith.
- What is *not* at stake is the preaching of repentance. I wholeheartedly affirm that the preacher must summon sinners to repentance of their sins, moral behavior, ascetical practices, and personal participation in the life of the Holy Spirit.
- What is *not* at stake is the horror of hell and the outer darkness. I wholeheartedly affirm that rejection of God necessarily results in spiritual death and misery. Preachers therefore need to warn their congregations of this terrible possibility.

And I'm sure there are several more "not at stakes" that I cannot think of at the moment.

So what is at stake? Nothing less than the good news of Jesus Christ!

Destined for Joy

"God is love," the Apostle John declares (1 Jn 4:8). In the life, death, and resurrection of Jesus Christ, God the Holy Trinity has been revealed as love—absolute, infinite, unconditional, abounding, ever-bestowing love. In the wonderful words of St Isaac, the Syrian:

> In love did He bring the world into existence; in love does He guide it during this its temporal existence; in love is He going to bring it to that wondrous transformed state, and in love will the world be swallowed up in the great mystery of Him who has performed all things; in love will the whole course of the governance of creation be finally comprised.[1]

All Christians affirm that God is love, though most disagree with the implications that the universalist draws from it:

- Universalists affirm that God unconditionally wills the eschatological well-being of every human being. They reject the Augustinian, Thomist, and Calvinist positions that God elects only a portion of humanity to eternal salvation.
- Universalists affirm that God never wills our eschatological ill-being. They reject the claim that God everlastingly punishes the wicked or abandons them to interminable torment or lacks the resources to restore every person to himself in freedom and faith.

The Love of God is Radically Unconditional

Most Christians balk at the description of the divine love as truly *unconditional*, even though they will sometimes use that word. They insist that God has in fact stipulated multiple conditions for the fulfillment of salvation, the most commonly mentioned being the

---

[1] Isaac of Nineveh, *Hom. II.38,* in *The Second Part (1995).*

free response of faith and repentance before the moment death. Thus St Basil the Great:

> The grace from above does not come to the one who is not striving. But both of them, the human endeavor and the assistance descending from above through faith, must be mixed together for the perfection of virtue ... Therefore, the authority of forgiveness has not been given unconditionally, but only if the repentant one is obedient and in harmony with what pertains to the care of the soul. It is written concerning these things: "If two of you agree on earth about anything they ask, it will be done for them by my Father in heaven" [Mt 18:19]. One cannot ask about which sins this refers to, as if the New Testament has not declared any difference, for it promises absolution of every sin to those who have repented worthily. He repents worthily who has adopted the intention of the one who said, "I hate and abhor unrighteousness" [Ps 119:163], and who does those things which are said in the 6th Psalm and in others concerning works, and like Zacchaios does many virtuous deeds.[2]

Patriarch Jeremias II cites this passage from Basil in his critique of the Lutheran construal of justification by faith, which he interpreted as undermining the necessity of good works. His critique is well worth reading, as are the responses by the Tübingen theologians. For the Patriarch, as for so many of the Eastern Fathers, the emphasis falls not on the *sola gratia*, as one finds in St Augustine of Hippo and St Bernard of Clairvaux, but on the robust repentance that draws to us the divine mercy: "Even if salvation is by grace," writes Jeremias, "yet man himself, through whose achievements and the sweat of his brow attracts the grace of God, is also the cause."[3]

---

[2] Basil of Caesarea, *Short Rules* PG 31.1085; quoted in George Mastrantonis, *Augsburg and Constantinople* (2005), p. 38.
[3] Ibid., p. 42.

Clearly, though, this is not the whole evangelical story. I understand these statements and others like them as expressions of pastoral care, as exhortations to devote our lives wholeheartedly to a life of holiness and discipleship; but I have also seen, and have experienced within myself, the spiritual and emotional damage that can be done by the rhetoric of "worthy repentance" and "worthy communion." We cannot but hear this language as speaking of a divine love that is contingent upon the human response: God will be merciful to us *if* we believe, *if* we repent, *if* we obey or at least try very hard. Despite all that Christ has done, the burden of salvation falls upon the sinner. The Orthodox emphasis on synergism only reinforces the point. The cooperative interaction of divine grace and human agency is, of course, *descriptively* true—God saves us within, not apart from, our personal involvement—but when it is translated into first- and second-person *prescriptive* preaching, it will always be heard as law; and law never generates faith and hope. The urgent question then becomes, How do we fulfill the stipulated conditions and how can we ever know, can we know, we have fulfilled them? Despair is the inevitable consequence of every exhortation to perfection that appears to call into question the all-embracing love of the Father: "those to whom the promise of the kingdom of heaven is proclaimed must fulfill all things perfectly and legitimately, and without them it shall be denied."[4] For Jeremias, justification before God is a purely future possibility and the threat of irrevocable failure is never far away.

It's not just a matter of achieving in our teaching a scholastic kind of harmony between divine grace and human effort but rather of understanding how authentic faith is grounded upon the unconditional promise of eternal salvation. Jeremias understands that the grace and mercy of God precedes and anticipates, yet he

---

[4] Ibid., p. 39.

cannot declare the love of God as unconditional, for fear of cultivating sloth, indifference, and presumption. Not unexpectedly the Tübingen theologians found wanting Jeremias's conditionalist construal of the gospel:

> But it is necessary that the divine promise be most clear and certain, so that faith may depend upon it. For were the assurance and steadfastness of the promise shaken, then faith would collapse. And if faith is overturned, then our justification and salvation will vanish.[5]

To a large extent the parties are talking past each other. Why so? I suggest the following: Jeremias is reflecting on justification from within the existential struggles and dynamics of the ascetical life, in anticipation of the coming judgment. The Lutherans are reflecting on justification from within the existential situation of having heard the Last Judgment spoken to them in the gospel, "ahead of time," as it were.[6] They understand that when God speaks his eschatological promise to us, we can no longer treat our salvation as a transaction. Life in Christ is not a matter of us doing our part and God doing his. In the right preaching of the gospel, God takes upon himself the responsibility for the fulfillment of the salvific promise: "In Christ your life is good and will be good—this I declare to you in the name of the crucified and risen Son." From this moment on, there can only be living and doing that is grounded upon the gospel. This is saving faith—a trusting and hopeful living within the Love who has grasped us. Whereas, the preaching of conditional promise produces either fervent effort to fulfill the soteriological conditions (hence the language of merit and reward), rejection ("I like my life

---

[5] Ibid., p. 126.
[6] "'Gospel!' is the news of God's completely remarkable affirmation of just this rebel [i.e., sinful man], the Last Judgment let out ahead of time and revealed as, of all things, acquittal." Robert W. Jenson, "A Dead Issue Revisited," *Lutheran Quarterly* (1962): 55.

of sin just as it is, thank you very much"), or despair ("this task is too much for me"), the preaching of unconditional promise generates either unshakable faith ("I trust you, O Lord, in all things") or offense ("How dare you violate my freedom!"). Robert W. Jenson puts it this way:

> "Faith" is *not* the label of an ideological or attitudinal state. Like "justification" the word evokes a *communication-situation*: the situation of finding oneself addressed with an unconditional affirmation, and having now to deal with life in these new terms. Faith is a mode of life. Where the radical question is alive all life becomes a *hearing*, a listening for permission to go on; faith is this listening—to the gospel.[7]

Faith does not liberate us from the churchly summons to repent of our sins; but the exhortations are now heard differently, for they are spoken within the evangelical context of the giftedness of salvation. Can we exploit the gift for our own to sinful ends? Of course. The Apostle Paul had to address that situation in Romans 6: "Are we to continue in sin that grace may abound?" Note his response: "You have died to sin in baptism and are no longer the kind of persons who would even ask that question!" The gospel performatively creates and fulfills the condition for its regenerate reception in the Spirit. Unconditional love calls forth unconditional discipleship. *Because* God loves you unconditionally, *because* he has assumed human flesh and defeated death and Satan by his resurrection on Easter morning, *because* he has poured out his Spirit upon humanity; *therefore*, believe and repent and return to the Lord; *therefore*, go forth into the world, preach the gospel, serve the poor, and love your neighbor as your Savior loves you.

Another oft-stipulated condition of salvation is the time limit. At some point, typically the moment of death, repentance becomes an

---

[7] Eric W. Gritsch and Robert W. Jenson, *Lutheranism* (1976), p. 41.

impossibility for the sinner. As Dumitru Staniloae puts it, the reprobate are "hardened in a negative freedom that cannot possibly be overcome."[8] At this point, God has no choice but to withdraw his offer of forgiveness. God abandons the wicked to their doom, or as St John of Damascus puts it, the condemned are "given over to everlasting fire."[9] The divine love is understood as truly conditional, at the practical level if not at the theological (absolute predestination creates its own problems). In traditional Western presentations, the divine love gives way to divine justice; in Orthodox presentations, the divine love remains theoretically inexhaustible but now rendered impotent, thus emptying it of existential relevance. If the sinner has become constitutionally incapable of repentance, then God must cease to desire his redemption. The Omnipotence is helpless before human freedom. He has made a rock that even he cannot lift. In both Eastern and Western construals, therefore, the gospel is necessarily presented as contingent promise: "If you repent before such-and-such a time, then you will be saved." Yet how do the infernalists know that final and irrevocable impenitence is even a possibility? In fact they do not *know*. They have inferred it from their prior dogmatic commitment to everlasting damnation. Once again we see how hell conditions theological reflection and corrupts faith. Once we accept perdition, we will configure our understanding of created freedom accordingly. The universalist, however, emphatically dissents. No matter the depth of our obduracy, our primordial desire for the Good abides. We cannot eradicate our innate hunger for union with the Holy Trinity. This is what it means to be made in the image of Christ. The fire may have diminished to near nothingness, yet always an ember remains that the Spirit can blow into flame.

---

[8] Dumitru Staniloae, *The Experience of God* (2013), VI:42.
[9] John of Damascus, *On the Orthodox Faith* IV.27.

Those who confess the universalist hope—whether in its weaker version (St Gregory Nazianzen, St Maximus the Confessor, Julian of Norwich, Hans Urs von Balthasar, Kallistos Ware) or its stronger version (St Gregory Nyssen, St Isaac the Syrian, Sergius Bulgakov, David Bentley Hart) —vigorously protest against the conditionalist portrayal of deity. Their objection is not grounded on the exegesis of a particular verse or two but rather upon a profound apprehension of the God they have encountered in Jesus Christ. How someone achieves this apprehension varies from person to person. Some experience it through their reading of Scripture, some through sacrament and liturgy, others through contemplative prayer and mystical experience or their service to the poor and oppressed, still others through the love bestowed upon them by their neighbors—or any combination of the above. But once the love of God is personally experienced in the fullness of its radical unconditionality, there can be no turning back. Once we know God as absolute love, we cannot unknow it. It is now the fundamental truth of our lives. The unconditionality of the divine love, therefore, can never be just one option among many options. Nor may it be qualified, subordinated, or dismissed in the name of dogma—*it is the dogma!* Unconditional love can only be affirmed unconditionally—categorically, uncompromisingly, immoderately, scandalously. The bounteous self-giving of the Father, Son, and Holy Spirit has become the prism through which all of reality is apprehended and experienced. It informs the hopes and dreams of every person who has heard the gospel of Jesus.

Yet, there is much in Scripture that seems to argue against the unconditionality of the divine love, including some of the parables and teachings of Jesus. We need not rehearse these texts. I imagine that we all have wrestled with them and continue to wrestle with them. I remember posing this question to Jenson in the late 80s. His reply: "Go back and reread the Bible." At the time, I didn't find the reply particularly helpful, but I eventually came to understand what I think he was saying: "Put on a different pair of spectacles!"

The Spectacles of Love

In his book *Imagining God,* Garrett Green invites us to consider the role of theological paradigms in our interpretation of Scripture. Analogous to the role of paradigms within modern science, theological paradigms and metanarratives organize the data available to us and help us to make sense of it. "Our perception of parts," he writes, "depends on our prior grasp of the whole."[10] Perhaps the greatest stumbling block to a serious consideration of the universalist reading of Scripture is our refusal to step outside the traditional paradigm of conditional love. How is it possible that the holy God of Israel could accept us in our sinfulness, "just as we are"? How is it possible that by his Spirit, God might convert even the most wicked and pervicacious of sinners? What is needed is an imaginative leap to a new, but also very old, paradigm. Only then will we be able to apprehend the universalist reading of Scripture as a coherent gestalt. Another way of putting it: we must read the Bible through a hermeneutic of Pascha.

Several years ago, a respected Orthodox priest asked and answered the question *Dare we hope that all men be saved?* "No," he declared, "we do not dare to hope for such a thing. It is a delirious fantasy, neither a proper object of Christian hope, nor a proper subject for Christian speculation." I was appalled. I understand why he and others believe that the universalist hope is heterodox; yet when I read their articles and books, I am shocked, nonetheless. I hear them declaring a different gospel than the one I have long believed, confessed, and preached. If God is *not* absolute, infinite, and unconditional love, then there is no good news of Jesus

---

[10] Garrett Green, *Imagining God* (1989), p. 50.

Christ to believe and proclaim, and our lives are not worth living and dying. We have reduced the God of the gospel to a punitive divinity who commands us to achieve our righteousness under the threat of eternal torment. In the end, we are saved or not saved according to our merits. If the word "merit" offends, then substitute faith, repentance, virtues, works, performance—it doesn't matter, for in this context all express the transactionality of the soteriological arrangement. But if God is absolute, infinite, unbounded love, then we may not restrict his willingness and power to accomplish his salvific ends for mankind; we may not put limits on his commitment to accomplish our good, for he most certainly puts no limits on it.

Even so, someone objects, universal salvation still sounds too good to be true. Our skepticism runs deep. Human history is replete with truly wicked persons. It's easier to believe that they will remain irreversibly fixed in their rejection of God's love and forgiveness, no matter how many chances they are given, than to believe that everyone, without exception, will eventually repent. To this concern George MacDonald has given the only possible gospel answer:

> We do not hope half enough. "This is too good to believe," we say. But, if there be a God, nothing is too good to believe; and, if Christ be His Son and messenger and image, humanity is divine and God is human. A father's heart, a heart like our own, only infinite in tenderness, will be found at the bottom of things."[11]
>
> If you find what I tell you untrue, it will only be that it is not grand and free and bounteous enough. To think anything too good to be true,

---

[11] Sermon delivered at All Soul's Unitarian Church, New York City, on 11 May 1873, as reported by Henry Witney Bellows and quoted in *Wingfold* (Winter 2007).

is to deny God—to say the untrue may be better than the true—that there might be a greater God than he.[12]

God wills our salvation and only wills our salvation. He never accepts no as our final answer. In the words of the Apostle Paul: "For all the promises of God find their Yes in him. That is why we utter the Amen through him, to the glory of God" (2 Cor 1:20). And again Paul:

> For I am sure that neither death, nor life, nor angels, nor principalities, nor things present, nor things to come, nor powers, nor height, nor depth, nor anything else in all creation, will be able to separate us from the love of God in Christ Jesus our Lord. (Rom 8:38-39)

What is at stake in this present debate? Nothing less than who God has revealed himself to be in the crucified and risen Jesus Christ. Any qualification of the unconditionality of the divine love is intolerable. If there should come a point, any point, where God abandons the one lost sheep or no longer searches for the one lost coin, then God is not the Father of Jesus Christ and our worst nightmares are true.

---

[12] George MacDonald, *Donal Grant* (1883), chap. 45.

Chapter Six

The Gospel as Story and Promise

Robert W. Jenson is known today as a brilliant theologian who sought to reenvision metaphysics from the perspective of the gospel: if Jesus Christ be crucified and risen, how does this impact our understanding of God and cosmos? This was an abiding theme throughout his theological career. Yet what drew me originally to Jenson four decade ago were not his metaphysical speculations but his unequivocal affirmation of the gospel as liberating proclamation and promise, grounded in the unconditional love of the Holy Trinity.

Jenson begins his 1973 mini-systematics *Story and Promise* with this passage:

> Since shortly after the execution of Jesus the Nazarene, a certain communication has passed through history and through the world. A few in each generation have told the story of this Jesus, and of his people Israel, as a message of destiny—of the destiny, indeed, of each new set of speakers and hearers. This story, its messengers have claimed, is the encompassing plot of all men's stories; it promises the outcome of the entire human enterprise and of each man's involvement in it. Let me try a premature summary formulation of the story and its promise, at some risk of ambiguity: "There has lived a man wholly for others, all the way to death; and he has risen, so that his self-giving will finally triumph."[1]

A story and a promise, a story with a promise, a story that is promise. The gospel is more than the communication of historical

---

[1] Robert W. Jenson, *Story and Promise* (1973), p. 1.

facts about a person who lived 2,000 years ago. It certainly includes "facts," for Jesus was a man who lived and died in human history, but from the beginning his biography has been presented in a unique way—specifically, as eschatological pledge, as gospel. Having surrendered himself to death on the cross for the salvation of all, Jesus now lives—he is risen!—his love for his fellow human beings must determine the final outcome of history. As the Church confesses: "he shall come again, with glory, to judge the quick and the dead."

Jenson describes Christ as a human being who lived by the Spirit fully and completely for others. This way of speaking—"a man for others"—can be traced back to Dietrich Bonhoeffer. It was popularized in the English-speaking world by J. A. T. Robinson in the 1960s. I've never particularly liked the expression and have never used it in my preaching. To my ears it makes Jesus sound like a great humanitarian, and that is light-years away from Jenson's intent. It's easy enough, though, to rephrase: the life of Jesus was perfectly determined by love—by love for his Father and by love for his brethren. Precisely as such he is the incarnate Son, the second person of the Holy Trinity.

Jesus as Eschatological Prophet

The young Jenson's understanding of the historical Jesus was formed by his graduate school immersion in German "second quest" scholarship—think especially of Ernst Käsemann and Günther Bornkamm, among many others. I do not know how well acquainted Jenson was with the "third quest" of Jesus scholarship (he would have found helpful support in the works of E. P. Sanders, N. T. Wright, and John P. Meier). In any case, he appears to have consistently maintained the second quest view of the Nazarene as eschatological prophet and herald of the Kingdom:

Destined for Joy

Jesus the Nazarene was a wandering preacher, a semi-rabbi. He went from place to place proclaiming the coming of the "Kingdom of God." "Kingdom of God" was a summary name for the fulfillment of all the promises which Israel's history with Jahve had left with her. With John "the Baptist," prophets were, surprisingly, again on the scene; also Jesus was a sort of prophet. He said: "The time is fulfilled, and the kingdom of God is at hand. Turn your lives around, and trust the good news."[2]

Of course, Jeremiah, Isaiah, and Ezekiel might also be described as eschatological prophets, so what was the difference? All prophets before Jesus urgently called Israel to repentance. All spoke of judgment. Some spoke of a coming new age. The time is short, declares St John the Forerunner. The judgment of God is at hand. Change your lives now, before it is too late. If you do, you will partake of the goodness and blessings of the reign of God; if you do not, you will know only tribulation and condemnation. The prophetic summons posits a temporal space for conversion: repent now . . . before it is too late. Jesus also spoke this way; but the difference, suggests Jenson, was the way he said it:

> Although what Jesus said about the Kingdom was not new, there was something new in the way he said it. The normal, law-like, pattern of utterance and life posits a span of time between my present and whatever future I am concerned with: the "then . . ." clause poses a future possibility, and the "if . . ." clause establishes a space of controllable time in which to take care of the indicated conditions. The "if . . ." clause posits a sort of expanded present, a space protected from the uncertainty of the future, in which I can do what I need, if I choose. So the standard way of meeting also the prophetic announcement of the coming Kingdom had been—and is—to put it five or five hundred years in the future, or five seconds, and take the interval as the time to get ready.

---

[2] Ibid., p. 35.

The interval can be used for postponement. "Repent," said the prophets; "Next year we will indeed," said most of the people. But it can also be used for frantic preparations, for the "works of the Law." This was the pattern of the Pharisees, a lay movement that had developed the religion of the Law to a consistency and sincerity nearly past our conceiving. They made a life's work of looking for conditions of the Kingdom and fulfilling them.

Jesus so spoke the Kingdom at the existence of his hearers as to short-circuit both responses, as to take away the space of time between the moment of their hearing him and the future he promised. He left them no time to get ready; instead he made the Kingdom the decisive reality for the decisions and hopes and fears which were the then-and-there of their lives. When men heard Jesus' call to the Kingdom, they either were thereby called into its citizenship, or found they had already rejected it. They either found that all other values defined themselves by the hope of the Kingdom ("they left all and followed him" [Matt 5:11]), or that they had already chosen to prefer other things ("and he went sadly away, for he had many possessions" [Mark 10:17-31]).[3]

By word and action, Jesus brought the Kingdom of God into the life of Israel as an immediate reality, anticipated yet still to be realized. There was no longer any time in which one might either prepare for its coming, no time in which to repent or not to repent. The Kingdom is dawning. As Jenson puts it: "Jesus took away from his hearers the possibility of neutralizing God's futurity, of mitigating its threat and challenge by cutting out a time of their autonomous own in which to plan and prepare for it, and so getting it—even a little bit—into present control."[4] Why is it, some asked, that the disciples of John and the Pharisees fast but yours do not? "Can the wedding guests fast while the bridegroom is with them?" Jesus replies (Mark 2:19). The wedding feast is already under way. All are bade to

---

[3] Ibid., pp. 36-37.
[4] Ibid., p. 38.

rejoice and celebrate. Come, join the festivities! Social and religious status is irrelevant. Whether Pharisee or publican, priest or whore, rich or poor, none are at advantage or disadvantage. "Zacchae′us, make haste and come down; for I must stay at your house today" (Luke 19:5). Jesus scandalized the religious elites by eating with tax collectors and sinners in proleptic actualization of the Messianic Banquet. He proclaimed the Kingdom *unconditionally* and embodied it as *gift*. There was no longer any time in which to fulfill "if . . . then . . ." clauses. There was only the present and decisive moment of *eschaton*.

> That is, Jesus proclaimed the Kingdom *unconditionally*; he left not time to fulfill "if . . ." clauses. . . . When the question is, "Will life achieve a meaning at all?" everyone heard from Jesus the same promise and was tempted to the same abnegation. We will all achieve our selves in spite of ourselves. . . .
>
> Jesus did not merely proclaim to the poor, the publicans, and the sinners that in God's future they would be new men, he treated them then and there as the new men they would be. His message had nothing in it of "pie in the sky by and by." This is the point of one of the most pervasive recollections about Jesus' actions: that he "ate with publicans and sinners." In all cultures, eating together is an expression of fellowship; in oriental cultures, it creates permanent brotherhood; and in Israel, because of the table prayers, it creates brotherhood before God. Jesus' chosen brothers before God were the outsiders.
>
> We regulate our relations with our fellows by what they have been; if a teenager is hooked on dope, we do not encourage our children to make him a friend. Jesus did the opposite: he brought his fellows into his life not in terms of what they had been, but of what they would be. And not in terms of what it could be predicted they would be, on the basis of a "little bit of good in everyone" or of what he planned to

reform them to, but in terms of what they could be only by God's miracle. He enacted God's future as his brothers' own present.[3]

Such was the prodigality of the love of the Nazarene, and it was precisely this love that led him to his death. But why should we believe that his love has anything to do with us today?

The Gospel of Pascha

"Jesus is risen!" Here is the gospel in its most compact, succinct, and exhilarating expression. The gospel can be proclaimed in a multitude of ways, yet all ultimately distil to Easter. Apart from the resurrection, Jesus' preaching of the coming Kingdom is proved empty and his agonizing death on the Cross meaningless. Apart from the resurrection, Jesus simply joins a long line of dead prophets and messianic pretenders. He may have exercised a powerful ministry back in the day, but why should subsequent generations pay him attention? If Jesus is dead, then he exists only in the past, and it would be folly to imitate him. It's one thing to die for a cause that one deems greater than oneself, but it's quite another to embrace a loving that inevitably leads to death and is at that moment undone. Love promises the gift of self to one's beloved, yet death destroys the gift and voids the promise. How is that salvation for the world? As the Apostle Paul reminded the church in Corinth: "If Christ be not raised, your faith is vain; ye are yet in your sins" (1 Cor 15:17). Apart from the resurrection, life in Christ is impossible. Faith rests on the unconditional promise of the Kingdom proclaimed by Christ and sealed in his obedience unto death:

---

[3] Ibid., pp. 38-39.

If Jesus were dead, following him would be the imitating of a figure of the past, and so self-defeating: for the life to which the past Jesus called was exactly that we give up all such clinging to the past, and live by hope for the future Kingdom. Precisely the historical facts of his words and his actions means that only if he is alive, only if he is free to surprise us and upset all our imitations of what has been, is it possible to be his followers. Christian faith is not a matter of knowing about what Jesus did back there, and then seeking how now to get benefit from it; it is a matter of the promise made right now in the name of a living man, Jesus—who is of course known to us only by what he did back there, and by the self-surrender unto death in which he did it.[6]

The message of resurrection, in other words, need not be heard as gospel. It all depends on who Jesus was. If Jesus had been an inconsequential fellow who lived down the block ("Can anything good come out of Nazareth?" [John 1:46]), we might well respond to the news of his resurrection with a yawn. "How curious," we'd remark, and then proceed with our lives as if nothing of import had happened.

If Jesus had lived a particularly wicked life, if he had in fact been a tyrant responsible for the oppression and death of millions, then we would probably be horrified by the news of his resurrection. Substitute the name "Josef Stalin, "Adolf Hitler," or "Pol Pot" and see how you feel. As Jenson wryly remarks: "Hitler is risen' would lift few hearts."[7]

But everything changes when Jesus of Nazareth is made the subject of the resurrection confession. Hearts are transformed and disciples are made—suddenly there is Church. "Jesus is risen!" becomes breathtaking news because "Jesus" names the love narrated

---

[6] Ibid., p. 44.
[7] Robert W. Jenson, *Systematic Theology* (2001), I:31.

in the four gospels. If Jesus lives, his love has a future, for us and for his God:

> Jesus lived and then died. Therefore we have a definition of what it means to be Jesus, we know what he is: he is the one who lived wholly in the hope he had to bring his fellows, giving himself to that hope even to death. If despite death he now lives, then his self-giving is not only an item of the past to be remembered, but a surprise in the future to be expected. And if that, then not merely one item of the future, but the last future, the conclusion of the human enterprise. For death is already behind him, and nothing can any more limit his hopeful self-giving; it will necessarily encompass all men and all man's history. To say "Jesus was dead and is alive" is to say something about the last future.[8]

Jesus now lives with *death behind him.* Here lies, Jenson contends, the eschatological significance of Jesus' proclamation of the coming Kingdom; and here lies, I contend, the driving conviction of Jensonian theology. That the God of Israel has exalted Jesus as Lord and Christ means not only that God has ratified the teaching and mission of Jesus, but that he has eternally established him as the eschatological consummation of humanity and the cosmos. Jesus is risen and his love must triumph! The Kingdom would not be Kingdom otherwise.

Death limits all the promises we may make to each other, yet Jesus dared to proclaim the Kingdom unconditionally to his hearers. When the Lord invited himself into the life of Zacchaeus, thereby incorporating the tax collector into the communion of the Kingdom, Zacchaeus responded with an act of sacrificial thanksgiving: "Behold, Lord, the half of my goods I give to the poor; and if I have defrauded any one of anything, I restore it fourfold" (Luke 19:8). "Today," Jesus immediately announced, "salvation has come to this

---

[8] Jenson, *Story*, p. 44.

house" (Luke 19:9). We misread the story if we interpret Zacchaeus' repentance as a precondition for his salvation. In the symbolic act of table fellowship, Jesus had already brought the Kingdom to him. Such was Jesus' faith in his Father and the eschatological mission entrusted to him. In this faith Jesus freely embraced the passion and death that was the inevitable conclusion of his mission. "Father, if thou art willing, remove this cup from me; nevertheless, not my will, but thine, be done" (Luke 22:42). Only Pascha would prove the faith of Jesus. "In that he interpreted his fellows' lives by God's future rather than by their own pasts," writes Jenson, "Jesus interpreted his own life by that same future. The outcome of his own life would be the fulfillment or failure of the promise he brought."[9]

By the mighty act of God, Jesus now lives. Death lies behind him, and therefore his promise of Kingdom is not only confirmed but has become sayable in the world:

> If Jesus died but now lives, his reality is open to the meaning and outcome of what he did, suffered, and was, without the condition that we must observe: he does not need to specify, "I am committed, of course, only insofar as my commitment does not lead me to death and so to its own negation." Since death is behind him, nothing can anymore separate him from his future. He is himself the one he evoked by his teaching, the one for whom the prophets' promises are the word to live by right now—without intervening space for preparation, postponement or failure, without intervening death, without intervening law. Alienation is no longer a possibility. . . .
>
> If Jesus died and lives, the fulfillment of his life opens unconditionally to him. But his life was speaking the promise of Israel's Kingdom to other men, acting it out with them, and doing both in a way that removed all conditions and refused all social and religious distinctions. Therefore the fulfillment now promised to Jesus, is exactly

---

[9] Ibid., pp. 39-40.

that the promises of Israel will be fulfilled for his fellows, and that his fellowship will reach to all men. "The Word of God" is first of all the word by which the man Jesus now lives; and what that word says to him is: "All men will be your brothers, despite their alienation and unconditionally, in the new order that will fulfill Israel's hope. Just so this word is equally addressed to us, without distinction; it is the word that each of us may speak to the other in Jesus' name, and in this form it says: "Israel's hope will be fulfilled for Jesus' sake, and for you; despite all past or future failed conditions, despite all alienation, and despite the death that rules in both."[10]

The Gospel as Unconditional Promise

"What happened to the world with Jesus," Robert W. Jenson avers, "was that at the end of the long history of Israel's promises, a sheerly unconditional promise was said and became sayable in the world."[11] But exactly what does he mean by unconditional promise? Here he offers a simple bit of linguistic analysis. In the exchange of verbal communication, we may ask of any given utterance, what does it do to us? Jenson proposes an either/or answer: an utterance either opens the future for us *as gift* or poses the future to us *as demand*.

An example of the former is the statement "I love you." "It is obvious," he notes, "how the speaking of it opens an entirely new life for the hearer—even if he rejects the offer, his life will never be quite the same again."[12] In the assertion of his love, the lover promises himself to his beloved. It's easy to think of other examples:

- I am going to deposit $1,000,000 to your bank account.
- You have won an all-expense paid vacation to the French Riviera.

---

[10] Ibid., pp. 48-50.
[11] Ibid., p. 50.
[12] Ibid., pp. 6-7.

- I am going promote you to regional manager.
- I have found your lost puppy.
- Yes, I will marry you and remain faithful to you for all our days.

In all such utterances, a good is communicated as to grant new possibilities. The hearer does not create these possibilities; they are freely given to him. The speaker assumes full responsibility for their fulfillment. In this sense such utterances function as performative speech-acts. Jenson groups them under the classification of *promise*.

Now examples of the alternative form of discourse:

- If you get straight A's on your report card, I'll permit you to attend the prom.
- If you pay me $500,000, I will give you the drug that will cure your bone cancer.
- If you are faithful to your marriage vows, I too will be faithful to mine.
- If you are naughty, Santa Claus will not bring you any presents this Christmas.
- Thou shalt not kill. If you do, it's straight to the gallows.

These utterances also pose a possible future, but they bind that future to a prior condition and thus function as demand and obligation: the realization of the promised possibilities, whether good or ill, depends upon the performance of the hearer. Jenson groups these utterances under the classification of *law*.

Conditional promises share a common grammatical structure, explicitly or implicitly: "if . . . then." The if-clause does not have to explicitly stated in order to be in force. This structure pervades the web of communal speech, and one might wonder how it could be otherwise. Even our strongest promises—as in traditional marriage vows—are conditioned by death. We may pledge to be faithful to our spouses "for better for worse, for richer for poorer, in sickness and in health"; yet always our mortality imposes itself: "until death do us part." We cannot commit ourselves beyond that point. Death steals from us our freedom for communion. In our fallen world verbal communication ultimately reduces to law and contract.

Yet we can still theoretically imagine the linguistic structure of a genuine unconditional promise, without any hidden clauses: "because . . . therefore." Jenson elaborates:

> A promise goes: "Because I will do such-and-such, you may await such-and-such." The pattern is "because . . . , therefore . . . , " the exact reverse of "if . . . , then . . ." Here a future is opened independent of any prior condition, independent of what the addressee of the promise may do or be beforehand. Indeed, we may say that whereas other communication makes the future depend on the past, a promise makes the past depend on the future, for it grants a future free from the past, and so allows us to appropriate the past in a new way. This is the point of all the biblical and churchly talk about "forgiveness;" if we are accepted in spite of what we have been, we are thereby permitted to appropriate what we have been afresh, as the occasion and object of that acceptance.[13]

A truly unconditional promise can only be made by one who lives with death behind him. Only he who has died and been raised into life eternal possesses the power to fulfill a vow beyond the death that conditionalizes existence. The narrative content of such a promise, if it is a true promise, is Pascha.

For 2,000 years, the Church has boldly proclaimed in the name of Jesus Christ a solemn pledge that transcends all circumstances, contingencies, and limitations. We call it the gospel:

---

[13] Ibid., p. 8.

- Because Jesus is risen, your sins are forgiven.
- Because Jesus is risen, you will be healed of your sorrows and fulfilled in happiness and bliss!
- Because Jesus is risen, you will dine with him in the banquet of the Kingdom.
- Because Jesus is risen, you may embrace a life of asceticism, sacrifice, self-denial, even martyrdom, without fear of losing yourself.
- Because Jesus is risen, "all shall be well, and all shall be well, and all manner of thing shall be well."

The Church dares to declare this gospel because he who originally spoke the gospel stands as surety. Jesus has been confirmed by God as divine Son and mediator of the goods of redemption. His salvific will must therefore triumph. "Behind the conditionality of our promises," Jenson elucidates, "is the certainty of death: by every promise I commit some part of my future, which I do not surely have. The gospel promise is unconditional, for behind it stands the victor over death. Just so, it is the word of God, who has all the future."[14] With Christ's death and resurrection a new age has been inaugurated, an age in which unconditional promises have become proclamable. It is the age of the Spirit, of life that is freedom, new creation, extravagant love, and confident hope. The Church proclaims Pascha and thereby demonstrates Jesus as alive in the final future:

> The gospel, spoken by one man to another, is Jesus' word: his address of himself into a common world with us. The gospel is Jesus' word because what it promises only he can rightly promise: the gospel promises that Jesus will give himself to us; it promises the total

---

[14] Robert W. Jenson, *Visible Words* (1978), p. 6).

achievement and outcome of his deeds and sufferings as our benefit; it promises his love. If the gospel-promise is true, its occurrence is Jesus' occurrence as a shaping participant in our world. It is the *truth* of the gospel-promise that is the presence of the promised. If the gospel is not true, then when we hear it we hear only each other.[15]

Jenson believes that it was the great gift of the 16th century *Lutheran* Reformation to have clarified for the Church the unconditionality of the gospel. (The Calvinist movement must be excepted, with its assertion of limited atonement and double predestination.) Given developments in medieval penitential practices and an ever-increasing homiletical emphasis on eternal perdition, the unconditional giftedness of salvation of Christ ceased to be experienced by many. The meaning of life was called into radical question. Am I *worthy*? Can I ever *become* worthy? How can I *possibly* become worthy? The despair of Luther is well-known. Against this threat of damnation, the Lutheran Reformers asserted the gratuity of divine grace: we are justified by faith, not by works. By this declaration, they did not intend to promote faith as a meritorious and justifying work; rather, they bespoke an eschatological existence beyond justifying works, freely bestowed by the Savior through the preaching of the gospel:

> The Reformers' fundamental *insight* was that the radical question about ourselves can accept as answer only an unconditional affirmation of the value of our life. An affirmation which sets a condition of any sort whatever, which in any way stipulates "you are good and worthy if you do/are such-and-such" only directs me back to that very self that is the problem. The point made by "without works" is: any affirmation of our life which says "if you do/are . . ." is not merely a poor answer to the Reformation question about justification, *it is no sort of* answer to the

---

[15] Jenson, *Story*, p. 160.

question being asked; for what is being asked is whether it is worth doing or being anything at all.[16]

According to the Reformation insight and discovery, the gospel is a wholly unconditional promise of the human fulfillment of its hearers, made by the narrative of Jesus' death and resurrection. The gospel, rightly spoken, involves no ifs, ands, buts, or maybes of any sort. It does not say, "If you do your best to live a good life, God will fulfill that life," or, "If you fight on the right side of the great issues of your time . . . ," or, "If you repent . . . ," or, "If you believe . . ." It does not even say, "If you *want* to do good/repent/believe . . . ," or, "If you are sorry for not wanting to do good/repent/believe . . ." The gospel says, "Because the Crucified lives as Lord, your destiny is good." The Reformation's first and last assertion was that any talk of Jesus and God and human life that does not transcend all conditions is a perversion of the gospel and will be at best irrelevant in the lives of hearers and at worst destructive.[17]

That the Reformers latched onto the language of justification by which to express their rediscovery of unconditional promise was determined by their cultural location in history. No doubt they would have found different conceptuality if they had lived in Greece or Russia. But in 16th century Germany, "justification" became determinative. In their reading of St Paul's epistles to the Romans and Galatians, Martin Luther, Philip Melanchthon, Martin Chemnitz, and Johannes Brenz came to see that the preaching of the gospel is nothing less than the *final* judgment of God spoken to sinners. "The image behind the word," Jenson explains, "is that of a court where I await decision on the meaning of my deeds; in this case, the judgment will cover the whole of my life. *The gospel claims to be the last judgment let out ahead of time*: 'Not guilty.' 'Justified.'

---

[16] Eric W. Gritsch and Robert W. Jenson, *Lutheranism* (1976), p. 41. In this volume, Gritsch wrote the historical chapters and Jenson the theological chapters.
[17] Ibid., p. 42.

'Good.'"[18] The point is not the elevation of a forensic doctrine of justification above other doctrines; the point is meta-linguistic: preach of the story of Christ in *the performative mode of unconditional promise*; proclaim the crucified and risen Jesus in such a way the future of his Kingdom is opened to your hearers.

This is where faith comes into play. When an unconditional promise is spoken to you, what is the first thing you have to do? You have to choose to believe or disbelieve it; indeed, you may discover that your response is even more immediate, skipping the choosing and jumping right to trust or distrust, joy or offense:

> In Reformation language, "faith" is not the label of an ideological or attitudinal state. Like "justification," the word evokes a communication-situation: the situation of finding oneself addressed with an unconditional affirmation, and having now to deal with life in these new terms. Faith is a mode of life. Where the radical question is alive, all life becomes a hearing, a listening for permission to go on; faith is this listening—to the gospel.[19]

Catholics, Orthodox, Reformed, and revivalist Protestants will inevitably raise a host of questions about Jenson's formulation of the unconditionality of the gospel. What about free will? What about the necessity of repentance, conversion, prayer, and good works? What about *theosis* and holiness? What about hell? These are important questions, yet Jenson refuses to back down. If we wish to speak gospel *as gospel*, as good news that liberates sinners from their egoism and rescues them from the existential threat of absurdity, we must dare to follow in the steps of our Lord and lavish upon sinners, to *do* to sinners, the gift of the Kingdom. By Word and Sacrament, we are called to justify the ungodly!

---

[18] Jenson, *Story*, p. 121; emphasis mine.
[19] *Lutheranism*, p. 41.

Hell as Narratival Aberration

But what about HELL? This is always the first question posed when confronted with Robert W. Jenson's understanding of the gospel as unconditional promise. If the Church is authorized to speak the Kingdom to all comers, does this not imply universal salvation? In his youthful *Story and Promise*, Jenson refuses to answer yay or nay:

> What is the point of the traditional language about damnation? Two points only. First, damnation is not part of the gospel. The gospel is not a carrot and a stick: it is *unconditional* promise. Damnation is a possibility I pose to myself when I hear the gospel and instead of believing it begin to speculate about it—which we all regularly do. Therefore, this book, which tries to explain the gospel, has talked only about Fulfillment and will continue to do so. Second, damnation would be that we were finally successful in self-alienation from our own destiny. Is this a real possibility? We do not know; and we do not need to, for the gospel says to us: "Jesus' love will find *you*, in spite of everything and anything." So much, and no more about damnation— which already is rather too much.[20]

To understand his reasoning, we must remember that for Jenson all theological reflection is grounded in God's self-revelation in Jesus Christ, presented to us in the gospel message. At no point do we stand outside the event of having been personally addressed by God, as if we could *objectively* validate or assess the gospel from a neutral philosophical position. No such neutral position exists. Jenson explains:

> Theology has most often been done from the location of an observer: the theologian observes the realities "God" and "creature" and the relation between them, and tries to describe and partly explain what he

---

[20] *Story.*, pp. 78-79.

sees. It may be doubted that there is any location from which to observe God; but whether there is or not, the doctrine of justification locates the theologian elsewhere. Proper Lutheran theology occurs *within* the event of hearing and speaking the gospel; it is the thinking involved in moving from hearing to speaking. Lutheran theology is reflection within the discourse of the church on how this discourse may be gospel and not only law.[21]

All we know as Christians—and this is a knowing of faith—is that we have been grasped by the story of Jesus as the guarantee of our salvation. We have heard the good news and cannot get away from it. Even when we try to escape, even when we depart into the darkness of rebellion and sin, we keep hearing the whisper: "Nevertheless . . . I *will* be your happiness and joy." God's decision to justify the ungodly in and by the preaching of the gospel is absolute, for it is identical to his eternal decision to be the God who dies on the Cross for the salvation of all.

But that then means (gulp) predestination. Absolutely right, replies Jenson. It most certainly does imply predestination—but not the predestination of the philosophers but the predestination of unconditional promise. Predestination is but the flip side of justification by faith, prophetically spoken in the active voice with God as subject: "I have chosen you in my Son for eternal glory, and I will make good on my promise, no matter what." Once the electing decree has been spoken to you, what choice do you have but to believe or disbelieve. Once God has told you that he has appointed you to his Kingdom, then that's simply that. Deal with it!

> A doctrine of predestination appropriate to the gospel has nothing to do with any sort of cause-effect "determinism" . . . and little to do with explaining why some are "saved" and some are "lost." A proper

---

[21] *Lutheranism*, p. 62.

doctrine of predestination is not a description of God's relation to mankind in general, done from some third-person observer standpoint—so as then to say: "That man came to a good end because God picked him, those others to a bad end because God did not." A proper doctrine of predestination is a first- and second-person doctrine: it reminds me, trying to speak gospel to you, not to take "No" for an answer; it reminds me that God chooses you and me here, despite everything. It says nothing one way or the other about some other fellows off there—until you or I turn to speak gospel to them.[22]

We want to think of predestination as God arbitrarily choosing some to be saved and some to be damned—a divine lottery of sorts, minus the element of chance. This has a long history in the Western theological tradition but is simply the wrong way to think about it. Predestination is not an explanation of the mechanics of salvation; it's not an explanation of anything at all: "As the reverse of the doctrine of justification, this doctrine also is instruction to gospel-speakers. It instructs us: to whoever will listen, promise fulfillment regardless of his 'works'; say, 'It will be yours simply because God wants it that way.'"[23] God elects sinners in the event of the gospel, proclaimed from the final future. As the Lord himself declared through the prophet: "So shall my word be that goes forth from my mouth; it shall not return to me empty, but it shall accomplish that which I purpose, and prosper in the thing for which I sent it" (Isa 55:11).

"But that implies that I am but a mere puppet," we respond. "What's happened to my freedom?" But reflect a bit more. You are seated in the pew and the preacher declares, "In the name of Jesus Christ, crucified and risen, I declare to you that God has destined you to his Kingdom." How is your liberty compromised? In fact, is

---

[22] Ibid., p. 122.
[23] Jenson, *Lutheranism*, p. 159.

The Gospel as Story and Promise

it not the case that because of this prophetic announcement you are now free for the first time in your life? The Creator of the universe has just spoken to you the most thrilling words imaginable. You are free—free for faith, free for repentance, free for ministry and service, free for joy, free for love! Here is genuine liberty, the freedom of the Spirit—the freedom to love God and neighbor unconditionally and selflessly, absent the taint of egoism, gain, and self-righteousness. All other considerations are moot:

> Whether predestination means tyranny or freedom depends entirely on which God is absolute. If a Decider throned outside of time settled our destinies as one might sort potatoes, this would indeed end human freedom. But the God who is absolute is the very event in time that opens our freedom. The decision that is absolute is the decision of love. Therefore God and we do not compete to determine our lives: just *because* there are no conditions on his choice, we are free. We are unfree and bound because we prefer to compete with God and each other. But—says the gospel to you and me—God will not let that stop our freedom either.[21]

But what about hell? In asking this question we have done what we must not do: we have abstracted ourselves from the promise God has spoken to us and begun to speculate on the fate of others from the position of a neutral observer. We engage in a kind of fiction. Let's pretend we do not know who God is. Let's pretend we have not met Jesus Christ and have not heard his Word. Let's pretend we have not been saved by baptism. What is this speculation but sin? If we are concerned about the salvation of others (and we damn'd well better be), then we should be busying ourselves with evangelism. That is the task of our love. Yet still we ask, "Am I not free to reject

---

[21] Jenson, *Story*, p. 122.

Destined for Joy

Christ's promise of the Kingdom?" The young Jenson refuses to answer.

Jenson returned to the question of hell and damnation in his celebrated *Systematic Theology*, written twenty-five years after *Story and Promise*. Here he cites the contradictory testimonies within the New Testament. On the one hand, the Apostle Paul can assert that "Those who do not obey the gospel of our Lord Jesus . . . will suffer the punishment of eternal destruction, separated from the presence of the Lord" (II Thess 1:8-9). Jenson reads Paul's statement as affirming an eternal perdition but does offer this qualifying observation: "We may also note . . . that Paul says this as *comfort* to the Thessalonican congregation—that his judgment is pronounced on third parties who when the letter is read will not be there to hear."[25] On the other hand, the same Apostle can declare: "Therefore just as one's man responses led to condemnation for all, so one man's act of righteousness leads to justification and life for all" (Rom 5:18) and "And so all Israel will be saved. . . . For God has imprisoned all in disobedience so that he may be merciful to all" (Rom:11-26-32). "The logic of Paul's own soteriology," comments Jenson, "can never stop short of universal affirmations."[26]

He then proceeds to examine the question of damnation under two aspects—the baptized and the unbaptized. I shall focus on the former, since that is the worrisome point:

> A believer's baptism is God's own promise of the Kingdom, sealed personally. Paul nevertheless warns the Corinthian baptized to take heed lest they "fall" [1 Cor 10:1-13]; exclusion is evidently a possibility. Yet if the promise of God cannot fail for the Israel that does not obey the gospel, as Paul also insists [Rom 11:26], how can it fail for those to

---

[25] *Systematic*, II:360.
[26] Ibid.

whom God has addressed his baptismal promise and who in baptism have in fact obeyed the gospel?

If I am baptized, should I fear exclusion? Paul apparently thinks I should, and in the referenced passage puts this fear into me. And yet were this fear to determine any part of my believing life, all would be undone. For to hear and believe the gospel and simultaneously to fear exclusion from the Kingdom is impossible. So Catholic-Reformation dialogue: having defined faith as "the giving over oneself to God and God's word or promise," the parties agreed, "No one can in this . . . sense believe, and simultaneously suppose that God in his word of promise is unreliable. In this sense Luther's dictum holds: . . . faith is certainty of salvation."[27]

How then do we reconcile the unconditionality of the gospel, confirmed and sealed in baptism, with the Scripture's apparent acknowledgement of the possibility of eternal reprobation? Jenson suggests that the biblical warnings can "only be understood as addressed to believers insofar as they do not believe," that is to say, insofar as they are involved in living their lives *as if* they had not been baptized. Jenson is thinking here of Romans 6:1-14: we have died to sin in baptism and have been given a new identity in Christ. Paul's warnings of the possibility of exclusion from the Kingdom, therefore, are intended to remind his readers that they no longer belong to the old age and are dead to the allurements of the world. "That is, the threat of exclusion is made precisely to turn us away from entertaining it. So again, if I am baptized, should I fear exclusion? Perhaps the confessor's proper answer is, 'Since you ask, No.'" Jenson concludes: "The third-person proposition, 'It is possible for the baptized to be lost,' can, it seems, only function as

---

[27] Ibid., II:362.

just that, a proposition about a third person not there to be addressed. It has no context in which to be actual."[28]

So far, Jenson's mature view on damnation is continuous with that of his younger self. Those who have been baptized into Christ are not in a position to entertain the possibility that God will not fulfill his salvific promise. To do so is to step outside the event of gospel-communication. At the same time, and for the same reason, Jenson is unwilling to explicitly affirm apokatastasis: "With respect to the baptized, the children of Israel, and those simply outside the covenant, in each case differently, 'Exclusion is possible' is a true theological, that is, second-level proposition, to which, however, no first-level believing discourse corresponds. . . . The Church must think that damnation is possible but is not to make it an article of faith, proclaim it, or threaten it except in such fashion as to obviate the threat. What sort of truth does 'Damnation is possible' then have? Perhaps God does not wish us to know."[29]

A true second-order proposition that fails to correlate with the primary language of faith. How can it then be *true*? I do not find Jenson's argument here convincing, though I respect his desire to take seriously the biblical threats of exclusion. Neither believer nor preacher can ignore these threats. Further historical exegesis may prove helpful in placing them in their proper historical and rhetorical context. We should not uncritically assume that either Jesus or the Apostles intended to teach as revealed truth a doctrine of everlasting perdition. Ultimately these texts of eschatological terror must be interpreted through a hermeneutic of Pascha. Did Christ empty hades just to create hell? Surely not. Is omnipotent Love impotent against our vaunted freedom and pride? Again, surely not. If such were the case, the unconditional gospel would be

---

[28] Ibid.
[29] Ibid., II:365.

nonsense and in the strongest sense incredible. Perhaps the challenge for the preacher is even greater. How does one preach the threats *today* in gospelwise fashion? The preacher does not need to introduce us to the torment of the outer darkness, for it exists within us as an ever-present existential reality. Sometimes we do need to be bluntly warned of the devastating consequences of our sin and impenitence. Yet Old Testament Israel teaches us that the summons to repentance cannot ultimately save, as well evidenced by her—and the Church's—interminable cycle of new beginnings followed by worn-out endings, failure, disobedience, and betrayal. As Jenson comments: "For history conceived as repeated recreation to be good, there must finally be new beginning that leads to no decrepitude."[30] The coming Kingdom of the risen Christ represents precisely this new, enduring, and decisive beginning. If the gospel is true, this Kingdom is freely and unconditionally granted to us in the proclaimed Word. Here is the real challenge of evangelical preaching, to *give* the final future of Christ:

> The promise is and is to be final. . . . This can be established simply by . . . noting that the coming of a crucified and risen one, a person with death behind him, must be an unsurpassable event, i.e., the promise in question is "eschatological." The rule is: What does this text promise, and what may I promise, eschatologically, as the last future that Jesus and he only can bring? . . . The final promise is and has to be . . . absolute, unconditional, entirely and utterly free of "if"s or "maybe"s of any sort. The point is again tautologous; an Eschaton *can* be promised only unconditionally—whatever problems that may raise about the significance of the hearer's acceptance, etc. I have not got things going until I hear from the text and can say to my hearers, "You will be . . . ,

---

[30] Robert W. Jenson, "The Preacher, the Text, and Certain Dogmas," *dialog* 21 (Spring 1982): 110.

in spite of all considerations to the contrary." This is the distinction of gospel from law; the law is any address with an "if."[31]

A conditional gospel, which is no gospel, necessarily distills to the terrifying threat of eternal perdition: "Repent or be damned." It's as simple and unavoidable as that. How does the preacher threaten hell without conditionalizing the promise?

My question for my departed teacher: When the word of unconditional promise is spoken to me by the Church, is it *only* spoken to *me*? Does not the gospel itself teach me that I am a person only in relation to others? Do I exist apart from my parents, my spouse and my children, my friends, neighbors, and enemies, past and future generations? If I believe that the unconditional love and forgiveness of God intends *me*, as the gospel assures me that it does, then surely, I may infer that it also intends all of humanity. In the words of the poet:

> No man is an island
> Entire of itself.

My brothers and sisters exist in me and I in them. On Great Saturday, the Orthodox Church sings:

> Uplifted on the Cross, Thou hast uplifted with Thyself all living people; and then, descending beneath the earth, Thou raisest all that lie buried there.

We will not be saved apart from all others, the total Adam, for whom the Second Adam died and rose again. To hear the predestinating gospel spoken to *me* is to hear the salvation of mankind—apokatastasis! Hence, as long as we indwell the gospel and feed upon the Body and Blood of the risen Christ, we must deny

---

[31] Ibid., p. 112.

the possibility of the eternal loss of our brethren. To do otherwise would be to repudiate the promise sealed to us in Baptism and renewed in Holy Eucharist. The God who is love will not renege on his promises. As the Apostle reminded the faithful in Corinth: "For the Son of God, Jesus Christ, whom we preached among you, Silva′nus and Timothy and I, was not Yes and No; but in him it is always Yes. For all the promises of God find their Yes in him. That is why we utter the Amen through him, to the glory of God" (2 Cor 1:19-20).

Chapter Seven

The Explosive Nothing of Grace

My adult Christian life, both pre- and post-seminary, has been marked by theological passions. Holy Trinity, Incarnation, Eucharist, feminist language for God, ecclesial polity and authority, the grammar of dogma; at any given point in time these topics have captured my intellect. I would read books voraciously, xerox journal articles, write letters (and later emails) to famous and not-so famous theologians. Once in a blue moon, my passion of the moment would find its way into an article; always it would find its way into my preaching. But there is one passion, indeed obsession, that has occupied my mind, heart, and soul for over forty years—the unconditionality of God's love for humanity. I have wrestled with it under different aspects—grace, justification, covenant and promise, sacramental absolution, worthy and unworthy communion—but always I am brought back to the grounding question: Does God love and forgive humanity—does God love and forgive *me*—gratuitously, unreservedly, unconditionally, absolutely, categorically, nontransactionally, without qualification, no hidden clauses, no ifs, ands or buts?

Over the decades, I have principally reflected upon the unconditionality of the divine love under the locus of *justification by faith*. The adventure began in seminary. How very odd that an Anglo-Catholic aspirant in an Anglo-Catholic seminary should stumble upon the writings of two Reformed theologians, James B. Torrance and his brother Thomas, and one Lutheran theologian, Robert W. Jenson. I emphasize the word "stumble." My Nashotah House instructors certainly did not direct me to them, nor do I recall my seminary friends recommending them. Yet, stumble upon them I did. One article by James Torrance especially impressed me: "The Unconditional Freeness of Grace." The following passage grabbed me:

> The important thing is that in the Bible, God's dealings with men in creation and in redemption—in grace—are those of a covenant and not of a contract. This was the heart of the Pauline theology of grace, expounded in Romans and Galatians, and this was the central affirmation of the Reformation. The God of the Bible is a covenant-God and not a contract-God. God's covenant dealings with men have their source in the loving heart of God, and the form of the covenant is the indicative statement, 'I will be your God and you shall be my people'. The God and Father of our Lord Jesus Christ is the God who has made a covenant for us in Christ, binding himself to man and man to himself in Christ, and who summons us to respond in faith and love to what he has done so freely for us in Christ. Through the Holy Spirit, we are awakened to that love and lifted up out of ourselves to participate in the (incarnate) Son's communion with the Father.
>
> Two things are therefore together in a biblical understanding of grace, the covenant of love made for man in Christ, between the Father and the incarnate Son. (a) On the one hand, it is unconditioned by any considerations of worth or merit or prior claim. God's grace is 'free grace'. (b) On the other hand, it is unconditional in the costly claims it makes upon us. God's grace is 'costly grace'. It summons us unconditionally to a life of holy love—of love for God and love for all men. The one mistake is so to stress free grace that we turn it into 'cheap grace' by taking grace for granted—the danger of the 'antinomianism' against which Wesley protested. The other mistake is so to stress the costly claims of grace that we turn grace into conditional grace, in a legalism which loses the meaning of grace.
>
> The fallacy of legalism in all ages—perhaps this is the tendency of the human heart in all ages—is to turn God's covenant of grace into a contract—to say God will only love you and forgive you or give you the gift of the Holy Spirit IF . . . you fulfill prior conditions. But this is to

invert 'the comely order of grace' as the old Scottish divines put it. In the Bible, the form of the covenant is such that the indicatives of grace are prior to the obligations of law and human obedience. 'I am the God of Abraham, Isaac and Jacob, I have loved you and redeemed you and brought you out of the land of Egypt, out of the house of bondage, therefore keep my commandments.' But legalism puts it the other way round. 'If you keep the law, God will love you!' The imperatives are made prior to the indicatives. The covenant has been turned into a contract, and God's grace—or the gift of the Spirit—made conditional on man's obedience.[1]

I cannot say that Torrance's article hit me like a thunderbolt, but I can say that it swung wide a door in my mind and heart through which rushed the liberating winds of the Spirit. Was this what the Reformation was about, the utter freeness of grace? A flurry of questions immediately came to mind. I have wrestled with them for decades, but Torrance's emphatic assertion that our sins and disobedience do not condition the divine love struck me then as impossibly true. Surely this is the heart of the gospel. Soon afterwards, I discovered Thomas Torrance's and Robert Jenson's writings on justification. I was converted and have not wavered since. The absolute love and mercy of God—this has been the evangelical engine that has powered my priesthood and preaching. I devoted the next two decades to immersing myself in the literature on justification by faith. Perhaps the most challenging I read during this time was a little book by the Lutheran theologian Gerhard Forde, *Justification by Faith—A Matter of Death and Life*. Forde's reflections dovetail nicely with the Torrances and Jenson but is expressed with even greater existential urgency. What must we do to be saved? asks Forde. His answer: *absolutely nothing!*

---

[1] James B. Torrance, "The Unconditional Freeness of Grace," *Theological Renewal* (June/July 1978): 7-15. The article has been reprinted in *Trinity and Transformation* (2016), ed. Todd Speidell, pp. 276-287.

The Explosive Nothing of Grace

> We are justified freely, for Christ's sake, by faith, without the exertion of our own strength, gaining of merit, or doing of works. To the age old question, "What shall I do to be saved?" the confessional answer is shocking: "Nothing! Just be still; shut up and listen for once in your life to what God the Almighty, creator and redeemer, is saying to his world and to you in the death and resurrection of his Son! Listen and believe!" When one sees that it is a matter of death and life one has to talk this way. The "nothing" must sound, risky and shocking as it is. For it is, as we shall see, precisely the death knell of the old being. The faith by which one is justified is not an active verb of which the Old Adam or Eve is the subject, it is a state-of-being verb. Faith is the state of being grasped by the unconditional claim and promise of the God who calls into being that which is from that which is not. Faith means now having to deal with life in those terms. It is a death and resurrection.[2]

Forde dares to grasp the nettle—and grasp it too we must. It's easy enough to speak of unconditional love. It is expounded in a plethora of books and articles, both academic and popular. Invariably the authors end up telling us that even God's love has its limits, set by the bounds of human freedom. God can only invite. It is up to us to accept the gift, and if we do not, the gift is effectively nullified. At the critical moment, God's unconditional love becomes conditional and we are abandoned to our self-chosen perdition. Love is replaced by law, and in its wake follows bondage and death.

Forde shares with Torrance the apprehension that every human being is determined by the deep need to justify and defend himself to God, to others, and to himself—hence our unshakeable commitment to legalism and works-righteousness. Let's call this the Reformation version of original sin. The old Adam lives in a world of conditionalist consciousness; he lives by the *if-then*; if we believe such-and-such, if we think such-and-such, if we do such-and-such,

---

[2] Gerhard Forde, *Justification by Faith—A Matter of Death and Life* (1990), p. 22.

Destined for Joy

then specific consequences, both good and ill, will obtain. At every step, the old Adam remains in charge of his life and eternal destiny. This is why we fight so hard against the proclamation of unconditional grace. It directly challenges our worldview and personal identity. Who am I if by eternal decree God predestines my final future, even if that future is good? How dare he interfere with my freedom? The *nothing* inevitably evokes indignation and fierce resistance. "Why is it," someone once asked Forde after one of his lectures on justification, "that when anyone talks about the sheer grace and absolute mercy of God people get so angry?"

> Why indeed? Because it is a radical doctrine. It strikes at the root, the radix, of what we believe to be our very reason for being. The "nothing," the *sola fide*, dislodges everyone from the saddle, Jew and Greek, publican and pharisee, harlot and homemaker, sinner and righteous, liberal and orthodox, religious and non-religious, minimalist and maximalist, and shakes the whole human enterprise to the roots. It strikes at the very understanding of life which has become ingrained in us, the understanding in terms of the legal metaphor, the law, merit and moral progress. Justification, the reformers said, is by imputation, freely given. It is an absolutely unconditional decree, a divine decision, indeed an *election*, a sentence handed down by the judge with whom all power resides. It is as the later "orthodox" teachers like to say, a "forensic" decree: a flat-out pronouncement of acquittal *for Jesus'* sake, who died and rose for us...
>
> The gospel of justification by faith is such a shocker, such an explosion, because it is an absolutely *unconditional* promise. It is not an "if-then" kind of statement, but a "because-therefore" pronouncement: Because Jesus died and rose, your sins are forgiven and you are righteous in the sight of God! It bursts in upon our little world all shut up and barricaded behind our accustomed conditional thinking as some strange comet from goodness knows where, something we can't really seem to wrap our minds around, the logic of which appears closed to us. How can it be entirely unconditional? Isn't

it terribly dangerous? How can anyone say flat-out "You are righteous for Jesus' sake"? Is there not *some* price to be paid, *some*-thing (however minuscule) to be done? After all, there *can't* be such a thing as a free lunch, can there?

You see, we really are sealed up in the prison of our conditional thinking. It is terribly difficult for us to get out, and even if someone batters down the door and shatters the bars, chances are we will stay in the prison anyway! We seem always to want to hold out for something somehow, that *little bit* of something, and we do it with a passion and an anxiety that betrays its true source—the Old Adam that just does not want to lose control.[3]

To proclaim the gospel rightly the preacher must find ways to speak the radical *nothing*: "There is nothing you can do to save yourselves. Without your permission, God has saved you in Christ and is saving you by the Spirit." To preach the good news of Pascha is to scandalously declare to sinners the Final Judgment *ahead of time*: "Come, O blessed of my Father, inherit the kingdom prepared for you from the foundation of the world" (Matt 25:34). Forde elaborates:

> For the point is that the unconditional declaration of justification, the imputation, the flat-out declaration, that which offends and shocks us so, that which shatters our ambitions for "something to do"—that declaration *is* our death and our life, the new beginning. It is the act which re-creates, redeems God's creation. Death, you see, is put in the position of not being able to do anything according to the ways of this world—the law, religion, the upward climb—with all its plans and schemes. They suddenly stop, come to an end: "I through the law died to the law that I might live to God." Both our vices and virtues come to

---

[3] Ibid., pp. 22-23.

Destined for Joy

a full stop. The justification declaration *is* precisely that: a full stop. "You have died," says Paul. It is all over![4]

The righteousness granted by the right preaching of the gospel enjoys an eschatological character. "It is," as Forde puts it, "the totality of the 'Kingdom of God' moving in upon us."[5] To be justified by the word of the risen Christ is to be made a new creation. The gospel of unconditional grace is eschatological speech, speech that performatively enacts the final future. To hear and trust the evangelical promise is to die and be raised into the Kingdom with Christ and in Christ. Forde understands the inadequacies of the imputational model of justification. He believes that those who formulated this doctrine in the 16th and 17th centuries were attempting to reinterpret the preaching of the gospel as speech that transforms and recreates by incorporating the hearer into the Kingdom, word that slays and makes alive and delivers us from the conditionalism of our fallen world into the new world of grace and Spirit. This liberation requires nothing less than our death and resurrection. The preacher is so much more than an encourager to live well and do good works. He is a prophet of the Kingdom, speaking the Word of God that accomplishes what it proclaims (Isa 55:11); he is a priest of the *eschaton*, giving to communicants the Body and Blood of the glorified Lord. "Receiving and believing the word of justification *is* death and resurrection," comments Forde. "It is the end and new beginning."[6]

Yet in those early years of priesthood, I continued to wrestle with the preaching of the unconditional gospel. So, I finally decided to write Dr Forde himself, and he graciously replied a few days later:

---

[4] Ibid., pp. 34-35.
[5] Ibid., p. 51.
[6] Ibid., p. 36.

The Explosive Nothing of Grace

3/18/85

Dear Rev. Kimel,

Thank you for your letter of March 14. I write what I fear will be a rather hasty reply, but I hope it will be better than putting it off and perhaps neglecting it altogether as I fear I have done in the past, for which I must apologize!

Is not the act of belief in "some sense" a condition for salvation, at least in the sense that without it one will not be saved? When we arrive at that question, I think, we arrive at what might be called the limits of language in this matter, the point at which the language is likely to trick us if we are not careful. So we can get on with the problem, I believe, by making a couple of moves. The first would be to note carefully what the language is doing and perhaps make some helpful distinctions and the second would be to shift to more personal categories like the language of love. The distinction I like to make is one between descriptive language and declarative language. Descriptively it is quite true to say that unless you believe you shall not be saved. But that is just description of what is the case, and even though it is quite true in and of itself, it is not legitimate to jump immediately to the conclusion or the inference that belief is a condition for salvation, because the description says nothing about how such belief is to come about. Descriptive language is always tricky in theology especially and tricks us because it is so easy to translate it immediately into law language, conditional language. It is the unconditional language, the proclamation, that creates the belief, the faith, without which one cannot be saved. Faith is not a condition for salvation, it is salvation already, since it is created by the living address.

Perhaps this becomes more evident if we make the second move and shift to the more personal language of love, or the language of relationship between persons. Descriptively it is quite true to say that without love the relationship between, say, husband and wife, parent and child, is not likely to be a happy or perfect one. But if the relationship goes sour and I immediately translate the (quite true!)

descriptive language into conditional language, I would then turn it into law, and turn on the alienated one with a demand. I would likely say, "Look here, you are supposed to love me." Again, that is quite true, but of course it only makes matters worse. It creates the mistaken impression that love is a condition to be fulfilled, a means to an end which the alienated one is supposed to accomplish. But if I know the difference between law and gospel, I will immediately realize that the only proper move is to direct, unconditional declaration: "I love you! No ifs, ands, or buts!" I would realize that love is not a condition, that it cannot be commanded, it can only be given as best and as unconditionally as one can.

Love is not the condition for the relationship, it is the relationship. To assume it is a condition is to assume that I can, by some means or other, master the situation, indeed, master and control the other. But that is not the case. Hans Urs von Balthasar has some helpful things to say on this score (in *Love Alone, The Way of Revelation*, p. 44): "No I has the possibility or the right to master intellectually the Thou who encounters him in his own freedom, nor can he understand or deduce his attitude prior to their meeting. For love granted to me can only be understood as a miracle; I can never account for it, either empirically or transcendentally—not even from knowledge of our common human nature. A Thou meets me as an Other." The moment I think that I have understood the love of another person for me—for instance, on the basis of laws or human nature or because of something in me—then this love is radically misused and inadequate, and there is no possibility of a response. True love is always incomprehensible, and only so is it gratuitous.

Perhaps that is why we say we simply "fall in love."

Faith, belief, is like that. More deeply, according to Paul, it is like dying and being raised to new life. I simply cannot say to Our Lord that I have fulfilled "the conditions" so that I now am a proper candidate for salvation. Indeed, without faith, I am lost. That is a true description. But it is the declaration, the unconditional word that raises the dead!

So I always counsel my students that descriptive language is indeed true and useful, but they should beware of translating it into conditional language or law. Especially is this true for preaching—for if we find ourselves preaching a description as though it were gospel, we will find ourselves in big trouble!

Grace and Peace!

Gerhard Forde

After decades of preaching the radical gospel of grace, I can confirm Forde's analysis. No sermons of mine have evoked as much consternation and discussion as those that declared the salvific "nothing." We would believe anything except the evangelical message that God has eternally elected us to glory. At any cost we would retain our "freedom" to irrevocably reject God's gift of joy. Let God be God, but please not in this. But I can also confirm that many who have heard and believed the gospel of grace have been born anew into the freedom of the Spirit!

Critics of Forde have raised the objection that Forde has eliminated the process of sanctification—or as we Orthodox would say, *theosis*. If there is nothing for us to *do*, what then is the role of repentance, prayer, fasting, and all the moral and ascetical practices that inculcate virtue and intimacy with Christ? It is a weighty but not irresolvable concern. The short answer (mine, not Forde's): they retain their necessary role, but they are now enveloped in God's love and promises. Their necessity is that of grace, not works. We have died to the law and have been reborn in Christ. "Now the Lord is the Spirit, and where the Spirit of the Lord is, there is freedom" (2 Cor 3:17). This is what saving faith is: life joyfully, even playfully, lived in the baptismal gift of resurrection. As the Apostle Paul declares:

> In him also you were circumcised with a circumcision made without hands, by putting off the body of flesh in the circumcision of Christ;

> and you were buried with him in baptism, in which you were also raised with him through faith in the working of God, who raised him from the dead. And you, who were dead in trespasses and the uncircumcision of your flesh, God made alive together with him, having forgiven us all our trespasses, having canceled the bond which stood against us with its legal demands; this he set aside, nailing it to the cross. (Col 2:11-14: cf. Rom 6:1-14)

The old Adam has been slain, and we now live in the Eucharist of the *eschaton*. We are saved by the *nothing* of grace because God's love is absolute and unconditional: God wills our good, and he will accomplish it. He has sealed his commitment in the death of his Son. Yet there remains the mystery of our synergistic cooperation with the Spirit in our repentance, healing, and purification. As St Augustine famously declared: "God created us without us: but he did not will to save us without us."[7] We do not need to know the mechanism of *theosis*. We need only to trust the promises of Christ and obey his commandments. We are enfolded in the liminal space between the death and resurrection of Christ.

In recent years, I have come to see that the justification by faith controversy that shook the Latin Church in the 16th century is now being replayed in the current controversy over universal salvation. The burning gospel question in both is the same, grammatical tense being the only difference:

- Does God justify sinners, apart from their works and merit?
- Will God justify sinners, apart from their works and merit?

Justification by faith proclaims the utter freeness of the grace of God, gratuitously bestowed on all through the preaching of the good

---

[7] *Sermo* 169,11,13:PL 38,923.

news of Jesus Christ. Apokatastasis is but the gospel of Christ's absolute and unconditional love sung in an eschatological key.

Chapter Eight

Preaching Very Good News: The Grammar of Apokatastasis

Preaching Law, Preaching Gospel

What difference does apokatastasis make to the churchly preaching of the gospel? All the difference in the world—and all the difference *to* the world. How we understand the conclusion of the gospel story informs how we tell the story of Jesus of Nazareth and how the story is heard and received. Those who love to read novels know that a wretched ending can ruin a very fine tale, while a brilliant and satisfying ending can redeem even a deeply flawed one. It's as if the conclusion seeps back into the narrative and rewrites the whole, for good or ill.

In 2006, I decided I could no longer remain a priest in the Episcopal Church. Suddenly, I found that instead of having to deliver Sunday sermons, I was "privileged" to listen to them. I have since heard hundreds of homilies. With a few exceptions, they have shared one dominant feature, *exhortation*—specifically, exhortation embedded within a conditionalist linguistic structure. Preachers apparently believe that their principal homiletical task is to *urge* their hearers to behave and live differently. No matter what gospel reading is assigned for the particular Sunday, the lesson drawn from the text is always "try harder." Some preachers tend to emphasize ascetical behavior, others moral behavior; but the message is the same—believe harder, convert harder, work harder, obey harder,

Preaching Very Good News: The Grammar of Apokatastasis

pray harder.[1] The joyous proclaiming of Jesus Christ is reduced to exhortation and admonishment, adjuring and imploring. To put the matter in the language of the sixteenth century Lutheran Reformers, preachers preach law, not gospel. And we wonder why our congregations are so toxic and moribund.

The discourse of law shares a common transactional structure: *if . . . then*, It can be presented in positive terms (the language of reward and merit) or negative terms (the language of penalty and punishment):

- If you confess your sins,
  God will forgive you.
- If you truly and fully repent,
  you will be reborn in the Spirit.
- If you feed the poor and house the homeless,
  you will experience God's blessings and merit eternal life.
- If you devote yourself to prayer and struggle against the passions,
  you will experience *theosis*.

Or:
- If you you do not not spend sufficient time in prayer and the ascetical disciplines,
  the Spirit will depart from you.
- If you partake of the Body and Blood of Christ unworthily,
  you will fall under divine condemnation.
- If you do not serve the poor,
  God will not indwell your heart.
- If you do not go out into the world and proclaim the gospel,
  well, you don't want to know the consequences.

---

[1] From what my friends tell me, preachers in the evangelical tradition tend to stress the "convert harder."

These and all similar pledges make the outcome contingent upon the performance of the promisee. They pose to us a future for which we ourselves are responsible to actualize. If we fulfill the specified conditions, we will bring about the promised result, either as reward or punishment. Conditionalist preaching also entails a destructive pastoral corollary: if we do not experience a promised blessing (spiritual renewal, healing, consolation, emotional or material flourishing, career success, a happy marital life), then the fault must lie with ourselves. "Your faith is not strong enough," as too many of us are told. "You haven't really repented," our confessor "helpfully" suggests. Even if the "It's your fault" remains unspoken, we already know this must be the case—God sure ain't responsible. We are left with three options:

- frantically strive to strengthen our faith and perfect our obedience (and if successful become self-righteous);
- descend into self-condemnation and despair;
- abandon the Christian adventure altogether.

We are all intimately acquainted with transactional communication. It is the discourse of industry and commerce, civil and criminal judicial systems, communal and family life, education . . . and religion. It is the language of our Pelagian world. We determine our future by the contracts we make. Law functions as demand upon our performance, and upon this performance falls the weight of the utterance. Once a conditional promise is spoken to us, we had best get busy, either to obtain or avoid the consequent. Conditional promise, in other words, presents the future to us as demand, obligation, and threat. It actualizes and confirms our fallen existence. Hence it is not surprising that anxiety and despondency, legalism and judgmentalism pervade congregational life. And this is true even in churches that pride themselves on their anti-Pelagian dogmas. As one of my friends likes to quip, "I get salvation the old-fashioned way. I earn it!"

Underlying the conditionalist preaching of the Church is the long-standing doctrine of hell. Once everlasting perdition is embraced, all preaching, theology, penitential discipline must and will be reworked around it. Hell generates conditionalist preaching, and conditionalist preaching leads to hell.

If you do ____ or do not do ____ ,
God will condemn you to everlasting suffering.

Given the magnitude of the punishment—damnation, after all, is the worst possible conclusion of anybody's life—this threat must condition how every sermon is heard by the congregation, even if not explicitly stated. Hell is eager to snatch the sinner into unrelieved torment and misery. The preacher of conditional promises is always the purveyor of fire and brimstone.

Unconditional promise, too, has its own characteristic grammatical pattern: *because . . . therefore . . .*

- Because Jesus is risen,
  your future will be glorious.
- Because you are baptized by water and the Spirit,
  you are now empowered to live a life of faithfulness and love.
- Because your Creator will see to your needs,
  you are free to give generously and sacrificially to the oppressed and destitute.
- Because God has forgiven you all your sins on the cross,
  you are now free from the bondage of the past and can give yourself wholeheartedly to the way of love and compassion.

- Because God is your Good and will bring you into overflowing happiness,
  you have nothing to gain from sin and wickedness.
- Because the Father of Jesus is absolute Love,
  you need not fear that he will ever abandon you, no matter what.

Just as conditional promise posits a specific kind of future, so does unconditional promise; but note how differently these two kinds of utterance impact our lives. When God speaks to us a conditional promise, the burden of its fulfillment falls totally upon us. We are back on Mt Sinai. Existentially, it doesn't matter if we are also told that God will assist us with his grace. What matters is doing or not doing what needs to be done. Herein lies the difference between heaven and hell. But when God speaks unconditional promise, he assumes responsibility for our future; he is its guarantor. God presents our destiny as eschatological gift.

The preacher who dares in the name of Christ to speak the gospel of cross and resurrection in the performative mode of promise—and there is no other gospel—will always be on the lookout for new ways to reinterpret our antecedent hopes and nightmares and subvert the existential conditions that enslave and bind us. Every "no" we utter to the LORD becomes an occasion for the prophetic "yes" of Pascha. The preacher thrives on these occasions, as Robert W. Jenson observes:

> Our alienated fear of the future will always seek safely conditional evocations of future possibility, that is, "law." "Rightly dividing" the law and the gospel is the knack of so making promises in Jesus' name as endlessly to transcend this turn back to law. "God loves you for Jesus' sake." "Yes, if I could believe that. But I can't." To which the gospel-sayer who knows his job responds, "Just by your unbelief you prove yourself the very man whom God loves, for he chooses above all the

ungodly!" In actual preaching, teaching, liturgical practice, counseling, etc., the game can go on forever. He "rightly divides law and gospel" who always finds the way to make new proposed conditions into so many objects and reasons for the promise; who in the speaking of the gospel discovers how never to take "but" for an answer.

The gospel tolerates no conditions. It is itself unconditional promise. And when it is rightly spoken, it takes the conditions we put on the value of our life as the very occasions of its promise.[2]

Yet, as attractive as all this talk about unconditional promise may be, we still cling to the conditional. We still must repent, we insist. Here we must distinguish between two kinds of repentance. When the preacher declares "If you repent of your sins, God will forgive you" (with emphasis on the hypothetical "if"), he is asserting that God only offers absolution upon our fulfillment of a prior condition. Our repentance moves God from wrath to mercy. We may call this *legal repentance*. Of course, somebody will need to explain to us what repentance involves—but that is by the by. The critical point is that the responsibility and burden of fulfilling the stipulated conditions of salvation falls totally upon our shoulders. And at every moment hangs the threat of failure: What if I am unable to achieve a wholehearted repentance? What if I cannot free myself from my disordered desires and addictions? What if I don't want to convert? Will God forgive? If I die in mortal sin, can God forgive?

But now consider the difference when forgiveness is declared in *the mode of unconditional promise*: "In the name of Jesus Christ, I say to you: God forgives you and will make all things right; therefore, repent and live in the unconquerable joy of the Spirit." Suddenly everything changes. By the gospel annunciation, God raises us from the condemnation of sin and grants us a future no longer bound to the past. He enters our lives as an emancipating and transforming

---

[2] Robert W. Jenson, *Lutheranism* (1976), p. 44.

power. Repentance is no longer a work that merits divine grace: it is the fruit of freely bestowed absolution. Forgiveness is logically prior to our penitential response. We may call this *evangelical repentance*. "Because Jesus has risen for you into the life of the Kingdom, you may repent of your iniquities and give yourself over totally to love." When the recreative promise of the gospel is spoken to us, our lives are reframed, *ex opere operato*, and set upon an eschatological foundation. "Therefore, if any one is in Christ, he is a new creation; the old has passed away, behold, the new has come" (2 Cor 5:17). The sermon does not seek, Jenson incisively explains, to induce or manipulate conversion. The hearer's transformation, rather, is

> accomplished as the act of gospel-speaking itself. Conversion is a change in the communication situation within which every person lives; a proper sermon or baptism liturgy or penance liturgy just *is* that change. Using penance as the simplest paradigm, when the confessor says, "You have confessed cheating and coveting. Now I forgive all your sins, in Jesus' name," these words do not seek to stimulate conversion as an event external to their being said. Rather, this utterance *is* conversion of the penitent's life, from a situation in which the word he or she hears and must live by is "you are a cheat and a coveter," to one in which the word he or she hears and must live by is "You are Jesus' beloved."[3]

Life in Christ thus becomes pure joy, celebrated in thanksgiving and tears, holy works, ascetical discipline, and the worship and praise of our Savior. At every moment we are surrounded and upheld by the divine mercy. We were lost but have been found, we were blind but now we see, we were dead but now we live in the power of the *eschaton*.

---

[3] Robert W. Jenson, "Pneumatological Soteriology," in *Christian Dogmatics* (1983), II:134.

Preaching Very Good News: The Grammar of Apokatastasis

The Challenges of Gospel Preaching

Immediately our minds raise a host of objections. I am acquainted, I think, with most of them. They boil down to a single concern: if God declares me unconditionally forgiven, does that mean that I am free to disobey the commandments of God with impunity? The Apostle Paul addressed a similar concern in his Epistle to the Romans: "Are we to continue in sin that grace may abound?" He must have been asked this question on multiple occasions. Note his answer:

> By no means! How can we who died to sin still live in it? Do you not know that all of us who have been baptized into Christ Jesus were baptized into his death? We were buried therefore with him by baptism into death, so that as Christ was raised from the dead by the glory of the Father, we too might walk in newness of life. (Rom 6:1-4)

Continue in sin that grace may abound? Absolutely not! Because the gospel has been done to us in baptism, Paul replies, we are no longer the kind of people who can ask that question. There is now only one way forward—to walk in in love in the freedom of the Spirit!

The same question can be restated in its universal scope: Will all therefore be saved? What about free-will and our cooperation with grace? What about faith and conversion, sin and wickedness? Can't we reject God forever? All of these questions have been effectively addressed by theologians, past and present. The critical move—and perhaps only God can bring the necessary illumination—is to see how our lives are already comprehended within the unconditional love of the incarnate Son. At every moment we are embraced by the eternal Creator who will never abandon us. He will always find a way. We do not need an abstruse metaphysics of human freedom or a contestable schema of salvation. All we need is for the gospel of love to be declared to us in the name of the Holy Trinity. To believe the unconditional promise of salvation is to experience its liberating truth.

What difference does apokatastasis make to the churchly preaching of the gospel? Above all, it should encourage and authorize our pastors to proclaim the good news of Jesus Christ precisely *as good news*. No more qualifications and compromises; no more ifs, buts, and maybes. The gospel is a message of triumphant hope, or it is not gospel at all. This does not mean that each homily must now be about universal salvation. Quite the contrary. As always, the pastor will continue to preach on the lectionary texts appointed for that day; but he or she now searches for ways to proclaim even the harshest biblical passage through the hermeneutic of Pascha. Every text now bespeaks Jesus Christ, crucified and risen. Every text summons to life made possible by the gift of the Holy Spirit. Every text is gospel.

Brothers and sisters, Jesus is risen! He has transcended death and lives with death behind him. In our fallen world, all of our promises ultimately turn to dust and ashes—we cannot pledge a future we do not possess. At any point death may intervene and nullify our commitments. But by his paschal victory, Jesus of Nazareth possesses the final future. Only the Risen Christ can make an unconditional promise and mean it unconditionally. "If Jesus has death behind him," states Jenson, "then his intention for his followers, defined by his particular life and death, must utterly triumph, there being no longer anything to stop him."[4]

If Jesus were Attila the Hun or Joseph Stalin, the resurrection would be horrifying news; but the resurrection of the Jesus to whom the gospels testify is the best, most wonderful transforming news

---

[4] Robert W. Jenson, "On the Problem(s) of Scriptural Authority," *Interpretation* 31 (1977): 238.

possible. Neither death nor life, neither principalities nor powers, not even our pathetic attempts to reject our Savior irrevocably and definitively, can defeat the illimited love by which Jesus lived and died. His omnipotent intentions for his brethren, his intentions for all of humanity, his intentions for you and me, must and will triumph—utterly, completely, gloriously. The preaching of the gospel is simply this—the proclamation of Easter, with all of its consequences and implications for our lives.

All Christians know this—surely, we know this. At the Paschal Vigil, Orthodox Christians declaim the words of St John Chrysostom:

> Enjoy ye all the feast of faith: Receive ye all the riches of loving-kindness. let no one bewail his poverty, for the universal Kingdom has been revealed. Let no one weep for his iniquities, for pardon has shown forth from the grave. Let no one fear death, for the Savior's death has set us free. He that was held prisoner of it has annihilated it. By descending into Hell, He made Hell captive. He embittered it when it tasted of His flesh. And Isaiah, foretelling this, did cry: Hell, said he, was embittered, when it encountered Thee in the lower regions. It was embittered, for it was abolished. It was embittered, for it was mocked. It was embittered, for it was slain. It was embittered, for it was overthrown. It was embittered, for it was fettered in chains. It took a body, and met God face to face. It took earth, and encountered Heaven. It took that which was seen, and fell upon the unseen.
>
> O Death, where is your sting? O Hell, where is your victory? Christ is risen, and you are overthrown. Christ is risen, and the demons are fallen. Christ is risen, and the angels rejoice. Christ is risen, and life reigns. Christ is risen, and not one dead remains in the grave. For Christ, being risen from the dead, is become the first fruits of those who have fallen asleep. To Him be glory and dominion unto ages of ages. Amen.

The indicatives of the gospel precede the imperatives; the evangelical narrative prefaces all doctrinal teaching and qualifies all ethical and ascetical exhortations. Pastors may dare to boldly bestow the Kingdom, for the Crucified lives and has given himself as surety.

But not only does Jesus guarantee the promise of eschatological fulfillment, he is its ultimate speaker. Every address is the personal presence of someone. In this article, I am presently intruding into your life with my controversial reflections on preaching and apokatastasis. But were I to stand before you and in the name of Jesus unconditionally promise you eternal salvation in his Kingdom, then it would not be only me addressing you. I cannot rightly make such a pledge, for I cannot implement its promised outcome. Only the One who has death behind him can do so. Only the conqueror of sin and death may bestow the final future. When the preacher dares to proclaim the gospel in its radicality and power, there is the gladdening and inspirited voice of Jesus the Christ. The making of eschatological promise must be *his* act, *his* presence, *his* Word, *his* Kingdom. "If the gospel promise is true and unconditional," Jenson writes, "then the event of the living word, of one person speaking the gospel to another, is the locus of God's reality for us. Where is God? He is where one man is promising good unconditionally to another, in Jesus' name."[5] Or as our Lord has taught us, "Where two or three are gathered in my name, there I am between you" (Matt 18:20). A homily rightly proclaimed is a sacrament of the risen and exalted King.

I propose the following grammatical rule for our preaching: *so proclaim the story of Jesus Christ that it elicits from our hearers nothing less than faith or offense.* Or to put the rule in its most succinct form: *proclaim the gospel in the performative mode of unconditional promise.* Robert Jenson calls this a meta-linguistic

---

[5] *Lutheranism*, p. 102.

rule, George Lindbeck a meta-theological rule. Their point is the *meta-*. The rule does not specify the content of our preaching—that content is given in the Scriptures and the Sacred Tradition of the Church. The rule, rather, *prescribes* and *instructs* how to rightly speak this content: preach the narrative of the crucified and risen Son of God, not as law and legal obligation, but as word that liberates sinners from the bondage of sin, conquers despair, and empowers believers to live lives of holiness, love, prayer, sacrifice, and radical discipleship. The proclamatory rule summons preachers to speak into the world the coming Kingdom of the Lord.

Christ is risen!

Chapter Nine

Redemption Eternal: The Caponian Vision of Grace

Robert Farrar Capon was not a systematic theologian, even though he taught theology at the seminary level for several years. He wrote his books for a popular audience. He also wrote in a colloquial idiom that resists the systematic articulation of his views. He does not develop his thoughts in a way that would satisfy academic scholars, and he rarely references those who have informed his thinking. First and foremost, Capon is a biblical theologian and preacher whose burning passion is the gospel of Jesus Christ. His vision can only be described as ... Caponian.

The Eternal Justification of the Ungodly

The scandalous grace of Jesus lies at the heart of all of Capon's writings. It is summed up in the Apostle Paul's declaration: "There is therefore now no condemnation for those who are in Christ Jesus" (Rom 8:1). This is the gospel—the final judgment spoken ahead of time. *We are justified by grace, not by works*—period. Capon preaches like Martin Luther *redivivus* but with one decisive difference: *every* human being, he avers, is justified in Christ, now and eternally. It's all been accomplished. There is nothing we need do or can do to make ourselves right with God, for Jesus has made us right on the cross. Salvation, therefore, is nontransactional. It comes to us as sheer gift, without conditions of any kind, and will never be withdrawn. Faith comes into the picture only because there's nothing else left for us to do. A gift has been irrevocably given. It's as if God has deposited to our banking account a million dollars. It's ours. We didn't do anything to acquire it. We didn't earn it. All we need do is enjoy the gift of our new wealth. Faith is believing that the gift has been given. It is the joyful writing of checks, a living into the Father's freely bestowed mercy and grace. Capon is emphatic: God's forgiveness covers all of our sins—past, present, and future. We have been given a blanket absolution. In Christ, all of humanity is reconciled to God. The Anglican Capon may be the most radical "Lutheran" any of us will encounter. He pushes grace to the nth degree. Every human being, including the most wicked, have died in Christ and been raised with him into the glory of the Trinity. "There is therefore now no condemnation . . ."

How can this be so? Capon's answer: Christ's work of reconciliation belongs to the eternal life of the Trinity. He calls it the *Mystery of Christ*:

> The Mystery, as the New Testament presents it, is not at all a transaction model poked into a universe that previously didn't have the benefit of it. Rather, it is a *cosmic dispensation* that has been present at all times and in all places but "kept secret for ages and generations" (Rom. 16:25). It is a dispensation, in fact, that has been hidden "from the foundation of the world" (Matt. 13:35), or even "before the foundation of the world" (Eph. 1:4) until it could finally be revealed in Jesus. In other words, the mysterious and reconciling grace that has been revealed in Jesus is not something that got its act in gear for the first time in Jesus; rather it is a feature of the very constitution of the universe—a feature that was there all along, for everybody and everything. And it was there, Christians believe, because the Person who manifest himself finally and fully in Jesus' humanity is none other than the Word of God, the Second Person of the Three Persons in One God who is intimately and immediately present to every scrap of creation from start to finish.[1]

---

[1] Robert Farrar Capon, *The Mystery of Christ* (1993), pp. 25-26.

Destined for Joy

> The Incarnation, accordingly, is a Mystery that is true **all through history**. Jesus is the **great sacrament** of that Mystery, the **real presence** of it in his historical time and place. But the Mystery of the Word incarnate in Jesus is also really and effectively present at **all times and places** because that Word is **God himself,** the second Person of the Trinity. In Jesus, the Mystery didn't **show up** in a world from which it was previously absent; rather **what had been there all along** was finally and fully **manifest** in him.[2]

Capon's proposal thus solves the longstanding problem of how God can save those who have never heard the gospel. There is no conundrum to solve. In a mystery all are included in the atoning work of Christ, now and forever. Or to put it differently, every human being indwells their Creator and Savior, Jesus the eternal Word:

> One of the perennial problems of theology is how to imagine, how to figure to ourselves, the way in which God, having made the world and let it get out of whack, manages to get it back in shape. The problem is usually solved by thinking of God as coming down from heaven and fixing something: putting in a new fuse, or doing a valve job on the world so it will run right again.
>
> But that introduces an impossible set of images. It suggests that God, in his deepest being, is at some distance from the world—that if he turns up at all, he comes as a kind of celestial road service doing incidental repairs after the damage has been done. But. If there is indeed therefore *now* no condemnation, it can mean only one thing: that from the most important point of view (God's), he was already on the scene before the damage was done, and he fixed it before it had a chance to do any final damage. Because if God can tell you that *now* you are uncondemned for some sin you are committing right now, or even will commit next week (and he does indeed tell you just that), then he's talking about something a lot more intimate to your being than

---

[2] Ibid., p. 72.

some ex post facto visit by a garage mechanic. He's talking about something he is present to *eternally*. He is telling you that as far as his *Word* is concerned (and his Word *goes*), you have never been out of line at all—or, more accurately, that anything you may have put out of line was, in the very moment of its misalignment, realigned then and there by the suave and forceful *Wisdom* that goes through all things and is more moving than any motion. And above all he is telling you that what was announced in Jesus by that Word, what was done in Jesus by that Wisdom, was not the temporal start of the repair of your wreck but the final accomplishment of it from the beginning by the Lamb slain from the foundation of the world—by the Ultimate Beloved whose voice creates and reconciles all.

Put that together, then, and ask the right question. Do not ask, "Where is God, and how does he get here, and what does he do when he arrives?" Ask instead, "Where is the world?"

And then, finally, you see. The world is in bed . . . with the Father and Saint Sophie. The world leaps out of nothing into being between the lips of the Word and the ear of the Father. The world is what the Ultimate Beloved whispers to the Ultimate Lover. Creation is the Pillow Talk of the Trinity. *The world is the Place the Divine Persons create by the power of their eternal Affair.*

Do you see now? Do you see why, in that bed, *there can be nothing wrong?* Why you are uncondemned and free, just by being? It is because, if the Wisdom of God be for you, nothing can be against you, nothing can separate you from the love of Christ. For you are the very body of that love, and if Wisdom speaks you into being in that bed, she speaks you reconciled forever. Whatever in you is evil, or nasty, or stupid, or said is not mentioned in that bed; it is taken down into the Silence of the Crucifixion of the Word that is the Forgetting of the Father.[3]

The reconciliation of humanity through the Cross belongs to the eternal act of creation, by the Father through the crucified and risen

---

[3] Robert Farrar Capon, *Between Noon and Three* (1996), pp. 120-121.

Son in the Holy Spirit. It is not an afterthought that requires God to intervene with plan B. Humanity is forgiven, justified, sanctified, glorified before the foundation of the world, eternally destined to share in the love and unity of the New Creation. Capon invites us to read Ephesians 1:3-10 with fresh eyes:

> Blessed be the God and Father of our Lord Jesus Christ, who has blessed us in Christ with every spiritual blessing in the heavenly places, even as he chose us in him before the foundation of the world, that we should be holy and blameless before him. He destined us in love to be his sons through Jesus Christ, according to the purpose of his will, to the praise of his glorious grace which he freely bestowed on us in the Beloved. In him we have redemption through his blood, the forgiveness of our trespasses, according to the riches of his grace which he lavished upon us. For he has made known to us in all wisdom and insight the mystery of his will, according to his purpose which he set forth in Christ as a plan for the fulness of time, to unite all things in him, things in heaven and things on earth. (Eph. 1:3-10)

The world is created from Calvary, and Calvary lies deep in the heart of God. In the words of the great Orthodox theologian Georges Florovsky: "The mystery of the Cross begins in eternity, 'in the sanctuary of the Holy Trinity, unapproachable for creatures.'"[4] From all eternity, for all eternity, God is Pascha:

> Christ, the Word of God by whom all things are made and offered to the Father, is also the Lamb of God by whom all things are reconciled—from the very foundation of the world. That means that the Mystery, the hidden, ever-present act by which he perpetually causes all things to leap out of nothing, is matched at every moment by another Mystery, another hidden, ever-present act by which he perpetually reconciles all things to the Father. And that means that the Creating, Reconciling

---

[4] Georges Florosvky, "Redemption," *Creation and Redemption* (1976): III:100.

Redemption Eternal: The Caponian Vision of Grace

Word himself is perpetually present to every single created thing at every moment of history, B.C. or A.D.[5]

But what about judgment? How can we reasonably say that the impenitent wicked are now justified in Christ? Capon acknowledges the scandal and concedes its seeming absurdity. It offends our sense of morality and justice. He directs us to two sayings of Jesus from the Gospel of John:

> The Father judges no one, but has given all judgment to the Son. (John 5:22)
>
> For I did not come to judge the world but to save the world. (John 12:47)

Do you see? Both the Father and the Son have abdicated their respective roles as hanging judge. They only will our good and salvation:

> There is therefore no condemnation for two reasons: first, there is nobody left to be condemned; and second, there is nobody around to do the condemning. And likewise, there is therefore *now* no condemnation for two reasons: you are dead now; and God, as the Lamb slain from the foundation of the world, has been dead all along. The blame game was over before it started. It really was. All Jesus did was announce that truth and tell you it would make you free. It was admittedly a dangerous thing to do. You *are* a menace. But he did it; and therefore, menace or not, here you stand: uncondemned, forever, *now*. What are you going to do with your freedom?[6]

Recall the Parable of the Unjust Judge (Luke 18:1-8): the judge justifies the persistent widow for no good reason whatsoever, and in

---

[5] *Noon and Three*, p. 220.
[6] Ibid., p. 114.

that act dies to his role as judge.[7] "There is therefore now no condemnation . . ."

Consider, or perhaps reconsider, the parables of judgment. We often miss the crucial point: the declaration of justification occurs *at the beginning* of the parables.

> Let's get straight what the Greek word for judgment is: it's *krisis*—the same word as "crisis" in English. And it means the same thing: an act or situation that, because it puts a new set of rules into the game, calls for a new decision about the game on our part. It does not, in the first instance mean "judgment" in the sense of *condemnation* (Greek has a number of other words for that). Because if you read Jesus' parables of judgment carefully, you'll see that the *krisis* in them—the primary judgment of God that calls us to decision—always comes at the *beginning* of those parables. Furthermore, it's always a *krisis* caused by God's *favorable* judgment about us: he starts out each of those parables with a declaration that every one of the characters that stand for humanity is okay. It's a *krisis*, in other words, that Jesus set up having the "God" character declare at the outset that he's going to act on the basis of *the presumption—the effective declaration—of innocence*. It's a *krisis* of *faith*, therefore: none of the "human" characters has to prove he's *not* guilty by doing something to establish his innocence; the only thing any of them needs to do is *believe* in the innocence already proclaimed over him.
>
> Look at a few instances. The guests invited to the king's son's wedding are all judged equally worthy of being at a royal wedding. All ten virgins are members of the bridal party. And all three servants, whether they receive five talents, or two, or one, are equally in their master's favor. They all receive a judgment of *acceptability*, of *inclusion*. They're all *presumed innocent*. Nobody is condemned to start with.

---

[7] See Capon's exegesis of the parable in *Kingdom, Grace, Judgment* (2002), pp. 329-336.

> Now obviously, at the ends of those parables, there's plenty of condemnation. But it's crucial to note what that condemnation is based on. The temptation, of course (since we're totally committed to justifying ourselves by our own goodness), is to read the hard-hearted endings as based on evil works—on the characters' failure to *perform properly*. But that just won't wash. What the final judgment is really based on is not their works but the presence or absence of *their faith* in the God-character who graciously included them in his favor from square one.[8]

In Jesus' parabolic teaching, the judgment of God is not a judgment of who is good and who is bad; it is not a judgment of works, righteous or evil. It is, rather, the recognition of who trusts the infinitely loving God and who does not. The wise virgins are rewarded even though they uncharitably refuse to share their oil with the foolish ones. The prodigal rake of a son is welcomed with open arms by his father, without proof of his contrition. And in the Parable of the Vineyard, "the Johnny-come-lately workers in the vineyard are given a full day's pay for next to no work."[9] Why the inequities? Why the lack of interest in who deserves or does not deserve the reward of the Kingdom? "It's because Jesus cares only about whether people are someplace where *trust alone* can get them," Capon explains, "not about whether they can claim to have worked their way there by noble efforts."[10] The judgment of the Almighty is not about justice at all:

> While we were still weak, at the right time Christ died for the ungodly. Why, one will hardly die for a righteous man—though perhaps for a good man one will dare even to die. But God shows his love for us in that while we were yet sinners Christ died for us. Since, therefore, we

---

[8] *Mystery*, pp. 86-87.
[9] Ibid., p. 90.
[10] Ibid.

are now justified by his blood, much more shall we be saved by him from the wrath of God. For if while we were enemies we were reconciled to God by the death of his Son, much more, now that we are reconciled, shall we be saved by his life. (Rom 5:6-10)

Yet still we balk. What about the bad people? Capon replies:

> But, but *Jesus* is in bad people. And Jesus hasn't turned his back on *them*. Don't you see? Jesus is all that counts. After all, he's the *Word of God* who made them, and he's the *Incarnate Word* who reconciles them. No matter what you or I may do or not do in our lives, the Gospel truth is that when we're dead, he's going to raise us, good or bad. And when he raises us, he's going to raise us *repaired*, not left in the mess of our sins. Of course, if you want to be like the guy in the parable of the King's Son's Wedding and refuse to put on the free tuxedo, then you can go to hell. But as I said, *not otherwise*.[11]

God has died for our sin and risen for our justification, and his eternal word of judgment is an astounding *not guilty!* Nor should we think that the "no condemnation in Christ Jesus" was an invention of Paul. It was embodied in Jesus' dining practices: he scandalously ate and drank with *sinners* in proleptic celebration of the Messianic Banquet. He did not first demand their repentance. He simply invited himself to dinner: "Zacchae'us, make haste and come down; for I must stay at your house today" (Luke 19:5). E. P. Sanders spells out the eschatological significance of Jesus' table fellowship:

> Table-fellowship has loomed large in recent discussion of Jesus. His eating with tax collectors and sinners has, probably correctly, been seen as a proleptic indication that they would be included in the kingdom: the meal looks forward to the 'messianic banquet', when many would come from east and west and dine with the patriarchs (Matt. 8.11). Several parables tell us that the kingdom is like a banquet, to which

---

[11] Ibid., p. 76.

many are called. And, most tellingly, before his death Jesus looked forward to drinking the fruit of the vine in the kingdom of God (Mark 14.25//Matt. 26.29//Luke 22.18). Thus it would appear that Jesus' eating with 'tax collectors and sinners' promised, as clearly as words, that they would inherit the kingdom; and thus it is likely that Jesus saw his eating with tax collectors and sinners as promising membership in the coming kingdom. . . . It seems to be the case. . . that Jesus offered the truly wicked—those beyond the pale and outside the common religion by virtue of their implicit or explicit rejection of the commandments of the God of Israel—admission to his group (and, he claimed the kingdom) if they accepted him.[12]

And this brings us to the Parable of the Great Judgment (Matt 25:31-46).[13] Capon's exegesis of the parable is distinctive and insightful. Given his interpretation of the other parables, he rightly maintains that the final judgment parable should not be interpreted as an abrupt retreat into justification by works. The sheep are justified because of their relationship *with Jesus* (of which they were unaware); the goats are condemned because of their non-relationship *with Jesus* (of which they too were unaware). "In as much as you did it (or didn't do it) to the least of my brethren, you did it (or didn't do it) to me." The sheep and goats are judged according to their actions as participation or non-participation in the love of Jesus. Their unknowing faith or non-faith is implied. The goats are condemned not because of their sins but because they have closed their hearts to the divine forgiveness already bestowed:

> Do you finally see? Nobody knows anything. The righteous didn't know they were in relationship with the King when they ministered to the least of his brethren, any more than the cursed knew they were

---

[12] E. P. Sanders, *Jesus and Judaism* (1985), pp. 209-210. Also see E. P. Sanders, *The Historical Figure of Jesus* (1993), pp. 230-237.
[13] See Capon's exegesis of the parable, *Kingdom*, pp. 504-512.

despising the King when they didn't so minister. Knowledge is not the basis of anybody's salvation or damnation. Action-in-dumb-trust is. And the reason for that is that salvation comes only by relationship with the Savior—by a relationship that, from his side, is already an accomplished eternal fact, and that therefore needs only to be accepted by faith, not known in any way. "No man," Luther said (if I may quote him one last time), "can know or feel he is saved; he can only believe it." At the final parousia, we will not be judged by anything except our response of faith or unfaith to the Savior whose presence was coterminous with our whole existence. And at that day he will simply say whether, from our side (by faith, that is—but with no other conditions specified as to knowledge or any other human achievement), we related to that presence. He will simply do the truth from his side—simply affirm his eternal, gracious relationship with all of creation—and honor what both the sheep and the goats did with that truth from their side.[14]

The sheep are not saved because they have a splendid moral record. They are saved by their acceptance of Christ's acceptance. "Or to put it even more precisely," writes Capon, "they are praised at his final parousia for what they did in his parousia throughout their lives, namely, for trusting him to have had a relationship with them all along."[15] Nor are the goats punished because of their evil deeds: they are condemned for not trusting in Jesus.

The Realization of the Eschaton in Jesus

By this time readers will have come to realize that Capon has one foot (maybe two) firmly placed in realized eschatology:

- the final judgment has already been spoken in the death and resurrection of Jesus;

---

[14] Ibid., pp. 510-511.
[15] Ibid., p. 510

Redemption Eternal: The Caponian Vision of Grace

- we are justified by grace, not by works;
- the Kingdom to come is already present;
- we are dead and risen in Jesus;
- in Christ all things have been made a new creation.

Capon is of course well aware that these are stupendous, perhaps unbelievable claims, given that nothing appears to have dramatically changed in the world since Easter and Pentecost. Death, pestilence, violence and war, hurricanes and earthquakes, horrific suffering—life pretty much goes on as it always has. Only by faith do we hear the music of the Kingdom:

> It's like a dance—a big formal party that everybody is already invited to and present at. Now what happens at a dance? When the band starts to play, almost everybody decides to trust the "new world" of the dance and to act accordingly: they move in harmony with the music. But when the band takes a break they go back to acting in accordance with the "old world" they know better: husbands and wives get into arguments; some people drink too much; others try to make real-estate deals; and so on.
>
> If you think about that, it gives you a much better picture of what Christians are really supposed to be up to. Because the dance that God has invited us to—the dance of the Mystery of Christ—is always going on: the band playing the music of forgiveness never takes a break. The music of the Mystery, of course, is *hidden* music: we have to *trust* that it's being played—and for anyone who doesn't trust, it's just as if there's no music going on at all. Christians, therefore, are not some select group who have music nobody else has; they're simply people who by faith—trust—always hear the music of the Mystery of Christ that the whole creation has been provided with. And so the real job of Christians as far as the world is concerned is simply to dance to the hidden music—and to try, by the joy of their dancing, to wake the world

up to the music it's already at, even though it thinks it doesn't hear any music at all.[16]

But how do we hear music that cannot be heard? Is the life of faith simply make-believe? At this point Capon takes a surprising contemplative turn:

> T. S. Eliot called the cross—the death of Christ—"the still point of the turning world"; and except for that point, he said, "there would be no dance." That was in the *Four Quartets*. And somewhere else in them he says, "So the darkness shall be the light, and the stillness the dancing." It's only when we can sit still in our deaths—present "deaths," like your inability to hold a book, or our final death in death itself—that we can hear the music at all. Everything else we might do is just noice that drowns it out. It's only when we listen in the stillness that grace can have its way with us. But grace is always there because Jesus is always there: and any time we stop our noice, the music comes up.[17]

Yet, realized eschatology strains credulity when taken too seriously. I sure don't feel like I'm living the Messianic Banquet. Where is the compelling evidence of its presence? If I'm risen from the dead, why does my back hurt all the time? Yes, the Gospel of John bespeaks a realized eschatology, but surely, it's just a figurative way of speaking we can jettison when convenient. But Capon refuses to let us off the hook. We need to take both present resurrection and future resurrection with equal seriousness, for it is under these two sets of images that the resurrection is proclaimed to us by Holy Scripture: "resurrection *now*, and resurrection *then*—resurrection presented under the the imagery of *immediacy*, and resurrection presented under the imagery of *history*."[18]

---

[16] *Mystery*, pp. 169-170.
[17] Ibid., pp. 169-170.
[18] Ibid., p. 221.

So how does Capon envision us holding both together. Begin, he suggests, with the most difficult—realized resurrection:

> Which is the harder reading? Resurrection *now* obviously. Accordingly, take that reading first, make resurrection now utterly real. Insist that, in him, we have always been as risen as we're going to get—that there will not be a single moment of our life at the end of the world that wasn't present, in the Mystery of the Word, from the foundation of the world. Say flatly that he's always had it all together, and that in him we've got it all together too *right now*. In short, take the vertical imagery of the Mystery at full force.[19]

By divine revelation we know that our lives are grounded upon the reality of present resurrection in Christ. God has declared to us the general resurrection of mankind—and indeed of all creation—under two signs: first under the historical sign of his own resurrection in A.D. 30; secondly under the promissory sign of our participation in the general resurrection at the end of time. "They are not, either of them, *when* the resurrection happens," Capon explains; "they are simply two times when the eternal happening of the resurrection is *sacramentalized*—historically manifested—as really present. They are simply two points at which the truth under all points is thrust up for our attention in faith."[20]

If all of this is true, *when* then is heaven? Right *now*, of course, despite the obvious reasons why we think it cannot be.

> If we are *now* in Christ, we are *now* in the new creation. Unless what we believe is a lie, it is just that simple, and the proof is as easy as the yoke of Christ. For if we are now dead with him, we are also now risen in him; and if we are now judged by him, we are also now reconciled in him. And therefore if heaven is the fullness of that reconciliation, it is

---

[19] Ibid.
[20] Ibid., 222.

that now, and we're in it already. The only important sense in which we are not in it is the least important sense of all; and the only catch to it turns out to be not a catch but the ultimate liberation: our apprehension of heaven-face-fo-face waits only for the easiest, most inevitable thing of all—our *literal, physical death*. That alone has yet to be true; everything else is true already. Therefore, we are as good as home *now*. Q.E.D.[21]

Almost Apokatastasis

If at this point, you are asking yourself, "Does not Capon's vision of the universality of grace within the divine life of the Trinity entail apokatastasis?" Know that I too, am asking that question. All the necessary ingredients are there—or perhaps not quite all. In *Between Noon and Three* Capon discusses humanity's innate desire for the Good. He doesn't name Thomas Aquinas as his inspiration, but I'm confident that he was. Capon has even caught something of Thomas's Neoplatonism. The following quotations are often phrased in the past tense, as Capon is describing his intellectual journey to a radical understanding of grace and the mystery of the Kingdom:

> Because the divine knowing—what the Father knows, and what the Word says in response to that knowing, and what the Spirit broods upon under the speaking of the Word—all that intellectual activity isn't just day-dreaming. It's the *cause* of everything that is. God doesn't *find out* about creation; he *knows it into being*. His knowing has hair on it. It is an *effective* act. What he knows, is. What he thinks, by the very fact of his thinking, jumps from no-thing into thing. He never thought of anything that wasn't.
>
> But that meant his knowing was determinative of the being of each and every thing. And not simply of its *static* being, its existence

---

[21] *Noon and Three*, p. 281.

considered as something just sitting there doing nothing. God's knowing (the knowing of the Trinity, to be precise) has also to be seen as determinative of the *dynamics* of the being of everything thing—of the way it *moves by desire* toward the Highest Good. For all things arise out of nothing for one reason only: because of the *desire* of the Word and the Spirit to offer to the Father what he delights to know. Everything that exists is a delightful present, gift-wrapped and given, at the Father's eternal un-birthday party. All creatures spring from and are borne upon a torrent of desire for the Father's good pleasure; there is a river of longing flowing from the Son and the Spirit to the Father, a river whose streams make glad the City of God.[22]

So very good! I love Capon's description of creation as rooted in the mutual knowing and loving of the Father, Son, and Holy Spirit. He then proceeds to talk about the self-knowing of creatures:

But that in turn meant something more. Since it is the very creatures themselves that are the gifts of the Beloved to the Father, the creatures themselves are participants of that flow of desire; and they are participants *by knowing themselves* on whatever level they can manage. The apples of his eye, to whatever degree they can know and love themselves *as apples*, to that degree they really do participate in the knowledge and love of the Son for a Father who is crazy about apples.

In other words, the proper self-knowledge and self-love of every created thing is ipso facto a participation in the knowledge and love of God. The entire universe moves by desire for the Highest Good simply because every part of it loves what God loves—namely, its own being. The stones on the beach, the grass in the field, the rabbits in the woods, and the stars in the sky all move toward him by the most dependable of all motions; their own desire to know and love themselves.[23]

---

[22] Ibid., pp. 235-236.
[23] Ibid., pp. 236-237.

Capon acknowledges the objection that ascribing desire to inanimate objects suffers from an extreme anthropomorphism, but he decides that it's closer to the mark than not, especially for animals. Finally, he comes to humanity's natural desire for God:

> The second objection, however, was less easily dismissed—though in the end, when I properly understood it, it turned out to be the biggest lead of all. It was that when you applied the grand rubric to human beings—when you said that every motion human beings make is a motion toward the Highest Good and works by means of our desire to know ourselves as the totality that God knows—you had to include Sin in the equation. All the horrible items in my list—Roberto and Vito at the moment the garrote was applied, Paul and Catherine at the fatal lunch in the Italian restaurant, and so on [Capon is referring to two stories around which the book is structured—a mob execution of a gangster and the tragic affair of an adulterous couple]—had to be said to fall under the same rubric. Even those acts of knowledge that end up desiring what God does not desire had to be seen as expressions of the desire for the Highest Good by means of a desire to know what God knows. Perverted desires, perhaps—knowings-in-contradiction, inconvenient and dangerous alterations in self-knowledge—but still the same desire to know which is the only root of all motion and which, despite its perversion, is still a desire for the Highest Good.[24]

The above movement of thought leads Capon into a "re-membering" of the story of Adam and Eve. He posits the Fall as an alteration in the self-knowledge of the couple. From knowing themselves as oriented to God as their true good, they begin to know themselves outside of themselves. As Capon puts it: "It was by knowing themselves that they were supposed to desire the Highest Good; but instead, they parked that knowledge in a dumb tree and

---

[24] Ibid., p. 238.

forsook their own center."[25] That was, of course, disastrous. When Adam and Eve then tried to know themselves, they couldn't do it anymore: "'And the eyes of them both were opened, and they knew that they were naked'—a discovery, of course, of nothing at all."[26] And from this alteration of human self-consciousness follows the tragic history of sin and death.

The Fall of humanity into disorder and death then leads Capon to speculate upon the dead mind of the dead Jesus before his resurrection: "For if the origin of evil lay in the alteration of human knowledge, then the end of evil—the quashing of it, the reconciliation of all its disastrous consequences—must lie somehow in a second alteration of that same knowledge."[27] The death of the Lord's human consciousness thus becomes, so Capon conjectures,

> the device by which all the perverted alterations in human knowledge could finally be terminated and our full historical existence be seen as reconciled in the unaltered remembering that the Word of God offers to the Father. For our sake, Christ dies not simply to the law but to that whole contradictory way of knowing the good for which the law condemns us. By the deadness of his human mind and ours, we are literally *absolved, set loose,* from the unreconciled knowledge of our times as we held them in our hands. And in the power of his resurrection, we are lifted up into nothing less than the reconciled knowledge of those times as they are held by the Second Person of the Trinity in both his unaltered divine mind and his risen human consciousness.[28]

A remarkable speculative proposal! As far as I know, it is original to Capon. The soteriological significance of the death of Jesus' human

---

[25] Ibid., p. 241.
[26] Ibid.
[27] Ibid., p. 243.
[28] Ibid., pp. 243-244.

consciousness has been ignored by even the best thinkers of the Church. Capon continues his speculation:

> And as Christ holds us risen in himself, the deadness of our own human minds—yours, mine, Vito's, anybody's—works the same way. All the horrible alteration, perversion, and contradiction in Vito's knowledge, for example—the one and only root of all the evil in his life—is absolved, dissolved, in his death. Because in his death he loses everything that was his, good and bad. And when he comes out of his death into the power of Christ's resurrection, he comes out with the full knowledge of everything in his life, good and bad, restored to him from the hand of God—held by him as it is in the risen mind of Christ. He sees it all with a knowing untainted by alteration, perversion, or contradiction (because the mind that knew it that way is dead forever); and he grasps it no longer as the evil it once tried to be but as the desire for the Highest Good it always was in the offering of the Word to the Father. If our Fall was our recognition, our re-knowing of the *good as evil*, then our Reconciliation is our re-cognition in Christ—our re-knowing in the risen humanity of the Word—of evil as *the good he has made it once more*.
>
> And there finally stood the dock, clearly visible. The grand image of it all turned out to be nothing other than the great sacrament of reconciliation itself, the Eucharistic offering: "Do this in remembrance of me. . . . As often as ye eat of this bread and drink this cup, ye do show the Lord's death till he come." Do *this*, he says, for my *anamnesis*, for a remembering, a re-cognition, a re-knowing, a re-presenting of *my death*. Take, he commands us, the worst thing you ever did to me—that most disastrous of all the disastrous alterations in your knowledge—and see it now, face it now, accept it now as I see it in my resurrection: as the best thing that ever happened to you. Take this worst of all the world's Fridays in thankful *anamnesis* and *recognize* it now, *celebrate* it now as the Good I always meant and saw—and that you meant, too, but could never achieve in your contradiction. By the grace of my unaltered risen knowledge, see even the disasters of your

history as the inexorable desire for the Highest Good I always knew them to be.

Nothing, therefore, is lost. Not a scrap of history. Not the smallest, whitest lie or the greatest genocidal holocaust. It is all held in a renewed knowledge—in an *anamnesis*, in a *re-membering*, a *re-cognition* by the grace that raises those whom death has absolved. . . . What God effects in the reconciliation does the work of forgetting without the *danger* of forgetting. He does better than forget: he remembers our evil in grace as *the only real thing it could have been.* He takes away the flaming sword between us and our self-knowledge and brings us home to ourselves.[29]

The vision is glorious! In the Kingdom of God that is the Father, Son, and Spirit we are are already forgiven, healed, sanctified, deified. However we might judge Capon's speculations, still we must applaud his accomplishment. Yet sadly, Capon was unable to divine the logically necessary conclusion of universal salvation. He devotes a few pages to the topic in *Between Noon and Three*, but his arguments are unconvincing. The weight of Scripture and ecclesial tradition holds him back. He does not see that when resurrected, transfigured, renewed human beings are brought into full knowledge of the risen Christ's knowledge, both of God and of themselves, they will be irresistibly drawn to unite themselves to the love, joy, happiness, and rapture that is the life of the Holy Trinity. For that is our true end and consummation.

So where are the damned? If realized and future eschatology are as intimately united as Capon proposes, the damned must be present somewhere at the eschatological festivities. The separation of the final judgment can never be a real separation. Love would not allow that:

---

[29] *Kingdom*, pp. 505-506.

> Jesus is the Good Shepherd, and the Good Shepherd lays down his life for the sheep. But he lays down his life for the goats as well, because on the cross he draws all to himself. It is not that the sheep are his but the goats are not; the sheep are his sheep and the goats are his goats. Any separation that occurs, therefore, must be read as occurring within his shepherding, not as constituting a divorce from it. . . . Accordingly, Jesus' drawing of all to himself remains the ultimate gravitational force in the universe; nothing, not even evil, is ever exempted from it. Hell has no choice but to be within the power of the final party, even though it refuses to act as if it is at the party. It lies not so much outside the festivities as it is sequestered within them. It is hidden, if you will, in the spear wound in Christ's side to keep it from being a wet blanket on the heavenly proceedings; but it is not, for all that, any less a part of Jesus' catholic shepherding of his flock.[30]

Capon's image that hell is sequestered within the spear wound of Christ is beautiful. The self-damned are separated neither from the risen Christ nor from his eschatological banquet. But because of their adamant refusal to embrace the Crucified and join in the dance of love, the Lord graciously hides them within himself. At all times, for all eternity, they are enveloped in his love and care.

A critical theological truth is at stake here. We must not think of damnation as something that happens apart from the Lord's saving work: "Everything that happens after the second coming of Jesus—judgment, heaven, and even hell—happens within the triumphantly reconciling power of his death and resurrection."[31] Whether they realize it or not, the damned are definitively and forever forgiven and reconciled in Christ. Their sins are nailed on the cross of the Savior. They have died with Christ and been raised in him. This truth must govern the Church's teaching on the final judgment.

---

[30] Ibid., pp. 244-245.
[31] Ibid., p. 96.

Chapter Ten

Sometimes Eternity Ain't Forever: *Aiónios* and the Universalist Hope

Words do not mean. People mean.
~ *Alfred Korzybski* ~

When I use a word,
it means just what I choose it to mean—
neither more nor less.
~ *Humpty Dumpty* ~

When discussing the question of eschatological punishment, defenders of the doctrine of everlasting damnation immediately appeal to our Lord's teaching on Gehenna.[1] It is simply *obvious*, they tell us, that Jesus taught the *eternal* damnation of the reprobate. Certainly that is how most English translations of the New Testament render the relevant texts. The classic passage is Jesus' Parable of the Last Judgment (Matt 25:31-46). It concludes with these words (Matt 25:46):

καὶ ἀπελεύσονται οὗτοι εἰς κόλασιν αἰώνιον, οἱ δὲ δίκαιοι εἰς ζωὴν αἰώνιον

And these shall go away into everlasting punishment: but the righteous into life eternal. (KJV)

---

[1] I am not a biblical scholar. I don't even read ancient Greek. My purpose in writing this article is quite modest: to present samples of the scholarship, past and present, that challenges the translation of *aionios* as "eternal" in the oft-quoted hell passages in the New Testament. These passages can be *plausibly* and *reasonably* interpreted in ways that do not deny apokatastasis. Please forgive the very lengthy quotations. I want you to see the words of the scholars rather than my paraphrases.

> And these will depart into eternal punishment, but the righteous into eternal life. (RSV)
>
> Then they will go away to eternal punishment, but the righteous to eternal life. (NIV)
>
> And these shall go away into age-abiding correction, but the righteous, into age-abiding life. (REB)
>
> And these shall go away to punishment age-during, but the righteous to life age-during. (YLT)
>
> And these shall be coming away into chastening eonian, yet the just into life eonian. (CLNT)
>
> And these will go to the chastening of that Age, but the just to the life of that Age. (DBHNT)

We immediately note that the King James, Revised Standard, and New International Versions speak of "*eternal* punishment" and "*eternal* life." The underlying Greek word is *aiónios*, the adjectival form (along with *aiónion, aioníou*, and others) of the noun *aión* (age, eon, era, epoch). A popular New Testament lexicon offers the following definitions for αἰώνιος, α, ον [αἰών]:

- 'relating to a period of time extending far into the past', long ages ago.
- 'relating to time without boundaries or interruption', eternal.
- 'relating to a period of unending duration', permanent, lasting.[2]

The translation of *aiónios* as "eternal" appears to accord perfectly with the lexicon's definitions (specifically #2 and #3). We are, after all, talking about the Last Judgment and the divine assignment of the righteous and the wicked to their final destinies. Everything seems to be in order. Nothing to see here. Move along.

---

[2] Frederick William Danker, *The Concise Greek-English Lexicon of the New Testament* (2009), p. 12.

Yet what about those other translations in the list? *Rotherham's Emphasized Bible* translates *aiónios* as "age-abiding" and *Young's Literal Translation* as "age-during." The *Concordant Literal New Testament* delivers something more like a transliteration ("chastening eonian," "life eonian"), entrusting to us the task of figuring out what "eonian" means. And David Bentley Hart's translation is more curious still and will be discussed below. Why did these translators choose to break from the infallible consensus? Simple answer: because the semantic range of *aiónios* is notoriously wider than the lexical entry might lead us to believe. Even in the context of the Last Judgment, *aiónios* need not, and perhaps should not, be rendered "eternal."

The Eonic Semantics of *Aiónios*

Two linguistic principles need to be kept in mind throughout this article:

- Words do not mean; people mean. Language is a living cultural reality by which people communicate.
- A word in one language is not equivalent to a word in another language. Translation is always an adventure.

We begin with Marvin Vincent's classic *Word Studies of the New Testament*:

> Αἰών, transliterated *aeon*, is a period of longer or shorter duration, having a beginning and an end, and complete in itself. Aristotle (περὶ οὐρανοῦ, i. 9, 15) says: "The period which includes the whole time of one's life is called the *aeon* of each one." Hence it often means *the life* of a man, as in Homer, where one's life (αἰών) is said to leave him or to consume away (*Iliad* v. 685; *Odyssey* v. 160). It is not, however, limited to human life; it signifies any period in the course of events, as the

period or age before Christ; the period of the millennium; the mythological period before the beginnings of history. The word has not "a stationary and mechanical value" (De Quincey). It does not mean a period of a fixed length for all cases. There are as many aeons as entities, the respective durations of which are fixed by the normal conditions of the several entities. There is one aeon of a human life, another of the life of a nation, another of a crow's life, another of an oak's life. The length of the aeon depends on the subject to which it is attached.

It is sometimes translated *world*; world represents a period or a series of periods of time. . . . Similarly οἱ αἰῶνες, *the worlds*, the universe, the aggregate of the ages or periods, and their contents which are included in the duration of the world. . . . The word always carries the notion of time, and not of eternity. It always means a period of time. Otherwise it would be impossible to account for the plural, or for such qualifying expressions as this age, or the age *to come*. It does not mean something endless or everlasting. . . .

In the New Testament, the history of the world is conceived as developed through a succession of aeons. A series of such aeons precedes the introduction of a new series inaugurated by the Christian dispensation, and the end of the world and the second coming of Christ are to mark the beginning of another series. . . . He includes the series of aeons in one great aeon, ὁ αἰὼν τῶν αἰώνων, *the aeon of the aeons* (Eph. 3:21); and the author of the Epistle to the Hebrews describes the throne of God as enduring unto the aeon of the aeons (Heb 1:8). The plural is also used, aeons of the aeons, signifying all the successive periods which make up the sum total of the ages collectively. . . . This plural phrase is applied by Paul to God only.

The adjective αἰώνιος in like manner carries the idea of time. Neither the noun nor the adjective, in themselves, carry the sense of *endless* or *everlasting*. They may acquire that sense by their connotation, as, on the other hand, ἀΐδιος, which means *everlasting*, has its meaning limited to a given point of time in Jude 6. Αἰώνιος means *enduring through or pertaining to a period of time*. Both the noun and the adjective are applied to limited periods. Thus the phrase εἰς τὸν αἰῶνα, habitually rendered *forever*, is often used of duration which is limited in the very nature of the case. . . . The same is true of αἰώνιος. Out of 150 instances in LXX, four-fifths imply limited duration. . . .

Words which are *habitually* applied to things temporal or material cannot carry in themselves the sense of endlessness. Even when applied to God, we are not forced to render αἰώνιος *everlasting*. Of course the life of God is endless; but the question is whether, in describing God as αἰώνιος, it was intended to describe the duration of his being, or whether some different and larger idea was not contemplated. . . .

There is a word for everlasting if that idea is demanded. That ἀΐδιος occurs rarely in the New Testament and in LXX does not prove that its place was taken by αἰώνιος. It rather goes to show that less importance was attached to the bare idea of everlastingness than later theological thought has given it.[3]

Note especially Vincent's claim that *aiónios* typically refers to a limited or indefinite period of time. In itself, it does not bespeak eternality. James Hope Moulton and George Milligan agree:

---

[3] Marvin Vincent, *Word Studies of the New Testament* (1900), IV:58-60. Writing around the same time, Thomas Allin states: "Let us next consider the true meaning of the words *aiōn* and *aiōnios*. These are the originals of the terms rendered by our translators 'everlasting,' 'for ever and ever': and on this translation, so misleading, a vast portion of the popular dogma of endless torment is built up. I say, without hesitation, misleading and incorrect; for *aiōn* means 'an age,' a limited period, whether long or short, though often of indefinite length; and the adjective *aiōnios* means 'of the age,' 'age-long,' 'aeonian,' and never 'everlasting' (of its own proper force). It is true that it may be applied as an epithet to things that are endless, but the idea of endlessness in all such cases comes not from the epithet, but only because it is inherent in the object to which the epithet is applied, as in the case of God." *Christ Triumphant* (2015), pp. 275-276.

> In general, the word [*aiónios*] depicts that of which the horizon is not in view, whether the horizon be at an infinite distance . . . or whether it lies no farther than the span of a Caesar's life.[1]

Vincent also notes that *aiónios* may be used in a qualitative sense. We see this especially in the Gospel of John:

> **Ζωή αἰώνιος** *eternal life*, which occurs 42 times in N. T., but not in LXX, is not endless life, *but life pertaining to a certain age or aeon*, or continuing during that aeon. I repeat, life may be endless. The life in union with Christ is endless, but the fact is not expressed by αἰώνιος. **Κόλασις αἰώνιος**, rendered *everlasting punishment* (Matt. 25:46), is the punishment peculiar to an aeon other than that in which Christ is speaking. In some cases ζωή αἰώνιος does not refer specifically to the life beyond time, but rather to the aeon or dispensation of Messiah which succeeds the legal dispensation. . . . John says that ζωή αἰώνιος is the present possession of those who believe on the Son of God. . . . The Father's commandment is ζωή αἰώνιος, . . . ; to know the only true God and Jesus Christ is *zoe aionios*. . . . Thus, while αἰώνιος carries the idea of time, though not of endlessness, there belongs to it also, more or less, a sense of quality. Its character is ethical rather than mathematical. The deepest significance of the life beyond time lies, not in endlessness, but in the moral quality of the aeon into which the life passes.[5]

Yet, most translations of Matt 25:41 and 46 render *aiónios* as "eternal," thus eliding the nuances of the word and perhaps importing into it later theological commitments.

In his translation of the Parable of the Last Judgment, David Bentley Hart leaves open the question of duration, emphasizing

---

[1] James Hope Milligan and George Milligan, *The Vocabulary of the Greek New Testament* (1929), p. 19.
[5] Vincent, IV:60-61.

instead the divine judgment as eschatological event, i.e., that which pertains to the aeon to come:

> Then he will say to those to the left, "Go from me, you execrable ones, into the fire of the Age prepared for the Slanderer and his angels." (Matt 25:41)

> And these will go to the chastening of that Age, but the just to the life of that Age. (Matt 25:46)

In his concluding postscript, Hart notes the wide semantic range of *aiónios* in ancient Greek literature, paralleled by an equally wide range of the Hebrew word *olam* and the Aramaic *alma*, "both of which most literally mean something at an immense distance, on the far horizon, hidden from view, and which are usually used to mean 'age,' or 'period of long duration,' or a time hidden in the depths of the far past or far future, or a 'world' or 'dispensation,' or even 'eternity,' and so on; but it can also mean simply an extended period, and not necessarily a particularly long one, with a natural term."[6] If we reasonably assume both that Jesus taught in his native

---

[6] David Bentley Hart, *The New Testament: A Translation* (2017), p. 541. Heleen Keizer devotes a chapter of her dissertation *Life Time Entirety* (1993) to the relationship between *aiōn* and *'olām* in the Septuagint. She contends that *aiōn* (and analogously *aiōnios*) is a time-word signifying the whole or entirety of time: "Aiōn is the encircling whole of time" (p. 177). At the end of the chapter she concludes: "To summarize, *'olām* = *aiōn* in its fundamental sense designates what constitutes the temporal horizon inside of which we, created beings, have our position: it denotes time, always bound up with creation, reaching as far as we are able to envisage. In relation to particular matters, this horizon can be wider or more narrow: the time of a life, the time of a particular condition" (p. 204).

In the conclusion of her dissertation, Keizer connects the LXX understanding of *'olām/aiōn* with the usage of Jesus: "Of decisive importance is the new usage of *aiōn* found in the New Testament, where we hear Christ speaking of 'this (present) *aiōn*', 'the end of this aiōn', and 'the coming (future) aiōn'. This new usage of the Greek term again reflects literally the usage of *'olām*. Rabbinic sources speak of *'olām hazze* and *'olām habbā'* ('this *'olām*" and "the coming

language of Aramaic and that the evangelists faithfully rendered his words into their Greek equivalents, it would then be irresponsible for the modern translator to insist on the *eternal* duration of the eschatological fire—unless, of course, the literary and historical context demands this reading. Hart concludes:

> It is almost certainly the case that in the New Testament, and especially in the teachings of Jesus, the adjective *aiōnios* is the equivalent of something like the phrase *le-olam*, but also the case that it cannot be neatly discriminated from the language of the *olam ha-ba* ["the age to come"] without losing something of the theological depth and religious significance it possessed in the time of Christ."[7]

Hence Hart's decision to translate *aiónios* and noun as "the fire of the Age," "the chastening of that Age," "the life of that Age."

In their book *Terms for Eternity*, Ilaria Ramelli and David Konstan offer a comprehensive survey of how *aiónios* is used in Greek secular literature, Septuagint, New Testament, and early Church Fathers and contrasts it with *aídios* ("eternal"). With respect to New Testament usage, they conclude:

> In the New Testament, then, ἀΐδιος, which is used far less often than αἰώνιος, would appear to denote absolute eternity in reference to God; in connection with the chains of the fallen angels, on the other hand, it seems to indicate the continuity of their chastisement throughout the

---

'*olām*'). The distinction between two *aiōns*/'*olāms* originated in the period before Christ; it is rooted in the soil of the Old Testament prophecies and firmly present in Jewish apocalyptic texts. To speak of 'this *aiōn*', its 'end' and 'the *aiōn* to come' clearly lends to *aiōn* the meaning of a limited time. But at this point our findings with regard to the Old Testament meaning of '*olām*/*aiōn* can be supportive and supported. The New Testament indicates that 'this' and the 'coming' *aiōn* are not simply successive 'ages' or 'periods': the coming *aiōn*, as a restored, reborn world, will in the future completely replace the present one, while as a new 'horizon' of life it is also present already now" (pp. 251-252).
[7] Ibid., pp. 542-543.

entire duration of this world—and perhaps too from before the creation of the world and time itself, that is, eternally *a parte ante*.

As for αἰώνιος, it has a much wider range of meanings, often closely related. It perhaps signifies "eternity" in the strict sense—without beginning or end—in reference to God or his three Persons or to what pertains to God, such as his glory or his kingdom; or it may mean "perpetual"—in the sense of "without end," "permanent," "uninterrupted"—in reference, for example, to the new covenant mentioned by Christ. Far the most common expression is ζωή αἰώνιος, which, we have argued, indicates life in the future *αἰών*, in contrast to the present καιρός (or χρόνος, "time," or κόσμος, "this world," often used in a negative sense), and which is expressly connected with Christ, faith, hope (for the future), the resurrection in the world to come, and above all to grace in numerous passages, especially Pauline, where grace is said to justify, and Johannine, where it is connected with love or ἀγάπη: for John, God himself is ἀγάπη, and the αἰώνιος life is directly identified with Jesus. This life, which is the goal or finality of the Gospel, is the true life, and is often designated simply by ζωή tout court; and it coincides with salvation. The adjective αἰώνιος is associated too with other nouns (e.g., glory, salvation), always with reference to life in the next world. Although one may infer that life in the world to come is eternal in the sense of unending, it appears that this is not the primary connotation of αἰώνιος in these contexts, but is rather the idea of a new life or αἰών.

On the other hand, αἰώνιος is also applied to punishment in the world to come, particularly in the expression πῦρ αἰώνιον: ἀΐδιος is never employed either for fire or for other forms of future punishment or harm of human beings, and on one occasion (in 4 Macc) ὄλεθρος αἰώνιος is contrasted specifically with βίος ἀΐδιος.[8]

---

[8] Ilaria Ramelli and David Konstan, *Terms for Eternity* (2011), pp. 69-70. Also see their article "Terms for Eternity," *Noua tellus*, 24/2 (2006): 21-39, which may be downloaded here: http://www.scielo.org.mx/pdf/novatell/v24n2/0185-3058-novatell-24-02-21.pdf. Because their book has been dismissed on social media as

Destined for Joy

Konstan was asked on an internet forum to provide a short summary of his and Ramelli's research on *aiónios*:

> Ancient Greek had two words that are commonly translated as "eternal": *aídios* and *aiónios*. The latter of these terms is an adjective clearly deriving from the noun *aión*, from which we get the English "eon": it is an old word, appearing already in Homer, where it refers normally to a lifetime, or else some definite period of time. It never suggests an infinite stretch of time, and in later writers it continues to mean, almost always, either a lifetime or some particular period of time.
>
> What, then, about the adjective *aiónios*? Here is where problems arise, since the adjective seems first to occur in Plato, and Plato adapts it to a very special sense. Plato had the idea that time was a moving image of eternity, with the implication that eternity itself does not move or change: it is not an infinite length of time, but a state of timelessness (think of what time must have been like before God created the universe). This is quite different from the common meaning of *aídios*, which the presocratic philosophers had already used to express precisely an infinite stretch of time, with no beginning and no end; and this is what *aídios* continued to mean.
>
> So, we have two adjectives in use: one of them clearly means "infinite," when applied to time; but the other does not, and what is more, it is connected with a common noun—*aión*—that means simply a lifetime, with no suggestion of eternity. *Aiónios* remains relatively rare in classical Greek, and then we come to the Septuagint, or the Greek translation of the Hebrew Bible, where it occurs very frequently (*aídios*, by contrast, only appears twice, and those in parts originally written in Greek). Now, *aiónios* here can refer to things that are very old (as we say in English, "old as the hills"), but by no means eternal—what in this world is eternal? This is a very common usage, based on the Hebrew

---

a piece of universalist propaganda, it should be noted that Dr Konstan is *not* a universalist. He doesn't even believe in the afterlife. He is a respected and widely-published scholar of the classics, with no universalist axe to grind.

term. But it can also be used in reference to the world to come, and here we face the fundamental issue.

If one speaks of the next life, or something that happens in the next life, as *aiónios*, does it mean simply the next era or eon, or does it carry the further implication of "eternal"? Many of the passages in the Septuagint seem to indicate that the meaning is "of that eon"—and after all, it is a very long, but still finite period of time, that elapses between our death and judgment day and the resurrection, and this could be called an era. What is more, there is some reason to think that, after the resurrection, time itself will come to an end. So, saying that punishment in the afterlife is *aiónios* may just mean "for that eon" or epoch, and not forever.

We argued that this sense was understood by many (or most) of the Church Fathers, and that when they used *aiónios* of punishment in the afterlife, they were not necessarily implying that punishment would be eternal. Of course, one can only show this by careful examination of specific passages in context, and this is what we tried to do in our book. Very often, the evidence is ambiguous; for example, when God is described as *aiónios*, it is very difficult to be sure whether the word means "of the other world" or simply "eternal," since God is both. We hope readers will decide for themselves, on the basis of the evidence we collected and the interpretations we offered.[9]

Hart presents a lexical analysis similar to that of Konstan and Ramelli:

There is a genuine ambiguity in the term in Greek that is impossible to render directly in an English equivalent. *Aiōnios* is an adjective drawn from the substantive αἰών (*aiōn* or *aeon*), which *can* sometimes mean a period of endless duration, but which more properly, throughout the whole of ancient and late antique Greek literature, means "an age," or

---

[9] *The Evangelical Universalist Forum* (January 2012):
https://forum.evangelicaluniversalist.com/t/terms-for-eternity-aionios-aidios-talk-part-2/1392/48.

"a long period of time" of indeterminate duration, or even just "a substantial interval." Its proper equivalent in Latin would be *aevum*. At times, it can refer to an historical epoch, to a time "long past" or "far in the future," to something as shadowy and fleeting as the lifespan of a single person (in Homer and the Attic dramatists this is its typical meaning), or even to a considerably shorter period than that (say, a year). It can also, as it frequently does in the New Testament, refer to a particular universal dispensation: either the present world or the world to come or a heavenly sphere of reality beyond our own. Moreover, the adjective *aiōnios*, unlike the adjective ἀΐδιος (*aïdios*) or adverb ἀεί (*aei*), never clearly means "eternal" or "everlasting" in any incontrovertible sense, nor does the noun *aiōn* simply mean "eternity" in the way that the noun ἀϊδιότης (*aïdiotēs*) does; neither does *aiōnios* mean "endless" as ἀτέλευτος (*ateleutos*) or ἀτελεύτητος (*ateleutētos*) does; and, in fact, there are enough instances in the New Testament where the adjective or the noun obviously does not mean "eternal" or "eternity" that it seems to me unwise simply to *presume* such meanings in any instances at all. Where it is used of that which is by nature eternal, God in himself, it certainly carries the connotation that, say, the English words "enduring" or "abiding" would do in the same context: *ever*lasting. But that is a connotation by extension, not the univocal core of the word.[10]

If Jesus, the evangelists, or the other New Testament writers had wanted to teach eternal punishment, Greek words were available to them, including *aïdios* (eternal), *aperantos* (unlimited, endless), *adialeiptos* (unceasing), and *ateleutos* (endless), in lieu of the ambiguous and unsuitable *aiónios*. Yet they did not avail themselves of them. But another first century Jew did, Josephus Flavius. He tells us that the Pharisees teach that the wicked suffer "eternal retribution" (ἀιδίῳ τιμωρίᾳ),[11] "eternal imprisonment" (εἰργμὸν

---

[10] Hart, p. 538.
[11] Josephus, *The Wars of the Jews* 2.155.

ἀίδιον),[12] while the Essenes teach that the wicked are condemned to "unending retributions" (τιμωριῶν ἀδιαλείπτων)[13] and "deathless retribution" (ἀθάνατον τιμωρίαν).[14]

Given its semantic range, the meaning of *aiónios* in any specific text must be determined by context and usage. Except when it modifies the noun "God," *aiónios* need not signify "eternal," and perhaps not even then, as Heleen Keizer points out.[15] Even when *aiónios* modifies the word "God" other meanings may be intended other than "absolute eternity." For an interesting example, take a look at Rom 16:25-26: in v. 25, the St Paul speaks of "the mystery which was kept secret for long ages [*aioníois*] but is now disclosed," which clearly refers to a span of time that has ended; and then in the very next verse he speaks of the *aioníou theou*, the everlasting God. My favorite example of *aiónios*'s polysemy: "Sodom and Gomorrah and the surrounding cities . . . serve as an example by undergoing a punishment of αἰωνίου fire" (Jude 1:7). Most translators render αἰωνίου as "eternal," yet we know that the fire that destroyed Sodom did in fact come to an end. So in what sense is the fire eternal?

Origen, the greatest exegete of the early Church and a native Greek speaker, was well aware of the meaning of *aión* and its adjectival forms:

> Whenever Scripture says, "from aeon to aeon," the reference is to an interval of time, and it is clear that it will have an end. And if Scripture says, "in another aeon," what is indicated is clearly a longer time, and yet an end is still fixed. And when the "aeons of the aeons" are

---

[12] Josephus, *Antiquities* 1814.
[13] Josephus, *Wars* 2.155.
[14] Ibid., 2.157.
[15] Heleen Keizer, Review of *Terms of Eternity*, *The Studia Philonica Annual* 23 (2011): 203.

mentioned, a certain limit is again posited, perhaps unknown to us, but surely established by God.[16]

Commenting on Rom 6.5, Origen writes:

> In Scriptures, *aión* is sometimes found in the sense of something that knows no end; at times it designates something that has no end in the present world, but will have in the future one; sometimes it means a certain stretch of time; or again the duration of the life of a single person is called *aión*.[17]

Origen explicitly connects *aiónios* life to final salvation and apokatastasis. Commenting on the Gospel of John, he writes:

> The Savior calls himself a harvester, and the recompense of our Lord is the salvation and reintegration of those who are harvested; the expression "And he gathers the fruit for *aiónios* life" means either that what is gathered is the fruit of *aiónios* life or that it itself is *aiónios* life.[18]

But even the *aiónes* will come to an end, Origen tells us: "After *aiónios* life a leap will take place and all will pass from the aeons to the Father, who is *beyond aiónios* life. For Christ is Life, but the Father, who is 'greater than Christ,' is greater than life."[19]

God the Father transcends all ages. In the apokatastasis the entirety of creation will participate in the *aídios* life that is the Creator. God will be all in all, as the Apostle teaches (1 Cor 15:24-

---

[16] Origen, *Hom. in Ex.* 6.13; quoted by Ilaria Ramelli, *The Christian Doctrine of Apokatastasis* (2013), p. 161. In the fifth century, Theodoret of Antioch gave the following definition of *aión*: "*Aión* is not any existing thing, but an interval denoting time, sometimes infinite when spoken of God, sometimes proportioned to the duration of the creation, and sometimes to the life of man." Quoted by John Wesley Hanson, *Aiōn–Aiōnios* (1878), p. 12.

[17] Origen, *Comm. in Rom.* 6.5; quoted by Ramelli, p. 163.

[18] Origen, *Fragments on John* 13.46.299; quoted by Ramelli and Konstan, p. 122.

[19] Origen, *Comm. in Io* 13.3; quoted by Ramelli, p. 160.

28). The Origenian notion of eschatological stages sounds strange to our ears today. When was the last time you heard a sermon on the Son delivering his kingdom to the Father in cosmic *theosis*? Origen's exegesis should at least challenge our default readings of eschatological *aiónios* punishment. The fire that belongs to the world to come, the *pur aiónion*, most definitely will come to an end once it has accomplished the purification of the condemned. It may last for a short or long time; but it is not eternal. Evil has no place in the universal restoration. Konstan and Ramelli elaborate:

> In this connection, it seems particularly significant that Origen calls the fire of damnation πῦρ αἰώνιον but never πῦρ ἀΐδιος. The explanation is that he does not consider this flame to be absolutely eternal: it is αἰώνιον because it belongs to the next world, as opposed to the fire we experience in this present world, and it lasts as long as the *aiónes* do, in their succession. It does not, however, endure into the ἀϊδιότης, that is, in the absolute eternity of the final apocatastasis.[20]

Origen clearly understood the semantic spectrum of *aiónios* and recognized that it does not compel a reading of "eternal."

Almost 300 years after Origen's death, the Emperor Justinian would command Menas, the Patriarch of Constantinople, to convene a synod to condemn Origen. In his edict he affirms the doctrine of eternal perdition:

---

[20] Ramelli and Konstan., p. 126. In *De Sectis* the following quotation is attributed to Origen: "There is a resurrection of the dead and there is punishment, but not everlasting [ἀπέραντος]. For when the body is punished the soul is gradually purified, and so is restored to its ancient rank." Quoted by John Behr, *On First Principles* (2017), II:610. On Origen's understanding of the purifying nature of the fire of Gehenna, see Brian Daley, *The Hope of the Early Church* (1991), pp. 56-58. St Gregory of Nyssa, following Origen, also taught that the purifying fire of God will effect the salvation of all rational beings, including even the demons. See Morwenna Ludlow, *Universal Salvation* (2000), pp. 82-85; Ilaria Ramelli, *A Larger Hope* (2019), pp. 109-129.

> The Holy Church of Christ teaches an endless *æonian* [*ateleutetos aionios*] life to the righteous and endless [*ateleutetos*] punishment to the wicked.[21]

Justinian uses the word *ateleutetos* to express the endlessness of both *aionion* life and final punishment. The clarification is necessary, given that Origen and his disciples happily taught *aiónios* punishment. John Wesley Hanson comments:

> If he [Justinian] supposed *aiónios* denoted endless duration, he would not have added the stronger word to it. The fact that he qualified it by *ateleutetos*, demonstrated that as late as the sixth century the former word did not signify endless duration.[22]

To confirm his point, Hanson then quotes the Neoplatonic philosopher Olympiodorus, a contemporary of Justinian:

> Do not suppose that the soul is punished for endless ages [*apeirous aionas*] in Tartarus. Very properly the soul is not punished to gratify the revenge of the divinity, but for the sake of healing. But we say that the soul is punished for an *æonian* period, calling its life, and its allotted period of punishment, its *æon*.[23]

Not only does the philosopher deny eternal punishment, but he explicitly employs *aiónion* to express the limited duration of post-mortem punishment.

Aiónios as Adjective: Qualitative or Quantitative?

In Matt 25:46 Jesus speaks of "*aiónios* punishment" (punishment pertaining to the aeon to come—the only place in the New

---

[21] Quoted by John Wesley Hanson, *Universalism the Prevailing Doctrine of the Christian Church* (1889), p. 283.
[22] Ibid.
[23] Ibid., pp. 283-284.

Testament where the phrase occurs) and "*aiónion* life" (life pertaining to the aeon to come). Given that the life given to us in Jesus Christ is eternal in the strong sense, does this not mean that the punishment of Gehenna is also eternal in the strong sense? St Basil of Caesarea appears to have made this inference in his brief rules for monastics: "for if there will be at a certain moment an end of *aiónios* punishment, there will also surely be an end of *aiónios* life."[24] The argument seems initially plausible, even compelling, given the parallelism; but the inference does not necessarily obtain. *Aiónios* is an adjective: it modifies the noun to which it is connected. Adjectives often vary in meaning when the nouns they qualify signify different categories of things, states, or events. When we read the sentence "Jack is a tall man standing in front of a tall building," we do not jump to the conclusion that Jack is as tall as the building. We recognize the relativity of height with respect to both. When Jesus states that the wicked are sent to *aiónios* punishment, we should not assume that it refers to a state of perpetual punishing or that the loss is irretrievable. Jesus is not necessarily threatening interminable suffering. He (or the evangelist) may, for example, have intended *aiónios* to signify indefinite duration, i.e., the duration proper to the aeon of the next world. If so, the parallelism holds, yet even still it does not entail endless punishment. Or Jesus may be referring to the divine requital (whether remedial, retributive, or annihilating) that *properly belongs* to the eschatological aeon. And this is the crucial lexical point: *aiónios* by itself does not tell us whether the fire of Gehenna is of limited, indefinite, or unlimited duration. By contrast, the life of the age to come, ζωή αἰώνιος, is truly eternal, for the life of Christ is indestructible and perduring. Adjectives modify nouns, yet nouns also modify adjectives.[25]

---

[24] Quoted by Ramelli and Konstan, p. 195.
[25] My thanks to Dan Heck for this observation.

Christopher Marshall rejects the claim that the parallelism of Matt 25:46 implies eternal punishment. We may not deduce the eternality of Gehenna, he argues, from the eternality of the Kingdom:

> The word "eternal" is used in both a qualitative and a quantitive sense in the Bible. It is sometimes urged that if eternal life in Matthew 25:46 is everlasting in duration, so too must be eternal punishment. But "eternal" in both phrases may simply designate that the realities in question pertain to the future age. Furthermore, inasmuch as life, by definition, is an ongoing state, "eternal life" includes the idea of everlasting existence. But punishment is a process rather than a state, and elsewhere when "eternal" describes an act or process, it is the consequences rather than the process that are everlasting (e.g., Heb. 6:2, "eternal judgment"; Heb. 9:12, "eternal redemption"; Mark 3:29, "eternal sin"; 2 Thess. 1:9, "eternal destruction"; Jude 7, "eternal fire"). Eternal punishment is therefore something that is ultimate in significance and everlasting in effect, not in duration.[26]

Note how misleading the English word "eternal" can be as a translation of *aiónios*. If the qualitative sense is intended by the speaker, then "eternal" is an inaccurate rendering, given that the dictionary definitions of "eternal" focus on temporal perpetuity and timelessness. The point is not the duration of the eschatological age but its character and tone, purpose and telos. In common usage "eternal" does not capture this nuance. David J. Powys concurs:

> The general primacy of the qualitative sense of *aiónion* in N.T. usage, is universally acknowledged. Seen as such it expresses the quality of the promised Age (*aión*), the age of the kingdom of God. This rather than the duration of the kingdom is the primary stress within the word *aiónios*. Matthew 25:31-46 is packed with imagery concerning the

---

[26] Christopher Marshall, *Beyond Retribution* (2001), p. 186, n. 123.

fulfilment of the kingdom: it tells of the coming of the Son of man (v.31), the coming of the King (v.34) and the gathering of the nations before the throne (vv.31,32).

It is thus natural and appropriate to take 'eternal' (*aiónios*) in each of its three instances in this passage as being primarily qualitative in sense. The point is not that the fire will burn for ever, or the punishment extend for ever, or the life continue for ever, but rather that all three will serve to establish the rule of God.[27]

Kim Papioannou offers a similar exegetical judgment: "It is therefore likely that in the New Testament the adjective αἰώνία goes beyond the quantitative sense of 'a period of time' to imply a quality to be associated with the age to come—the age that God will set up."[28] In these cases "pertaining to the age to come" would be a more accurate translation, Papioannou suggests. It should be noted that Marshall, Powys, and Papioannou are not proponents of universal salvation.

Taking a somewhat different tack, Thomas Talbott has proposed that *aiónios*, both in Matt 25 and elsewhere in the New Testament, should be understood in a causal sense, except when it is used directly of "God":

> Whether God is eternal (that is, timeless, outside of time) in a Platonic sense or everlasting in the sense that he endures throughout all of the ages, nothing other than God is eternal in the primary sense (see the reference to 'the eternal God' in Rom. 16:26). The judgements, gifts, and actions of God are eternal in the secondary sense that their causal source lies in the eternal character and purpose of God. One common function of an adjective, after all, is to refer back to the causal source of some action or condition. When Jude thus cited the fire that consumed Sodom and Gomorrah as an example of *eternal fire*, he was *not*

---

[27] David J. Powys, *Hell: A Hard Look at a Hard Question* (2007), p. 292.
[28] Kim Papioannou, *The Geography of Hell* (2013), p. 47.

making a statement about temporal duration at all; in no way was he implying that the fire continues burning today, or even that it continued burning for an age. He was instead giving a theological interpretation in which the fire represented God's judgement upon the two cities. So the fire was eternal not in the sense that it would burn forever without consuming the cities, but in the sense that, precisely because it was God's judgement upon these cities and did consume them, it expressed God's eternal character and eternal purpose in a special way.

Now even as the adjective *aiónios* typically referred back to God as a causal source, so it came to function as a kind of eschatological term, a handy reference to the age to come. This is because the New Testament writers identified the age to come as a time when God's presence would be fully manifested, his purposes fully realized, and his redemptive work eventually completed. So just as eternal life is a special quality of life, associated with the age to come, whose causal source lies in the eternal God himself, so eternal punishment is a special form of punishment, associated with the age to come, whose causal source lies in the eternal God himself. In that respect, the two are exactly parallel. But neither *concept* carries any implication of unending temporal duration; and even if it did carry such an implication, we would still have to clarify what it is that lasts forever. If the life associated with the age to come should be a form of life that continues forever, then any correction associated with that age would likewise have effects that literally endure forever. Indeed, even as eternal redemption is in no way a temporal process that takes forever to complete, neither would an eternal correction be a temporal process that takes forever to complete.[29]

Talbott's proposal illustrates the variety of interpretive possibilities open to the exegete.

Now consider how Matt 25:46 reads when the word *kólasis*, traditionally rendered "punishment" in English translations, is given

---

[29] Thomas Talbott, "A Pauline Interpretation of Divine Judgement," in *Universal Salvation?*, ed. Robin Parry and Christopher H. Partridge (2004), pp. 46-47.

an alternative, but very possible, rendering—chastisement. As seen above, Hart translates *kólasis* in Matt 25:46 "chastening of that Age." God chastises not to exact vengeance (*timoria*) but to correct, convert, discipline, and purify. Although *kólasis* can be used in a retributive sense (e.g., 2 Macc 4:38), it may also signify *remedial* punishment. If Jesus intended *kólasis* to signify chastisement, then the adjective *aiónion* cannot mean "eternal." Chastisement comes to an end when its corrective purpose is accomplished. In the late 2nd century, Clement of Alexandria clearly distinguished between *kólasis* and *timoria*:

> For there are partial corrections which are called chastisements [*kólasis*], which many of us who have been in transgression incur by falling away from the Lord's people. But as children are chastised by their teacher, or their father, so are we by Providence. But God does not punish, for punishment [*timoria*] is retaliation for evil. He chastises, however, for good to those who are chastised collectively and individually.[30]

Just as *aiónios* does not compel "eternity," so *kólasis* need not mean "retribution," i.e., deserved punishment for its own sake. The corrective function of Gehennic punishment was explicitly stated by Theodore of Mopsuestia:

> Those who have here chosen fair things will receive in the world to come the pleasure of good things with praises; but the wicked who have turned aside to evil things all their life, when they are become ordered in their minds by penalties and the fear that springs from them, and choose good things, and learn how much they have sinned by having persevered in evil things and not in good things, and by means of these things receive the knowledge of the highest doctrine of the fear of God, and become instructed to lay hold of it with a good will, will be deemed

---

[30] Clement, *Strom.* 7.16.

worthy of the happiness of the Divine liberality. For He would never have said, "Until thou payest the uttermost farthing," unless it had been possible for us to be freed from our sins through having atoned for them by paying the penalty; neither would He have said, "he shall be beaten with many stripes," or "he shall be beaten with few stripes," unless it were that the penalties, being meted out according to the sins, should finally come to an end.[31]

Yet even if biblical exegetes should determine, however unlikely, that *kólasis* in Matt 25:46 denotes the retributive infliction of suffering, this is perfectly compatible with the doctrine of universal salvation, *as long as the punishment is finite and temporary.*

I propose the following as a plausible translation of Matt 25:46: "Then they will go away to eonion punishment, but the righteous to eonion life." The advantage of this translation is that it leaves open legitimate interpretive possibilities and does not read into the text later dogmatic developments.

The Hermeneutics of *Aiónios*

The polysemy of *aiónios* explains why most universalists of the patristic period were native Greek speakers. They knew its semasiological scope and exploited it to advance their universalist convictions. Hence they had no problems asserting that the punishments of Gehenna would come to an end.[32] They knew that Jesus' assertion of *aiónios* punishment in Matt 25:46 did not mean, or at least need not mean, what we mean today by the words

---

[31] Theodore of Mopsuestia, fragment; quoted by Solomon of Akhlat, *The Book of the Bee*, chap. 60. John Wesley Hanson (pp. 216-217) also quotes this passage (minus the first sentence) and cites Assemani's *Bibliotheca orientalis*, tom. iii, as its source.

[32] On the challenges of translation of ancient Greek into other languages, see Orville Jenkins, "Time or Character, The Ages or A Time Sequence in *aionios*": http://orvillejenkins.com/theology/aionios.html.

"eternal" and "everlasting." If they had wanted to clearly assert eternal punishment, they had other adjectives available to them. When the Greek New Testament was translated into Latin, the translators made a fateful decision: they chose to render both *aiónios* and *aïdios* by *aeternus* (forever, everlasting, eternal, perpetual). While *aeternus* renders *aïdios* well, it's a disaster for *aiónios*. The aeonic significance of the word is completely lost. The deal was sealed with the eventual adoption by the Latin Church of St Jerome's translation of the Bible (now known as the Vulgate) as its preferred translation. Jerome renders Matt 25:46 as follows: *et ibunt hii in supplicium aeternum iusti autem in vitam aeternam* ("And these shall go into everlasting punishment: but the just, into life everlasting"). Faced with the Lord's apparent assertion of eternal perdition, the dogmatic rejection of universalism by the Latin Church was, tragically, the only faithful response.[33]

The lexical evidence is neither decisive nor probative; but it does indicate that *aiónios* need not—and some would say, cannot—be interpreted to support the traditional doctrine of eternal damnation. "True," writes Robin Parry (aka Gregory MacDonald), "the age to come is everlasting, but that does not necessitate that the punishment of the age to come lasts for the duration of that age,

---

[33] In her review of *The Terms of Eternity*, Keizer writes: "A positive observation can be made in as much as the hypothesis investigated by *Terms for Eternity* appears to be largely confirmed—a nuanced reformulation of the conclusion is, however, called for, which may be as follows: Scripture and the Church Fathers offer a basis to say that the *aionios* life is to be understood as really without end, whereas *aionios* death can be understood as once meeting its limit; *aidios* appears to be used by the Fathers far more frequently for future life than for death or punishment. This state of affairs, it can be stated, is bound up with the fact that *aionios* is very much more a biblical term than *aidios* as an obvious result of the respective frequency of the two terms in the Bible (OT + NT): *aionios* 222 and *aidios* 4 times. It can be concluded moreover that *aidios* regularly expresses endless duration in time, while *aionios*, as derived from *aion*, regularly refers to an entirety of time, the limits of which are not known or not there; both adjectives may also be employed to refer to a supra-temporal condition" (p. 206).

simply that it occurs during that age and is appropriate for that age."[34] At this point proponents of the greater hope commonly invoke the character of God to guide their interpretation:

> Any interpretation of Gehenna must be compatible with the claim that God is love and would never act in a way towards a person that was not ultimately compatible with what is best for that person. Any interpretation of Gehenna as a punishment must be compatible with the claim that divine punishment is more than retributive but has a corrective intention as well (for divine punishment of the sinner must be compatible with, and an expression of, God's love for that sinner). Any interpretation of Gehenna must be compatible with God's ultimate triumph over sin and the fulfilment of his loving purpose of redeeming all his creatures.[35]

Elsewhere, I have argued that Christians should and must read the Holy Scriptures through a "hermeneutic of love" or, as I prefer, a "hermeneutic of Pascha," precisely because God has revealed himself in Jesus Christ as absolute love. This gospel revelation must guide our interpretation of the Scriptures. The point is the eschatological passages in the Scriptures are theologically underdetermined. In many cases, the language is ambiguous, polysemous, metaphorical. When Jesus taught that the wicked will be condemned to Gehennic punishment, what exactly did he intend to communicate? It is by no means obvious. Will this punishment be eternal? Exegetes vigorously disagree, and their disagreements seem to be irresolvable, even at the basic level of historical investigation. The wide semantic range of *aiónios* precludes a dogmatic conclusion. Jesus is not here in the flesh to explain himself, and there are no oracles to whom we may go to receive infallible answers. Even so, interpret we must, if we are going to

---

[34] Robin Parry, *The Evangelical Universalist*, 2nd ed. (2013), p. 148.
[35] Ibid.

preach the good news of Jesus Christ. We must therefore choose our hermeneutical paradigm wisely—for choose we inevitably will, one way or the other.

But one thing I think we may safely say: sometimes eternity ain't forever.

PART TWO

The Greater Hope in History

Chapter Eleven

St Augustine and the Misericordes

Contrary to popular belief, Origen of Alexandria did not invent the doctrine of universal salvation. He did not concoct it out of thin air. He received it from the theological tradition. The greater hope took on distinct forms both before and after the great third-century theologian put his unique speculative stamp upon it.[1]

In his great work *The City of God*, St Augustine of Hippo identifies seven different universalist and semi-universalist positions present in the Church in the early fifth century, each group employing different biblical texts to support its convictions.[2] He famously dubs them "*misericordi nostri*" ("our own compassionate ones"). With the exception of Origen and his followers, he does not regard the other six groups as heretical. His tone might even be described as cordial:

> I must now, I see, enter the lists of amicable controversy with those tender-hearted Christians who decline to believe that any, or that all of those whom the infallibly just Judge may pronounce worthy of the punishment of hell, shall suffer eternally, and who suppose that they shall be delivered after a fixed term of punishment, longer or shorter according to the amount of each man's sins. (XXI.17)

Richard Bauckham has helpfully provided a table listing the seven doctrinal positions and favorite texts:[3]

---

[1] See Ilaria Ramelli's magisterial monograph *The Christian Doctrine of Apokatastasis* (2013).
[2] *De Civitate Dei* XXI.17-25.
[3] Richard Bauckham, *The Fate of the Dead* (1998), pp. 150-151.

(1) Origen: All, including the devil and his angels, will be saved, after purgatorial punishments.

De civ. Dei 21.17; reply: 21.23.
Also *Ad Orosium* 5-7 (415 C.E.)

(2) All human beings (but not devils) will be saved, after punishments of varying duration.

De civ. Dei 21.17; reply: 21.23.
Also *Ad Orosium* 5-7 (415 C.E.)

(3) All human beings (but not devils) will be saved by the intercession of the saints on the Day of Judgment. Thus no one will be punished at all. Hell is a threat of what the wicked deserve, but mercy will overrule it. Scripture is largely silent on this in order to promote the repentance of those who fear hell.

Texts: Psalm 76:10(77:9); Jonah 3; Psalm 30:20(31:19); Rom 11:32.
De civ. Dei 21.18; reply: 21.24.
Also *Enchiridion* 29 (112) (421 C.E.)
Text: Psalm 76:10(77:9)
and perhaps *Serm.* 75.9 (? 400 C.E.)

(4) All who participate in the Christian sacraments, including heretics, will be saved.

Text: John 6:50-51.
De civ. Dei 21.19; reply: 21.25.

(5) All who participate in the Catholic eucharist will be saved.

Text: 1 Corinthians 10:17.
De civ. Dei 21.20; reply: 21.25.

(6) All who remain in the Catholic church (hold the Catholic faith) will be saved, those who lived wickedly after temporary punishment.

Text: I Corinthians 3:11-15.
De civ. Dei 21.21; reply: 21.26.
Also *De fide et operibus* 15 (24-26) (413 C.E.)
Text: I Corinthians 3:11-15.
Enchiridion 18 (67-69) (421 C.E.)
Text: 1 Corinthians 3:11-15.
De octo Dulcitii quaestionibus 1 (423-5 C.E.)
Texts: Matthew 5:26; 1 Corinthians 3:11-15.

(7) All who perform works of mercy will be saved.

Texts: James 2:13; Matthew 23:34-46; 6:12, 14-15.
De civ. Dei 21.22; reply 21.27.
Also *Enchiridion* 19-20 (70-77) (421 C.E.)
Text: Luke 11:41.

Origen: all shall be saved

Augustine begins with Origen, whom he describes as the most indulgent of the *misericordes* because of his extension of compassion to Satan and the unholy angels. After severe and prolonged purifying suffering, Origen teaches, God will deliver all rational beings from their wickedness and restore them to the company of the saints. For this belief and others (specifically, "his theory of the ceaseless alternation of happiness and misery, and the interminable transitions from the one state to the other at fixed periods of ages"), the Church has condemned Origen. He does not tell us when and where this condemnation took place. This is unsurprising. History has not recorded a formal synodical repudiation of the universalist views of Origen during the third through fifth centuries. Perhaps Augustine is invoking a growing consensus in the Latin Church. Perhaps he is referring to St Epiphanius' letter to the patriarch of Jerusalem (394), in which he excoriates Origen for teaching that Satan "will return to his former dignity and rise again to the kingdom of heaven."[4] Perhaps he is thinking of Patriarch Theophilus' synodal, in which he summarizes the eight condemnations of Origen by the 400 Synod of Alexandria (apokatastasis is not mentioned).[5] Perhaps he is mesmerized by St Jerome's abrupt conversion from being a supporter of the Adamantine to being his zealous adversary.[6] Whatever his sources and reasons, the bishop of Hippo is convinced that Origen has been condemned by the Church because of his profession of apokatastasis.

For the doctor of grace, the eternal reprobation of the incorrigibly wicked, demons and humans alike, is a biblical given that overrides compassion. He wheels out the usual proof texts: Matt 25: 31-46; Rev 20:10. The Scriptures clearly state that final judgment is eternal, which of course it does if one is relying on either the *Vetus Latina* or the Vulgate. He is particularly impressed by the parallelism in Matt 24:46:

---

[4] On Epiphanius, see Elizabeth A. Clark, *The Origenist Controversy* (1992), pp. 86-104. Regarding Origen's own beliefs on the salvation of the demons, see C. A. Patrides, "The Salvation of Satan," *Journal of the History of Ideas* 28 (1967): 467-478; Lisa Holliday, "Will Satan Be Saved?" *Vigiliae Christianae* 63 (2009): 1-23; Ramelli, *Apokatastasis*, pp. 141-156.

[5] On Theophilus, see Clark, pp. 105-121.

[6] On Jerome, see Clark, pp. 121-151. While Augustine does not explicitly name Origen a "heretic," Jerome certainly does:

"Origen is a heretic, true; but what does that take from me who do not deny that on very many points he is heretical? He has erred concerning the resurrection of the body, he has erred concerning the condition of souls, he has erred by supposing it possible that the devil may repent, and—an error more important than these—he has declared in his commentary upon Isaiah that the Seraphim mentioned by the prophet are the divine Son and the Holy Ghost" (Ep. 61).

> Then what a fond fancy is it to suppose that eternal punishment means long continued punishment, while eternal life means life without end, since Christ in the very same passage spoke of both in similar terms in one and the same sentence, "These shall go away into eternal punishment, but the righteous into life eternal." If both destinies are "eternal," then we must either understand both as long-continued but at last terminating, or both as endless. For they are correlative—on the one hand, punishment eternal, on the other hand, life eternal. And to say in one and the same sense, life eternal shall be endless, punishment shall come to an end, is the height of absurdity. Wherefore, we the eternal life of the saints shall be endless, so too the eternal punishment of those who are doomed to it shall have no end. (*Civ. Dei* XXI.23)

Why is the brilliant Augustine unwilling to consider alternative readings of the damnation texts? At no point does he ask, *Is eternal torment worthy of the God who is absolute goodness and cruciform love?* In his *On Christian Doctrine*, Augustine instructs us that we have misunderstood a biblical text if our interpretation does not build up our love of God and neighbor (I.36.40), yet throughout his analysis of the *misericordes*, he urges the reader to restrict their love and compassion before the sovereignty of the divine will. I have to wonder if Augustine's developing reflection on divine predestination and the *massa damnata* now precludes the evangelical question posed above. Already in 397, he could write:

> So the apostle represses the impudent questioner. "O man, who art thou that repliest against God?" A man so speaks back to God when he is displeased that God finds fault with sinners, as if God compelled any man to sin when he simply does not bestow his justifying mercy on some sinners, and for that reason is said to harden some sinners; not because he drives them to sin but because he does not have mercy upon them. He decides who are not to be offered mercy by a standard of equity which is most secret and far removed from human powers of understanding. (*Ad Simplicianum* 2.16)

Here we have the beginnings of Augustine's doctrine of preterition. Why do some sin? Because God chooses not to bestow upon them his justifying mercy. At this point Augustine has introduced a cleavage in the heart of God. Once the schism between the divine love and justice is accepted, who are we to object to God's decision to everlastingly punish the wicked? The "standard of equity" is inscrutable.[7]

Origen Lite: all shall be saved, except Satan

If Origen's universalist views are heretical, then the second position should also be considered heretical, declares Augustine—*if only* its proponents were logically consistent in their reasoning:

> Very different, however, is the error we speak of, which is dictated by the tenderness of these Christians who suppose that the sufferings of those who are condemned in the judgment will be temporary, while the blessedness of all who are sooner or later set free will be eternal. Which opinion, if it is good and true because it is merciful, will be so much the better and truer in proportion as it becomes more merciful. Let, then, this fountain of mercy be extended, and flow forth even to the lost angels, and let them also be set free, at least after as many and long ages as seem fit! Why does this stream of mercy flow to all the human race, and dry up as soon as it reaches the angelic? And yet they dare not extend their pity further, and propose the deliverance of the devil himself. Or if any one is bold enough to do so, he does indeed put to shame their charity, but is himself convicted of error that is more unsightly, and a resting of God's truth that is more perverse, in proportion as his clemency of sentiment seems to be greater. (Civ. Dei I.17)

---

[7] Which comes first for Augustine, everlasting damnation or divine predestination? The chicken-and-egg problem can be run both ways. Also see Ilaria Ramelli's fascinating article "Origen in Augustine," *Numen* 60 (2013): 280-307.

If compassion and mercy are to be our guide, then at least be consistent! Why should God's compassion and ours stop with human beings? Limiting the divine mercy to humanity is purely arbitrary. Does not God also love the unholy angels? If you are willing to allow Satan to suffer eternal torment, have you not betrayed and violated pity itself? Augustine confronts the anthropic universalist with a stark choice: to follow Origen into heresy or to embrace the teaching of Christ and affirm the justice of everlasting damnation.

Note: Augustine does not name this compassionate view heretical. Apparently, it was still permissible in the fifth century for Christians to believe that the Holy Trinity will bring all mankind to salvation, *as long as they also taught the eternal punishment of the unholy spirits.*

Augustine knew something about Origen's theology from Jerome, but he learned of this "anthropic universalism" from Orosius, who had contacted Augustine in 415 about the growing influence of Priscillianism and Origenism in Spain. "A certain Avitus had brought a volume of Origen (probably the *Peri Archon*) back from Jerusalem to Spain," Bauckham explains, "and Origen's views on universal salvation were being propagated in Spain. But the salvation of devils seems not to have been adopted by the Spanish."[8]

Intercessory Universalism

Whereas Augustine's knowledge of Origen and Spanish Origenism is largely based on second-hand reports, his knowledge of this third group, what we might call "intercessory universalism," has been acquired through personal conversation with its proponents. Unlike the Origenists, who propose a purgatorial fire by which the damned will be transformed and made fit for heaven, the intercessory

---

[8] Bauckham, p. 152.

universalists maintain that at the last judgment God will revoke his eschatological sentence of eternal punishment in response to the entreaties of the saints:

> There are others, again, with whose opinions I have become acquainted in conversation, who, though they seem to reverence the holy Scriptures, are yet of reprehensible life, and who accordingly, in their own interest, attribute to God a still greater compassion towards men. For they acknowledge that it is truly predicted in the divine word that the wicked and unbelieving are worthy of punishment, but they assert that, when the judgment comes, mercy will prevail. For, say they, God, having compassion on them, will give them up to the prayers and intercessions of His saints. For if the saints used to pray for them when they suffered from their cruel hatred, how much more will they do so when they see them prostrate and humble suppliants? For we cannot, they say, believe that the saints shall lose their bowels of compassion when they have attained the most perfect and complete holiness; so that they who, when still sinners, prayed for their enemies, should now, when they are freed from sin, withhold from interceding for their suppliants. Or shall God refuse to listen to so many of His beloved children, when their holiness has purged their prayers of all hindrance to His answering them? And the passage of the psalm which is cited by those who admit that wicked men and infidels shall be punished for a long time, though in the end delivered from all sufferings, is claimed also by the persons we are now speaking of as making much more for them. The verse runs: "Shall God forget to be gracious? Shall He in anger shut up His tender mercies?" [Ps 77.9]. His anger, they say, would condemn all that are unworthy of everlasting happiness to endless punishment. But if He suffer them to be punished for a long time, or even at all, must He not shut up His tender mercies, which the Psalmist implies he will not do? For he does not say, Shall He in anger shut up His tender mercies for a long period? but he implies that He will not shut them up at all. (*Civ. Dei* XXI.18)

Intercessory universalists do not deny that God has spoken clearly about the eternal punishment of the wicked, but this need not be determinative, they reply. Scripture also teaches that God may declare his retributive intent in the most absolute terms yet choose *not* to enact his intent. Jonah and the Ninevites is the paradigmatic example. When Jonah prophesied the destruction of Nineveh, he did not say that the city will be destroyed *if* its inhabitants do not repent and change their ways. He spoke without qualification: Nineveh *will* be overthrown in forty days. No ifs, ands, or buts. Yet even so, God forgave the Ninevites when they beseeched his mercy. God threatens punishment in order to terrify the wicked and thus hopefully evoke their repentance.[9] The condition of repentance need not be explicitly stated; indeed, the threat is more effective if it is not. The example of Nineveh, therefore, teaches us that "the great and hidden sweetness of God's mercy is concealed in order that men may fear" (*Civ. Dei XXI.18*). "If, then," Augustine continues, speaking on behalf of the intercessory universalists, "He spared those whom His own holy prophet was provoked at His sparing, how much more shall He spare those more wretched suppliants for whom all His saints shall intercede?" (*Civ. Dei* XXI.18). Surely this is the meaning and intent of the words of the Apostle: "For God hath concluded all men in unbelief, that He may have mercy upon all" (Rom 11:32).

Are you surprised by this particular formulation of universal salvation? I know I was when I first read about it. Yet it goes back at least to the first half of the second century! In the *Apocalypse of Peter*, which the Muratorian canon lists as an inspired text that was read in the churches, the risen Christ declares:

---

[9] St Jerome notes that this interpretation of Jonah was prevalent in his day: "I know that most persons understand by the story of Nineveh and its king, the ultimate forgiveness of the devil and all rational creatures" (*Comm. in Jon.* 3).

> Then I will grant to my called and elect ones whomsoever they request from me, out of the punishment. And I will give them [those for whom the elect pray] a fine baptism in salvation from the Acherousian lake a portion of righteousness with my holy ones.[10]

In the context of the *Apocalypse*, the words of the Lord are not explicitly universalist. The damned are identified as those who have persecuted the faithful, and the mercy of Christ reaches only as far as the compassion of the saints. Bauckham elaborates:

> Thus Peter's desire for mercy, so severely rebuked in chapter 3, is granted eventually, when taken up by the elect on the Day of Judgment and after the justice of hell has been carefully demonstrated. . . . There is a kind of logic in the sequence. The justice of the punishment of the persecutors is a justice owed primarily to the persecuted. But in that case it is a punishment that can be remitted if the martyrs themselves desire mercy for their persecutors. No one else has the right to forgive oppressors, but those whom they have oppressed do have this right. So if it is for his people's sake that God must punish their oppressors, then for his people's sake (as *SibOr* 2:355, interpreting *ApPet* 14, states) he can save those for whom they desire mercy. In this way the conflict of justice and mercy is resolved. One obstacle to universal salvation—that of which the apocalyptic tradition, because of its origins in situations of injustice and persecution, was most aware—is effectively removed by the compassion and forgiveness of the saints. Other obstacles are not considered, and it is not, of course, actually stated that salvation will be universal, but as extensive as the compassion of the elect.[11]

But if the saints will have compassion on their oppressors, will they not also extend their compassion to all the damned? For their wills are perfectly aligned with the will of their Savior, "who desires all

---

[10] Rainer fragment, quoted by Bauckham, p. 145.
[11] Ibid, p. 146.

men to be saved and come to the knowledge of the truth" (1 Tim 2:4).

Bauckham believes that the beliefs of the third group of the *misericordes*, the intercessory universalists, clearly has its source in the *Apocalypse of Peter*:

> This group of people, then, envisage that at the Day of Judgment (a) the damned will implore the saints to pray for them, (b) the saints will indeed pray for them, and (c) God 'will grant them to the prayers and intercessions of his saints.' It is clear that this expectation must derive from the apocalyptic tradition about the intercession of the saints for the damned at the Last Judgment. . . . The oldest source in which tradition is now extant is the *Apocalypse of Peter*, which contains all three points (a, b, c) in Augustine's report of what the Christians he knew expected: (a) in 13:4; (b) and (c) in 14:1, which reads: 'I will give to my called and elect ones whomsoever they request from me, out of the punishment' (Rainer fragment). The phraseology is strikingly close to Augustine's: God 'will grant them to the prayers and intercessions of his saints.'[12]

Augustine does not mention the *Apocalypse of Peter*. Perhaps the members of the group did not refer to it in their conversations with him, knowing that he was skeptical of apocryphal writings. Instead, they invoked Scriptural texts to support their convictions. As Bauckham notes: "The appeal to Scripture must be understood as defence of a doctrine Augustine's interlocutors had derived from extra-canonical apocalyptic literature but now needed to defend in a period when apocryphal literature was being increasingly discredited."[13]

Augustine offers a lengthy critique of the intercessory position, combined with a fair amount of *ad hominem* polemic. He appeals

---

[12] Ibid., pp. 155-156.
[13] Bauckham, p. 157.

to the liturgical practice of the Church, observing that the Church does not pray for Satan and his fellow fallen angels or for incorrigible departed sinners:

> The reason, then, which prevents the Church from now praying for the wicked angels, whom she knows to be her enemies, is the identical reason which shall prevent her, however perfected in holiness, from praying at the last judgment for those men who are to be punished in eternal fire. At the present she prays for her enemies among men, because they have yet opportunity for fruitful repentance. For what does she especially beg for them but that "God would grant them repentance," as the apostle says, "that they may return to soberness out of the snare of the devil, by whom they are held captive according to his will?" [2 Tim 2:25-26]. But if the Church were certified who those are, who, though they are still abiding in this life, are yet predestinated to go with the devil into eternal fire, then for them she could no more pray than for him. But since she has this certainty regarding no man, she prays for all her enemies who yet live in this world; and yet she is not heard in behalf of all. But she is heard in the case of those only who, though they oppose the Church, are yet predestinated to become her sons through her intercession. But if any retain an impenitent heart until death, and are not converted from enemies into sons, does the Church continue to pray for them, for the spirits, *i.e.*, of such persons deceased? And why does she cease to pray for them, unless because the man who was not translated into Christ's kingdom while he was in the body, is now judged to be of Satan's following?
>
> It is, then, I say, the same reason which prevents the Church at any time from praying for the wicked angels, which prevents her from praying hereafter for those men who are to be punished in eternal fire; and this also is the reason why, though she prays even for the wicked so long as they live, she yet does not even in this world pray for the unbelieving and godless who are dead. For some of the dead, indeed, the prayer of the Church or of pious individuals is heard; but it is for those who, having been regenerated in Christ, did not spend their life

so wickedly that they an be judged unworthy of such compassion, nor so well that they can be considered to have no need of it. As also, after the resurrection, there will be some of the dead to whom, after they have endured the pains proper to the spirits of the dead to whom, after they have endured the pains proper to the spirits of the dead, mercy shall be accorded, and acquittal from the punishment of the eternal fire. For were there not some whose sins, though not remitted in this life, shall be remitted in that which is to come, it could not be truly said, "They shall not be forgiven, neither in this world, neither in that which is to come" [Matt 12:32]. But when the Judge of quick and dead has said, "Come, ye blessed of my Father, inherit the kingdom prepared for you from the foundation of the world," and to those on the other side, "Depart from me, ye cursed into the eternal fire, which is prepared for the devil and his angels," and "These shall go away into eternal punishment, but the righteous into eternal fire" [Matt 25:34, 41, 46], it were excessively presumptuous to say that the punishment of any of those whom God has said shall go away into eternal punishment shall not be eternal, and so bring either despair or doubt upon the corresponding promise of life eternal. (*Civ. Dei* XXI.24)

Augustine's objection is simple: the saints will not pray for the damned at the last judgment because they will see that the wicked are frozen in their impenitence and therefore incapable of changing their fundamental orientation.[14] Hence they are justly excluded from the divine mercy, just as the unholy angels now are. To pray for the

---

[14] But is God incapable of changing their orientation? Even the old *Catholic Encyclopedia* is forced to admit, in Augustinian-Thomistic fashion, that he is not: "The proximate cause of impenitence in hell is God's refusal of every grace and every impulse for good. It would not be intrinsically impossible for God to move the damned to repentance; yet such a course would be out of keeping with the state of final reprobation." J. Hontheim, "Hell," in *The Catholic Encyclopedia* (1910): http://www.newadvent.org/cathen/07207a.htm.

Why then does God not bring the damned to repentance? Hontheim's answer is hardly convincing. And while it is true that the traditional liturgical prayers for the dead are restricted to the faithful departed, it is also true that the Latin Church has also prayed for all the departed, as documented by Hans Urs von Balthasar.

damned at this eschatological moment would be to set oneself against the holy will and judgment of God, which is impossible for the saints.

The intercessory universalists have at hand a ready rejoinder: if the damned were incapable of repentance, as Augustine presupposes, they would not be crying out to the saints for their supplications. The key difference between Augustine and the universalists is the latter's refusal to limit the grace and mercy of God. Bauckham summarizes the conflicting theological principles:

> In the debate between Augustine and these 'merciful Christians' there is a serious clash of theological principles. On the side of the apocalyptic tradition taken up by the 'merciful Christians' there are two key principles. The first is the solidarity of the human race, such that the compassion of the saints extends to all humans, however wicked, since they understand themselves to be bound up with them, to some extent even in their sin. Therefore they feel bound to plead the case of the damned with God. The second principle is an understanding of prayer in which the saints persist in prayer even against the apparent will of God. They plead God's mercy against God's justice and, as it were, win God over. On Augustine's side of the debate, the overriding principle is the sovereign will of God. As a result the solidarity of the human race is radically severed by God's will in the form of predestination. Even in this life the church prays for the reprobate only through ignorance. If she knew who the elect were, she would pray only for them. Prayer, in Augustine's understanding, is wholly subordinated to God's will. Therefore, once the will of God with regard to the reprobate is known, as it will be at the Last Judgment, the perfection of the saints will show itself in their absolute concurrence with that divine will.[15]

---

[15] Bauckham, pp. 158-159.

St Augustine and the Misericordes

At this point, I bring this chapter to a close. I will not discuss the remaining *misericorde* parties, as they do not represent a genuine universalist hope, restricting, as they do, their eschatological expectations to the baptized and merciful. But it is germane to note that by St Augustine's standards, St Ambrose and St Jerome qualify as *compassionate* Christians.[16]

---

[16] Brian Daley, *The Hope of the Early Church* (2002), pp. 97-104.

Chapter Twelve

The Scourge of Love

God has created humanity for eternal communion with himself. *By love* he has created us *for love* to share in the Trinitarian paradise *of love*. For this purpose, St Isaac the Syrian so eloquently writes, Jesus Christ came into the world. He is the tree of life:

> Paradise is the love of God, wherein is the enjoyment of all blessedness, and there the blessed Paul partook of supernatural nourishment. When he tasted there of the tree of life, he cried out, saying "Eye hath not see, nor ear heard, neither have entered into the heart of man, the things which God hath prepared for them that love Him." Adam was barred from this tree through the devil's counsel.
>
> The tree of life is the love of God from which Adam fell away, and thereafter he saw joy no longer, and he toiled and labored in the land of thorns. Even though they make their way in righteousness, those who are bereft of the love of God eat in their work the bread of sweat, which the first-created man was commanded to eat after his fall. . . . But when we find love, we partake of heavenly bread, and are made strong without labor and toil. The heavenly bread is Christ, Who came down from Heaven and gave life to the world. This is the nourishment of the angels. The man who has found love eats and drinks Christ every day and hour and hereby is made immortal. "He that eateth of this bread," He says, "which I will give him, shall not see death unto eternity." Blessed is he who eats the bread of love, which is Jesus! He who eats of love eats Christ, the God over all, as John bears witness, saying, "God is love."
>
> Wherefore, the man who lives in love reaps life from God, and while yet in this world, he even now breathes the air of the resurrection; in this air the righteous will delight in the resurrection. Love is the Kingdom, whereof the Lord mystically promised His disciples to eat in

His Kingdom. For when we hear Him say, "Ye shall eat and drink at the table of my Kingdom," what do we suppose we shall eat, if not love? Love is sufficient to nourish a man instead of food and drink.[1]

We are created for Paradise, yet at the moment of death not all are ready for Paradise. At death a separation of sheep and goats takes effect, anticipating the final separation of which Jesus speaks (Matt 25:31-46); but this separation is not definitively set. Isaac does not advance a hard-and-fast schema of judgment and eschatological life. His terminology and vision are fluid. Upon repose the soul enters immediately into either Paradise or Gehenna. There is no intermediate realm between them, though within each "there are varying degrees of recompenses."[2] The general resurrection remains future for Isaac; but he does not make a clear distinction between Hades and Gehenna, as is commonly done in contemporary Orthodox circles.

In the Kingdom, the Blessed will together adore and delight in the Holy Trinity, each person deriving "a unique benefit from this visible sun through a single enjoyment of it common to all, each according to the clarity of his eyesight and the ability of his pupils to contain the sun's constant effusion of light."[3] Yet, while the vision of the uncreated light is distinct and particular to each, no one will notice differences of rank and noetic abilities, lest it become "a cause of sadness and mental anguish."[4] All will experience the love of God in fullness and perfection, to the degree enabled by his or her spiritual condition. No one will feel jealous or envious. All will rejoice. All will know and glory in love.

---

[1] Isaac, *The Ascetical Homilies of St Isaac the Syrian* (2011), I.46, pp. 357-358.
[2] Ibid., I.6, p. 173.
[3] Ibid., I.6, p. 172.
[4] Ibid.

But what of those who do not love God and do not desire his company? What of the damned? Here we enter into the most striking dimension of Isaac's mystical vision. We begin with one of the most frequently quoted passages from his homilies:

> I also maintain that those who are punished in Gehenna are scourged by the scourge of love. For what is so bitter and vehement as the punishment of love? I mean that those who have become conscious that they have sinned against love suffer greater torment from this than from any fear of punishment. For the sorrow caused in the heart by sin against love is sharper than any torment that can be. It would be improper for a man to think that sinners in Gehenna are deprived of the love of God. Love is the offspring of knowledge of the truth which, as is commonly confessed, is given to all. The power of love works in two ways: it torments those who have played the fool, even as happens here when a friend suffers from a friend; but it becomes a source of joy for those who have observed its duties. Thus I say that this is the torment of Gehenna: bitter regret. But love inebriates the souls of the sons of Heaven by its delectability.[5]

God's love for his creatures does not stop at the borders of hell. The Creator does not cease to will the salvation of the damned. His mercy does not suddenly turn into wrath. Though we may speak of the damned as separated from God, we must not think that he has separated himself from them. Those in hell are not deprived of his grace. They remain the objects of his mercy and compassion—and that is their torment! The damned hate God because they despise his forgiveness; they hate God because they regret the happiness they have lost through their pride and foolishness; they hate God because they can neither abide nor escape his presence. They are "scourged by the scourge of love."

---

[5] Ibid., I.28, p. 266.

The Scourge of Love

Long before I became acquainted with St Isaac the Syrian, the above represented my understanding of hell. I learned it first from C. S. Lewis. He taught me that hell is locked from the inside. The damned freely choose their perdition, refusing all solicitations to return to their Creator and Redeemer. For all eternity they obstinately refuse to make even the smallest step toward the Good, for they have reached the point where they are irredeemably defined by their preference for self and autonomy. The condemned individual "has his wish," writes Lewis—"to live wholly in the self and to make the best of what he finds there. And what he finds there is Hell."[6] This view isn't quite identical to Isaac's, but close enough. Lewis's disciple, philosopher Peter Kreeft, draws even closer to the great Syrian mystic:

> In reality, the damned are in the same place as the saved—in reality! But they hate it; it is their Hell. The saved love it, and it is their Heaven. It is like two people sitting side by side at an opera or a rock concert: the very thing that is Heaven to one is Hell to the other. Dostoyevski says, "We are all in paradise, but we won't see it.". . .
>
> Hell is not literally the "wrath of God." The love of God is an objective fact; the "wrath of God" is a human projection of our own wrath upon God, as the Lady Julian saw—a disastrous misinterpretation of God's love as wrath. God really says to all His creatures, "I know you and I love you," but they hear Him saying, "I never knew you; depart from me." It is like angry children misinterpreting their loving parents' affectionate advances as threats. They project their own hate onto their parents' love and experience love as an enemy—which it is: an enemy to their egotistic defenses against joy. . . .
>
> Since God is love, since love is the essence of the divine life, the consequence of loss of this life is loss of love. . . . Though the damned do not love God, God loves them, and this is their torture. The very fires of Hell are made of the love of God! Love received by one who

---

[6] C. S. Lewis, *The Problem of Pain* (1940), chap. 8.

only wants to hate and fight thwarts his deepest want and is therefore torture. If God could stop loving the damned, Hell would cease to be pure torture. If the sun could stop shining, lovers of the dark would no longer be tortured by it. But the sun could sooner cease to shine than God cease to be God.

"Our God is a consuming fire." All that can be consumed, will be consumed, so that only the unconsumable will remain. Self must be consumed, must die, in order to rise. There is no other way to eternity. The blessed embrace that blessed death of the sinful self they hate, and it is to them supreme bliss. The damned refuse it (but that does not make it any less necessary; the fire burns on whether we feel it as life-giving warmth or destructive pain), and it is their supreme torture. Thus Heaven and Hell are the very same objective reality, the only one there is, the only game in town: the fire of God's love, which is His essential being. In a sense, everything is Heaven. Earth is Heaven as a seed. Purgatory is Heaven's kindergarten. Hell is Heaven refused. Heaven is Heaven accepted.[7]

The reprobate experience God's self-communication as wrath and judgment, for they project their own wrath and self-hatred upon him. Hell, we might say, is heaven experienced differently. I embraced Kreeft's construal as soon as I read it in the mid-80s and incorporated it into my parochial catechesis. It represents the ecumenical doctrine as presently taught in 21st century Orthodoxy, Catholicism, and mainline Protestantism. Retributivists can still be found in all Christian traditions, but the Lewis-Kreeft construal of hell as self-exclusion from joy has established itself as the normative position. Various differences can be discerned in these accounts of hell; but they are united in the judgment that it is from love, and not out of a determination to punish, that God honors the eschatological

---

[7] Peter Kreeft, *Every Thing You Ever Wanted to Know About Heaven* (1990), pp. 230-235.

finality of creaturely decision. Jonathan Kvanvig classifies this as the issuant model of hell:

> An adequate conception of hell must be an issuant conception of it, one that portrays hell as flowing from the same divine character from which heaven flows. Any other view wreaks havoc on the integrity of God's character.[8]

Hell *issues* from the divine love, for in love God allows the final decision of the creature to stand. He will not force anyone into his Trinitarian communion of life and joy.

The one critical difference we find among the various ecclesial traditions relates to the question of the irreversibility of the state of perdition. For Catholicism and most forms of Protestantism, once an individual finds himself in the condition of damnation, he is frozen in it forever. He is incapable of repentance, incapable of altering his fundamental decision to reject God. He can only suffer the destruction and misery he has chosen. Pope Benedict XVI well represents this position:

> With death, our life-choice becomes definitive—our life stands before the judge. Our choice, which in the course of an entire life takes on a certain shape, can have a variety of forms. There can be people who have totally destroyed their desire for truth and readiness to love, people for whom everything has become a lie, people who have lived for hatred and have suppressed all love within themselves. This is a terrifying thought, but alarming profiles of this type can be seen in certain figures of our own history. In such people all would be beyond remedy and the destruction of good would be irrevocable: this is what we mean by the word Hell.[9]

---

[8] Jonathan Kvanvig, *The Problem of Hell* (1993), p. 136.
[9] Benedict XVI, *Spe salvi* 45.

Many Orthodox agree. St John of Damascus writes that the "fall is to the angels just what death is to men. For, just as there is no repentance of men after their death, so is there none for the angels after their fall."[10] Others, however, point to the Orthodox practice of praying for the departed. They believe that some, though perhaps not the most incorrigibly impenitent, may be saved through the prayers of the Church and the divine mercy. This appears to have been the position of St Mark of Ephesus. This, I take, is the majority opinion within Orthodoxy today. But there are also theologians, for instance Kallistos Ware, who believe that we may genuinely hope that all may be saved.[11] Ware's position strongly resembles the contingent universalism articulated by Hans Urs von Balthasar.[12] In any case, the majority of Orthodox agree that those who are condemned to Gehenna at the Final Judgment are beyond hope. For the damned there is only unrelenting torment and agony: they cannot but experience God as their hell. Greek theologian George Metallinos states the dominant Orthodox position:

> Paradise and hell are not two different places. (This version is an idolatrous concept.) They signify two different situations (ways), which originate from the same uncreated source, and are perceived by man as two, different experiences. Or, more precisely, they are the same experience, except that they are perceived differently by man, depending on man's internal state. This experience is: the sight of Christ inside the uncreated light of His divinity, of His "glory." From

---

[10] John of Damascus, *De Fide Orthodoxa* 2.4; see David Bradshaw's article "Patristic Views on Why There Is No Repentance after Death," in *The Unity of Body and Soul in Patristic and Byzantine Thought*, ed. A. Usacheva, S. Bhayro, and J. Ulrich (Brill, 2021), pp. 192-212.

[11] Kallistos Ware, "Dare We Hope for the Salvation of All?" *The Inner Kingdom* (2000), pp. 193-215.

[12] Hans Urs von Balthasar, *Dare We Hope That All Men Be Saved?: With a Short Discourse on Hell*, 2nd ed. (2014).

the moment of His Second Coming, through to all eternity, all people will be seeing Christ in His uncreated light. . . .

Paradise and hell are the same reality. This is what is depicted in the portrayal of the Second Coming. From Christ a river flows forth: it is radiant like a golden light at the upper end of it, where the saints are. At its lower end, the same river is fiery, and it is in that part of the river that the demons and the unrepentant ("the never repentant" according to a hymn) are depicted. This is why in Luke 2, 34 we read that Christ stands "as the fall and the resurrection of many". Christ becomes the resurrection into eternal life, for those who accepted Him and who followed the suggested means of healing the heart; and to those who rejected Him, He becomes their demise and their hell.

The righteous and the unrepentant shall both pass through the uncreated "fire" of divine presence, however, the one shall pass through unscathed, while the other shall be burnt. He too is "saved," but only in the way that one passes through a fire. Efthimios Zigavinos (12th century) observes in this respect: "God as fire that illuminates and brightens the pure, and burns and obscures the unclean." And Theodoritos Kyrou regarding this "saving" writes: "One is also saved by fire, being tested by it", just as when one passes through fire. If he has an appropriate protective cover, he will not be burnt, otherwise, he may be "saved", but he will be charred!"[13]

The contemporary Orthodox understanding of hell is often portrayed, particularly in apologetic contexts, as morally superior to the Catholic and Protestant conceptions of hell. This certainly holds if we are comparing it to traditional juridical models; but as we have seen, mainline Catholicism and Protestantism appear to have adopted non-retributive views very similar to the Orthodox. What I want to ask now is, What would St Isaac think about the river of fire formulation of hell? His statement that the damned are "scourged

---

[13] George Metallinos, "Paradise and Hell according to Orthodox tradition" (2005): http://www.oodegr.com/english/swthria/kol_par1.htm.

by the scourge of love" is often quoted by Eastern writers and pastors. They do not see eternal torment as a moral problem. The lost have freely chosen their doom. They have shaped themselves into the kind of people who despise their Creator. They hate the demands he makes upon them. They abhor his self-giving and loathe his presence. Their rejection of his love is definitive and irrevocable. The lost, therefore, are alone responsible for their fate. That they should suffer everlastingly is meet and right. Proponents of the river of fire model, however, fail to observe that the cause of their suffering is precisely God himself. Unlike the self-separation presentation of hell that we find in C. S. Lewis's *The Great Divorce*, the river of fire model thrusts the damned into the midst of fiery Love. The veil of divine hiddenness is removed. There is no place to run, no cave in which to hide. Everywhere there is only the consuming fire that is the Father, Son, and Holy Spirit. The uncreated Light blazes forth throughout creation. The walls of narcissistic consciousness collapse. The One who is all in all invades the soul. The agony is unbearable, yet no relief can be found. The conflagration cannot be extinguished. Do not speak to the reprobate of the joys of heaven. God is their hell.

Here we have the loving God *imposing himself* upon those who reject him *to their eternal torment and agony*. Given that the damned are incapable of repentance, given that they are incapable of responding to the divine love with anything other than hatred, given that they cannot escape from what, for them, is an intolerable state, how is this not punishment of the worst imaginable kind? This is not chastisement, for the damned are beyond education and reform. This is torture.

With the final condemnation of the impenitent, has not the God of love in fact become the God of wrath? The time for mercy is over; now is the time for the punishment of love. *God's antecedent salvific will has collapsed into his consequent retributivist will.*[14] Precisely at the point when humanity loses its freedom to embrace God's offer of salvation—and therefore becomes subject to *interminable* anguish—we have no choice but to appeal to divine justice. Only if the damned *deserve* to suffer can the horror of hell be morally justified. Such was the view of St Gregory Palamas: "For then it is a time of revelation and punishment, not compassion and mercy; then is a time of revelation of the wrath, the anger, and the just retribution of God. . . . Woe to him who falls into the hands of the living God."[15] Yet recall the Syrian's bracing dictum: "God is not one who requites evil, but He sets evil aright."[16]

What then has become of the God of infinite Love? Is the Final Judgment the end of mercy? How can Gehenna be the good that the heavenly Father eternally wills for the damned?

The "scourge of love," however, is not St Isaac of Nineveh's last word on Gehenna.

---

[14] As David Bentley Hart observes: "Under the canopy of God's omnipotence and omniscience, the consequent is already wholly virtually present in the antecedent." *That All Shall Be Saved* (2019), p. 82. Also see David Bentley Hart, "What God Wills and What God Permits," *Public Orthodoxy* (5 May 2020): https://publicorthodoxy.org/2020/05/05/what-god-wills-and-what-god-permits/.
[15] Quoted in Nikolaos P. Vassiliadis, *The Mystery of Death* (1993), pp. 509-510.
[16] Isaac of Nineveh, *The Second Part* (1995), II.39.15. For a helpful presentation of Isaac's eschatology, see Hilarion Alfeyev, "The Life of the Age to Come: The Eschatology of St Isaac the Syrian," *The Orthodox Life* (11 September 2013): https://orthodoxchurchlife.wordpress.com/2013/09/11/the-life-of-the-age-to-come-the-eschatology-of-st-isaac-the-syrian/.

Chapter Thirteen

The Triumph of the Kingdom Over Gehenna

"Those who are punished in Gehenna are scourged by the scourge of love"—these famous words of St Isaac the Syrian have profoundly influenced the Orthodox understanding of hell and damnation. For centuries, readers of St Isaac's writings have assumed that this mystical insight represents the apex of his reflections on damnation. But in 1983, Sebastian Brock discovered in the Bodleian Library the complete text of a group of discourses virtually unknown in the Byzantine and Latin Churches. Unlike his published ascetical homilies, these discourses had never been translated into Greek nor into any other language (except perhaps Arabic). That they existed was known to scholars, but the one extant text in Iran was lost in 1918. And then Brock made his remarkable discovery. In 1995, he published an English translation under the riveting title *The Second Part*. In this volume, we find three homilies specifically devoted to the last things (chapters 39, 40, and 41). The eschatological homilies reveal an Isaac whose understanding of hell was far more original and daring than previously suspected: the damned may be "scourged by the scourge of love," but the scourging is not forever!

St Isaac and the Horror of Eternal Damnation

Underlying Isaac's reflections on eschatology is his fierce conviction that retributive punishment is incompatible with the God of absolute and infinite love. Our Father wills our good, always and eternally. He does not inflict unnecessary pain and suffering. If he chastises, it is always with the aim of our conversion and sanctification:

The Triumph of the Kingdom Over Gehenna

> For it would be most odious and utterly blasphemous to think that hate or resentment exists with God, even against demonic beings; or to imagine any other weakness, or passibility, or whatever else might be involved in the course of retribution of good or bad as applying, in a retributive way, to that glorious divine Nature. Rather, He acts towards us in ways He knows will be advantageous to us, whether by way of things that cause suffering, or by way of things that cause relief, whether they cause joy or grief, whether they are insignificant or glorious: all are directed towards the single eternal good, whether each receives judgement or something of glory from Him—not by way of retribution, far from it!—but with a view to the advantage that is going to come from all these things.[1]
>
> That is how everything works with Him, even though things may seem otherwise to us: with Him it is not a matter of retribution, but He is always looking beyond to the advantage that will come from His dealing with humanity. And one such thing is this matter of Gehenna.[2]

Even perdition is encompassed within God's salvific plan for humanity; even hell can be used by the Creator for our good and eternal happiness. The claim that the Father of Jesus Christ will abandon his children to eschatological misery is unthinkable, indeed impious. Eternal damnation is unworthy of the God revealed in Jesus Christ. Isaac solemnly announces the liberating and godly alternative:

> I am of the opinion that He is going to manifest some wonderful outcome, a matter of immense and ineffable compassion on the part of the glorious Creator, with respect to the ordering of this difficult matter of Gehenna's torment: out of it the wealth of His love and power and

---

[1] Isaac, II.39.3, *The Second Part* (1995).
[2] II.39.5.

wisdom will become known all the more—and so will the insistent might of the waves of His goodness.[3]

Isaac speaks to us from his profound mystical illumination. He knows that an eternal hell is irreconcilable with the divine love and goodness he has experienced. Isaac is not simply engaging in philosophical speculation. He is speaking to us as a mystagogue and holy ascetic who has been transfigured by union with the Holy Trinity. This is why his words possess such revelatory and compelling power. From the solitude of the mountain, the anchorite prophetically proclaims: the Kingdom of God will triumph over Gehenna.

Isaac is horrified by the teaching of eternal reprobation. It cannot be reconciled, he insists, with God's self-revelation of love given in the death and resurrection of Jesus Christ. The suggestion that God might have created the universe knowing full well that many souls would be condemned to interminable punishment must be dismissed as absurd and morally intolerable:

> It is not the way of the compassionate Maker to create rational beings in order to deliver them over mercilessly to unending affliction in punishment for things of which He knew even before they were fashioned, aware how they would turn out when He created them—and whom nonetheless He created.[4]

Like other Church Fathers, Isaac believes in God's foreknowledge of the future. God created the world knowing full well that humanity would fall from grace, with death, sin, and Gehenna as the consequences. It cannot be the case that Adam's decision to eat the apple totally took the Creator by surprise. Such ignorance would reduce him to the status of a finite being and introduce mutability

---

[3] II.39.6.
[4] II.39.6.

The Triumph of the Kingdom Over Gehenna

into the divine nature. In his foreknowledge of angelic and human sin, therefore, God has included Gehenna within his providential plan to accomplish the final reconciliation of the wicked:

> If the Kingdom and Gehenna had not been foreseen in the purpose of our good God as a result of the coming into being of good and evil actions, then God's thoughts concerning these would not be eternal; but righteousness and sin were known by Him before they revealed themselves. Accordingly the Kingdom and Gehenna are matters belonging to mercy, which were conceived of in their essence by God as a result of His eternal goodness. It was not a matter of requiting, even though He gave them the name of requital.
>
> That we should further say or think that the matter is not full of love and mingled with compassion would be an opinion full of blasphemy and insult to our Lord God. By saying that He will even hand us over to burning for the sake of sufferings, torment and all sorts of ills, we are attributing to the divine Nature an enmity towards the very rational being which He created through grace; the same is true if we say that He acts or thinks with spite and with a vengeful purpose, as though He was avenging Himself.[5]

I confess I still find the topic of divine foreknowledge difficult, even after decades of theological reading. I affirm, of course, the omniscience of God—God knows everything that happens—but is *what has not yet happened* something to be known? At this point we are brought into the unfathomable mystery of the relationship between eternal divinity and temporal reality. Perhaps some philosophers might want to accuse Isaac of a naive understanding of eternity and time; but whatever divine foreknowledge means, it certainly means that God was surprised neither by the disobedience of Adam nor by the iniquities of human beings that necessitate Gehenna. Yet, he created humanity regardless—and that is the

---

[5] II.39.22.

essential point. If the omniscient and benevolent Deity created the world knowing, or at least fully anticipating, that mankind was going to rebel against his love and authority and fall into corruption, then he must have made redemptive provision for this eventuality from before the beginning. He *must* have—because hell is that intolerable. Isaac will not allow us to invoke our inadequate notions of justice to justify a doctrine of unending perdition. God acts in love, always in love, only in love. "Among all His actions," Isaac concludes, "there is none which is not entirely a matter of mercy, love and compassion: this constitutes the beginning and the end of His dealings with us."[6]

If we do not share St Isaac's horror of a perduring Gehenna, then perhaps that says something very important *about us*. This, I suggest, is St Isaac's unstated premise. Our opposition to apokatastasis ultimately flows not from biblical exegesis or intellectual reasoning. Once one has experienced the extraordinary love and mercy of God and been drawn into the embrace of the Father through the Son in the Spirit, one **knows** the truth of God and therefore **knows** the impossibility of eternal punishment. If we *do not* know, then we are suffering from ignorance, moral and spiritual incompetence, or faithlessness—or some combination of the three. Isaac intends to offend and convict. He confronts us with two irreconcilable possibilities: the Holy Trinity is either absolute love (apokatastasis) or absolute justice (everlasting damnation). There is no safe middle ground to which we may retreat, no distinction between the antecedent and consequent wills of the Creator to which we may appeal. The truth does not lie in the mean. We must pray for the illumination that only the Spirit can give.

But Isaac also believes that he is speaking from within the Holy Tradition of the Church. He is not presenting his readers with a

---

[6] II.39.22.

doctrinal innovation. He is not teaching, he assures us, "things of which our former orthodox Fathers never spoke, as though we were bursting out with an opinion which did not accord with truth."[7] He invokes two respected Oriental Fathers specifically in support—Theodore of Mopsuestia and Diodore of Tarsus.[8] The following quotation from Theodore is of particular interest:

> In the world to come, those who have chosen here what is good, will receive the felicity of good things along with praise; whereas the wicked, who all their life have turned aside to evil deeds, once they have been set in order in their minds by punishments and the fear of them, choose the good, having come to learn how much they have sinned, and that they have persevered in doing evil things and not good; by means of all this they receive a knowledge of religion's excellent teaching, and are educated so as to hold on to it with a good will, and so eventually they are held worthy of the felicity of divine munificence. For Christ would never have said "Until you pay the last farthing" unless it had been possible for us to be freed from our sins once we had recompensed for them through punishments. Nor would He have said "He will be beaten with many stripes" and "He will be beaten with few stripes" if it were not the case that the punishments measured out in correspondence to the sins, were finally going to have an end.[9]

Clearly Theodore does not understand repentance and purification as being impossible after death. He declares the expectation that the wicked will eventually come to see the gravity of their sin and choose the good—and thus be saved. Divine chastisement is educative, rehabilitative, and of limited duration.

---

[7] II.39.7.
[8] For more on the universalist convictions of Diodore and Theodore, see Ilaria Ramelli, *A Larger Hope* (2019), pp. 129-146. Both men are venerated as saints in the Assyrian Church of the East.
[9] II.39.8.

St Isaac presents us with a simple choice—the punishment of Gehenna is either retributive or remedial, punitive or medicinal. If the former, then God, and we, are trapped in the past; if the latter, then God, and we, are open to a future beyond our imaginings:

> So then, let us not attribute to God's actions and His dealings with us any idea of requital. Rather, we should speak of fatherly provision, a wise dispensation, a perfect will which is concerned with our good, and complete love. If it is a case of love, then it is not one of requital; and if it is a case of requital, then it is not one of love. Love, when it operates, is not concerned with the requiting of former things by means of its own good deeds or correction; rather, it looks to what is most advantageous in the future: it examines what is to come, and not things that are past.[10]

Isaac's eschatology is soundly biblical and must be distinguished from the exotic construal of apokatastasis condemned in the sixth century.

The Scourge of Love as Purifying Fire

In light of the eschatological homilies, the famous words of St Isaac that the damned are "scourged by the scourge of love" take on a very different meaning. Read the passage once again:

> I also maintain that those who are punished in Gehenna are scourged by the scourge of love. For what is so bitter and vehement as the punishment of love? I mean that those who have become conscious that they have sinned against love suffer greater torment from this than from any fear of punishment. For the sorrow caused in the heart by sin against love is sharper than any torment that can be. It would be improper for a man to think that sinners in Gehenna are deprived of the love of God. Love is the offspring of knowledge of the truth which,

---

[10] II.39.18.

as is commonly confessed, is given to all. The power of love works in two ways: it torments those who have played the fool, even as happens here when a friend suffers from a friend; but it becomes a source of joy for those who have observed its duties. Thus I say that this is the torment of Gehenna: bitter regret. But love inebriates the souls of the sons of Heaven by its delectability.[11]

The scourging of love, his river of fire, is nothing less than God's work of purification in the hearts of the wicked. The chastisement that God imposes in hell is educative, remedial, and reparative. God scourges in order to bring the damned to salvation, to bring them into a knowledge both of his mercy and of their sin and its terrible consequences for themselves and for God's creation. Even Gehenna falls into God's redemptive purposes. Its goal is to generate within the hearts of the condemned the stirrings of faith and repentance, thus allowing them to experience God precisely as love and not as torture. Only thus are the torment and anguish of the damned, caused by the eschatological invasion of love, rendered morally acceptable.

St Isaac emphatically rejects any suggestion that the damned are beyond redemption. God would never have created a cosmos whose history would conclude, even for a small portion of rational beings, with an eternal Gehenna. And it is inconceivable that he would have so constructed the afterlife that the wicked would be incapable of turning their hearts to Christ and appealing to his mercy. The Lord's face is set "all the time towards forgiveness."[12] His grace is like an ocean that knows no measure.

The Syrian ascetic does not conjecture on the specifics of how God might accomplish the conversion of the damned. Apparently, he did not feel the need to offer explanation. His teaching is

---

[11] I.28, *The Ascetical Homilies of St Isaac the Syrian*, p. 266.
[12] II.40.13.

governed by an adamantine hope, revealed in Scripture and confirmed in mystical experience. This hope trumps all counterarguments, all objections, all other considerations. As Patrik Hagman notes: "Ultimately, Isaac bases his belief on hope on his firm trust in God as a loving father. Gehenna was created with our future good in mind."[13] Despite hell, and even because of hell, the final destiny of humanity will be glorious. God will be all in all. It would be blasphemous, suggests Isaac, to think otherwise.

Here is where philosophy ends and mystery begins. Philosophers tell us that God so values libertarian freedom that an eternal populated hell must remain a possibility. Every human being is given an opportunity to definitively accept or reject God, and God will respect this choice, even if it means the individual's unending suffering. This has become the ecumenical justification for everlasting perdition. Freedom triumphs over love. But the Syrian mystic refuses to be trapped by this philosophical problem, for the God who rose from the dead on Easter morning is not trapped by it:

> Accordingly we say that, even in the matter of the afflictions and sentence of Gehenna, there is some hidden mystery, whereby the wise Maker has taken as a starting point for its future outcome the wickedness of our actions and willfulness, using it as a way of bringing to perfection His dispensation wherein lies the teaching which makes wise, and the advantage beyond description, hidden from both angels and human beings, hidden too from those who are being chastised, whether they be demons or human beings, hidden for as long as the ordained period of time holds sway.[14]

Gehenna will end. Through his goodness and beauty God will overcome evil. The damned will be saved, not by force or coercion but by the chastisement of mercy that will ultimately bring them into

---

[13] Patrik Hagman, *The Asceticism of Isaac of Nineveh* (2010), p. 202.
[14] II.39.20.

the true happiness they have always hoped and dreamed for. St Isaac does not speculate further. He simply presents us with the confident hope that the infinitely wise and good God will restore and consummate his creation in love.

Wacław Hryniewicz summarizes Isaac's understanding of apokatastasis and the temporary duration of Gehennic punishment:

> Isaac belongs to those Christian mystics who do not exaggerate the power of evil. In his eyes human sin is infinitely small in comparison with the infinite mercy of God. The torments of Gehenna are caused by self-exclusion from the great feast in the Kingdom of heaven, by a person's inability to participate in the love of God. Yet they will come to an end, although here on earth we do not know when it will take place. Gehenna is a consequence of sin which also will have its end. If God punishes, He does it out of love, in order to heal a sick freedom of rational creatures. Sinners in Gehenna are not deprived of the compassionate love of God. The purpose of punishment is change for the better, purification and conversion. The punishment ceases when this purpose is achieved. The sinners are not deprived of God's love even in their infernal state. They can always count on His help. God's justice and mercy are inseparable. He awaits with love all His creatures at the end of their purification. If evil, sin and Gehenna do not have their origins in God, how can they be eternal? . . .
>
> According to Isaac, Gehenna can only be temporary and provisional, permeated by God's love and mercy. He would not allow a punishment which would deny His own nature. The punishment has a therapeutic and correctional meaning. It is always connected with His "compassionate intentions and purpose" to set us on the upright path, and not to bring us to perdition. Gehenna's torment is "a matter of immense and ineffable compassion." It must have its end and achieve its purpose. For this reason it is subject to a limit. It is not for eternity and will last only for a fixed period, decreed by God's wisdom. The punishments, measured out in correspondence to the sins, are finally going to have an end. The eternal punishment would be a monstrous

reality unworthy of God. Who thinks otherwise has not overcome an"infantile way of thinking," "the childish opinion of God."[15]

Isaac is well aware that the eschatological hope of apokatastasis can and will be exploited by sinners to justify their laxity and wickedness. This does not lead him to dilute the glorious revelation of final triumph, however. Isaac forthrightly summons his readers to repentance. No one wants to experience the torments of hell, he tells us, even for a single moment. Far better to begin the ascent to God now. *Now* is the time to repent; *now* is the time to accept the forgiveness of God and to begin living the union of love:

> Let us beware in ourselves, my beloved, and realize that even if Gehenna is subject to a limit, the taste of its experience is terrible, and the extent of its bounds escapes our very understanding. Let us strive all the more to partake of the taste of God's love for the sake of perpetual reflection on Him, and let us not have experience of Gehenna through neglect.[16]

The call to repentance flows from the gospel and the hope of universal salvation. All shall be saved—therefore believe on Jesus Christ and embrace his call to discipleship.

St Isaac of Nineveh has presented us with a glorious vision of the future, a vision grounded in his mystical experience of the God of Jesus Christ and his contemplative reading of the Scriptures. "In every epoch," writes Hilarion Alfeyev, "the Christian world needs to be reminded of this universal love of God for his creation because in every epoch there is a strong tendency within Christianity to replace the religion of love and freedom taught by Jesus with a

---

[15] Wacław Hryniewicz, "Universalism of Salvation: St Isaac the Syrian," *The Challenge of our Hope* (2007), pp. 82-83.
[16] II.40.1.

The Triumph of the Kingdom Over Gehenna

religion of slavery and fear."[17] We need not fear the twin proclamation of the unconditional love of God and the triumph of his Kingdom. It is this gospel that transforms our lives and sustains the Church. As the saint reminds us, "Divine hope uplifts the heart, but fear of Gehenna crushes it."[18]

Isaac knows well the paralyzing power of the threat of eternal damnation. No doubt he has heard it declared by his fellow monks. He knows the terror it generates in the hearts of the faithful and rejects it as a corruption of the gospel. We are called to proclaim the absolute goodness of the Creator who makes all things new in Jesus Christ:

> O the astonishment at the goodness of our God and Creator! O power for which all is possible! O immeasurable kindness toward our nature, that He will even bring sinners back into existence! . . . Where is Gehenna, that can afflict us? Where is the torment that terrifies us in many ways and quenches the joy of His love? And what is Gehenna as compared with the grace of His resurrection, when he will raise us from Sheol and cause our corruptible nature to be clad in incorruption, and raise up in glory what has fallen into Sheol? Come, men of discernment, and be filled with wonder! Whose mind is sufficiently wise to wonder worthily at the bounty of our Creator? His recompense of sinners is that instead of a just recompense, he rewards them with resurrection, and instead of those bodies with which they trampled upon His law, He robes them with the glory of perfection. That grace whereby we are resurrected after we have sinned is greater than the grace which brought us into being when we were not.[19]

Amen. Amen. Amen.

---

[17] Hilarion Alfeyev, *The Spiritual World of Isaac the Syrian* (2000), pp. 300-301.
[18] I.51, p. 384.
[19] I.51, p. 388.

Chapter Fourteen

Will Satan Be Saved?

St Paisios the Athonite once fasted and prayed for two weeks for the eternal salvation of the devil. While praying he saw a dog's head sticking his tongue out and mocking him. Paisios concluded from this incident that "God is ready to accept the demons provided they repent, but they themselves do not want their salvation."

Kallistos Ware tells the story of a four-hour car journey he once had with a Greek archbishop. Hoping to enjoy a long conversation on the question of the salvation of Satan, he asked him: "If it is possible that the devil, who must surely be a very lonely and unhappy person, may eventually repent and be saved, why do we never pray for him?" The hierarch peremptorily replied, "Mind your own business." End of discussion. Ware comments:

> He was right. So far as we humans are concerned, the devil is always our adversary; we should not enter into any kind of negotiations with him, whether by praying for him or in other ways. His salvation is quite simply none of our business. But the devil has also his own relationship with God, as we learn from the prologue of the book of Job, when Satan makes his appearance in the heavenly court among the other "sons of God" (Job 1:6-2:7). We are, however, altogether ignorant of the precise nature of this relationship, and it is futile to pry into it. Yet, even though it is not for us to pray for the devil, we have no right to assume that he is totally and irrevocably excluded from the scope of God's mercy.[1]

---

[1] Kallistos Ware, "Dare We Hope for the Salvation of All?" *The Inner Kingdom* (2000), pp. 202-203.

Ware has a point. Satan has never been the object of the prayers of the Church. In the baptismal liturgies, he is decisively renounced. We pray for protection from his malignant agency, and we pray for the deliverance of those who come under his oppressive power. But the Church has not taught the baptized to pray for his salvation. "Mind your own business" enshrines a spiritual wisdom that must be heeded. The depth and power of demonic evil cannot be comprehended by embodied creatures. Perhaps the saints and holy elders may safely pray for the salvation of our great adversary, but the Church as a whole has not been called by her Lord to do so. The demons are none of our business.

St Isaac the Syrian and God's Love for Satan

Nevertheless, St Isaac the Syrian did not hesitate to affirm that the fallen angels are as much objects of God's love and salvific will as are human beings. We cannot speak of the one without speaking of the other. God loves the demons and desires their reconciliation:

> Nor are we able to say that the love of the Creator is diminished towards those rational beings who have become demons as a result of their demonic action, and is any less than the fulness of love which He has towards those who remain in the angelic state; or that it is less for sinners than for those who are justly named righteous. This is because the divine Nature is not affected by what happens and by opposition, nor does there spring up within it any causal stirring which takes its origin from creation, and which is not to be found with Him from eternity; nor does He have a kind of love which originates as a result of events which take place in time.
>
> Rather, everyone has a single place in His purpose in the ranking of love, corresponding to the form He beheld in them before He created them and all the rest of created beings, that is, at the time before the eternal purpose for the delineation of the world was put into effect. For it was not with an adventitious love that He had, without any beginning,

the stirring that initiated the establishment of the world. He has a single ranking of complete and impassible love towards everyone, and He has a single caring concern for those who have fallen, just as much as for those who have not fallen.

And it is clear that He does not abandon them the moment they fall, and that demons will not remain in their demonic state, and sinners will not remain in their sins; rather, He is going to bring them to a single equal state of perfection in relationship to His own being—in a state in which the holy angels are now, in perfection of love and a passionless mind. He is going to bring them into that excellency of will, where it will not be as though they were curbed and not [free], or having stirrings from the Opponent then; rather, they will be in a state of excelling knowledge, with a mind made mature in the stirrings which partake of the divine outpouring which the blessed Creator is preparing in His grace; they will be perfected in love for Him, with a perfect mind which is above any aberration in all its stirrings.[2]

Isaac prophesies the ultimate salvation of Satan and the demonic company. His argument is identical to his argument offered for the salvation of humanity: God's love does not change. It is immutable and impassible; it is not affected by what happens within the creaturely realm. Despite the disobedience and rebellion of rational creatures, whether angelic or human, God continues to love them with the same love that he possessed before the ages. And just as God made provision to save impenitent sinners by the Gehennic "torments of love," so he has made analogous provision for the restoration of Satan and the fallen angels. How? By the enchantment of his divine goodness and beauty, Isaac answers. In the mystery of parousial self-revelation, the LORD will overcome the resistance of both humans and demons and restore them to himself:

---

[2] Isaac of Nineveh, *The Second Part*, trans. Sebastian Brock (1995), II.40.2-4.

The Fathers tell us that at the hour when the saints will be attracted by the divine wave, they will be raised to that beatitude by meeting our Lord Who will attract them with His power, like a magnetic stone drawing iron particles into itself. Then all the legions of heavenly hosts and Adam's descendants will gather together into one Church. And then the purpose of the Creator's providence will be fulfilled which He prepared from the beginning of the world, making the creation by His benevolence. To this purpose the long course of various events of this world was prepared, serving to rational (beings) as to its master. And henceforth the exiles of the Kingdom will enjoy a life in peace in which there is no end or change.[3]

And since in the new World the Creator's love rules over all rational nature, the wonder at His mysteries that will be revealed (then) will captivate to itself the intellect of (all) rational beings whom He has created so that they might have delight in Him, whether they be evil or whether they be just.[4]

Even now, our Great High Priest prays to his Father for the salvation of all rational beings:

"You are a Priest forever" (Ps 110.4). This "forever" (means) that our Lord Jesus Christ is a priest now and ministers to us for our redemption. It always continues (and will continue) until He elevates us all to Himself.[5]

The ministry of Christ consists in saying prayers on behalf of all rational natures to the Divine nature which dwells in Him. . . . The Apostle testifies: "He entered heaven itself, now to appear for us in God's presence" (Heb 9.24). This "for us" should be understood (as follows): He rose for the sake of us all and sat down on the right hand

---

[3] Isaac, *Cen.* I.92; quoted by Alexey Fokin, "Apocatastasis in the Syrian Christian Tradition: Evagrius and Isaac," in *St Isaac the Syrian and his Spiritual Legacy* (2015), pp. 133-134.
[4] Isaac, II.38.2.
[5] Isaac, Cent. I.21; quoted by Fokin, p. 131.

Destined for Joy

of God and intercedes for us. He did it not only for the sake of human beings but also for the sake of holy angels.[6]

Isaac speculates that the fallen spirits may be elevated to an even more brilliant noetic level than the unfallen!

> Maybe they will be raised to a perfection even greater than that in which the angels now exist; for all are going to exist in a single love, a single purpose, a single will, and a single perfect state of knowledge; they will gaze towards God with the desire of insatiable love, even if some divine dispensation [i.e., Gehenna] may in the meantime be effected for reasons known to God alone, lasting for a fixed period, decreed by Him in accordance with the will of His wisdom.[7]

Who can put limits on the Father's love? Who can fathom his transcendent wisdom?

We may wonder how Isaac can assert his opinion so confidently, given the testimony, for example, of the Book of Revelation: "And the devil who had deceived them was thrown into the lake of fire and sulphur where the beast and the false prophet were, and they will be tormented day and night for ever and ever" (Rev 20:10). No problem. Revelation was not included in the 7th century Syrian canon of the Bible, the Peshitta. Regardless, the verse does not pose an insurmountable problem for Isaac. He reads the Bible through a *hermeneutic of love*, the very love he finds portrayed in the crucified Christ and experiences in prayer. What else then can the lake of fire be but the purifying flames of divine love?

The demons may not presently want to be saved, as Paisios learned, but that hardly constitutes an insuperable obstacle for omnipotent Love:

---

[6] Isaac, Cent. I.22; quoted by Fokin, p. 131.
[7] Isaac, II.40.5.

Will Satan Be Saved?

> No part belonging to any single one of all rational beings will be lost, as far as God is concerned, in the preparation of that supernal Kingdom, which is prepared for all worlds. Because of that goodness of His nature by which He brought the universe into being and then bears, guides and provides for the worlds and all created things in His immeasurable compassion, He has devised the establishment of the Kingdom of heaven for the entire community of rational beings—even though an intervening time is reserved for the general raising of all to the same level. And we say this in order that we too may concur with the magisterial teaching of Scripture.[8]

God will bring his creation to perfection in the Love that he is— Father, Son, and Holy Spirit. He has made provision for both demonic and human evil, which he foresaw before the ages. This is the deep truth of Holy Scripture: Christ's love will ultimately prove irresistible for all, even for the demons. As Wacław Hryniewicz comments:

> Sin and Gehenna will be ultimately abolished, although their end is a mystery surpassing human understanding. The final outcome of the history of the created world must correspond to the beauty of the beginning and to the goodness of God. If we suppose the truly eternal punishment of sinners and demons, this would mean that the creation of the world was an enormous failure and mistake. God is able to overcome, by His goodness and beauty, every evil, even the opposition of the devil himself.[9]

Sergius Bulgakov and the Battle to Save the Demons

Few theologians in the Christian tradition have spoken as boldly as Isaac about the ultimate salvation of Satan and his fellow demons.

---

[8] Isaac, II.40.7.
[9] Wacław Hryniewicz, "Universalism of Salvation: St Isaac The Syrian, *The Challenge of Our Hope* (2007), p. 85.

Even the great Origen appears to have hesitated.[10] But in the mid-20th century Orthodox theologian Sergius Bulgakov dared to declare the eschatological restoration of the unholy spirits.[11] He follows closely the logic of love as laid out by Isaac: just as God will not and cannot abandon human beings to evil, so he will not and cannot abandon the fallen angels. He wills to be all in all. In particular I note two of Bulgakov's speculative insights that complement the teachings of the Syrian.

First, by their expulsion from the immediate presence of their Creator, the fallen angels are cut off from the bread of heaven. They now live in the world as parasites, drawing upon its life and being to sustain themselves in their diminished demonic existence:

> The two worlds—angelic and human—are inseparably linked. The supreme angel, together with his minions, was called to become man's first friend, and this service could have been based only on self-renouncing love. When this love faded, its place was taken by the lust for power, fed by envy, for, originally, from his creation, man was placed ontologically higher than the angels, having his own world, which the angels serve. From the guardian angel of the world Satan is transformed into "the prince of this world," who wants to gain possession of it. He becomes a conquering predator, governed not by love but by envy and the lust for power, not by truth but by falsehood. The devil "was a murderer from the beginning, and abode not in the truth, because there is no truth in him" (John 8:44). Satan's relation to

---

[10] See C. A. Patrides, "The Salvation of Satan," *Journal of the History of Ideas* 28 (1967): 467-478; Lisa Holliday, "Will Satan Be Saved?" *Vigiliae Christianae* 63 (2009): 1-23; Ilaria Ramelli, *Apokatastasis* (2013), pp. 141-156; Ambrose Andreano, "The True Fate of the 'So-called Devil' in Origen" (2020): https://www.academia.edu/44789518/The_True_Fate_of_The_So_Called_Devil_in_Origen.

[11] Bulgakov addresses the question of demonic salvation in *The Bride of the Lamb* (2001), trans. Boris Jakim; and in his essay "On the Question of the Apocatastasis of the Fallen Spirits (in Connection with the Teaching of Gregory of Nyssa)," *The Sophiology of Death* (2021), pp. 76-91.

the world is based upon his all-devouring subjectivism, for he finds for himself a kingdom in which he can rule parasitically, until he is "cast out" (John 12:31). As an angel he retains access to the life of the world and his own place of action in it. As Satan he retains this possibility of action in the world, but he uses it now to pervert the world according to his own likeness, to sow his chaff in the world, to poison and ruin the world. As an angel he is not transcendent to the world but belongs to it; as Satan he is hostile to the world. And by this creative capacity of evil, he acquires objective life. If the life of the holy angels is cohuman by their positive service, then in the case of Satan too it is cohuman, but now only because of parasitic infection. Satan's insane desire to become God's equal and to take God's place in the human world finds a temporary and apparent realization, whence the creative action of evil in the world and the battle for the world with God.[12]

Second, the battle for the salvation of the unholy spirits only begins with their banishment from the world that sustains their pseudo-objective existence. They must be cast into the void. Only then can they suffer the full depth of their ontological impotence and thus be forced to confront the futility of their quest for radical independence from the LORD. Finally, they will know what they have lost and cannot recover. Such is their freedom and their hell:

> Insofar as unlimited freedom is without bottom or support, satanism is the infinite rebellion of malice and hatred. The pseudo-creative activity of evil is rooted in this emptiness, which determines the pose of the "prince of this world," who pretends to be the absolute center of creation. For a time there exists the possibility of such an illusion here and even a place for the authentic creative activity of evil, as long as the kingdom of this world exists. The world here is in some sense stolen from God, who permits this on the pathways of creaturely freedom. But this trial of freedom has its limit; it can and will be experienced to the end. And the end of the trial will come by the power of God, in the

---

[12] Bulgakov, *Bride*, pp. 158-159.

parousia, when Satan, despite his solipsistic affirmation, will be expelled from this world, will remain void of being, in the pose of a metaphysical charlatan, no longer deceiving anyone, not even himself. Satan will not stop being a creature of God, for, outside of this, only annihilation would await him. But God does not annihilate His creatures. With hatred and against his will, Satan knows that he is a creature of God, but he does not find joy in this, for he hates God precisely owing to this consciousness of his creatureliness. This consciousness of self is for him the primal source of the burning in hell, of the hatred of God as the source of life, of ontological envy. But after the expulsion of the prince of this world, Satan's duel with God begins.[13]

We can barely imagine the desolation of this terrible existence. Alive but not alive. Nothingness and gloom. Frigidity. Impotence. Inertness and immobility. Infecundity. Defeat. Absolute aloneness.

How can this emptiness that is left by the "casting out" be filled? How can this spasm accompanied by a pose be resolved? Can this caprice of self-willfulness find in itself a positive power, and how? For if this caprice is suspended in emptiness, can the latter be infinite and (if only in this sense) eternal? The nature of the creaturely spirit is characterized by creative activity, which is its life—as self-creative activity. As long as Satan was the "prince of this world," of God's creation that he had stolen, he was characterized by a parasitical pseudo-creative activity of evil, whose material and content, whose given, taken from the world, were "stolen goods" from the ontological point of view. But when, in the parousia, God takes possession of the world and Satan is expelled from the latter, he will be compelled to see that he is nothing, that his pseudo-creative activity has no content and creates nothing. Can the life of the spirit ground itself in such emptiness except by a gyration in eternal repetition? Can even creaturely freedom be realized in such objectless emptiness? But such a possibility would signify a subject without object or nature, a

---

[13] Ibid., pp. 507-508.

life without the content of life, the burning fire of the thirst for life without any satisfaction, an absolute dead end. Such is satanical eternity. When freedom is arbitrary and irrational, it contains all possibilities, in particular the bad infinity of satanism as the only stable existence of the now-powerless anti-god.[14]

Thus, begins the ages-long process of demonic repentance. Cast into the void of the outer darkness, "condemned to sustain themselves in an objectless solipsism,"[15] the malignant spirits must inevitably exhaust themselves in their struggle against their Creator. Try as they will to continue their rebellion, the undeniable *fact* of creaturehood abides. As long as they possessed the cosmos as an arena of action and sustenance, they were able to suppress awareness of their existential contradiction; but in the abyss of their nothingness, their consciousness is now flooded with one thought: "I am not God!" They are powerless to maintain their delusions and phantasies, powerless to evade the torments of their impotent existence, powerless to deny the futility of their quest for total freedom. Surrender is inevitable:

> The living out of this contradiction constitutes the only and exhaustive content of the life of the prince of this world in his exile from this world. Can this struggle extend for an infinite (and in this sense "eternal") duration, a bad infinity, or, having been weakened by the struggle, must he at some point in exhaustion lay down his arms? If his strength inexhaustible for this hopeless and endless struggle with what is self-evident, such that it can fill the ages of ages, or is even such a supposition impossible because . . . Satan, in point of fact, is a creature and only a creature, making his strength and his capabilities limited? What can save him in this situation is precisely that same creaturehood he rejects as a reality outstripping his creaturely freedom. He can grow exhausted in this unequal struggle—rather, he cannot *not* grow

---

[14] Ibid., p. 509.
[15] Ibid., p. 511.

exhausted from it, in the end capitulating before reality and acknowledging that not he himself, but rather God, is his creator, and this means: falling down and worshipping him. Then will there occur an ontological coercion on the part of reality, by force of fact.[16]

Bulgakov calls this the "ontological postulate" of demonic existence. "This pathway can end," he comments, "only with the filling of the void that appeared in heaven as a consequence of the fall, with the return of the fallen angels, the 'lost sheep,' to the fullness of the kingdom of God, where God is definitively all in all *without any limitation or exception*, and creation is without any failure or even minus: 'He shall have put down all rule and all authority and power. For he must reign till he hath put all enemies under his feet' (1 Cor. 15:24-25)."[17] By the transforming grace of the Father, Satan will once again become Lucifer, "star of the morning" (Isa 14:12).

This matter is beyond us. It is none of our business—yet perhaps it is. The fallen angels may be beyond our comprehension and sympathy, much as psychopaths are, yet they are our fellow creatures. As alien as they are to human experience, we are bound together by cross and resurrection. All we know is that devils are dangerous, destructive, malevolent, malignant.

Satan is our enemy—not only our enemy but the enemy of our family, friends, and fellow Christians. His hatred for mankind appears to know no bounds. As long as Satan remains in the world, parasitically drawing on its being and life, he remains incapable of repentance. We must leave his destiny in the hands of Christ and the saints. Bulgakov offers this warning:

> Indeed, as long as the prince of this world and his armies do battle against Christ and all humankind in this world, a sentimental attitude

---

[16] Bulgakov, "Apocatastasis," pp. 78-79.
[17] Bulgakov, *Bride*, p. 512.

toward the enemies of the name of Christ would constitute an utterly false pity. The Church severely rejects and condemns such false sentimentality under the pretext of love. The Lord Himself not only chased away demons, forbidding and annulling the works of their malignity, but also addressed the words of His holy indignation to them: "O faithless generation, how long shall I be with you? How long shall I suffer you?" (Mark 9:19; Matt. 17:17; Luke 9:41). The Book of Revelation is full of such holy wrath, which is a manifestation of God's love for creation. And, in general, before the expulsion of the prince of this world, during the state of battle with him and his continuing power, there can be no reconciliation with him. It is as if a limit to love were erected in the hearts of people and even in the Church itself.[18]

But if we are not called to pray for the conversion of Satan, perhaps we can be glad that St Isaac the Syrian does. We must each pray for a merciful heart:

> And what is a merciful heart? It is the heart burning for the sake of all creation, for men, for birds, for animals, for demons, and every created thing; and by the recollection of them the eyes of a merciful man pour forth abundant tears. By the strong and vehement mercy which grips his heart and by his great compassion, his heart is humbled and he cannot bear to hear or to see any injury or slight sorrow in creation. For this reason he offers up tearful prayer continually even for irrational beasts, for the enemies of the truth, and for those who harm him, that they be protected and receive mercy. And in like manner he even prays for the family of reptiles because of the great compassion that burns without measure in his heart in the likeness of God.[19]

Prayer for a merciful heart—that is our business.

---

[18] Bulgakov, *Bride*, p. 513.
[19] Isaac, *The Ascetical Homilies of Saint Isaac the Syrian* (2011), 2nd edition, I.71, p. 491.

Chapter Fifteen

The Shewings of Julian of Norwich: How Well is Hell?

Alle shall be well,

and alle shalle be wele,

and alle maner of thinge shall be wel.[1]

Does Julian of Norwich advocate the salvation of every human being? The question haunts readers of her *Shewings*. On the one hand, one may find numerous statements that strongly suggest universal salvation, including the famous "All shall be well." On the other hand, Julian repeatedly qualifies (twenty-five times, to be exact) God's salvific work in Christ with the phrase "that shalle be saved." For example:

> For in this onehede stondeth the life of alle mankind that shalle be saved. (LT 9)
>
> Crist, having knit in him all man that shalle be saved, is perfete man. (LT 57)

Nicholas Watson and Jacqueline Jenkins comment that the phrase appears to "pull against" the universalizing thrust of "All shalle be welle" and similar expressions.[2] Granted, "that shalle be saved" is ambiguous. It need not exclude a universalist reading, yet why

---

[1] All Middle English quotations of Julian are from Nicholas Watson and Jacqueline Jenkins, *The Writings of Julian of Norwich* (2007). All modern quotations are from Edmund Colledge, *Julian of Norwich: Showings* (1977). The quotations are from the long text (LT).
[2] Watson and Jenkins, p. 154.

introduce it if the author intended apokatastasis? The phrase appears to mediate between the universality of the salvific will of God, as clearly revealed in her shewings, and its particularity, as stated in the Church's teaching of the necessity of baptism, faith, and repentance. It may even reflect the belief that the number of the elect is eternally set. More likely, though, Julian intended the open-endedness of the phrase. It gives her the space to reflect on her shewings without committing herself on the doctrinal questions which they raise. I take the anchoress at her word when she states that nothing in them led her to question the common teaching of Holy Church (LT 46). And at a critical juncture in her reflections she explicitly affirms the doctrine of eternal damnation:

> Our faith is founded on God's Word, and it belongs to our faith that we believe that God's word will be preserved in all things. And one article of our faith is that many creatures will be damned, such as the angels who fell out of heaven because of pride, who now are devils, and many men upon earth who die out of the faith of Holy Church, that is to say those who are pagans and many who have received baptism and who live unchristian lives and so die out of God's love. All these will be eternally condemned to hell, as Holy Church teaches me to believe. And all this being so, it seemed to me that it was impossible that every kind of thing should be well, as our Lord revealed at this time. (LT 32)

The last sentence highlights the tension between the teaching of the medieval Latin Church on eternal damnation and the shewings Julian has received. She is a faithful daughter of the Church—"it was not my intention to make trial of anything which belongs to our faith" (LT 33)—but she recognizes that the revelations are irreconcilable with the doctrine of final retribution. In her heart, she knows that hell is not well: it may be just, but it is certainly not well. Eternal punishment testifies not to the triumph of love but to its failure. "For this is good and acceptable in the sight of God our

Saviour, Who will have all men to be saved, and to come to the knowledge of the truth," writes the Apostle Paul (1 Tim 2:3-4 [Douay-Rheims]); yet in the end, so the Church teaches and Julian affirms, many whom the Savior desires to save will be condemned by the Savior. That Julian is troubled by hell and its torments is telling. Everyone in the 14th century believed in the justice of eternal retribution, as evidenced by sermons, paintings and passion plays, theological and spiritual writings. It is manifestly meet and right that God should punish the wicked for their sins and impenitence. There's no conundrum to be solved, no antinomy to upon which to ponder—yet still Julian is troubled. To resolve her perplexity, she might have availed herself of the medieval distinction between the antecedent and consequent will of God. In the words of St Thomas Aquinas: "In the same way God antecedently wills all men to be saved, but consequently wills some to be damned, as His justice exacts."[3] But surprisingly divine retribution has no place in Julian's vision of divinity. There is no suggestion in the *Shewings* that when love fails, justice steps in; no suggestion that the perditional punishment of the wicked is an expression of divine charity. Against everything she has been taught, Julian does not see retribution in God. When she looks at her own sins and those of her fellow human beings, she acknowledges that "we deserve paine, blame and wrath," yet when she looks at God, she sees only mercy (LT 46). God does not blame his children for their sins. And so she wonders how hell can be well.

We will return shortly to this tension, but here I wish to record Denys Turner's judgment regarding the alleged universalism of Julian:

---

[3] Summa Theologiae I.19.6.

The Shewings of Julian of Norwich: How Well is Hell?

Moreover, Julian appears to be certain not just of the possibility that God can be rejected, but that in fact at least some people actually make that choice, and that they get what they want—to be in hell. Disputed as the matter is, there is much less textual support to be found in Julian's Revelation for the 'universalist' doctrine that all will be saved and none that is as explicit as her emphatic assertion that many are not.[1]

When Turner writes that Julian recognizes that the damned get "what they want," he goes beyond the text. Who desires unbearable torment? She never suggests that the damned have chosen condemnation and punishment, as if she were an early exponent of the free-will defense of hell. She simply acknowledges that by their wicked acts and impenitence the reprobate have died "out of God's love" and in consequence have received their just desserts.

Yet even still . . . when I concluded my first reading of the Showings, having noted along the way the various texts supporting the traditional position, I had nonetheless developed the clear impression that Christ had led Julian into the greater hope, perhaps not as a theological judgment but most assuredly as rhetorical performance, and this impression was confirmed in subsequent rereadings. Julian discourses as if she is a committed universalist. Missing are prophetic threats of perdition, as well as the countless summonses to repentance that often characterize homilies and spiritual writings. The note of exhortation is occasionally struck, but it plays only a minor role. Missing also are the expected qualifications of her universalist-sounding statements, lest her readers misunderstand. That which one hears in her words is the divine word of absolute love; that which one remembers is the divine word of promise, spoken in a striking and emphatic mode of

---

[1] Denys Turner, Julian of Norwich, Theologian (2013), p. 106; cf. Robert Sweetman, "Sin Has Its Place, but All Shall Be Well," in All Shall Be Well (2011), pp. 66-92.

unconditionality: "Alle shalle be wele, and alle shalle be wele, and alle maner of thinge shalle be wele" (LT 27).

I submit the following: even though Julian herself did not assert an explicit universalism, both the content and logic of her revelations challenges the traditional doctrine of eternal damnation. They therefore invite the Church to a deeper understanding of the good news of Jesus Christ. I note four features of her shewings in support of this thesis. Perhaps none are individually decisive, yet cumulatively they produce conviction.

God is Absolute and Inclusive Love

All Christians affirm that God is love. Yet preachers and theologians, particularly in the Latin tradition, have also sought to balance this attribute with the attribute of retributive justice. God is merciful, they say, but he is also holy and righteous. He rewards the virtuous and punishes the wicked. On the last day, Scripture tells us, he will "render to every man according to his deeds" (Rom 2:6). Yet in Julian's visions the attribute of justice recedes into the background. She sees only love in God. "Charite unmade is God," she declares (LT 84). God does not begin to love his creatures; it is from love he has created them and to love he destines them:

> For I saw that God never began to love mankind; for just as mankind will be in endless bliss, fulfilling God's joy with regard to his works, just so has that same mankind been known and love in God's prescience, from without beginning in his righteous intent. And by the endless intent and assent and the full accord of all the Trinity, the mediator wanted to be the foundation and the head of his fair nature, out of whom we have all come, in whom we are all enclosed, into whom we shall all go, finding in him our full heaven in everlasting joy by the prescient purpose of all the blessed Trinity from without beginning. (LT 53)

The Shewings of Julian of Norwich: How Well is Hell?

Love is both beginning and consummation. Julian does not hesitate to speak categorically in the first-person plural: we have come from Christ, we are enveloped by Christ, and to Christ we shall return, according to the eternal plan and foreknowledge of the Holy Trinity. No ifs, ands, or buts. Was perdition too a part of the plan? I find it difficult to believe that Julian would unreservedly assent, despite the passage quoted above. Perhaps she might whisper in reply: "God did not show me hell."

In the conclusion of her book, Julian shares that she long wanted to know the meaning of what God had shown her:

> And from the time that it was revealed, I desired many times to know in what was our Lord's meaning. And fifteen years after and more, I was answered in spiritual understanding, and it was said: What, do you wish to know your Lord's meaning in this thing? Know it well, love was his meaning. Who reveals it to you? Love. What did he reveal to you? Love. Why does he reveal it to you? For love. Remain in this, and you will know more of the same. For you will never know different, without end. So I was taught that love is our Lord's meaning. And I saw very certainly in this and in everything that before God made us he loved us, which love was never abated and never will be. And in this love he has done all his works, and in this love he had made all things profitable to us, and in this love our life is everlasting. In our creation we had beginning, but the love in which he created us was in him from without beginning. In this love we have our beginning, and all this we shall see in God without end. (LT 86)

God wills our good and never ceases to will our good. And so, we may ask, How can eternal damnation be an expression of love?

Julian arrestingly elaborates on the divine love in her figurative identification of Jesus as Mother:

> Our great Father, almighty God, who is being, knows us and loved us before time began. Out of this knowledge, in his most wonderful deep

> love, by the prescient eternal counsel of all the blessed Trinity, he wanted the second person to become our Mother, our brother and our saviour. From this it follows that as truly as God is our Father, so truly is God our Mother. Our Father wills, our Mother works, our good Lord the Holy Spirit confirms. And therefore it is our part to love our God in whom we have our being, reverently thanking and praising him for our creation, mightily praying to our Mother for mercy and pity, and to our Lord the Holy Spirit for help and grace. For in these three is all our life: nature, mercy and grace, of which we have mildness, patience and pity, and hatred of sin and wickedness; for the virtues must of themselves hate sin and wickedness. (LT 59)

Perhaps we can entertain with St Augustine and John Calvin the possibility that the Father of Jesus might restrict his atoning love to the elect; but Julian's bold maternal identification of Christ excludes such limitation. Mothers love all their children, in all times and all situations. They are devoted in their care, ferocious in their protection. The metaphor highlights the universality, inclusivity, unconditionality, as well as tenderness and passion, of the divine love.

> The moders service is nerest, rediest, and sekerest: nerest, for it is most of kind: rediest, for it is most of love; and sekerest, for it is most of trewth. This office ne might nor coulde never none done to the full but he alone. (LT 61)

The love of Jesus for humanity is put on full display in his passion and death. On the cross our Lord yearns and thirsts for the salvation of every human being (LT 31). "If I might suffer more," he tells Julian, "I wolde suffer more" (LT 22). One can hardly imagine a stronger affirmation of the absolute love of God. How much does a mother love her children? God loves his infinitely more. He is willing to experience any and every suffering in order to accomplish the deification of his children.

Divine love excludes wrath and condemnation

In a book full of theological surprises, perhaps the most startling is Julian's statement that in her shewings she does not see any sign of the divine wrath. Its absence surprises her (and the reader), for she has been taught by Holy Church that "we be sinners and do many evilles that we oughte to leve, and leve many good dedes undone that we oughte to do, wherfore we deserve paine, blame, and wrath" (LT 46). Yet despite the undeniable actuality of human wickedness, at no point does God blame his people for their sins. God's anger is absent, she tells us, (a) because anger cannot exist within the God who is absolute goodness and unconditional love, and (b) because the oneing between God and human beings in Jesus Christ is inalienable:

> And despite all this, I saw truly that our Lord was never angry, and never will be. Because he is God, he is good, he is truth, he is love, he is peace; and his power, his wisdom, his charity and his unity do not allow him to be angry. For I saw truly that it is against the property of his power to be angry, and against the property of his wisdom and against the property of his goodness. For it is that goodness which cannot be angry, for God is nothing but goodness. And between God and our soul there is neither wrath nor forgiveness in his sight. For our soul is so wholly united to God, through his own goodness, that between God and our soul nothing can interpose. (LT 46)

The first reason is easily grasped. If God genuinely and always wills the good and wellness of those whom God has freely created in his goodness, then he will never act in ways that might irreparably harm them. Whatever justice might mean, therefore, it cannot mean anything less than the realization of their good. She does not see wrath or retributive punishment in God because it has no place in the One who is Love. This apprehension of divinity leads Julian to the conclusion that God does not *literally* forgive:

> For it was a great marvel, constantly shown to the soul in all the revelations, and the soul was contemplating with great diligence that our Lord God cannot in his own judgment forgive, because he cannot be angry—that would be impossible. For this was revealed, that our life is all founded and rooted in love, and without love we cannot live. And therefore to the soul which by God's special grace sees so much of his great and wonderful goodness as that we are endlessly united to him in love, it is the most impossible thing which could be that God might be angry, for anger and friendship are two contraries; for he dispels and destroys our wrath and makes us meek and mild—we must necessarily believe that he is always one in love, meek and mild, which is contrary to wrath. For I saw most truly that where our Lord appears, peace is received and wrath has no place; for I saw no kind of wrath in God, neither briefly nor for long. For truly, as I see it, if God could be angry for any time, we should neither have life nor place nor being; for as truly as we have our being from the endless goodness, just as truly we have our preservation in the endless power of God and in his endless wisdom and in his endless goodness. For though we may feel in ourselves anger, contention and strife, still we are all mercifully enclosed in God's mildness and in his meekness, in his benignity and in his accessibility. (LT 49)

God cannot forgive because God does not get angry with the sins of humanity. They do not make a difference to him. God does not change his mind about us. He does not move from a state of disapproval to approval, from condemnation to acceptance. Or as Fr Brendan Pelphrey puts it: "Forgiveness does not describe our relationship to God, because forgiveness implies a change from displeasure."[5] God simply loves—totally, passionately, unconditionally, redemptively. This leads Julian to the conclusion that our sins cannot disrupt our friendship with God, at least not from God's side. Consider the parable of the prodigal son. When the son returns home, the father runs out to greet him, cuts short the prodigal's confession, and orders the making of a feast. He speaks no words of absolution. There is only celebration. As Turner observes: "He offers no forgiveness after the event because he does not need to; the forgiveness was always there before the event of the son's betrayal, because forgiveness was in the very nature of his fatherhood."[6] Consider the ramifications for our understanding of the sacrament of penance: we make our confession not to fulfill a condition for reconciliation with God but to celebrate the forgiveness that God's love eternally is. "In Christ," as Pelphrey remarks, "we do not encounter a Judge who graciously accepts out contrition, and magnanimously 'forgives' us. Instead, we discover that he has always been with us, in 'homely' love."[7]

The second reason Julian offers for the absence of divine wrath is a bit more complex. That God continues to conserve and sustain us in existence witnesses to his abiding love: "For sothly, as to my sight, if God might be wroth a touch, we shuld neither have life, ne sted [locality], ne being" (LT 49). But Julian also seems to be making a stronger claim: because of our abiding union with our Creator, not only can we not undo our existence, but we cannot extinguish our desire for God as our supreme good and eschatological end. She posits in every human being (or at least in every human being "that shalle be saved") a bestial will and a godly will. The godly will, Julian tells us, has "never assented to sinne, nor

---

[5] Brendan Pelphrey, *Lo, How I Love Thee! Divine Love in Julian of Norwich* (2013), p. 151.
[6] Turner, p. 127.
[7] Pelphrey, p. 408.

never shalle" (LT 37). Fallen humanity is so immersed in the sensual world that it has lost sight of its fundamental orientation to God, yet it remains deep within each of us. "This godly will," comments Denys Turner, "is the level of true desire that is indeed there already in us."[8] Neither original sin nor our actual sins has obliterated it. No matter how mortal our transgression, it is never quite mortal (or as Miracle Max explained to Inigo Montoya: "There's a big difference between mostly dead and all dead"). Turner continues: "There is nothing that we have to get ourselves to do except allow ourselves to be drawn by grace to see that we love God anyway, for loving God comes with our being created by God's love for us. It is only sin that prevents us from seeing this and causes us to misrelate to our selves and our truest loves."[9] The Christian life is a seeking for that which we already possess and need to repossess. Julian then makes the following astounding claim:

> For before he made us he loved us, and when we were made we loved him; and this is made only of the natural substantial goodness of the Holy Spirit, mighty by reason of the might of the Father, wise in mind of the wisdom of the Son. And so is man's soul made by God, and in the same moment joined to God. . . . In this endless love man's soul is kept whole, as all the matter of the revelation means and shows. In this endless love we are led and protected by God, and we never shall be lost. (LT 53)

"We shall never be lost"—to whom is the promise spoken? to Julian and her readers, to the baptized, the elect, all mankind? In our determination to conform Julian to doctrinal orthodoxy, we hasten to reframe the promise into the subjunctive mood. Hidden within the promise there must be an *if*, we think, followed by stipulated

---

[8] Turner, p. 170.
[9] Ibid., 170-171.

conditions. Yet the shewings argue against the addition of the *if.* Christ tells her quite directly: he will keep us close to him, will protect us, will prevent us from getting lost. Our grasp of our Mother's hand is enclosed within the safety of her grasp. <u>We may let go, but she will never let go</u>. Our ultimate desire for wholeness in Christ abides, and by this desire we are clasped by Christ. How then can we entertain an everlasting alienation of humanity from God? How can we entertain the possibility that our Lord will abandon us to interminable torment? Humanity's desire for full and complete union with God (our godly will) remains intact, despite our sin. Will not Love find a way, even after death, even for the obdurately wicked and selfish, to bring to full blaze our yearning for the perfection of salvation?

Sinful Humanity is Eternally Oned to Jesus Christ

That Julian does not see wrath in God confronts Julian with a contradiction. On the one hand, Holy Church teaches her that we are responsible for our actions and that our sinful acts rightly incur guilt and blame. <u>On the other hand, she does not see wrath and judgment in God</u>: "Then was this my merveyle, that I saw oure lorde God shewing to us no more blame that if we were as clene and as holy as angels in heven" (LT 50). And so she cries out to Christ for enlightenment. In response he shares with her the parable of the lord (God) and the servant (Adam) (LT 51-52).

In the parable we learn that by the Incarnation God has united himself to sinful humanity so intimately that the Son is Adam and Adam is the Son. The corporate Son and the corporate Christ are one: "For in alle this, oure good lorde shewed his own son and Adam but one man" (LT 51). When Adam fell into the abyss of darkness and sin, the Son simultaneously fell into the womb of

Mary. Each human being is Adam and Adam is Christ. Our story is his and his ours.

Every human being is joined to Christ in ontological solidarity. Together they are one man, one Adam, one Son. This is the deepest reason why God does not condemn the sinner. To do so would be to condemn Jesus himself. God does not ultimately hold the sinner responsible for his sin and therefore does not reject him. "And thus hath oure good lorde Jhesu taken upon him all oure blame, and therfore oure fader may nor will no more blame assigne to us than to his owne derwurthy son, Jhesu Crist" (LT 51). God does not judge us as human beings judge one another: "For man beholdeth some dedes wele done and some dedes eville, and our lorde beholdeth them not so" (LT 11). We judge each other according to our virtues and vices, our good and bad actions—and always from the perspective of our fallen experience. "But God judges us," Pelphrey explains, "as he sees us, which 'beholding' . . . is always to see us as oned to him."[10] By the Spirit the Lord teaches us to replace our judgments with his judgments, to see ourselves through the eyes of divine mercy rather than wrath.

> In the servant is comprehended the second person of the Trinity, and in the servant is comprehended Adam, that is to say all men. And therefore when I say 'the Son', that means the divinity which is equal to the Father, and when I say 'the servant', that means Christ's humanity, which is the true Adam. By the closeness of the servant is understood Son, and by his standing to the left is understood Adam. The lord is God the Father, the servant is the son, Jesus Christ, the Holy Spirit is the equal love which is in them both. When Adam fell, God's Son fell; because of the true union which was made in heaven, God's Son could not be separated from Adam, for by Adam I understand all mankind. Adam fell from life to death, into the valley of this wretched world, and

---

[10] Pelphrey, p. 409.

after that into hell. God's Son fell with Adam, into the valley of the womb of the maiden who was the fairest daughter of Adam, and that was to excuse Adam from blame in heaven and on earth; and powerfully he brought him out of hell. (LT 51)

Julian's visions lead her into a understanding of two judgments: the judgment of the Church and the judgment of God. Both are needful, she believes:

> The first judgment, which is from God's justice, is from his own great endless love, and that is that fair, sweet judgment which was shown in all the fair revelation in which I saw him assign to us no kind of blame. And though this was sweet and delectable, I could not be fully comforted only by contemplating it, and that was because of the judgment of Holy Church, which I had understood before, and which was continually in my sight. And therefore it seemed to me that by this judgment I must necessarily know myself a sinner. And by the same judgment I understood that sinners sometimes deserve blame and wrath, and I could not see these two in God, and therefore my desire was more than I can or may tell, because of the higher judgment which God himself revealed at the same time, and therefore I had of necessity to accept it. And the lower judgment had previously been taught me in Holy Church, and therefore I could not in any way ignore the lower judgment. This then was my desire, that I might see in God in what way the judgment of Holy Church here on earth is true in his sight, and how it pertains to me to know it truly, whereby they might both be reconciled as might be glory to God and the right way for me. (LT 45)

Julian was never given a solution to the riddle of the two judgments, except for the parable itself.

Julian's long contemplation upon her revelations brought to her a deep understanding of time, eternity, and our oneing in Jesus Christ. She takes the Church's teaching on the timelessness of God with decisive seriousness. God does not abide in time but is the transcendent Creator of time. He sees all temporal events simultaneously, with important consequences for both the Incarnation and the salvation of humanity. And so, Julian understands humanity's oneing with God as having occurred in the womb of the Virgin Mary: "For in that same time that God knit him to oure body in the maidens wombe, he toke oure sensual soule. In which taking—he us all having beclosed in him—he oned it to oure substance, in which oning he was perfit man" (LT 57). Pelphrey summarizes:

> Because there is no time for God, God sees us as already dwelling within him, and Jesus living within us. We are already in substantial union with him, and have always been from the beginning of creation. . . . From God's perspective there is no time (God having created time for our lives), and therefore the whole question of temporal "fall" and forgiveness is limited to an earthly point of view. For God, our salvation occurs at the same "time" as our own creation: "When Adam fell, God's son fell" (into the womb of Mary). There is, therefore, no "time" in which we are unredeemed, although in our own experience the process of redemption and sanctification seems to be a slow one. Christ lives in our souls already, and from God's point of view always has.[11]

---

[11] Ibid., 82-83. In his unpublished paper "Cosmic Science: Julian's Vision of Space, Time and the Resurrection in Pastoral Care" (2017), Pelphrey writes: "We may ask, for example: How long after the Fall of Adam, did God provide for the salvation of mankind in Jesus Christ? Julian answers, No time; for 'when Adam fell, God's Son fell' into the womb of the Mother of God. A different question is, 'when will I die?' Julian's answer is, At the same time that Christ died, which is the same time Adam died, although we will have suffered death at different times. Therefore, my Grandmother died at the same time that I will die, although I am still alive. In the traditional triple-immersion baptism of the ancient Church, the catechumen is seen to die with Christ and is then raised with Christ—although in the context of time, the Resurrection happened two thousand years ago, and the general resurrection has not happened yet. This language is not simply metaphorical (it is not as though we died in Christ), but quite real from the point of view of Julian's Christological science. . . . Since the work of God is without-

Julian then elaborates this ontological oneing of Christ and humanity into a sublime vision of the eschaton:

> Therefore this meaning was shown for understanding of Christ's humanity. For all mankind which will be saved by the sweet Incarnation and the Passion of Christ, all is Christ's humanity, for he is the head, and we are his members, to which members the day and the time are unknown when every passing woe and sorrow will have an end, and everlasting joy and bliss will be fulfilled, which day and time all the company of heaven longs and desires to see. And all who are under heaven and will come there, their way is by longing and desiring, which desiring and longing was shown in the servant standing before the lord, or, otherwise, in the Son standing before the Father in Adam's tunic. For the longing and desire of all mankind which will be saved appeared in Jesus, for Jesus is in all who will be saved, and all who will be saved are in Jesus, and all is of the love of God, with obedience, meekness and patience and the virtues which befit us. (LT 51)

By and in the eternal Son's embodiment as the man Jesus of Nazareth, every human being has already been brought into the life and glory of the Holy Trinity. "For Jhesu is all that shall be saved, and all that shall be saved is Jhesu."

I do not doubt that competent theologians can offer various solutions. qualifications, and caveats to bring Julian into conformity with the traditional doctrine of perdition, yet not into full conformity, I would think. Julian clearly understands Christ's revelations to her as rejection of eternal retribution, which is an essential component of the Latin doctrine. As she repeatedly asserts, there is no wrath in God. God does not condemn his children: to do

---

time, Julian is able to say that salvation is inherent in the original act of creation. It was always God's plan (or rather, there is no 'always' but simply 'now') for humanity to share the humanity of Christ. It is not that God became human like us, but that our humanity is God's; it was created for Christ and is fulfilled in Christ. Christ is all, in all" (pp. 9-10, 11).

so would be to condemn his Son and thus sunder the unity of the Holy Trinity.

The Impossible Possibility

"There is a deed the which the blisseful trinite shalle do in the last day," the anchoress prophesies (LT 32). What this deed will be and when it will occur is unknown to all creatures. It is, as we say, a mystery. All we need to know is this:

> This is the great deed ordained by our Lord God from without beginning, treasured and hidden in his blessed breast, known only to himself, through which deed he will make all things well. For just as the blessed Trinity created all things from nothing, just so will the same blessed Trinity make everything well which is not well. (LT 32)

Julian does not know how to rationally harmonize her shewings with the teaching of the Church on hell: "And stonding alle this, methought it was unpossible that alle maner of thing shuld be wele, as oure lorde shewde in this time" (LT 32). In response Christ reiterates his promise: "That that is unpossible to the is not unpossible to me. I shalle save my worde in alle thing, and I shalle make althing wele." Watson and Jenkins interpret Christ's words as promising "the reconciliation of orthodox teaching on damnation with God's message of love to Julian."[12] Still we wonder. How well is well? Is hell well, can it be well? Turner construes the pledge as eschatological manifestation of the behoveliness of perdition. Just as we will be given to see the befittingness of evil within the economy of salvation, so we will come to understand the inconceivable befittingness of damnation and everlasting loss and suffering. The conflict between magisterial teaching on hell and the revelation to Julian of God's infinite love is therefore only apparent. We cannot

---

[12] Watson and Jenkins, p. 224.

see the reconciliation now because we grasp only a fragment of the story:

> The Church teaches that many are damned. Her shewings reveal to her a God whose love is so universal and inclusive as to be beyond the need even to forgive sins, never mind any desire to punish for them. But that is the point: the tension between her two sources is troublingly present in a way that it would not be were Julian to have seriously challenged the Church's teaching in a universalist manner. Moreover, what does seem to be clear is that her frequently repeated references to "all that shalle be saved," though theoretically open to the possibility that every soul is to be saved, is more naturally read against the background of her unambiguous declarations that many are not. It is therefore true that, as Watson and Jenkins say, Julian is caused to be anxious by the difficulty of reconciling the universal love of God with the fact that some place themselves by their own choices outside that love. But when she tells God of this anxiety Julian admits that "as to this, I had no other answere in shewing of oure lorde but this: 'that that is unpossible to the[e] is not unpossible to me. I shalle save my worde in alle thing, and I shalle make althing wele.'" It does not seem right to conclude that the Lord's answer "I shalle make althing wele" entails that, contrary to the teaching of the Church, God will pull off the "impossibility" of saving everyone. It seems a more natural reading of what Julian says that the impossibility of which the Lord speaks refers to her problem of seeing how the damnation of many can be made consistent with God's making "althing wele," that what seems impossible to her is not an impossibility to God.[13]

I am unconvinced. If Turner's reading is correct, then the shewings seem all too inconsequential, even trivial and banal. Julian's problem with hell would merely be the consequence of the lack of scholastic schooling. All the Lord needed to do was quote a passage on eternal damnation from St Bonaventure's *Breviloquim*, and all

---

[13] Turner, pp. 106-107.

would have been made clear. As it is, the traditional teaching is preserved at the cost of being made even more intolerable. Do not be anxious. One day you too will see that hell is well.

Surely, though, "All shall be well" and "I shall make all things well" intimate something far more glorious, more wondrous and astonishing than the behoveliness of eternal damnation. The divine promise, after all, portends an eschatological act, an unexpected "gret deed" that redeems, heals, and makes whole. Hence I propose an alternative reading, along the lines of the illumination given to St Isaac the Syrian:

> I am of the opinion, that He is going to manifest some wonderful outcome, a matter of immense and ineffable compassion on the part of the glorious Creator, with respect to the ordering of this difficult matter of Gehenna's torment: out of it the wealth of His love and power and wisdom will become known all the more—and so will the insistent might of the waves of His goodness.[14]

How is it possible that the God of love might save the incorrigibly impenitent? It all seems quite impossible. Like Julian, we cannot see beyond the limits of human freedom and the constraints of dogma. If God has brought into being a world in which human beings may irrevocably reject him, how can we confidently hope and pray for the salvation of all? Yet that which is impossible for man is not impossible for God. The Lord Jesus Christ will return in glory, Thomas Merton assures us, bearing an "eschatological secret":

> I pray much to have a wise heart, and perhaps the re-discovery of Lady Julian of Norwich will help me. I took her book with me on a quiet walk among the cedars. She is a true theologian with greater clarity, depth, and order than St Theresa: she really elaborates, theologically, the content of her revelations. She first experienced, then thought, and

---

[14] Isaac of Nineveh, The Second Part (1995) 39.16

the thoughtful deepening of experience worked it back into her life, deeper and deeper, until her whole life as a recluse at Norwich was simply a matter of getting completely saturated in the light she had received all at once, in the "shewings," when she thought she was about to die.

One of her most telling and central convictions is her orientation to what one might call an eschatological secret, the hidden dynamism which is at work already and by which "all manner of thing shall be well." This "secret," this act which the Lord keeps hidden, is really the full fruit of the Parousia. It is not just that "He comes," but He comes with this secret to reveal, He comes with this final answer to all the world's anguish, this answer which is already decided, but which we cannot discover (and which, since we think we have reasoned it all out anyway) we have stopped trying to discover. Actually, her life was lived in the belief in this "secret," the "great deed" that the Lord will do on the Last Day, not a deed of destruction and revenge, but of mercy and of life, all partial expectations will be exploded and everything will be made right. It is the great deed of "the end," which is still secret, but already fully at work in the world, in spite of all its sorrow, the great deed "ordained by Our Lord from without beginning."

She must indeed believe and accept the fact that there is a hell, yet also at the same time, impossibly one would think, she believes even more firmly that "the word of Christ shall be saved in all things" and "all manner of thing shall be well." This is, for her, the heart of theology: not solving the contradiction, but remaining in the midst of it, in peace, knowing that it is fully solved, but that the solution is secret, and will never be guessed until it is revealed.[15]

Merton has offered a penetrating interpretation of how it was possible for Julian to sincerely affirm the Church's teaching on eternal reprobation and yet expound her shewings with such power and beauty that many readers are left with a puissant hope, nay certainty, that all shall be saved. Julian acknowledges the contrariety

---

[15] Conjectures of a Guilty Bystander (1968), pp. 211-212.

between the Lord's shewings of his absolute love and the magisterial teachings of the Church on repentance and determines to be faithful to both, abandoning premature resolution of the antinomies. In faith and humility, she will wait until the great eschatological deed of the glorified Lord when all will be made known and made well.

In conclusion listen again to the transcendent words of the Anchorite:

> And thus oure good lorde answered to alle the questions and doutes that I might make, sayeng full comfortabely: "I may make alle thing wele, and I can make alle thing welle, and I wille make alle thing wele, and I shalle make alle thing welle. And thou shal se thyselfe that alle maner of thing shall be welle." There he seyth "I may," I understonde for the father; and there he seyth "I can," I understond for the sonne; and there he seyth "I wille," I understonde for the holy gost; and there he seyth "I shalle," I understonde for the unite of the blessed trinite, thre person and on truth. And there he seyth "thou shalt se thyselfe," I understond the oning of alle mankinde that shall be saved into the blissful trinite. (LT 31)

Christ is risen and his love will triumph! Christ is risen and all shall be well! Christ is risen and all is well!

Chapter Sixteen

Did the Fifth Ecumenical Council Condemn Universal Salvation?

When first presented with the universalist hope, many Orthodox and Roman Catholics immediately invoke the authority of the Fifth Ecumenical Council (A.D. 553), citing the famous fifteen anti-Origenist anathemas: "Apokatastasis has been dogmatically defined by the Church as heresy—see canon 1 . . . case closed." Over the past three centuries, however, historians have seriously questioned whether these anathemas were officially promulgated by II Constantinople. The council was convened by the Emperor Justinian for the express purpose of condemning the Three Chapters. Justinian does not mention the Origenist debate in his letter announcing the council nor in his letter that was read to the bishops at the formal opening of the council; nor do the acts of the council, as preserved in the Latin translation (the original Greek text having been lost), cite the fifteen anathemas. Hence when church historian Norman P. Tanner edited his collection of the *Decrees of the Ecumenical Councils* in 1990, he did not include the anti-Origenist denunciations, offering the following explanation: "Our edition does not include the text of the anathemas against Origen since recent studies have shown that these anathemas cannot be attributed to this council."[1]

But the Fifth Ecumenical Council did condemn Origen, right? No and yes. *No*, in that it did not directly anathematize him. As St Gregory the Great would later observe, the general synod only anathematized one person—Theodore of Mopsuestia (*Ep.* 51). *Yes,*

---

[1] Norman P. Tanner, *Decrees of the Ecumenical Councils* (1990), I:106.

in that Origen is named alongside the heretics denounced in canon 11:

> If anyone does not anathematize Arius, Eunomius, Macedonius, Apollinarius, Nestorius, Eutyches and Origen, as well as their heretical books, and also all other heretics who have already been condemned and anathematized by the holy, catholic and apostolic church and by the four holy synods which have already been mentioned, and also all those who have thought or now think in the same way as the aforesaid heretics and who persist in their error even to death: let him be anathema.

The canon does not specify which of Origen's teachings are condemned, nor do the acts record any discussion of them by the council fathers. Origen is simply included among the anathematized. This is where things get tricky. The others in the list were denounced, directly or indirectly, by previous ecumenical councils and their heresies were well known; but those councils had never condemned Origen. Which teachings of Origen, therefore, did the bishops of the Fifth Council believe to be antithetical to the apostolic faith and to which synod or synods were they appealing? We do not know—neither the canons nor the acts of the council tell us. This point needs to be stressed. We may not assume that because the council fathers condemned Origen by name, they specifically intended to condemn his teaching on apokatastasis. The establishment of conciliar dogma requires more than guesswork and conjectural inference. F. Nutcombe Oxenham, 19th century Roman Catholic theologian and historian, succinctly states the historical problem and interpretive task:

> Let me say to any who may consider it an important matter to be assured whether Origen was, or was not condemned, by some ancient Synod, two things—(1) That if it could be ever so conclusively proved

that "Origen was condemned" by the Fifth Council, this would afford no evidence whatever that he was condemned *on account of* his doctrine of restitution, since he held a great many other doctrines much more open to blame than this one. And then (2) Supposing Origen's doctrine of restitution had been "by itself condemned," this would be no condemnation of the doctrine of restitution, as now held e.g. by Mr. Jukes or by Dr Farrar [two 19th century exponents of universal salvation]; since their two doctrines of restitution are in many important points essentially different.[2]

But Origen's teachings were condemned by earlier local synods, right? Yes, the most noteworthy being the Synod of Alexandria (A.D. 399 or 400), convened by Patriarch Theophilus. Theophilus identifies the anathematized teachings of Origen in his synodical epistle, i.e., official account of the proceedings. He states that the synod condemned eight teachings supposedly found in *On First Principles*, but Origen's teaching on the restoration of all human beings to God is *not* named! The Synod of Alexandria was quickly followed by councils held in Jerusalem and Cyprus under the leadership of St Epiphanius, each subscribing to Theophilus's synodal. Once again, final restoration is not named. Nor do Origen's principal critics include the doctrine among his alleged errors. As Thomas Allin remarks: "Jerome, Theophilus, and Epiphanius literally scrape together every possible charge against Origen, but *never allude to his teaching of the larger hope as heretical.*"[3]

---

[2] F. Nutombe Oxenham, *What is the Truth as to Everlasting Punishment?* (1882), p. 35. Though dated, this book is essential reading. The author discusses the principal first millennium sources for our knowledge of the Fifth Ecumenical Council with regards to its condemnation of Origen and apokatastasis. For an accessible 19th century account of the affair, see F. W. Farrar, *Mercy and Judgment* (1882), chap. 12; see especially Farrar's discussion of the patristic period: chaps. 9-12.
[3] Thomas Allin, *Christ Triumphant* (1905), p. 178.

This may come as a surprise, until we recall that in the fourth and fifth centuries the great disciple of Origen, St Gregory of Nyssa, was never censured for his universalist convictions. Nor was Diodore of Tarsus. I mention Diodore because he was the founder of the Antiochian school of biblical interpretation and an opponent of Origen's allegorical exegesis. Not all confessors of final reconciliation were followers of Origen! Diodore was present with Gregory at the First Council of Constantinople (A.D. 381), chaired by the hopeful universalist St Gregory of Nazianzus. Immediately following the council Gregory Nyssen and Diodore were appointed by Emperor Theodosius as guardians of the Nicene faith. Fifty years earlier at the Council of Nicaea (A.D. 325), Eusebius of Caesarea and Marcellus of Ancyra, both universalists, played important roles in the ecumenical denunciation of Arianism. Christians in the early centuries may have disagreed with each other regarding everlasting damnation; but at no point did this disagreement rise to the level requiring dogmatic definition or excommunication. Universalist bishops gathered in local and general synods right alongside their infernalist brothers, and neither anathematized the other.

Nor should we think that the universalists were always in the minority. In the *Shorter Rules of St Basil*, for example, we find a passage that asserts that "many [*hoi polloi tōn anthrōpōn*: most?] human beings, by disregarding such weighty and solemn words and declarations of the Lord, award to themselves an end of [eternal] punishment in order that they may sin with greater bravado" (*SR* 267). The statement suggests that in the fourth century the universalist position enjoyed significant popularity among the faithful in Asia Minor, having been taught by universalist theologians such as St Gregory Thaumaturgus, St Pamphilius, Methodius of Olympus (a vocal critic of Origen), Eusebius of Caesarea, Marcellus of Ancyra, Diodore of Tarsus, St Macrina the Younger, St Gregory of Nyssa, and St Gregory the Theologian. The same was no doubt the case in the province of Alexandria, home of universalists such as Clement of Alexandria, Origen, Theognotus, Pierius, St Dionysius of Alexandria, Didymus the Blind, St Anthony the Great (and perhaps even St Athanasius). Even as late as A.D. 420, St Augustine numbers the opponents of eternal perdition in the Latin West as "indeed very many [*immo quam plurimi*: vast majority?]" (*Enchiridion* XXIX.112). John Wesley Hanson summarizes the early Church's tolerance—and in some quarters, we would need to say *acceptance*—of the greater hope:

> The state of opinion on the subject of universal salvation is shown by the fact that through Ignatius, Irenaeus, Hippolytus and others wrote against the prevalent heresies of their times, Universalism is never named among them. Some of the alleged errors of Origen were condemned, but his doctrine of universal salvation, never.[1]
>
> Now let the reader recapitulate: (i) Origen during his life-time was never opposed for his Universalism; (2) after his death Methodius, about A. D. 300, attacked his views of the resurrection, creation and pre-existence, but said not a word against his Universalism; (3) ten years later Pamphilus and Eusebius (A. D. 310) defended him against nine charges that had been brought against his views, but his Universalism was not among them; (4) in 330 Marcellus of Ancyra, a Universalist, opposed him for his views of the Trinity, and (5) Eustathius for his teachings concerning the Witch of Endor, but limited their arraignment to those items; (6) in 376 Epiphanius assailed his heresies, but he did not name Universalism as among them, and in 394 he condemned Origen's doctrine of the salvation of the Devil, but not of all mankind;

---

[1] John Wesley Hanson, *Universalism, the Prevailing Doctrine of the Christian Church During Its First Five Hundred Years* (1899), p. 150. As the title suggests, Hanson firmly believed that the larger hope was widely affirmed, and prayed, by Christians during the first five centuries of the Church. It was, as he states, "the prevailing doctrine." This is a strong claim—perhaps too strong a claim. Even so, *Universalism* merits careful reading; but be sure to supplement, and correct, Hanson's scholarship in light of the published works of Ilaria Ramelli (cited below).

Destined for Joy

(7) in 399 and 401, his views of Christ's death to save the Devil were attacked by Epiphanius, Jerome and Theophilus, and his advocacy of the subordination of Christ to God was condemned, but not his teachings of man's universal salvation; and (8) it was not till 544 and again in 553 that his enemies formulated attacks on that doctrine...With the exception of Augustine, the doctrine which had been constantly advocated, often by the most eminent, did not evoke a frown of opposition from any eminent scholar or saint. . . .

There is no evidence whatever to show that it was not entirely allowable for five hundred years after Christ, to entertain the belief in universal salvation. Besides, the Council of Nice, A. D. 325, had, as an active member, Eusebius, Origen's apologist, a pronounced Universalist; the Council of Constantinople, A. D. 381, had as active members the two Gregories, Nazianzus and Nyssa, the latter as outspoken a Universalist as Origen himself. The Council of Ephesus, A. D. 431, declared that Gregory Nyssen's writings were the great bulwark against heresy. The fact that the doctrine was and had been for centuries prevalent, if not the prevailing sentiment, demonstrates that it must have been regarded as a Christian doctrine by the members of these great councils, or they would have fulminated against it.[5]

Origen was a controversial figure. His teachings were often misunderstood and misrepresented, yet many who objected to Origen's teachings honored him for his sanctity and faithfulness under persecution. Most importantly for our purposes, Origen was not the inventor of apokatastasis, nor was he criticized for his doctrine of restitution. The greater hope indwelt the Christian heart long before the Adamantine gave it systematic expression. But all of this changed in the sixth century. Our story jumps to A.D. 543, almost 300 years after Origen's death.

---

[5] Ibid., pp. 289-290.

Did the Fifth Ecumenical Council Condemn Universal Salvation?

Justinian, Origen, and the 543 Synod

According to the 6th century historian Liberatus, the papal legate Pelagius journeyed to Egypt and Palestine in the early 540s. While in Jerusalem he met anti-Origenist monks who described to him the heresies of the Origenist monks and the conflicts they were generating, presented him an indictment (*libellus*) against the teachings of Origen, and prevailed upon him to present their indictment to the emperor. Upon his return to Constantinople, he did precisely that. In A.D. 543 Justinian sent an edict (unfortunately not translated into English) to St Menas, Patriarch of Constantinople, commanding him to convene the home synod (*synodus endemousa*) and condemn the troublesome Alexandrian. He appended extracts from Origen's *On First Principles* (several of which may be spurious) and nine anathemas. Justinian also sent the edict and anathemas to Pope Vigilius and the patriarchs of Alexandria, Antioch, and Jerusalem—each acknowledging their compliance. No more is heard about the nine anathemas until the 13th century. Nikephoros Kallistos Xanthopoulos quotes them in his *Ecclesiastical History*, copied, he says, from a commentary (author and date unknown), and identifies them as official canons of the Fifth Ecumenical Council![6] Historians now believe this identification to be mistaken, but the fact that one or more of the sources Nikephoros had consulted make this error testifies to the confusion in the manuscript tradition. The reprobations read as follows:

> 1. If anyone says or holds that the souls of human beings pre-exist, as previously minds and holy powers, but that they reached satiety with

---

[6] Oxenham, p. 81. Following the lead of Nikephoros, more than a few pre-20th century historians (including E. B. Pusey) attributed the nine anathemas to Constantinople II, but recent scholarship supports their attribution to Justinian and the 543 Synod of Constantinople. See Price, II:271-272.

divine contemplation and turned to what is worse and for this reason grew old in the love of God and are therefore called souls, and were made to descend into bodies as a punishment, let him be anathema.

2. If anyone says or holds that the Lord's soul pre-existed and came into being united to God the word before the incarnation and birth from a virgin, let him be anathema.

3. If anyone holds or says that the body of our Lord Jesus Christ was first formed in the womb of the holy Virgin and that afterwards both God the word and the soul, being pre-existent, were united to it, let him be anathema.

4. If anyone says or holds that the Word of God became like all the heavenly orders, becoming cherubim for the cherubim, seraphim for the seraphim, and becoming (in a word) like all the powers above, let him be anathema.

5. If anyone says or holds that at the resurrection the bodies of human beings will be raised spherical and does not profess that we shall be raised upright, let him be anathema.

6. If anyone says or holds that heaven, sun, moon, stars, and the waters above the heavens are ensouled and rational powers, let him be anathema.

7. If anyone says or holds that in the age to come Christ the Master will be crucified on behalf of demons as well as on behalf of human beings, let him be anathema.

8. If anyone says or holds that God's power is finite and that he created [only] what he could grasp and comprehend, or that creation is coeternal with God, let him be anathema.

9. If anyone says or holds that the punishment of demons and impious human beings is temporary and that it will have an end at some time,

and that there will be a restoration of demons and impious human beings, let him be anathema.[7]

Because of Justinian's edict, the above anathemas are read as condemning Origen (which was clearly the Emperor's intent), yet Origen's name is not mentioned in the anathemas themselves. This in itself is suggestive or at least raises a question. Unfortunately, the 543 synodical acts are nonextant, so we are left only with our conjectures. Disentangling the authentic teachings of Origen from the sixth century Origenist doctrines denounced in the anathemas is no easy task. Origen most certainly, for example, did not teach that at the *eschaton* Christ will be crucified anew for demons and humanity or that human beings will be raised in spherical shape or that God's power is finite. But that is the crucial contextual point. The anathemas cannot be taken as condemnation of the positions of the *real* Origen (despite Justinian's irresponsible attempt to locate the heresies in *On First Principles*) but only of the 6th century "Origenist Origen." By this time Origenism (at least in some of its variants) had morphed into an exotic religious-metaphysical project Origen would have neither recognized nor approved. Regardless Justinian was determined to discredit the Adamantine. Most importantly, the nine anathemas do not possess dogmatic authority: they represent only the views of the emperor. Richard Price explains: "As regards the canons of 543, they were issued as an imperial decree, and sent to the patriarchs (including the patriarch of Constantinople) not for their confirmation but for their circulation. Their authority was imperial rather than synodal."[8] An

---

[7] Richard Price, *The Acts of the Council of Constantinople of 553* (2012), II:281. Also see Alois Grillmeier's discussion of Justinian's 543 edict against Origen in *Christ in Christian Tradition*, II/2:389-402.

[8] Richard Price, email message to Alvin Kimel, 9 September 2020. The great Church historian Karl Joseph von Hefele judiciously sidesteps the question of dogmatic authority of imperial pronouncements: "The question of ecclesiastical

imperial doctrinal pronouncement does not possess infallible authority in the Church catholic. Emperors and kings cannot define dogma.

For our purposes, it is anathema 9 that interests us: "If anyone says or holds that the punishment of demons and impious human beings is temporary and that it will have an end at some time, and that there will be a restoration of demons and impious human beings, let him be anathema." If abstracted from the nine canons as a whole and its 6th century context, it would seem to condemn every form of apokatastasis. Perhaps Justinian intended precisely that. Perhaps the synodical bishops joined in that intention, though we have no record of their discussions. Perhaps the patriarchs agreed, but history has not documented anything more than their subscription to the edict. Let us ask the decisive clarifying question: **Did either Justinian or the synodical bishops believe they were condemning the universalist views of St Gregory of Nyssa?** Bring forth the evidence—there is none. Anathema 9 was prompted not by the abstract question of eternal damnation nor by dispassionate scholarly study of the theology of Origen but by the exotic formulations of the restoration of souls to their *original* disembodied state then being advanced by troublesome monks in Palestine. Anathema 9, in other words, is *intrinsically* linked to the condemnation of the preexistence of souls in anathema 1, which in turn is grounded in the metaphysics of sixth century Origenism.

---

authority, as to whether the Emperor was entitled or not to issue an edict of this kind, belongs to another department. It seems to me that we have here before us one of those many and great, even if well-meant, Byzantine encroachments, which does not disappear even when we assume that the Emperor acted in agreement with Mennas and Pelagius" (*History of the Councils of the Church*, IV:240). In any case, Hefele confidently opines that the 543 synod did not formally approve Justinian's nine anathemas but instead issued the fifteen anti-Origenist canons (IV:221-228).

Oxenham reminds us that this condemnation is *"the only decree purporting to come from any ancient council, general or local, in which the doctrine 'that the punishment of the wicked will come to an end,' is even mentioned."*[9] This should caution us about universalizing its scope and application. Historical context constrains us. The doctrinal authority of anathema nine, moreover, is compromised by Justinian's clear intent to impose everlasting damnation on Church and empire for the sake of social order, political and ecclesial unity, and the favor of God.[10] The fear that apokatastasis will encourage immorality and civil disorder enjoys a long history. The threat of everlasting suffering can be a powerful inducement to obedience to moral norms, Church dogmas, and the laws of the imperium. But social utility is not a theological argument. God's self-revelation in Christ as absolute Love will always subvert imperial theology and challenge the violence and power structures of the state. Jesus is Lord, not Caesar. For this reason alone, emperors should not dictate doctrine. When they succeed in doing so, the Church must be free to go back and reassess.

---

[9] Oxenham, p. 117. It must also be observed that given that the synodical acts are not extant, we do not know with certainty that the bishops formally confirmed the nine anathemas, though it's reasonable to assume they bowed to the wishes of the Emperor. I am unaware of any independent historical sources that document their confirmation—hence the willingness of so many pre-20th century historians to deny that they did.

[10] Regarding Justinian's understanding of the role of the emperor in promoting an Orthodox empire, see Price, I:8-41. Price comments: "The condemnation of Origen is evidence of an increasing narrowness of outlook, and is an indelible blot on the ecclesiastical policy of Justinian" (II:280). Cf. Istvan Perczel, "Clandestine Heresy and Politics in Sixth-Century Constantinople," in *New Themes, New Styles in the Eastern Mediterranean* (2017): "In the years between 535 and 553, Justinian adopted a new conception of the orthodox Christian empire—apparently he tried to transform it to a land only inhabited by orthodox Christians and to eliminate all dissenting groups or religious formations from the folds of the empire" (p. 140).

But why blame Origen for teachings he never taught? Surely Justinian and his imperial theologians must have recognized the difference between the beliefs of Origen and the heretical beliefs of Palestinian Origenism. It appears they did not. Panayiotis Tzamalikos is scathingly blunt in his assessment of the depth of ignorance among the anti-Origenists regarding the authentic theology of Origen:

> Justinian had no idea of who Origen was, or what he had taught. His advisors, abbot Gelasius and his band, had only an oblique knowledge of Origen's doctrine, namely, a no longer extant fifth-century book by Antipatrus of Bostra, which was studied by the anti-Origenists of the Great Laura. All possible and impossible interpolations and extrapolations were laid at the door of Origen, probably based on hearsay by monks of the era, who styled themselves 'Origenists'.[11]

St Antipatrus (or Antipater) lived in the mid-fifth century and wrote a lengthy refutation of the *Apology for Origen* by St Pamphilus of Caesarea. His book was highly regarded by the fifth and sixth century opponents of Origen. After Gelasius of Isauria became abbot of the Great Laura of Mar Saba monastery in A.D. 537, he ordered it to be read to the monks. The supporters of Origen were incensed by what they heard and engaged in vigorous, and apparently disruptive, disputation. They were expelled from Great Laura and relocated to New Laura, joining there Nonnus and Leontius of Byzantium. Tzamalikos describes Antipatrus's monograph as the "black book" upon which the anti-Origenists relied for their attacks upon Origen:

---

[11] Panayiotis Tzamalikos, *The Real Cassian Revisited: Monastic Life, Greek Paideia, and Origenism in the Sixth Century*, p. 259. The entirety of chap. 6 is necessary and illuminating reading.

Did the Fifth Ecumenical Council Condemn Universal Salvation?

The treatise by Antipatrus of Bostra was the 'black book' used by the anti-Origenist band. For all his hostility, Cyril's testimony allows for the assumption that the Origenist monks were outraged at the reading of that treatise, presumably because this was not only an inimical account, but also an inaccurate and distorting story instilling outrageous interpolations in Origen's theology. Nevertheless, the book was put to ample use, and in c. 540 it was read in the churches of the East as an antidote to the widespread Origenism.[12]

In the early 540s, anti-Origenists read extracts from Antipatrus's book to Patriarch Ephraem of Antioch. Ephraim immediately convened a synod and anathematized the doctrines of Origen. In response the Origenist party, including Nonnus, Domitian, and Theodore Ascidas, pressed Patriarch Peter of Jerusalem to remove Ephraim from the diptychs; but this intervention only succeeded in convincing Peter to ask Gelasius and Sophronius, abbot of the monastery of Theodosius, to compose a *libellus* against Origen, which he in turn signed. The *libellus* was eventually shared with Pelagius, leading to the 543 Edict of Justinian. "It seems, therefore," Tzamalikos concludes,

> that the source of the hearsay about this legendary 'Origenism' was the distortion contrived by Antipatrus of Bostra in the fifth century. This was the guide and companion of the anti-Origenists of the Great Laura in their polemics. Justinian did not mention Antipatrus at all. He was advised by the libellus composed by Gelasius, the head of the Great Laura and Sophronius the Armenian, the head of the monastery of Theodosius the Coenobiarch, at the request of Patriarch Peter, in 542. Whether Antipatrus of Bostra was the sole culprit and source of a caricature of Origenism prevailing during the sixth century is not easy to determine. It is anyway clear that, in the years that followed, this parody produced various fruits: it was all too easy for anyone to style

---

[12] Ibid., p. 179.

anything 'teaching of Origen', drawing on obscure or hardly expected sources.[13]

Tzamalikos conjectures that Antipatrus' refutation is the source for the spurious citations attached to Justinian's letter to Menas. No matter. "Origen" has now become the whipping boy for the ills of the empire. Any stick may be picked up to pummel him:

> The problem of what Origenism meant in the sixth century is a real one. 'Origen' was simply a cloudy catchword used in order to either authorise or besmirch active people of the sixth-century dangerous and volatile world of imperial and ecclesiastical politics the world of all those plots, which made up the complex tangle of personal, political, and ecclesiastical relationships of the times. This is a dark period of palace intrigue, of concocting forgeries, of cooking up devious attributions to authors deemed compromising the imperial hegemony, of whisperings in corridors and shadowy deals.[14]
>
> At all events, it was convenient to attack Origen. In the sixth-century setting hardly anyone was aware of his theology, whereas his name was a symbol used to either praise or stigmatize occasional enemies, rather than a well-perused corpus of writings. Attacking the name of Origen was an alternative for declaring oneself prepared to endorse whatever Justinian set forward as the legitimate Christian doctrine. In other words, an attack on Origen by name was tantamount to declaring one's allegiance to the imperial orthodoxy.[15]

In the world of Justinian, "Origen" no longer denotes the historical Origen: it functions as a cipher, collectively naming those who disturb civil and ecclesial peace with their controversial teachings.

---

[13] Ibid., p. 280.
[14] Ibid., p. 259. "Therefore, there is good reason to sustain that several tenets ascribed to Origen had nothing to do with the Alexandrian's actual teaching. Whether consciously or not (as the case of Anastasius of Sinai shows), false attributions to Origen were the rule rather than the exception" (p. 283).
[15] Ibid., p. 299.

Did the Fifth Ecumenical Council Condemn Universal Salvation?

The Fifth Ecumenical Council and the Anathema Conundrum

The 543 imperial edict did not resolve the Origenist crisis in Palestine, and so in 553 Justinian decided to revisit the matter. And that brings us to the famous fifteen anti-Origenist anathemas, discovered in the late 17th century by Peter Lambeck, librarian of Vienna:

> 1. If anyone advocates the mythical pre-existence of souls and the monstrous restoration that follows from this, let him be anathema.

> 2. If anyone says that the origin of all rational beings was incorporeal and material minds without any number or name, with the result that there was a henad of them all through identity of substance, power and operation and through their union with and knowledge of God the Word, but that they reached satiety with divine contemplation and turned to what is worse, according to what the drive to this in each one corresponded to, and that they took more subtle or denser bodies and were allotted names such that the powers above have different names just as they have different bodies, as a result of which they became and were named some cherubim, some seraphim, and others principalities, powers, dominations, thrones, angels, and whatever heavenly orders there are, let him be anathema.

> 3. If anyone says that the sun, the moon and the stars, belonging themselves to the same henad of rational beings, became what they are through turning to what is worse, let him be anathema.

> 4. If anyone says that the rational beings who grew cold in divine love were bound to our more dense bodies and were named human beings, while those who had reached the acme of evil were bound to cold and dark bodies and are and are called demons and spirits of wickedness, let him be anathema.

5. If anyone says that from the state of the angels and archangels originates that of the soul, and from that of the soul that of demons and human beings, and from that of human beings angels and demons originate again, and that each order of the heavenly powers is constituted either entirely from those below or those above or from both those above and those below, let him be anathema.

6. If anyone says that the genus of demons had a double origin, being compounded both from human souls and from more powerful spirits that descend to this, but that from the whole henad of rational beings one mind alone remained constant in divine love and contemplation, and that it became Christ and king of all rational beings and created the whole of corporeal nature, both heaven and earth, and what is intermediate, and that the universe came into being containing real elements that are older than its own existence, that is, the dry, the liquid, heat and cold, and also the form according to which it was fashioned, and that the all-holy and consubstantial Trinity did not fashion the universe as the cause of its creation but that mind, as they assert, existing before the universe as creator, gave being to the universe itself and made it created, let him be anathema.

7. If anyone says that Christ, described as existing in the form of God, united to God the Word even before all the ages, and as having emptied himself in the last days into what is human, took pity, as they assert, upon the multifarious fall of the beings in the same henad and, wishing to restore them, passed through everything and took on various bodies and received various names, becoming all things to all, among angels an angel, among powers a power, and among the other orders or genera of rational beings took on appropriately the form of each, and then like us partook of flesh and blood and became for human beings a human being, [if anyone says this] and does not profess that God the Word emptied himself and became a human being, let him be anathema.

8. If anyone says that God the Word, consubstantial with God the Father and the Holy Spirit, who was incarnate and became man, one of the holy Trinity, is not truly Christ but only catachrestically, on account of the mind which, as they assert, emptied itself, because it is united to God the Word and is truly called Christ, while the Word is called Christ because of this mind and this mind is called God because of the Word, let him be anathema.

9. If anyone says that it was not the Word of God, incarnate in flesh ensouled by a rational and intelligent soul, who descended into hell and the same ascended back to heaven, but rather the mind they mention, whom impiously they assert to have truly been made Christ through knowledge of the monad, let him be anathema.

10. If anyone says that the Lord's body after the resurrection was ethereal and spherical in form, and that the same will be true of the other bodies after the resurrection, and that, with first the Lord himself shedding his own body and [then] all likewise, the nature of bodies will pass into non-existence, let him be anathema.

11. If anyone says that the coming judgment means the total destruction of bodies and that the end of the story will be an immaterial nature, and that thereafter nothing that is material will exist but only pure mind, let him be anathema.

12. If anyone says that the heavenly powers, all human beings, the devil, and the spirits of wickedness will be united to God the Word in just the same way as the mind they call Christ, which is in the form of God and emptied itself, as they assert, and that the kingdom of Christ will have an end, let him be anathema.

13. If anyone says that there will not be a single difference at all between Christ and other rational beings, neither in substance nor in knowledge nor in power over everything nor in operation, but that all

will be at the right hand of God as Christ beside them will be, as indeed they were also in their mythical pre-existence, let him be anathema.

14. If anyone says that there will be one henad of all rational beings, when the hypostases and numbers are annihilated together with bodies, and that knowledge about rational beings will be accompanied by the destruction of the universes, the shedding of bodies, and the abolition of names, and there will be identity of knowledge as of hypostases, and that in this mythical restoration there will be only pure spirits, as there were in their nonsensical notion of pre-existence, let him be anathema.

15. If anyone says that the mode of life of the minds will be identical to that earlier one when they had not yet descended or fallen, with the result that the beginning is identical to the end and the end is the measure of the beginning, let him be anathema.[16]

Various hypotheses have been advanced to account for these anathemas. In the 17th, 18th and 19th centuries, many historians, including the two Catholic colossi Karl Joseph Hefele and Ignaz von Döllinger and the eminent Protestant scholar Johann K. L. Gieseler, contended that they should be attached to the A.D. 543 Synod of Constantinople. Hefele was insistent that the fifteen anathemas should not be assigned to the Fifth Council. Not only are they not mentioned in the conciliar acts; but Popes Vigilius, Pelagius, and Gregory the Great do not mention them, even though they speak at some length on the decrees of the council. "It is by no means probable," concludes Hefele, "that this Fifth Ecumenical Council occupied itself with Origen in particular, or pronounced against him the fifteen condemnations of which we are speaking."[17] In 1899

---

[16] Price, II:284-286.
[17] Quoted by Oxenham, p. 102; *History of the Councils*, §257. Johann Gieseler too was convinced that the 15 anathemas were to be attributed to the 543 Synod: "and from this σύνοδος ενδημούσα proceeded, without doubt, the fifteen canons

Did the Fifth Ecumenical Council Condemn Universal Salvation?

Franz Diekamp offered an alternative hypothesis which has been embraced by most modern scholars and may now be considered the standard view.[18] In the Spring of 553, in response to an embassy from Palestine, the Emperor Justinian and his theological advisors composed the fifteen anathemas and ordered the patriarch, St Eutychius, to present them to the bishops then present in Constantinople. This meeting would have taken place **before** the great synod formally opened on May 5th. "The opening of the council was delayed by unavailing negotiations with Pope Vigilius," Price wryly remarks: "condemning Origenism was one of the activities that filled the bishops' time."[19] We do not know how long before the council this assembly took place nor who attended. Daniel Hombergen suggests March or April 553 as the most likely time.[20] Alois Grillmeier summarizes the now-standard historical assessment of the fifteen canons:

> Because the condemnation of the Origenists [i.e., the fifteen anathemas] clearly belongs to the Council of 553, but cannot be placed after the opening of it on 5 May 553, an interim solution has to be sought. It consists in the fact that Emperor Justinian instructed the bishops to deal with the question of the Origenists, which, contrary to his expectation, had not been settled by his decree of 543. These bishops had already arrived months before the opening of the Council

---

against Origen." *A Textbook of Church History*, trans. Samuel Davidson (1857), I:478, n. 10.

[18] Franz Diekamp, *Die Origenistische Streitigkeiten In VI. Jh* (1899). (Alas, I do not read German.) It should be noted that the Anglican priest-scholar H. H. Jeaffreson appears to have anticipated Diekamp's thesis by a decade. In his historical appendix to Alfred Gurney's book *Our Catholic Inheritance in the Larger Hope* (1888), Jeaffreson hypothesizes that the 15 anathemas, which scholars of his time attributed either to the 543 synod or the 553 general council, were in fact promulgated by an undocumented home synod convened by Patriarch Eutychius in 552 or early 553 (pp. 73-76).

[19] Price, II:271-272.

[20] Daniel Hombergen, *The Second Origenist Controversy* (2001), p. 307.

which was intended to be devoted to the question of the Three Chapters. This 'synodal action' took place on the level of a *synodus endemousa* and was not considered by the Emperor himself as a session of an ecumenical council.[21]

---

[21] Alois Grillmeier, *Christ in Christian Tradition*, II/2:403-404. For a reading of the Fifth Council that rejects the central theses presented in the present essay, see Georgi Maximov, "Will the Torments of Hades Have an End?" *The Orthodox Word* 56 (January-April 2020): 68-89. Maximov dismisses Diekamp's proposal of a pre-synod:

"Inasmuch as there is no analysis of the teaching of Origen in the acts of the Council that have been preserved, many modern researchers, following Diekamp, assume that the discussion of Origenism took place at the preliminary session of the Council, before its official opening. Basing themselves on this assumption, some have maintained that Origen was condemned, not by the Ecumenical Council, but by some private, 'local' one. Such an opinion is expressed by [A. V.] Kartashev: 'Actually, strictly formally, Origen was not condemned by the Ecumenical Council' [*Vselenskie Sobory*, p. 353]. This opinion is, to put it mildly, extravagant" (p. 76).

Maximov uncritically assumes that Evagrius Scholasticus' account of the Fifth Council can be trusted in all respects. He goes so far as to claim that the council's genuine anathemas against Origenism have been lost to history, despite the fact that the conciliar *acta* makes no mention of them. As far as the famous fifteen, Maximov tells us, their authorship and provenance are anybody's guess: "Evagrius Scholasticus saw the decrees of the Fifth Ecumenical Council concerning Origen and quotes excerpts, and not one of them is contained in the document from the Vienna library" (pp. 78-79). The fifteen anathemas are thus left hanging without historical context. As noted above, many early historians assigned the fifteen to the 543 Synod of Constantinople. Since the publication of Diekamp's *Die origenistischen Streitigkeiten* (1899), most historians have adopted his hypothesis that the fifteen were approved by an unrecorded 553 *synodus endemousa*. Some, like Price and Antoine Guillaumont, are still willing to entertain the possibility that they were approved by the bishops of the Fifth Council, despite the silence of the acts. To my knowledge, though, no respected scholar has suggested that the Fifth Council issued detailed but non-extant anti-Origenist anathemas.

Ironically, Maximov fails to see that his thesis of anathemas now lost to history in fact strengthens the case that apokatastasis was not condemned by Constantinople II, as will become clear in the course of the present essay. Contrary to the testimony of Evagrius (and contrary to the fantasies of Maximov), the council did *not* officially legislate dogmatic canons addressing the specific

Did the Fifth Ecumenical Council Condemn Universal Salvation?

Grillmeier invites us to imagine the situation something like this: Before the opening of the great council, Emperor Justinian summons the bishops then residing in the capital (the *endemountes*) to confirm his condemnation of Origenist theology.[22] The convocation of a patriarchal *endemousa* to address ecclesial and political concerns was already a long-standing practice. Originally, Grillmeier notes, the *endemousa* "had little to do with the episcopal throne, but in contrast more to do with the Emperor, who, depending upon the occasion, could for serious reasons summon together the bishops who were residing right there at the court."[23] Given that the bishops who attended the home synod undoubtedly attended the Fifth Ecumenical Council, the anti-Origenist anathemas were understandably, perhaps inevitably, associated with the latter. As with the synod of 543, we must not rush to identify the endemousal ratification of the imperial anathemas as an ecclesial or dogmatic act. The anathemas were as much political as theological. The emperor hoped to quell the civil unrest in Palestine and restore peace between the monastic communities. Failure to assent to the anathemas would most likely have been viewed by Justinian as treason. Confronted with the command of the emperor, when is assent free and genuine? The spectre of Caesaropapism haunts the proceedings.

In his history of the first-millennium Church, John Anthony McGuckin proposes a bit of palace intrigue to explain how the anathemas so quickly became linked to the 553 Council:

> In the early part of this great synod, when Pope Vigilius had been summoned to the capital but refused to appear at the sessions, a letter

---

teachings of sixth-century Origenism. The acts of the Fifth Ecumenical Council are historically determinative.
[22] Justinian's cover letter may be found in Appendix I of Price's book (II:282-284).
[23] Grillmeier, II/2:5-6, n. 1.

(*homonoia*) seems to have been issued by the emperor's personal cabinet to the assembled bishops denouncing the Isochristoi who were being led astray by Origen. Fifteen objectionable items were drawn up, a list of things to be anathematized. Peculiarly, the *anathemata* are all taken from the works of Evagrius of Pontus. The anathemata did not get themselves attached to the official acts of the council of 553, but to strengthen the legal case against the Origenist "disturbers of the peace" the *anathemata* were quietly added to the synodal acts at a later date and have consequently been received as conciliar records from the end of the sixth century onward, a sleight of hand made possible by those who held the key to the archives.[24]

As one of my seminary professors liked to say, "Interesting, if true." McGuckin's proposal has the merit of reconciling the presumably undoctored Latin version of the acts with the conviction among post-6th century Greeks that the Fifth Council issued detailed canons against Origenism.

Price has recently resurrected the proposal of the 18th century historians Pietro and Girolamo Ballerini that the anathemas were officially promulgated by Constantinople II but not included in the Latin translation of the acts because the controversy was of little interest to the Western Churches.[25] This seems a particularly weak conjecture, given that it was the papal legate who had urged Justinian

---

[24] John Anthony McGuckin, *The Path of Christianity* (2017), p. 615.
[25] See Price's 2017 unpublished lecture "East and West at the Ecumenical Councils." Hefele dismisses the Ballerini hypothesis as arbitrary and lacking evidentiary support (Hefele, IV:296). Cf. Price's earlier judgment:

"There was once a protracted debate over whether the council of 553 issued a series of canons condemning Origenism. The acts contain no such canons and no discussion of Origenism and, since the numbering of the sessions is continuous and corresponds to that cited at the ecumenical council of 680-1, they appear to be complete. Moreover, the letter from Justinian that was read out at the opening of the council (Acts I. 7) makes no reference to the Origenist controversy; nor does the long summary of the work of the council read out at the beginning of the eighth session (Acts VIII. 4)" (*Acts*, II:270).

Did the Fifth Ecumenical Council Condemn Universal Salvation?

to condemn Origenism back in A.D. 543. Did the Latins suddenly lose interest? But most decisively, the conjecture implausibly assumes that the translators would have omitted the fifteen anathemas on their own authority. Price himself acknowledges that the Latin translation was likely composed shortly after the publication of the Greek text. The translators had every reason to be produce an accurate and complete rendering of the *acta*; indeed, it was their solemn obligation to do so. So how is it that no one in the first millennium, either in the East or the West, ever noticed this important discrepancy between the Greek and Latin texts? The simple, most probable, and obvious answer: there was no discrepancy to be noticed! The Fifth Council never formally addressed Origenism nor promulgated any special canons against it. Including Origen's name in its list of heretics was deemed sufficient. Hence there is no need to speculatively posit the incomplete status of the Latin *acta*. Whether Price's hypothesis will prove persuasive to other historians remains to be seen. My money's on Diekamp.

But the absence of the fifteen canons in the Latin version of the acts of Constantinople II raises an intriguing question. When the Latin patriarchate received Constantinople II as a general council of the Church, did it do so in the form of the original Greek text or the Latin translation? It was the Latin version that was read to the bishops of the A.D. 649 Lateran Synod.[26] In the fourth session Pope Martin commanded that the decrees of the five ecumenical councils should be read in order. When the notary came to the decrees of Constantinople II, he read the fourteen canons related to the Three

---

[26] Oxenham, pp. 58-60, 91. Origen, Didymus, and Evagrius are also included in the Lateran Synod's list of heretics (canon 18). As documented below, the mistaken claim that the Fifth Ecumenical Council condemned Didymus and Evagrius can be traced back to the sixth century, despite the fact that neither are named in the authentic canons of the council. Nor does the inclusion of the three in the heresiological list tell us which of their teachings were judged heretical. What is the function of a heresiological list in a synodical decree?

Chapters *and no others*. The fifteen anti-Origenist anathemas were not read—they are not part of the Latin *acta*. Pope and bishops, therefore, heard the condemnation of Origen in canon 11, but they did not hear—and therefore did not receive—the fifteen anathemas. If the Latin Church never received them, and if reception by the entire Church, represented by the five patriarchates, is necessary for the establishment of dogma, how can they be said to possess dogmatic authority for the Church catholic?

Ignatius Green contends (1) that the fifteen anathemas, "signed beforehand at a preparatory council, . . . apparently won the approval of all five patriarchs at the time," and (2) that the general council accepted the anathemas.[27] Regarding the first claim, Green references the council's discussion of posthumous condemnations during the fifth session. Recall that the bishops were being asked by the emperor to condemn the person of Theodore of Mopsuestia, who had died in communion with the catholic Church. Multiple examples of posthumous condemnations are noted as precedents, including that of Origen:

> And we find indeed many others who were anathematized after death, including also Origen: if one goes back to the time of Theophilus of holy memory or even earlier, one will find him anathematized after death. **This has been done even now in his regard by your holinesses and by Vigilius the most religious pope of Elder Rome.**[28]

Green believes, as does Price, that the bolded sentence references the *endemousa*. Sounds plausible—yet the fifteen anathemas do not mention Origen, and are directed, as we shall see below, against beliefs held not by Origen but by Evagrius. In any case, even if the

---

[27] Ignatius Green, Introduction to *St Gregory of Nyssa's Catechetical Discourse* (2019), p. 42.
[28] Price, I:338; emphasis mine.

sentence is referring to the pre-synod, it cannot be construed as a conferral of dogmatic authority upon its anathemas. That would have required an official act, of which there is none. Regarding the second claim, Green provides no evidence, nor am I aware of any. The acts of the council do not mention the fifteen anathemas. It would be more accurate to say that the council fathers knew of the anathemas, given that some, many, most, or all of them (we do not know how many) had attended the *endemousa* and had presumably expressed their assent or at least acquiescence. Whether they wholeheartedly approved of them, whether they believed that they were condemning all formulations of apokatastasis (including St Gregory of Nyssa's), or just signing off on the emperor's attempt to resolve the Origenist controversy in Palestine, we do not know. Justinian was, like emperors before him, a tyrant and did not brook opposition well, as Pope Vigilius learned firsthand. When Justinian tells you to approve a document, whether by voice acclamation or signature, you do so—unless you are prepared for deposition, imprisonment, torture, exile. The house arrest of Vigilius would have served as a vivid example of the consequences of disobeying the emperor. (That Justinian is celebrated as a saint within the Orthodox Church witnesses to the tremendous mercy of our God and gives hope to us all. It might even be considered as a proleptic manifestation of apokatastasis!) Green contends that II Constantinople's insertion of Origen's name in its list of heretics implicitly ratifies the anathemas submitted to the *synodus endemousa*; yet the claim is unprovable—it is mere assertion on Green's part. Conjecture, guesses, and speculative inferences will not suffice. We do not have access to the hidden intentions of the council fathers. **The simple but decisive fact: the Second Council of Constantinople did not formally promulgate the fifteen anathemas. That it did not do so must determine our evaluation of their dogmatic authority.**

Cyril of Scythopolis is always the first witness summoned to support the traditional view that the Fifth Ecumenical Council formally approved the fifteen anathemas. His book *The Lives of the Monks of Palestine* was composed sometime before his death in 558, only five years after the council. Cyril relates that Abba Conon and others were sent from Palestine to Constantinople to petition the emperor to intervene in the Origenist conflict, arriving in September 552. After hearing their report, Justinian "gave orders for there to be an ecumenical council. . . . When the fifth holy ecumenical council had assembled at Constantinople **a common and universal anathema** was directed against Origen and Theodore of Mopsuestia and against the teaching of Evagrius and Didymus on pre-existence and a universal restoration, in the presence and with the approval of the four patriarchs."[29] Hombergen argues we should not take Cyril's account at face value. Cyril was himself an anti-Origenist partisan. In the above quotation, he claims that II Constantinople was convened to condemn Origenism, yet we know that Justinian summoned the bishops for the express purpose of condemning the Three Chapters, reiterated in his letter read to the council fathers. We also have good reasons to believe that the imperial summons was sent to the bishops *before* the delegation from Palestine had arrived in Constantinople. Cyril's "representation of the facts," comments Hombergen, "seriously contradicts the historical evidence."[30] Was the monastic hagiographer simply misinformed about the events surrounding the council,

---

[29] Cyril of Scythopolis, *The Lives of the Monks of Palestine* (1991), pp. 207-208; emphasis mine.
[30] Hombergen, p. 293. Price also questions Cyril's reliability as a historian because of his misrepresentation of Leontius of Byzantium's theological views (II:272-273).

Did the Fifth Ecumenical Council Condemn Universal Salvation?

Or did Cyril perhaps *need* this inaccuracy for his claim that it was due to Conon's *libellus* that Justinian convoked the Ecumenical Council? In fact, by shifting the date of the convocation as he did, Cyril could compose his account of a providential Origenist defeat by a "common and universal anathema", pronounced at an ecumenical council through the agency of Sabas' heir, without being forced to say too much about the painful (to Cyril and his party) Three Chapters affair. In reality, the Origenist coup in Jerusalem, followed by Conon's action in Constantinople, was only a matter of minor importance. This local crisis was not the one that led to the Fifth Ecumenical Council.[31]

In other words, while Cyril is an important witness to the events in Constantinople, he's not an impartial one. He and his sources have skin in the game. So what exactly does he say about the Fifth Council's condemnation of Origen? He states that a *single* anathema ("common and universal") was issued by the council. This would be an odd (albeit not impossible) way to speak if he were referring to the fifteen anathemas, but it makes perfect sense if he were referring to the inclusion of Origen's name in the list of heretics (canon 11). In that case, Cyril's testimony does not support the argument that apokatastasis was specifically condemned by the council. There is an important difference, as Oxenham comments, "between condemning *a man in general*, and condemning *certain opinions in particular*."[32] Note also that Cyril says that the council denounced Didymus and Evagrius Ponticus for their affirmation of the preexistence of souls and the universal restoration, yet our surviving records do not mention either the home synod or II Constantinople as having done so. Intentionally or unintentionally, Cyril has conflated the imperial condemnations ratified by the home synod (and perhaps even the condemnations of the 543 Synod of

---

[31] Hombergen, p. 301. On what the 6th century Origenists may *actually* have believed and taught, see Hombergen's discussion in chap. 3.
[32] Oxenham, p. 46.

Constantinople) and the Fifth Council's blanket condemnation of Origen in its 11th canon. Secondary sources cannot be taken at face value; they must be critically assessed and weighed for their accuracy.

Consider two more examples of the need to exercise *critical* assessment of the sources. Firstly, the decree of the Sixth Ecumenical Council (680-681): as had become customary, the council fathers announced in the preface of the decree their acceptance of the previous ecumenical councils. After naming the councils of Nicaea, Constantinople I, Ephesus, and Chalcedon, they then named Constantinople II:

> in addition to these, with the fifth holy synod, the latest of them, which was gathered here against Theodore of Mopsuestia, Origen, Didymus and Evagrius, and the writings of Theodoret against the twelve chapters of the renowned Cyril, and the letter said to have been written by Ibas to Mari the Persian.

The council fathers demonstrate their knowledge of the council's condemnation of the Three Chapters. They also associate with the council a condemnation of Origen, Didymus, and Evagrius, yet we know (contra Cyril of Scythopolis) both that the Fifth Council was not convened to address the Origenist problem in Palestine and that it did not explicitly condemn Didymus and Evagrius. Neither the Catholic nor Orthodox understanding of ecclesial infallibility require us to affirm historical errors, even if published by an ecumenical council. And please note: no mention is made of apokatastasis. We may not infer from the above citation a dogmatic affirmation of eternal damnation: that question was not formally addressed by either the Fifth or Sixth Ecumenical Councils.

Secondly, at the Seventh Ecumenical Council an epistle of Patriarch Tarasius of Constantinople was read to the council fathers.

Did the Fifth Ecumenical Council Condemn Universal Salvation?

In it Tarasius expresses his agreement with the six preceding general councils. Here is what he has has to say about II Constantinople:

> With the fifth, I also agree, which as a sword of the Spirit, cut off the lawless heresies, which prevailed from ancient times, and openly exposed those who originated them, Origen, Didymus, and Evagrius—which heresies I also reject as strange and deceitful babblings.[33]

Either the good patriarch is reciting what he knows by hearsay or has read the wrong manuscript. If he had read the authentic acts of the council, he would have known that it was principally concerned with the Three Chapters, but of this he makes no mention nor of the heresies that were actually condemned. He would also have known that the synodical bishops did not formally comminate Evagrius and Didymus. Regardless, it had become part of conciliar lore that "Origen, Didymus, and Evagrius" had been denounced by the Fifth Ecumenical Council. "All later writers, who assert that Origen was condemned by the Fifth Council," Oxenham explains, "always relate that Didymus and Evagrius were condemned at the same time and

---

[33] *The Seventh General Council*, ed. John Mendham, p. 95. Oxenham comments on St Tarasius's failure to mention the real work of the Constantinople II, namely, the condemnation of the Three Chapters, and asks:

"Is it reasonable to suppose that if Tarasius had before him, or in his mind, the genuine acts of the Fifth Council, he would have wholly ignored the chief purpose and work of that Council, and would have recorded, as if it were the sole outcome of the Council, a condemnation, which (if it belonged to that Council at all) was admittedly a secondary matter, brought before the Council which had met for other business? Is it not much more reasonable to suppose that Tarasius had in mind the act of that Synod which *was* exclusively with Origen and his followers [viz., the 543 Synod of Constantinople], and that—having no special reason to inquire what was or was not done by the Fifth Council—he took these acts to belong to the Fifth Council, as others had done before, though in reality they were not the acts of that Council, but of another held a few years previously?" (p. 68).

In its listing of the six preceding ecumenical councils, Nicaea II does not mention the Three Chapters and simply repeats Tarasius's blunder.

together with Origen; but Origen's name stands alone in this eleventh Canon, and no mention is made of Didymus or Evagrius."[34] The 6th century Byzantine historian Evagrius Scholasticus, writing four decades after Constantinople II, is the second witness always summoned into the box. Evagrius provides, so it is claimed, the strongest testimony for the traditional account that the fifteen anathemas were promulgated by the Fifth Ecumenical Council. He places the discussion of Origen and the Origenists *within the council proceedings,* coming after the discussion by the bishops of the propriety of pseudonymous condemnation and the ratification of the fourteen conciliar canons:

> And after other things they expounded fourteen chapters concerning the correct and blameless faith. And thus did these matters proceed. But when depositions against the doctrines of Origen, who is also called Adamantine, and those who follow his impiety and error, were submitted by the monks Eulogius, Conon, Cyriacus and Pancratius, Justinian asked the assembled Synod concerning these matters, after attaching both a copy of the deposition and the missives to Vigilius the correct and blameless faith concerning these things. From all of these one can gather how Origen attempted to fill up the simplicity of apostolic doctrines with Hellenic and Manichaean tares. Accordingly a reply to Justinian was given by the Synod, after it had made acclamations against Origen and his companions in error....
>
> To this they also attached the chapters which revealed what those who hold the doctrines of Origen were taught to profess, both their agreements as well as their disagreements, and their many-sided error. Among these there is a fifth chapter for the blasphemies of individual members of the so-called New Lavra, which ran thus: 'Theodore Ascidas the Cappadocian said: "If now the apostles and martyrs accomplish miracles and are held in the same honour, if in the restoration they are not equal to Christ, what sort of restoration is there

---

[34] Oxenham, p. 38.

for them?'" Many other blasphemies of Didymus, Evagrius and Theodore were also reported by them, since they had collected relevant material with great diligence.[35]

Evagrius records a discussion by the bishops of the Origenist heresies but of the fifteen anathemas he is silent. The fifth chapter that he quotes referring to Theodore Ascidas is not found in the famous fifteen.[36] It is probable, therefore, that Evagrius is referring to a different document or collection of documents—quite likely the (nonextant) depositions passed on to Justinian by the Palestinian monastic delegation in 552 and in turn made available to the synod.[37] But which synod? As noted by Michael Whitby, the translator of

---

[35] Evagrius, *Ecclesiastical History* (2008), trans. Michael Whitby, pp. 248-259.

[36] Hefele's comment on Evagrius' reference to Theodore Askidas is to the point:
"This proposition is not to be found among the fifteen anathemas, there is not even anything that recalls it, which proves that this passage of Evagrius has no feature in common with any of the fifteen anathemas; besides, he does not allude in any way to this number fifteen" (quoted by Oxenham, p. 103; *History of the Councils,* §257).
Hefele notes that the 17th century French scholar Henri Valois (Henricus Valesius) believed that Scholasticus "confounded the conclusions of the Synod of Constantinople held under Mennas (in 543, or else according to the opinion of Valois in 538), with those of the Fifth Ecumenical Council, and we are inclined to think him in the right, as other ancient documents, for example, the acts of the Synod of Constantinople, which was held in 536, have equally through error, been attributed to the Fifth Ecumenical Council" (quoted by Oxenham, p. 103; *History of the Councils,* §257). Gieseler opines that both Cyril Scythopolis and Evagrius confounded the condemnation of Origen, attributed to the Fifth Council, with the 543 Synod convened by Menas (*Church History*, I:480, n. 23).

[37] "Evagrius treats the anti-Origenist *libellus* presented to Justinian by a group of Palestinian monks, a letter of Vigilius on the same subject, and a *relatio* which the synod made to Justinian, extracts from which are given by Evagrius (188,24 - 189,16). To these *acta*, says Evagrius (189,17-20), was appended a list of Origenist errors, suitably refuted. The fifth chapter contained the teaching of Theodore Ascidas. None of these documents appears in the *acta* of the council of 553; the proceedings belong, as Diekamp has shown, to a preliminary meeting of the oecumenical council." Pauline Allen, *Evagrius Scholasticus, the Church Historian* (1981), p. 204.

Evagrius' *Ecclesiastical History*, Evagrius has confused the home synod and the general synod and has therefore mistakenly incorporated the proceedings of the former into the latter: "These proceedings concerning Origen are not included among the incomplete *acta* of the Fifth Council; they preceded the Council and were not regarded as a formal part of proceedings."[38] Hombergen identifies several mistakes in Evagrius' account of the council but offers this exculpation: "Evagrius depended not only on the documents he had at his disposal, but also, as it seems, on existing contradictory traditions concerning the issue of the Council."[39] Except for the obscure doctrine attributed to Theodore Ascidas, Evagrius does not provide any information about the teachings that the bishops may have discussed; he does not mention apokatastasis or the question of everlasting damnation. He does assert that Origen and his "companions in error" (presumably Didymus and Evagrius Ponticus) were condemned by the bishops by acclamation, but he does not specify their errors.[40] And as far as the fifteen anathemas,

---

[38] Whitby, p. 248, n. 131. Early historians such as Cave, Valois, Garnerius, and Hefele suggested that in his study of the manuscripts, Scholasticus mistakenly confused documents from the 543 and 553 synods.
[39] Hombergen, p. 304, n. 236. Cf. Hefele, IV:221-225.
[40] Responding to Edward Pusey's reference to Evagrius Scholasticus in support of the thesis that the Fifth Council condemned apokatastasis, Oxenham writes:

"I will, however, add further that *supposing* all the conciliar proceedings, here related by Evagrius and quoted by Dr Pusey, did belong to the Fifth Council, even then this witness of Evagrius would be of little worth for Dr Pusey's purpose. He says certainly that there were general 'acclamations made against Origen and those who went astray like him.' He says that Didymus, Evagrius, and Theodorus were condemned as well as Origen. No doubt they were. That Origen was on several occasions condemned for many of his opinions, no one disputes: but Evagrius says nothing about Origen being here condemned *for the opinion* that future punishment will not be endless—he says nothing about such an opinion having been condemned or considered; and as to the 'nine specific anathemas,' which Dr Pusey attributes to the Fifth Council, one of which condemns this opinion, Evagrius does not seem to have heard of them. He mentions the fourteen

perhaps Evagrius was acquainted with them, perhaps not. We can plausibly read them *into* the "between the lines" but less plausibly *out* of the lines.

We may also reference the testimony of Bishop Victor of Tunnuna (died c. 569), who wrote a contemporaneous year-by-year chronicle. For the year 553, he states that Justinian convened a synod in Constantinople, during which the Three Chapters were condemned. He mentions neither the condemnation of Origen nor the promulgation of the fifteen anathemas. However, for the year 565 he writes that "Justinian sent into exile Eutychius, Bishop of Constantinople, the condemner of the Three Chapters and of Evagrius, the eremite deacon, and of Didymus, monk and confessor of Alexandria." Unfortunately, he does not provide the specifics of Eutychius' condemnation of Evagrius and Didymus, neither how nor when. Oxenham comments:

> We are certainly not at liberty to cite this passing allusion as a proof that Victor held Evagrius and Didymus to have been condemned *at the same time as* "The Three Chapters," i.e. by the Fifth Council, since in his own record of that council he makes no mention of their condemnation. Of Origen, be it observed, he says nothing at all in either Chronicle.[11]

Curious and curiouser. One is tempted to assign Eutychius' condemnation of Evagrius and Didymus to the pre-synod, even though they are named neither in Justinian's introductory letter nor in the anathemas. Even more curious is the failure to mention Origen at all! Victor's testimony leads Hefele to speculate that Eutychius may in fact have been the origin of the false report that

---

Canons, which undoubtedly are the genuine canons of this Council; but about these other "nine" he is entirely silent" (pp. 49-50).

[11] Oxenham, p. 54

the Fifth Council condemned Didymus and Evagrius. We all know how news gets twisted through the retelling:

> This points to the fact that the Patriarch Eutychius, after the holding of our Synod at which he presided, published an edict in his diocese, and therein made known the decrees of the fifth Council, at the same time pronounced anathema on Evagrius and Didymus, and also on Origen (perhaps renewed the decrees of the Synod under Mennas). If this was so, then Cyril [of Scythopolis], living as a hermit in the remote Laura, might easily confound the edict of Eutychius following the fifth Synod with this, and so arrive at his conclusion respecting Origen.[42]

We jump back and ahead seven centuries to Nikephoros. In addition to providing us with the nine anti-Origenist anathemas, which he attributed to the Fifth Council, Nikephoros also provides a description of the heresies purportedly repudiated by the Council. The description leads one to suspect that at least one of his sources was acquainted with Justinian's letter to the bishops and the fifteen anathemas:

> The soul existed before the body, and it may have committed sins in heaven. And also that the heaven, the sun, the moon, the stars, and the water which are above the heavens are animated, and are, as it were, reasonable powers. Besides that, in the resurrection the bodies of men will be raised in a round and orbicular form, and that the torments of all impious men, and of the devils themselves, will have an end, and that the wicked and devils shall be restored to their former order. Moreover, that it behoves Christ to be crucified also for the devils, and often to suffer in future ages for the spirits of wickedness who are in heavenly places.[43]

---

[42] Hefele, IV:297.
[43] Quoted by Oxenham, p. 80.

How is it that ancient scribes and historians could get things both so right and so wrong? Seventeenth century historians William Cave (Anglican) and Jean Garnier (Jesuit) conjecture that the documents from the three synods under Menas and the general synod under Eutychius were collected together in one codex identified by the name "Fifth Synod."[44] If we throw in the documents from the pre-synod, this might explain the confusions among so many (including Evagrius Scholasticus) regarding which synods did what and when.

Be that as it may, catholic Christendom came to believe that the fifteen anti-Origenist anathemas had been promulgated by the Fifth Ecumenical Council.[45] But as I look back at this sentence, I'm not sure if it's accurate, given that the famous fifteen are, as far as I can discover, neither mentioned nor quoted during the first millennium, though one does find possible allusions to them. One might even argue that they had been forgotten by ecclesiastical writers. What was remembered and passed down in the tradition was that Constantinople II had condemned Origen, Didymus, and Evagrius and all their "mythical speculations."

Apokatastasis and the Hermeneutics of Dogma

Argumenti causa—let us assume, contrary to the weighty evidence presented above, that the council did officially publish the fifteen anathemas. There still remains—and this is the crucial issue—the challenge of *interpretation* and *application*. Not all universalisms are the same. Just as there are both heretical and orthodox construals of, say, the atonement or the Incarnation, so there are heretical and orthodox construals of the larger hope. The apokatastasis advanced by St Gregory of Nyssa, for example, differs in decisive ways from

---

[44] Oxenham, pp. 94-99.
[45] For a brief summary of the evidence, see Green, pp. 42-46; cf. Oxenham, pp. 44-84.

the sixth-century construal against which the anathemas were directed. The latter belongs to an esoteric metaphysical system cut loose from the Scriptures, as even a cursory reading reveals. The chasm between the two is enormous. Augustine Casiday suggests that we should think of the anti-Origenist canons as a rejection of this system as a whole, each denouncing one of its particulars.[46] Kallistos Ware made a similar point in 1998:

> There is, however, considerable doubt whether these fifteen anathemas were in fact formally approved by the Fifth Ecumenical Council. They may have been endorsed by a lesser council, meeting in the early months of 553 shortly before the main council was convened, in which case they lack full ecumenical authority; yet, even so, the Fathers of the Fifth Council were well aware of these fifteen anathemas and had no intention of revoking or modifying them. Apart from that, however, the precise wording of the first anathema deserves to be carefully noted. It does not speak only about apocatastasis but links together two aspects of Origen's theology: first, his speculations about the beginning, that is to say, about the preexistence of souls and the precosmic fall; second, his teaching about the end, about universal salvation and the ultimate reconciliation of all things. Origen's eschatology is seen as following directly from his protology, and both are rejected together.

That the first of the fifteen anathemas should condemn protology and eschatology in the same sentence is entirely understandable, for in Origen's thinking the two form an integral unity. At the beginning, so he believed, there was a realm of *logikoi* or rational intellects (*noes*) existing prior to the creation of the material world as minds without a body. Originally all these *logikoi* were joined in perfect union with the Creator Logos. Then followed the precosmic fall. With the exception of one *logikos* (which became the human soul of Christ), all the other *logikoi* turned away from the Logos and became, depending on the gravity of their deviation, either angels or human beings or demons. In

---

[46] Augustine Cassiday, email message to Alvin Kimel, 24 January 2015.

each case they were given bodies appropriate to the seriousness of their fall: light-weight and ethereal in the case of angels; dark and hideous in the case of demons; intermediate in the case of human beings. At the end, so Origen maintained, this process of fragmentation will be reversed. All alike, whether angels, human beings, or demons, will be restored to unity with the Logos; the primal harmony of the total creation will be reinstated, and once more "God will be all in all" (1 Cor 15:28). Origen's view is in this way circular in character: the end will be as the beginning.

Now, as we have noted, the first of the fifteen anti-Origenist anathemas is directed not simply against Origen's teaching concerning universal reconciliation, but against his total understanding of salvation history—against his theory of preexistent souls, of a precosmic fall and a final *apocatastasis—seen* as a single and undivided whole. Suppose, however, that we separate his eschatology from his protology; suppose that we abandon all speculations about the realm of eternal *logikoi*; suppose that we simply adhere to the standard Christian view whereby there is no preexistence of the soul, but each new person comes into being as an integral unity of soul and body, at or shortly after the moment of the conception of the embryo within the mother's womb. In this way we could advance a doctrine of universal salvation—affirming this, not as a logical certainty (indeed, Origen never did that), but as a heartfelt aspiration, a visionary hope—which would avoid the circularity of Origen's view and so would escape the condemnation of the anti-Origenist anathemas.[17]

Most scholars would now question Ware's identification of the views of Origen with the views of the sixth century Origenists. Brian E. Daley, for example, asserts that the denounced theses

> represent a radicalized Evagrian Christology and cosmology, and a doctrine of *apokatastasis* that went far beyond the hopes of Origen or

---

[17] Kallistos Ware, "Dare We Hope for the Salvation of All," *The Inner Kingdom* (2000), pp. 199-200.

Gregory of Nyssa. They envisage not only a spherical, ethereal risen body, but the complete abolition of material reality in the world to come, and the ultimate absorption of all created spirits into an undifferentiated unity with the divine Logos, so that even the humanity and the Kingdom of Christ will come to an end.[48]

E. M. Harding agrees that the views of the sixth century Origenists were rooted not in Origen himself but in the teachings of Evagrius Ponticus. "It is clear enough," she writes, "that Origen was condemned at the council mainly as a figure who synopsized the sixth-century Isochristoi, who themselves were predominantly following Evagrian themes and speculations"[49] Casiday concurs, with a caveat: just as there are significant differences between Origen and sixth-century Origenism, so there are important differences between Evagrius and sixth-century Evagrianism.[50] Neither Origen nor Evagrius should be tarred by the speculative excesses and innovations of their followers.

In her magisterial monograph *The Christian Doctrine of Apokatastasis*, Ilaria Ramelli argues that the fifteen anathemas do not speak to the authentic teachings of Origen:

> The so-called "condemnation of Origen" by "the Church" in the sixth century probably never occurred proper, and even if it occurred it did so only as a result of a long series of misunderstandings, when the anthropological, eschatological, and psychological questions were no longer felt as open to investigation—as Origen and still Nazianzen

---

[48] Brian Daley, *The Hope of the Early Church* (2002), p. 190.
[49] E. M. Harding, "Origenist Crises," in *The Westminster Handbook to Origen* (2004), p. 166. For an irenic Orthodox attempt to rehabilitate Origen, see Mario Baghos, "The Conflicting Portrayals of Origen in the Byzantine Tradition," *Phronema* 30 (2015): 69-104; also Serafim Seppälä, "Anathematized Church Fathers," RES 11 (1/2019), 10-28.
[50] Augustine Casiday, "Translation, Adaptations, and Controversies at St Sabas Monastery in the Sixth Century," *Journal of Medieval Monastic Studies* 2 (2013): 11.

considered them—, but dogmatically established. The aforementioned condemnation was in fact a condemnation, not at all of Origen, but rather of a late and exasperated form of Origenism; moreover, it was mainly wanted by emperor Justinian—or better his counselors, given that he was not a theologian—and only partially, or even not at all, ratified by ecclesiastical representatives.

This "condemnation" was triggered by the development of a radical kind of Origenism in the first half of the sixth century, especially in Palestine, in the monasteries of St. Saba, the "Great Laura" and "New Laura." . . . Justinian received reports about the Origenistic doctrines and promoted a condemnation of this kind of Origenism, which he mistook for Origen's own doctrine, at first in 543 CE.

The Council that is usually cited as that which "condemned Origen" is the fifth ecumenical council, the second Constantinopolitan Council, in 553 CE. . . . The anathemas, fifteen in number, were already prepared before the opening of the council. Here, Origen is considered to be the inspirer of the so-called Isochristoi. This was the position of the Sabaite opponents of Origen, summarised by Cyril of Scythopolis who maintained that the Council issued a definitive anathema against Origen, Theodore, Evagrius, and Didymus concerning the preexistence of souls and apokatastasis, thus ratifying Sabas' position (V. *Sab.* 90). One of these previously formulated anathemas, which only waited to be ratified by the Council, was against the apokatastasis doctrine: "If anyone supports the monstrous doctrine of apokatastasis [τὴν τερατώδη ἀποκατάστασιν], be it anathema." Other anathemas concern the "pre-existence of souls," their union with bodies only after their fall, and the denial of the resurrection of the body. These doctrines have nothing to do with Origen; in fact, Origen is not the object of any authentic anathema. And Vigilius's documents, which were finally emanated by a council that was not wanted by him, most remarkably do not even contain Origen's name.[51]

---

[51] Ilaria Ramelli, *The Christian Doctrine of Apokatastasis* (2013), pp. 724-726, 736-737; also see Ramelli, "Christian Soteriology and Christian Platonism,"

Ramelli demonstrates that Emperor Justinian and his theological advisors misunderstood and misrepresented the views of Origen on universal reconciliation, ensoulment, the resurrection body, and a host of other subjects; but the damage was done. Origen was named a heresiarch and his theology identified with the bizarre views of his sixth century "disciples." However we judge their dogmatic status, the anti-Origenist anathemas should not be interpreted as condemning the universalist position of Origen himself—despite the inclusion of his name in the council's heresiological list—much less that of the revered bishop of Nyssa, of whom the bishops of the Fifth Ecumenical Council approvingly refer on several occasions in the acts and whom the Seventh Ecumenical Council named "the Father of Fathers."

Ware's key point stands: the home synod condemnation of apokatastasis does not apply to construals similar to those of St Gregory of Nyssa or St Isaac the Syrian. Consider canon 1: "If anyone advocates the mythical pre-existence of souls and the monstrous restoration that follows from this, let him be anathema." The content of the "monstrous restoration" is then unpacked in canons 10-15. Note the intrinsic connection between the preexistence of souls and the universal restoration: the latter necessarily flows from the former, as clearly explained in canon 14, which speaks of the eschatological annihilation of hypostases and bodies and the restoration to a state of pure spirit, akin to the

---

Vigiliae Christianae 61 (2007): 313-356, and John R. Sachs, "Apocatastasis in Patristic Theology," 54 *Theological Studies* (1993): 617-640. In the quoted passage Ramelli writes that "The so-called 'condemnation of Origen' by 'the Church' in the sixth century probably never occurred proper." Here she echoes a long-standing view of some historians (but not Hefele and Price) that Origen's name was interpolated into canon 11 shortly after the adjournment of the Fifth Council. This question is still debated today, but the thesis of this essay does not hinge upon it. Lacking competence to even entertain an opinion, I have adopted Price's position that Origen's name properly belongs to canon 11.

original state of preexistence. As Ramelli puts it: "It is a doctrine of apokatastasis *embedded within that of the transmigration of souls* that was condemned by Justinian's Fifth Ecumenical Council (553), *not* Origen's own doctrine of apokatastasis."[52] Neither Gregory of Nyssa nor Isaac of Nineveh advocate the preexistence of souls (nor Origen, if Ramelli's reading is sustained). Their presentations of the universalist hope are grounded solely upon God's infinite love and the power of purgative suffering to bring enlightenment to the damned. The fifteen anathemas, therefore, condemn neither the soteriological universalism of patristic saints like Gregory and Isaac nor of modern theologians such as Sergius Bulgakov, Kallistos Ware, Hans Urs von Balthasar, Wacław Hryniewicz, and David Bentley Hart. As Hanson writes: "The theory here condemned is not that of universal salvation, but the 'fabulous pre-existence of souls, and the monstrous restitution that results from it.'"[53]

But we need not rely exclusively upon the assessment of modern scholars. I summon into the box Justinian himself. His letter to the bishops clearly states his principal theological concerns and the intent of the anathemas, which I quote in full:

> Our zeal was and is to protect from disturbance the holy, catholic and apostolic church of God and to condemn whatever springs up in any way that is contrary to the orthodox faith. Since therefore it has become known to us that there are indeed some monks at Jerusalem who follow Pythagoras, Plato, Origen the Adamantine and their impiety and error and teach accordingly, we have thought it necessary to take thought and carry out an investigation concerning them, lest through their pagan and Manichaean deceit they utterly destroy many. For, to mention a few things out of many, they assert that there were minds

---

[52] Ilaria Ramelli, *A Larger Hope? (2019)*, p. 171. In his introduction to *Origen: On First Principles*, John Behr confirms that Origen did not teach the preexistence of souls (I:lxiii-lxv, lxxx-lxxxviii).
[53] Hanson, chap. 21.

without any number or name, with the result that there was a henad of all the rational beings through identity of substance and operation and through power and their union with and knowledge of God the Word, and that when they reached satiety with divine love and contemplation, corresponding to the turning of each to what is worse, they clothed themselves with more subtle or denser bodies and were allotted names, and that this is the origin of the existence of the heavenly and ministering powers. Moreover, [they assert] that the sun, the moon and the stars, belonging themselves to the same henad of rational beings, became what they are through turning to what is worse, while the rational beings who for the greater part grew cold in divine love were named souls and were decked in our more dense bodies, and those who had reached the acme of evil were bound to cold and dark bodies and became and are named demons; and that from the state of the angels originates that of the soul, and from that of the soul that of demons and human beings, and from the whole henad of rational beings one mind alone remained undeviating and constant in divine love and contemplation, and it became Christ and King and a human being; and that there will be a total destruction of bodies with the Lord himself first shedding his own body and [then] of all the others; and that all will be raised again to the same henad and become minds (as they were in their pre-existence), when indeed the devil himself and the other demons are restored to the same henad, and when impious and godless human beings will be with godly and inspired men and the heavenly powers and will enjoy the same union with God that Christ too enjoys, just as in their pre-existence, with the result that there will be no difference at all between Christ and the remaining rational beings, neither in substance nor in knowledge nor in power nor in operation. For Pythagoras said that the origin of everything was the monad; and again Pythagoras and Plato, after asserting there is a whole company of bodiless souls, say that those who fall into some sin or other are made to descend into bodies as a punishment. Plato in consequence called the body a fetter and a tomb, since the soul is (as it were) fettered and buried in it.

Then about the coming judgement and retribution of souls he says again, 'The soul of one who has been a lover of boys and lived guilelessly with philosophy is set free in a third thousand-year cycle, and having thereby grown wings is released and departs in the thousandth year, while as for the others, when they end this life, some will enter the places of punishment under the earth and pay the reckoning and penalty, while others, raised by justice into a place in heaven, will lead a life worthy of how they have lived.' It is easy to realize the absurdity of this account; for who taught him the cycles of thousands of years, and that after the elapse of a thousand years each of the souls then departs to its own place? As for what is said incidentally, it would be unsuitable for the utterly licentious, let alone such a philosopher; for to those who had achieved pure philosophy he united the dissolute and lovers of boys and declared that both would enjoy the same rewards. So Pythagoras, Plato, Plotinus and their followers, who agreed that souls are immortal, declared that they exist prior to bodies and that there is a great company of souls, of which those that transgress descend into bodies and that there is a great company of souls, of which those that transgress descend into bodies, as I said above, the vindictive and wicked into leopards, the ravenous into wolves, the treacherous into foxes, and those made after women into horses. But the Church, following the divine scriptures, affirms that the soul is created together with the body, not first one and the other later, according to the insanity of Origen.

On account of these wicked and destructive doctrines, or rather ravings, we bid you most sacred ones to assemble together, read the appended exposition attentively, and condemn and anathematize each of these articles together with the impious Origen and all those who hold or have held these beliefs till death.[54]

---

[54] Price, II:282-284. For an ingenious reconstruction of what the Isochrists taught on apokatastasis, see Istvan Perczel, "Universal Salvation as an Antidote to Apocalyptic Expectations," in *Apocalypticism and Eschatology in Late Antiquity* (2017), pp. 125-161.

Justinian speaks of pagan teachings, of henads, of the preexistence and transmigration of souls and of their final absorption into Christ, and so forth. This is not the apokatastasis taught by St Gregory of Nyssa, Sergius Bulgakov, and David Bentley Hart!

But perhaps in speaking of apokatastasis I have confused matters. Let me rephrase the question before us: Did the Fifth Ecumenical Council reject the belief that the punishments of hell (whether understood as the infliction of retributive suffering or self-chosen alienation from the divine presence and love) will be temporary? The question can only be answered with a resounding no!

> In fine, that although there is ample evidence that Origen and many of his opinions were on several occasions condemned by local Synods, there is absolutely no reliable historical evidence that the doctrine of the finality of future punishment was ever condemned either by the Fifth General Council, or by any of the other councils, whose records have been confounded with it. No one has ever pretended that any other General Council condemned this doctrine, although it is simple matter of history that the doctrine was rife through the period during which the first four General Councils were held, and that no one of them took any notice of it.[55]

The fifteen anathemas reject the necessary restoration of pre-existent souls, but they do not address the simple claim that in his love God will bring to an end the sufferings of the damned. Nor do they address the belief that God will eschatologically reconcile all humanity to himself in the crucified and risen Jesus Christ (1 Cor 15:28).

To condemn Origen "generally," as the Fifth Council did in canon 11, is not to condemn him in all respects. The council named

---

[55] Oxenham, pp. 118-119.

him a heretic, but which of his teachings did it have in mind? We do not know. We aren't mind-readers. Ah, some say, they must have been thinking about the condemnation of Origen in the home synod a month or two earlier. Maybe, maybe not. But one does not establish irreformable dogma on the basis of maybes. The 5th Council did not officially make those anathemas its own. For this reason (and others) canon 11 is dogmatically useless to us today. The fifteen anathemas were politically important in the 6th century as a means to crush the Origenist movement in the Eastern Church; but they have little theological value today, since no one teaches what the sixth century Origenists apparently believed and taught—not even Origen taught what they taught!

We simply cannot take a dogmatic definition or conciliar anathema and make it apply to whatever views we disapprove. We must interpret it within its historical, cultural, and theological context. Not to do so would be a kind of *conciliar fundamentalism*, akin to someone who rips a commandment from the book of Leviticus and then insists that it remains obligatory upon Gentile Christians today. Similar hermeneutical considerations obtain when evaluating the dogmatic authority and application of the eleventh-century Byzantine condemnation of the eccentric views of John Italus, repeated in the 1583 version of the Synodikon, as if it is at all relevant to the present universalist debate. The historical exegesis of dogmatic statements is essential to our constructive employment of these statements in our theological reflection and is mandatory for the proper distinguishment of orthodoxy and heresy.

The universalist hope is, of course, a minority view within Orthodoxy, but being a minority view does not make it heretical. The fact that Orthodox bishops and priests have long taught a doctrine of eternal perdition does not mean that the matter is definitively closed; it does not mean that the Church may not reexamine its popular teaching in light of Holy Scripture, the

Fathers, and deeper theological reflection. Sergius Bulgakov accurately describes the dogmatic status of the doctrine of everlasting hell within Orthodoxy:

> The Church *has not yet established a single universally obligatory dogmatic definition in the domain of eschatology*, if we do not count the brief testimony of the Nicaeno-Constantinopolitan Creed concerning the second coming ("He will come again in glory to judge the living and the dead, and His kingdom will have no end"), as well as concerning the resurrection of the dead and the life of the future age. These dogmas of the faith, attested to by the Creed and based on the express promises of the Lord, have not, all the same, been developed by theology. They are considered to be self-evident for the dogmatic consciousness, although that is not, in reality, the case. All the rest, referring to various aspects of eschatology, has not been defined dogmatically; it is an object of dogmatic doctrine that has yet to undergo free theological investigation.
>
> If it is maintained that the absence of an ecclesial definition is compensated by the existence of a firm ecclesial tradition, patristic and other, one must call such an assertion inaccurate or even completely erroneous. Aside from the fact that this tradition is insufficient and disparate, the most important thing here is *the absence of a single tradition*. Instead, we have at least *two* completely different variants: on the one hand, a doctrine originating in Origen and stabilized in the teaching of St. Gregory of Nyssa and his tacit and open followers; and, on the other hand, a widespread doctrine that has had many adherents but none equal in power of theological thought to those mentioned above. (Perhaps in this group we can put Augustine, the greatest teacher of the Western Church, but the originality of his worldview sets him apart in general, especially for Eastern theology.) As regards both particular patristic doctrines and the systematization of biblical texts, an inquiry that would precede dogmatization has yet to be carried out.
>
> Given such a situation, it would be erroneous to maintain that the dogmatic doctrine expounded in the scholastic manuals represents the

authoritative and obligatory dogmas of the Church, and to demand subordination to them as such. In response to such a demand it is necessary to established decisively and definitively that this is an exaggeration and a misunderstanding. The doctrine expounded in the manuals can by no means be accepted without inquiry and verification. It only expresses the opinion of the majority, corresponding to the current status of theological thought on this subject, not more. Characteristic of a specific period of the past, this doctrine is losing its authority more and more at the present time and at the very least requires revision. There is insufficient justification to accept theological opinions as the dogmatic definitions of the Church, especially when these opinions are proper to only one type of thought. Eschatological theology remains open to inquiry even at the present time.[56]

We now arrive at the most "accursed" question of eschatology, that of the eternal torments of sinners. Those who understand eternity as temporal infinity (i.e., theologians of all confessions) attempt to affirm the infinite, or "eternity," of the torments of hell in all manner of ways—apologetically, patristically, exegetically. They attempt to prove the justice of the infinite duration of punishment even for temporal sins and the conformity of this punishment with God's wisdom and love. A whole theodicy of eternal torments is thus constructed. Of the great mass of judgments of this kind, of special interest are the opinions of Origen and especially St. Gregory of Nyssa, who are virtually the only ecclesiastical writers (besides Augustine with his rigorism) who made questions of eschatology an object of special inquiry. The Church has not issued a precise determination on this issue, although the doctrine of scholastic theology attempts to pass itself off as such a determination. But, actually, this doctrine only expresses the "opinion" of one of the two tendencies that have opposed each other and continue to oppose each other in theology. Even the definitions that condemn Origenism, which previously had been attributed to the fifth ecumenical council, have been shown by recent historical inquiry not to originate in this

---

[56] Sergius Bulgakov, *The Bride of the Lamb,* (2001), pp. 379-380.

council. Even if they had so originated, they would still require interpretation and very careful commentary.[57]

Hilarion Alfeyev categorically asserts: "There is also an Orthodox understanding of the *apokatastasis*, as well as a notion of the non-eternity of hell. Neither has ever been condemned by the Church and both are deeply rooted in the experience of the Paschal mystery of Christ's victory over the powers of darkness."[58] Paul Evdokimov concurs:

> The general view of eternal torment is only a textbook opinion, simplistic theology (of the penitential sort) which neglects the depth of texts such as John 3.17 and 12.47. Can we really believe that, alongside the eternity of the Kingdom of God, God has provided another eternity of hell? Surely, this would amount to a failure in the divine plan, even a partial victory of evil? Now, St Paul, in 1 Cor. 15.55, states quite the opposite. St Augustine did indeed oppose the more generous interpretations of the tender mercies of God, but that was out of a concern to avoid libertinism and sentimentality; besides, fear would not only be useless in pedagogical argument today, but would make Christianity dangerously like Islam. A healthy trembling before holy

---

[57] Bulgakov, p. 482.
[58] Hilarion Alfeyev, *The Mystery of Faith* (2002), p. 271. In *Doctrine and Teaching of the Orthodox Church* (2012), Hilarion appears to have moved toward a more traditional view of eternal damnation. He repeatedly appeals to the (alleged) dogmatic rejection of apokatastasis by the Fifth Ecumenical Council. This uncritical invocation of a questionable anathema severely undermines his presentation. Surely a theologian of Hilarion's caliber is well aware of the historical debate regarding the attribution of the fifteen anathemas to II Constantinople, yet he makes no reference to this debate. Hilarion also assumes that the anathema against apokatastasis accurately speaks to the authentic views of Origen; nor does he convincingly explain why the Council Fathers, if they intended to anathematize all forms of apokatastasis, did not include St Gregory of Nyssa's name among the condemned. I am at a loss to explain Hilarion's poor scholarship at this point.

> things keeps the world from becoming bland, but real fear is driven out by perfect love (1 John 4.18)....
>
> The Fifth Ecumenical Council did not occupy itself with the duration of the torments of hell. The Emperor Justinian (who for a while resembled Jonah, who was righteously angry because the wicked escaped punishment) presented his personal teaching to the Patriarch Menas in 543. The Patriarch used it to elaborate some arguments against neo-Origenism. Pope Vigilius confirmed them. By mistake, they have been attributed to the Fifth Ecumenical Council itself, but the teaching was only a personal opinion, and the contradictory teaching of St Gregory of Nyssa has never been condemned. The question remains open, the answer depending perhaps on human charity. St Anthony's explanation is one of the most profound: apocatastasis, the salvation of all, is not a doctrine, but a prayer for the salvation of all except me, for whom alone hell exists.[39]

One might claim, I suppose, that it really doesn't matter whether the Fifth Ecumenical Council *formally* approved the anti-Origenist anathemas. The Church subsequently came to believe that it had and that's what really counts. Consider the declaration of the Synod of Trullo in 692:

> Also we recognize as inspired by the Spirit the pious voices of the one hundred and sixty-five God-bearing fathers who assembled in this imperial city in the time of our Emperor Justinian of blessed memory, and we teach them to those who come after us; for these synodically anathematized and execrated Theodore of Mopsuestia (the teacher of Nestorius), and Origen, and Didymus, and Evagrius, all of whom reintroduced feigned Greek myths, and brought back again the circlings of certain bodies and souls, and deranged turnings [or transmigrations] to the wanderings or dreamings of their minds, and impiously insulting the resurrection of the dead. (Canon 1)

---

[39] Paul Evdokimov, Orthodoxy (2011), p. 338.

Though it does not explicitly mention apokatastasis, the text arguably suggests an acquaintance with the fifteen anathemas, though again we note the mistaken attribution of the threefold execration of "Origen, and Didymus, and Evagrius" to the Fifth Council. One might then maintain that when subsequent ecumenical councils confirmed II Constantinople as ecumenical, they implicitly confirmed the anathemas. So the Second Council of Nicaea: "We anathematize the mythical speculations of Origen, Evagrius and Didymus, as did the fifth synod, that assembled at Constantinople." Yet were the bishops actually acquainted with the acts of the Fifth Council or the fifteen anathemas of the pre-synod? I presume few if any had read the relevant texts of Origen, Didymus, and Evagrius. Come to think of it, how many of the bishops who attended either the 543 Synod of Constantinople or the Second Council of Constantinople had seriously studied Origen, Didymus, and Evagrius?

Perhaps we might call this the "as if" theory of dogmatic reception: the Church has received the anti-Origienist anathemas *as if* they had been officially promulgated by an ecumenical council and *as if* they condemned the universalist views of Origen, St Gregory Nyssen, and St Isaac the Syrian. Rejection of apokatastasis, after all, has been the standard teaching of Latin and Eastern Christianity for over a millennium. Doesn't that qualify as ecumenical dogma, even if initially based upon a historical blunder? If we believe hard and long enough that an ecumenical council has dogmatically condemned all forms of universal salvation, then surely it must have. Fifty million Frenchmen can't be wrong, as the saying goes. Perhaps we'll even throw in the work of the Spirit to seal the deal. But while one might expect an old-school Roman Catholic to argue in such a fashion, no doubt invoking papal authority and the infallibility of the ordinary magisterium, it seems odd for an Eastern Christian to take this route. It presumes a magisterial authoritarianism alien to the Orthodox spirit, as if the Church could or would impose universally binding dogmatic formulations without consideration of their historical origin and theological content. Even many Roman Catholic theologians now reject such a legalistic approach to dogma:

> The notion that there could be doctrines immune to historical limitations and capable of being imposed by the sheer weight of extrinsic authority reflects the nonhistorical and juridical type of thinking prevalent in the Church of the Counter Reformation. The roots of this mentality may be traced to Greek intellectualism and Roman legalism. More proximately, the absolutistic view of dogma reflects the characteristics of Catholic theology in a rationalistic era. To ward off naturalistic rationalism, orthodox theology adopted a supernaturalistic rationalism in which revelation was conceived as a divinely imparted system of universal and timeless truths entrusted to the Church as teacher.[60]

Unlike their Roman Catholic counterparts, contemporary Orthodox theologians have hardly begun to address the prerequisites of doctrinal irreformability or the hermeneutics of dogma (Bulgakov's essay "Dogma and Dogmatic Theology" being a notable exception). How and when does a doctrinal teaching achieve irreformable dogmatic status? Does it need to be formally defined by an ecumenical council? How long does it take for a doctrine to be properly received, and what are the criteria for reception? May the Church revisit either a dogmatic definition or a long-standing doctrine for theological, historical, and pastoral reasons? Ask Orthodox theologians these and related questions, and one will receive multiple, and contradictory, answers. Hence we should not be surprised when internet apologists, parish priests, and even

---

[60] Avery Dulles, "Dogma as an Ecumenical Problem," *Theological Studies* 29.3 (1968): 400; also see Francis Sullivan, *Creative Fidelity* (2003).

respected theologians who should know better dismiss the hope of universal salvation with the mere wave of a dogmatic hand. "The Fifth Ecumenical Council settled that long ago," some tell us. "The Synodikon has infallibly anathematized the universalist hope," others pontificate. But dogma is too important to be so superficially treated. And the universalist hope is too important to be so cavalierly and hastily dismissed. Substantive and cogent arguments have been raised against the traditional doctrine of everlasting damnation. They must be addressed head-on, not dismissed by lazy appeals to authority. And if these arguments should prove compelling, then the question of apokatastasis must also be reopened, for nothing less than the gospel of Jesus Christ is at stake.

I conclude with this eloquent plea from Nutcombe Oxenham:

> This question, whether the doctrine of never-ending sin and never-ending torments is true, or false, can not be decided on mere historical grounds. Whatever may have been the prevalent opinion in the Christian Church in early or in later ages; whatever may have been the teaching of this or that illustrious theologian in ancient days, or in our own day; whatever may have been the decrees of ancient councils, local or even general; whatever may be the apparent, literal meaning of any text of Scripture; whatever may have been the interpretation with more or less authority assigned to it; whatever may be the evidence which the most honest, laborious, and impartial historical inquiry may supply on any or all of these points, still there remain one question to be asked of vastly greater importance than all these, namely this, What is the moral aspect of this doctrine, which now claims to be *de fide* in the Christian Church? Is it in keeping with the general scope and tenor of the teaching of Christ and His apostles, or is it in violent contrast? is it in harmony with the revealed character of God? or is it painfully and shockingly discordant? Is it agreeable with those great and unquestionable "everlasting" principles of justice, or mercy, and of love, which must ever be the discriminating and the final test of the

Did the Fifth Ecumenical Council Condemn Universal Salvation?

truth or the falsehood of any doctrine which claims to be from God? or is it utterly and defiantly subversive of all those principles?[61]

Amen. Amen. Amen.

---

[61] Oxenham, pp. 119-120.

PART THREE

The Gospel of Universal Salvation

Chapter Seventeen

Freedom for Hell?

But what about free will? This is one of the most frequent objections posed to the universalist, second only to the Lord's teachings on Gehenna. Can Almighty God effect the universal reconciliation of human beings, while respecting their freedom and autonomy? The free-will theist answers with a clear *no*. Freedom is incompatible with divine determinism. A free choice, precisely to be a free choice, must be outside of God's causal control; and because God desires his relationship with his rational creatures to be characterized by freedom and mutual respect, he refuses to coercively interfere with their decisions and choices. God desires a relationship of love with free agents, not with automatons. St John Chrysostom well states the argument:

> Beloved, God being loving towards man and beneficent, does and contrives all things in order that we may shine in virtue, and as desiring that we be well approved by Him. And to this end He draws no one by force or compulsion: but by persuasion and benefits He draws all that will, and wins them to Himself. Wherefore when He came, some received Him, and others received Him not. For He will have no unwilling, no forced domestic, but all of their own will and choice, and grateful to Him for their service. Men, as needing the ministry of servants, keep many in that state even against their will, by the law of ownership; but God, being without wants, and not standing in need of anything of ours, but doing all only for our salvation makes us absolute in this matter, and therefore lays neither force nor compulsion on any

of those who are unwilling. For He looks only to our advantage: and to be drawn unwilling to a service like this is the same as not serving at all.[1]

The free-will theist logically maintains that given the gift of libertarian freedom not only must it be possible for human beings to irrevocably reject God and damn themselves to eternal perdition, but God is ultimately helpless to do anything about it. While free-will theists do not pretend to *know* whether hell will be populated, they will not be surprised if such turns out to be the case. The eternal damnation of one or many is the unavoidable consequence of human freedom—collateral damage, as it were. If we should freely determine final separation from our Creator, our Creator will respect and honor our decision. God can do everything, except constrain us to love him. In the words of C. S. Lewis, the gates of hell are locked from the inside. God does not damn, but he does permit us to damn ourselves.

The libertarian case against universal salvation appears to be impregnable. Perhaps we may hope, hope against hope, that all will be saved, yet we may not claim anything stronger. Freedom requires at a bare minimum the *possibility* of self-damnation. Yet is the free-will model of hell as irrefutable as it seems? Philosopher Thomas Talbott thinks not. He advances three propositions.

(1) "The very idea of someone freely rejecting God forever is deeply incoherent and therefore logically impossible."[2]

Talbott asks us to consider the example of a young boy who puts his head into a fire and keeps it there, despite the excruciating pain, despite all pleas from parents and friends. What would we say about this boy? Is he acting rationally? morally? freely? Would we not think, rather, that something must be terribly wrong with him?

---

[1] John Chrysostom, *Hom. in John* 10.1.
[2] Thomas Talbott, *The Inescapable Love of God*, 2nd ed. (2014), p. 170.

Freedom for Hell?

Perhaps he suffers from congenital analgesia. Perhaps he is overwhelmed by self-destructive impulses. The point Talbott is making is that other conditions, besides the absence of coercion, must obtain in order for an action to be judged a *free* action. At the very least, a minimal degree of rationality is needed. "That which is utterly pointless, utterly irrational, and utterly inexplicable," he writes, "will simply not qualify as a free choice for which one is morally responsible."[3]

Everyone agrees that eternal damnation represents the absolutely worst thing that can happen to a human being. It is not just tragic; it is the maximal tragedy. So why would a rational being make such a choice for himself when it contradicts his fundamental good and makes impossible his own happiness? We can entertain such a decision if it rests upon ignorance, disordered desire, vice, deception, pathology, addiction; but all such conditions result in diminished capacity and therefore diminished freedom. Of decisive consideration here is the coincidence between the ultimate happiness that we will for ourselves and the ultimate happiness that God wills for us:

> Let us now begin to explore what it might *mean* to say that someone freely rejects God forever. Is there in fact a coherent meaning here? Religious people sometimes speak of God as if he were just another human magistrate who seeks his own glory and requires obedience for its own sake; they even speak as if we might reject the Creator and Father of our souls without rejecting ourselves, oppose his will for our lives without opposing, schizophrenically perhaps, our own will for our lives. . . . But if God is our loving Creator, then he wills for us exactly what, at the most fundamental level, we want for ourselves; he wills that we should experience supreme happiness, that our deepest yearnings should be satisfied, and that all of our needs should be met. So if that is

---

[3] Ibid., p. 172.

true, if God wills for us the very thing we *really* want for ourselves, whether we know it or not, how then are we to understand human disobedience and opposition to God.[4]

When I first read Talbott's book, this paragraph immediately grabbed my attention. Perhaps here is the secret of the universalist hope. The good we desire for ourselves and the good God desires for us are identical! At any given moment we may not be able to see this profound truth, due to our egotism, viciousness, and alienation; but no matter how hardened our hearts become, we remain creatures made in the image of God. God, and only God, can satisfy our deepest desires.

In order, therefore, for a person to irrevocably reject God and the happiness that union with him brings, he must irrevocably reject the happiness he yearns for. "So if a fully informed person should reject God nonetheless, then," Talbott concludes, "that person, like the boy in our story above, would seem to display the kind of irrationality that is itself incompatible with free choice."[5]

Would God permit this to happen? We might hope that he would not, yet isn't the libertarian Deity impotent before our self-chosen hells?

(2) "Even if such an idea [i.e., of someone freely rejecting God forever] were perfectly coherent, a loving God could never permit his loved ones to make such a choice, because he would never permit them to do irreparable harm either to themselves or to others."[6]

---

[4] Ibid.
[5] Ibid., p. 173.
[6] Ibid., pp. 170-171.

Freedom for Hell?

The key word is *irreparable*. Dr Talbott is not speaking of injury that is beyond normal healing or damage beyond human rectification. Clearly God does permit evils and horrors that surpass the creaturely ability to make right. He is speaking, rather, of a kind of damage that not even God can repair:

> So even if a loving God could sometimes permit murder, he could never permit one person to annihilate the soul of another or to destroy the very possibility of future happiness in another; and even if he could sometimes permit suicide, he could never permit his loved ones to destroy the very possibility of future happiness in themselves either. Just as loving parents are prepared to restrict the freedom of the children they love, so a loving God would be prepared to restrict the freedom of the children he loves, at least in cases of truly irreparable harm.[7]

The influence of George MacDonald upon Talbott's theology is manifest. MacDonald was horrified by the Reformed teaching on election and limited atonement, which effectively restricts the love of God to only some human beings. In MacDonald's novel *David Elginbrod*, Mrs. Elton reads a homily on divine predestination to a young boy named Harry, who bursts into tears and runs out of the room, exclaiming, "I don't want God to love me, if he does not love everybody." For MacDonald, God cannot be less loving than the best fathers and mothers we know, and the best parents are those who will do all that is within their power to achieve the good of their children. As MacDonald declares in his remarkable sermon "The Voice of Job":

> The idea that God would be God all the same, as glorious as he needed to be, had he not taken upon himself the divine toil of bringing home his wandered children, had he done nothing to seek and save the

---

[7] Ibid., pp. 177-178.

lost, is false as hell. Lying for God could go no farther. As if the idea of God admitted of his being less than he is, less than perfect, less than all-in-all, less than Jesus Christ! less than Love absolute, less than entire unselfishness! As if the God revealed to us in the New Testament were not his own perfect necessity of loving-kindness, but one who has made himself better than, by his own nature, by his own love, by the laws which he willed the laws of his existence, he needed to be! They would have it that, being unbound, he deserves the greater homage! So it might be, if he were not our father. But to think of the living God not as our father, but as one who has condescended greatly, being nowise, in his own willed grandeur of righteous nature, bound to do as he has done, is killing to all but a slavish devotion. It is to think of him as nothing like the God we see in Jesus Christ. . . . God could not be satisfied with himself without doing all that a God and Father could do for the creatures he had made—that is, without doing just what he has done, what he is doing, what he will do, to deliver his sons and daughters, and bring them home with rejoicing.[8]

Like Job, Talbott too is willing to contend with the inscrutable Whirlwind. If the Creator truly is our good Father, as Jesus most certainly taught us that he is, then he will not permit his children to cast themselves into the lake of everlasting torment. He will not allow them to do irreparable harm, either to themselves or to others. Talbott is even willing to speak, as does MacDonald, of God having a moral obligation to human beings: just as parents have a natural obligation to do what good they can for the children they bring into the world, so God freely assumes the responsibility to secure the ultimate welfare of the human beings he brings into existence. "God could no more choose to create persons without accepting that responsibility," comments Talbott, "than human parents can choose

---

[8] George MacDonald, "The Voice of Job," Unspoken Sermons, Series Two (1886).

to raise children without acquiring an obligation to promote their welfare."[9]

I question the philosophical appropriateness of imposing moral obligations upon the transcendent source of moral obligation, but perhaps my concern is inapposite. If God is absolute love in his inner Trinitarian being, then we may certainly trust him to act for our benefit and ultimate welfare. The Father of Jesus Christ fulfills his promises. He wills our good and seeks to realize our good. But is God obliged to do so? Is he properly characterized as a moral agent subject to a code of ethics? To put it crassly, is God good because he is well-behaved?

It's unclear to me how hard Talbott wishes to push the notion of God's obligation to humanity. This may be a figurative way to speak forcefully of the unconditionality of the divine love. Yet it rings of anthropomorphism, as if the ineffable Creator is a being whose actions we may applaud or censure. I understand the cogency of this tack in responding to Calvinists and Augustinians who divorce love and justice and thus end up reducing grace to an arbitrary election of some from the sinful mass of humanity. At the very least, perhaps we need to say that while the holy God of Israel is not properly described as moral, he is not less than moral.

Yet having raised this concern, I still find myself assenting to the truth expressed by MacDonald: "This is the beginning of the greatest discovery of all—that God owes himself to the creature he has made in his image, for so he has made him incapable of living without him."[10]

---

[9] Talbott, p. 149.
[10] "Voice of Job."

3) "The free will theist's understanding of hell is, in any case, utterly inconsistent with the New Testament teaching about hell."[11]

God does not damn; we damn ourselves. God does not inflict eternal suffering; we bring this suffering upon ourselves through our obdurate impenitence. This is the central contention of the free-will model of eternal perdition, which has become dominant in Eastern Orthodoxy, Roman Catholicism, and mainline Protestantism. Talbott contends that this model is in fact inconsistent with the New Testament's terrifying imagery of Gehenna in two ways.

First, the biblical imagery argues against the suggestion that eternal perdition is a freely-embraced condition. Eschatological condemnation is typically presented as a judgment by God of sinful deeds, and for some, this judgment will come as a complete surprise: "Then they also will answer, 'Lord, when did we see thee hungry or thirsty or a stranger or naked or sick or in prison, and did not minister to thee?" (Matt 25:44). Yet if the judgment comes as a surprise, it can hardly be described as an outcome chosen and accepted by the condemned. Moreover, Gehenna is presented as a place of intolerable suffering and anguish: "The Son of man will send his angels, and they will gather out of his kingdom all causes of sin and all evildoers, and throw them into the furnace of fire; there men will weep and gnash their teeth" (Matt 13:41-42)—not a condition one might freely and irrevocably choose. Equally clearly, the rich man in Jesus' parable hardly displays a preference for his condition. He begs Father Abraham to warn his five brothers, lest they too find themselves in that "place of torment" (Lk 16:19-31). One might argue that the rich man had fair warning of the consequences of his neglect of the poor and homeless, but having now experienced those consequences, he is desirous of being delivered from them. His attitude may not yet count as genuine

---

[11] Talbott, p. 171.

repentance, but perhaps, like Ebenezer Scrooge, he would avail himself of a second chance if given the opportunity. "Indeed," writes Talbott, "insofar as the whole point of the New Testament imagery is to provide a warning and a motive for repentance in the present, it makes little sense to suggest that some people might prefer a hellish condition over a heavenly one."[12]

Second, whereas Scripture presents Gehenna as a place of intolerable suffering, the advocates of the free-will model often seek to minimize the suffering of the damned. That they do so is understandable, for the more intense the suffering, the more incomprehensible the eternal rejection of God becomes. Jerry Walls speculates that "those in hell may be almost happy, and this may explain why they insist on staying there. They do not, of course, experience even a shred of genuine happiness. But perhaps they experience a certain perverse sense of satisfaction, a distorted sort of pleasure."[13]

Walls's suggestion strikes me as initially plausible. I imagine that we have all experienced this kind of degenerate self-satisfaction. Talbott rightly notes, however, that the biblical image of torment excludes all such pleasure. Perhaps the Lucifer of John Milton's imagination initially thought he would find the experience of ruling hell superior to service in heaven, yet as the poem unfolds, his despair grows and intensifies:

> Be then his Love accurst, since love or hate,
> To me alike, it deals eternal woe.
> Nay curs'd be thou; since against his thy will
> Chose freely what it now so justly rues.
> Me miserable! which way shall I flie
> Infinite wrauth, and infinite despaire?

---

[12] Ibid., p. 182.
[13] Jerry Walls, Hell: The Logic of Damnation (2016), p. 126.

> Which way I flie is Hell; my self am Hell;
> And in the lowest deep a lower deep
> Still threatning to devour me opens wide,
> To which the Hell I suffer seems a Heav'n.

"My self am Hell"—does Lucifer here come close to the self-awakening that leads to repentance? Milton cannot entertain this possibility, given the received doctrine of perditional eternality.

Walls acknowledges that the "happiness" of hell is ultimately based on self-deception. The damned have convinced themselves that their infernal satisfactions must be greater than whatever joys heaven offers. "They must take some corrupt pleasure," he reflects, "in choosing evil because it is evil. Perhaps such a choice represents the epitome of self-assertion and independence from moral norms. Maybe it gives an illusion of complete autonomy that no other sort of choice does. It is admittedly hard to conceive of such a choice, but if real perversity is an option for free persons, it must be possible to see some advantage in choosing evil because it is evil."[14] But is it really possible to choose evil because it is evil? I am reminded of this passage from Herbert McCabe:

> To do good is to choose the highest good; but to fail to do this, to sin, is not to choose evil. Nobody chooses evil, it cannot be done. When we sin what we do is choose some trivial good at the expense of God's friendship. Sin is sin not because of the thing we positively choose: the human satisfaction, the pleasure or the power. It is sin because of what we fail to choose, what we sacrifice for the sake of a minor good. Sin is sin because we have opted not to grow up to our flourishing, our happiness which is life in God's love and friendship.[15]

---

[14] Ibid., p. 129.
[15] Herbert McCabe, God Still Matters (2005), p. 185.

Freedom for Hell?

In his pride and egoism, Milton's Lucifer thought he could choose evil for the sake of evil ("All good to me is lost;/Evil, be thou my Good"), but this declared intent only reflects the depth of his delusion. What happens when all creaturely goods are withdrawn from the damned, and they find themselves deprived of all sources of pleasure, including the pleasure of tormenting others? What happens when they are abandoned to the hellish anguish that must inevitably deepen and intensify? Here is the fatal vulnerability of Walls's position. He acknowledges that it is not within the power of human beings "to endure ever-increasing misery. We do not have the constitutional strength or capacity to absorb ever greater amounts of torment."[16] As the CIA operative in Zero Dark Thirty says when he is torturing a prisoner: "In the end, everyone breaks. It's biology." So why do the damned not break? Because God will not allow their suffering to reach the critical point. "To be sure," Walls explains, "if God added such pressure, the person would be forced to see that sin causes misery and would find it impossible not to submit to the pressure. But the choice to submit under these circumstances would not qualify as a free choice."[17] How odd. Out of ostensible respect for the personal integrity of the person the libertarian Deity steps in to prevent the person from achieving salvific insight. Like the lawyer who always walks through the door just at the moment when his client is about to buckle under the pressure of police interrogation and confess his crime, so God intervenes to protect the damned from the full consequences of their sin, thereby interrupting the process of illusion-demolition and allowing them to do irreparable harm to themselves and to all who love them. How is this authentic respect for freedom? How is this love? Alcoholics Anonymous insists that every addict must be

---

[16] Walls, p. 133.
[17] Ibid., p. 132.

allowed to hit bottom to begin the road to recovery, yet Walls envisions God as inhibiting the downward disintegrating spiral precisely to prevent sinners from ever reaching their bottom. At this point, the moral and theological power of the universalist position becomes evident:

> We can appreciate, of course, why many free will theists would reject the barbaric picture of an eternal torture chamber in which no repentance and no escape from unbearable suffering is even possible. For an eternity of such suffering would seem utterly pointless, and a "god" who would actually inflict such suffering on someone forever would be unspeakably barbaric, even demonic. But here, I would suggest, the universalists are in a far better position to accept the images and language of the New Testament than are the Arminians and other free will theists. For the universalists can regard the misery of hell as both an inevitable consequence of sin and as a means of correction for it; that is, precisely because they reject the idea of a freely embraced condition, they have no need to water down the New Testament image of unbearable suffering.[18]

Might it just be possible that Gehenna is God's last resort to reconcile humanity to himself through Jesus Christ? Consider the two principal biblical images of eschatological punishment:

> Then Death and Hades were thrown into the lake of fire. This is the second death, the lake of fire; and if any one's name was not found written in the book of life, he was thrown into the lake of fire. (Rev. 20:14-15)
> Then the king said to the attendants, "Bind him hand and foot, and cast him into the outer darkness; there men will weep and gnash their teeth." (Matt 22:13)

---

[18] Talbott, p. 183.

Freedom for Hell?

Unquenchable fire and outer darkness—two very different images, yet when held together in creative tension, they may well hold the key to understanding the redemptive possibilities of Gehenna.

Why is it, asks Thomas Talbott, that most of us do not in this life experience alienation from our Creator as the objective horror that it truly is? The Bible tells us that sin is destructive to our spiritual and psychological lives, yet these consequences somehow remain hidden from us. Why so? Talbott offers this answer:

> Because we initially emerge and begin making choices in a context of ambiguity, ignorance, and illusion, we do not typically experience our initial separation from God, or even our continuing separation from him in this life, as a horror. To the contrary, the very conditions that make an earthly life possible leave God at least partially hidden from us; they also protect us from experiencing our separation from him as a kind of horror.[19]

"Show me thy glory," entreats Moses of the Lord. And the Lord replies, "I will make all my goodness pass before you and will proclaim before you my name 'The Lord'; and I will be gracious to whom I will be gracious and will show mercy on whom I will show mercy. But you cannot see my face; for man shall not see me and live" (Ex 33:18-20). And so, the Lord hides Moses in the cleft of the rock and covers him with his hand, permitting him only to see the divine backside. Whether because Moses is a finite corporeal creature or because he is insufficiently sanctified, God protects him from the full revelation of the divine nature. Even in theophany, divinity remains hidden. Moses only sees the LORD's backside. But this hiddenness—or epistemic distance—characterizes human life in this world. Talbott proposes that it is a necessary condition for human beings to grow into freedom and authentic personhood, yet

---

[19] Ibid., p. 185.

it also brings with it the risk of error and sin. Because we do not presently enjoy the vision of our supreme Good, it becomes considerably easier to seek our happiness in temporal goods.

Presumably, however, all of this changes at some point after death, when each person is brought into immediate face-to-face encounter with the living God in his uncreated light and glory. Talbott indulges in a bit of creative speculation about this prospect. Consider again the images of the lake of fire and the outer darkness. Talbott suggests that we can plausibly think of them as metaphorically signifying "two very different realities."[20] The lake of fire represents the holy presence of God, a presence that brings forgiveness and refreshment of the Spirit to the penitent but misery and torment to the impenitent. "The misery of the lake of fire, therefore, is simply the way in which the rebellious and the unrepentant experience God's holy presence," Talbott comments.[21] Orthodox Christians will immediately think of a popular booklet by Alexandre Kalomiros, *The River of Fire*:

> God is a loving fire, and He is a loving fire for all: good or bad. There is, however, a great difference in the way people receive this loving fire of God. Saint Basil says that "the sword of fire was placed at the gate of paradise to guard the approach to the tree of life; it was terrible and burning toward infidels, but kindly accessible toward the faithful, bringing to them the light of day." The same loving fire brings the day to those who respond to love with love, and burns those who respond to love with hatred.
>
> Paradise and hell are one and the same River of God, a loving fire which embraces and covers all with the same beneficial will, without any difference or discrimination. The same vivifying water is life eternal for the faithful and death eternal for the infidels; for the first it is their element of life, for the second it is the instrument of their eternal

---

[20] Ibid., pp. 185-186.
[21] Ibid., p. 186.

suffocation; paradise for the one is hell for the other. Do not consider this strange. The son who loves his father will feel happy in his father's arms, but if he does not love him, his father's loving embrace will be a torment to him. This also is why when we love the man who hates us, it is likened to pouring lighted coals and hot embers on his head.[22]

Those who hate God and obstinately reject his mercy, in other words, can only experience "the consuming fire of God's perfecting love" as retribution and torture. They are incapable of recognizing and embracing love as love. They cannot welcome the divine agape; they can only resist, curse, and abominate it—this is the source of their suffering. Immersed in the divine goodness, the damned inevitably endure the river of fire as a "forcibly imposed punishment."[23] "It is simply not possible," Talbott continues, "for those who cling to their selfish attitudes, to their lust for power over others, or to their delusions of personal grandeur to experience God's holy presence as anything but unbearable torment."[24]

Talbott then proposes a surprising interpretive twist. If the lake of fire symbolizes the holy presence of God, may not the outer darkness symbolize the "separation from the divine nature as far as is metaphysically possible short of annihilation"?[25]

> Even in the lake of fire one may yet retain the power to continue resisting God's purifying love. For even as such resistance inevitably makes contact with the divine nature increasingly unbearable, it may also open up a theoretical possibility, at least, for this further choice: either one can submit freely to the purification that the lake of fire represents and begin to discover the bliss of union with the divine

---

[22] Alexandre Kalomiros, "The River of Fire" (1980): https://afkimel.wordpress.com/2021/01/29/the-river-of-fire-2/.
[23] Talbott, p. 186.
[24] Ibid.
[25] Ibid.

nature, or one can separate oneself altogether from God's holy presence. The latter option implies separation from every implicit experience of God, including even an experience of the material universe. The brief New Testament allusions to the outer darkness suggest further that God may indeed honor such a choice. If, perchance, anyone in the lake of fire should retain the delusion that some good is possible apart from God, such a person would be free to act upon it and put it to the test. So even as Hitler tried to escape intolerable misery through suicide, perhaps some of those in the lake of fire may try to escape God's presence altogether and thus leap from the lake of fire into sheer nothingness, otherwise known as the outer darkness. By this I do not mean to suggest annihilation (as if God would destroy forever what remains of his own image in even the worst of sinners); I merely mean to imply the loneliness and terror of living apart from every implicit experience of God. Nor is it even possible that someone rational enough to qualify as a free moral agent could both experience such a condition and continue to regard it as a desirable state.[26]

Is Talbott speaking here of an objective or subjective state of affairs? Perhaps the distinction is meaningless. The undeniable point is that our personal orientation to God informs and determines our experience of God. If we have exercised our fundamental option in repudiation of the Holy Trinity and consequently find ourselves immersed in the infernal fire, would we not seek a way of escape? And if physical escape is impossible, might we not retreat into our consciousness, building up wall upon wall of interior defenses, making nothingness our reality? Yet when we have succeeded in creating as perfect a seclusion as we can manage, what would be the result? Happiness? Impossible. Perhaps while we live in the world we can entertain the possibility of happiness without God, but imagine a post-mortem life stripped of creaturely goods and society,

---

[26] Ibid., p. 188.

Freedom for Hell?

a dreary existence of isolation, monotony, tedium, sterility, emptiness, death. Talbott cites a few lines from George MacDonald, embedded in a splendid passage that deserves full quotation:

> The man whose deeds are evil, fears the burning. But the burning will not come the less that he fears it or denies it. Escape is hopeless. For Love is inexorable. Our God is a consuming fire. He shall not come out till he has paid the uttermost farthing.
>
> If the man resists the burning of God, the consuming fire of Love, a terrible doom awaits him, and its day will come. He shall be cast into the outer darkness who hates the fire of God. What sick dismay shall then seize upon him! For let a man think and care ever so little about God, he does not therefore exist without God. God is here with him, upholding, warming, delighting, teaching him—making life a good thing to him. God gives him himself, though he knows it not. But when God withdraws from a man as far as that can be without the man's ceasing to be; when the man feels himself abandoned, hanging in a ceaseless vertigo of existence upon the verge of the gulf of his being, without support, without refuge, without aim, without end—for the soul has no weapons wherewith to destroy herself–with no inbreathing of joy, with nothing to make life good;—then will he listen in agony for the faintest sound of life from the closed door; then, if the moan of suffering humanity ever reaches the ear of the outcast of darkness, he will be ready to rush into the very heart of the Consuming Fire to know life once more, to change this terror of sick negation, of unspeakable death, for that region of painful hope. Imagination cannot mislead us into too much horror of being without God—that one living death. Is not this
>> to be worse than worst
>> Of those that lawless and in certain thoughts
>> Imagine howling?
>
> But with this divine difference: that the outer darkness is but the most dreadful form of the consuming fire—the fire without light—the darkness visible, the black flame. God hath withdrawn himself, but not

lost his hold. His face is turned away, but his hand is laid upon him still. His heart has ceased to beat into the man's heart, but he keeps him alive by his fire. And that fire will go searching and burning on in him, as in the highest saint who is not yet pure as he is pure.

But at length, O God, wilt thou not cast Death and Hell into the lake of Fire—even into thine own consuming self? Death shall then die everlastingly,

And Hell itself will pass away,

And leave her dolorous mansions to the peering day.

Then indeed wilt thou be all in all. For then our poor brothers and sisters, every one—O God, we trust in thee, the Consuming Fire—shall have been burnt clean and brought home. For if their moans, myriads of ages away, would turn heaven for us into hell—shall a man be more merciful than God? Shall, of all his glories, his mercy alone not be infinite? Shall a brother love a brother more than The Father loves a son?—more than The Brother Christ loves his brother? Would he not die yet again to save one brother more?[27]

Perhaps not two different Gehennic realities, therefore, but one indivisible reality experienced differently. There is only the consuming fire that is the living God—the fire of love, the fire of judgment, the fire of purgation, the fire of Nothingness and Being.

The Evangelical and Logical Necessity of Universal Salvation

Talbott finds in the outer darkness the solution to the problem posed by libertarian free will. God need not violently impose himself upon the wicked. He need only allow them to experience the nothingness they desire, in utter confidence they will find the condition a harrowing and intolerable horror. Finally, ineluctably, all resources exhausted, overwhelmed by despair and guilt, all avenues

---

[27] George MacDonald, "The Consuming Fire," *Unspoken Sermons*, Series One (1867).

of escape closed off, the soul cannot but abandon her loveless existence—"O Lord, save me!"

Thus Talbott boldly speaks of predestination unto glory. When read through the glasses of the greater hope, the words of the Apostle take on fresh meaning:

> We know that in everything God works for good with those who love him, who are called according to his purpose. For those whom he foreknew he also predestined to be conformed to the image of his Son, in order that he might be the first-born among many brethren. And those whom he predestined he also called; and those whom he called he also justified; and those whom he justified he also glorified. (Rom 8:28-30)

No need to indulge in the strained exegesis of the Calvinists and Augustinians (who restrict the elect to only a portion of humanity) or the Arminians (who insist that Paul is only thinking of the corporate election of the Church) or the Eastern Orthodox (who construe predestination in terms of divine foreknowledge). In Christ, declares Talbott, all humanity is divinely predestined to eternal bliss in the communion of the Father, Son, and Holy Spirit. Nor should we think that human freedom is therefore compromised. Why should the shattering of our illusions be judged a violation of personal integrity? The shattering is nothing less than its restoration.

> We thus return to the well-worn analogy of the grandmaster in chess.... When a grandmaster plays a novice, it is foreordained, so to speak, that the grandmaster will win, not because he or she causally determines the novice's every move or even predicts each one of them; the end is foreordained because the grandmaster is resourceful enough to counter any combination of moves that the novice will in fact freely decide to make. And similarly for the infinitely wise and resourceful God. He has no need to exercise direct causal control over our individual choices in order to "checkmate" us in the end; he can allow

us to choose freely, perhaps even protect us from some ill-advised choices for a while, and still undermine over time every conceivable motive we might have for rejecting his grace. For once we learn for ourselves—after many trials and tribulations, in some cases—why separation from God is an objective horror and why union with him is the only thing that can satisfy our deepest yearnings and desires, all resistance to his grace will melt away like wax before a flame.[28]

Talbott goes so far as to speak of a "necessary universalism" and a "guarantee" of salvation." Given the nature of God's love, wisdom, and power," he avers, "it is logically impossible that his grace should fail to reconcile all sinners to himself."[29] I understand the argument and gladly assent to it, yet even still I try to avoid the language of necessity when speaking of God's love and salvific work. I am thrilled to proclaim the victory of our Lord's resurrection and his eschatological transfiguration of the cosmos. God will be all in all (1 Cor 15:28)—this is my fervent hope. Yet, I still judge the language of necessity alien to the language of faith. This may be a fine point I am raising—a difference, perhaps, without a difference. Perhaps we must speak of a necessity that is freedom and a freedom that is necessity. It's a question of how we make the move from speculative reflection to proclamatory gospel. To speak unconditional promise in the name of the crucified and risen Christ is different from describing a metaphysical necessity embedded in the structures of creation and the human psyche. When we preach, we tell a story of judgment and grace, death and resurrection, freedom and indomitable hope. Back in 1949, Thomas F. Torrance criticized an article on universalism by John A. T. Robinson: "If universalism is true—is a necessity," he writes—"then every road whether it had the cross planted on it or not

---

[28] Talbott, pp. 194-195.
[29] Ibid., p. 191.

would lead to salvation."[30] Universalism would thus remain a necessary truth even if Jesus had not died for our sins and risen into immortal life. Torrance's concern is misplaced, however. If we believe the gospel, we cannot entertain the possibility that God would not do precisely what he has done for us in Jesus Christ. The necessity of universal salvation is simultaneously evangelical and metaphysical. "For God has consigned all men to disobedience, that he may have mercy upon all" (Rom. 11:32).

My confident hope in apokatastasis ultimately flows from Pascha, not from the conclusions of discursive reason. I'm a preacher, dammit, not a philosopher.

---

[30] Thomas F. Torrance, "Universalism or Election?" Scottish Journal of Theology, 2 (1949): 312; reprinted as an appendix in John A.T. Robinson, In the End, God, sp. ed. (2011).

Chapter Eighteen

Revealing the God Behind the Curtain

The publication of David Bentley Hart's *That All Shall Be Saved* has brought the question of universal salvation back to theological center stage in a way that no other book has in recent memory. Karl Barth raised the issue with his powerful expositions of election and atonement in the *Church Dogmatics*, but he also insisted that the freedom of God prevents us from drawing the logical universalist conclusion. Sergius Bulgakov sounded the clarion call of apokatastasis in his posthumously published *The Bride of the Lamb*, yet his penetrating arguments received little attention from theologians. In the 1980s, Hans Urs von Balthasar advanced a contingent universalism: we may, and indeed should, hope and pray for the salvation of all, yet like Barth he too believes that the divine freedom prevents us from affirming its necessity. But then *That All Shall Be Saved* appeared on the scene in 2019. In this little book, Hart unequivocally, passionately, pugilistically pronounces: the doctrine of everlasting damnation represents nothing less than a denial of God's absolute love. Suddenly, universal salvation has become a topic theologians can no longer ignore.

The Eschaton as Revelation of the True God

Hart begins his reflections with the classic Christian doctrine of the *creatio ex nihilo*. The doctrine declares that the infinite and perfect God created the cosmos in absolute freedom, without need of anything outside himself. On this all orthodox Christians agree. But Hart then draws our attention to an often overlooked feature of the divine act—namely, its telos and goal:

Revealing the God Behind the Curtain

> Perhaps the first theological insight I learned from Gregory of Nyssa is that the Christian doctrine of *creatio ex nihilo* is not merely a cosmological or metaphysical claim, but also an eschatological claim about the world's relation to God, and for that reason a moral claim about the nature of God in himself. In the end of all things is their beginning, and only from the perspective of the end can one know what they are, why they have been made, and who the God is who has called them forth from nothingness. Anything willingly done is done toward an end; and anything done toward an end is defined by that end.[1]

The meaning of the cosmos is revealed in its consummation. The beginning is directed toward the *eschaton*; the *eschaton* contains the beginning. There's nothing particularly obscure about this observation. Every good story journeys toward a fitting conclusion. The cowardly lion is gifted with courage, the tin man a heart, the scarecrow a brain, and Dorothy clicks her ruby slippers and returns home. Narrative threads and character arcs are brought to satisfying closure. Quests are fulfilled, lovers united, conflicts resolved, rewards and punishments meted out, truths revealed and falsehoods exposed, important questions answered—and if they are not, we see why this too was necessary. If the conclusion fails to provide the fulfillment both story and aesthetic enjoyment demands, then the story is called into question. A bad ending can ruin a splendid tale. The obverse also obtains: a brilliant ending can save a problematic story. We hope that our lives will ultimately constitute a coherent narrative, that they are more than a series of plotless, absurd happenings; we hope that somehow our ending will justify our beginning. If Macbeth is right and life should prove to be nothing more than "a tale / Told by an idiot, full of sound and fury, / Signifying nothing," then it was never worth the telling.

---

[1] David Bentley Hart, *That All Shall Be Saved* (2019), p. 68.

The God of the Bible freely creates from the final future—the final future that is God himself—in his timeless telling of the cosmos. "I am the alpha and the omega, the beginning and the end" (Rev 22:13). The infinite and ineffable divinity bespeaks himself in the mode of finitude. All is theophany. All is divine self-presentation and iconic manifestation. The *eschaton* constitutes the apocalyptic disclosure of the divine character:

> Here my particular concern is the general principle that the doctrine of creation constitutes an assertion regarding the eternal identity of God. The doctrine in itself is, after all, chiefly an affirmation of God's absolute dispositive liberty in all his acts—the absence, that is, of any external restraint upon or necessity behind every action of his will. And, while one must avoid the pathetic anthropomorphism of imagining God's resolve to create as an arbitrary choice made after deliberation among options, one must still affirm that it is free, that creation can add nothing to God, that God's being is not dependent on the world's, and that the only "necessity" present in the divine act of creation is the impossibility of any hindrance being placed upon God's expression of his own goodness in making the world. Yet, for just this reason, the moral destiny of creation and the moral nature of God are absolutely inseparable. As the transcendent Good beyond all beings, God is also the transcendental end that makes every single action of any rational nature possible. Moreover, the end toward which he acts must be his own goodness; for he is himself the beginning and end of all things. This is not to deny that, in addition to the "primary causality" of God's act of creation, there are innumerable forms of "secondary causality" operative within the created order; but none of these can exceed or escape the one end toward which the first cause directs all things. And this eternal teleology that ultimately governs every action in creation, viewed from the vantage of history, takes the form of a cosmic eschatology. Seen as an eternal act of God, creation's term is the divine nature for which all things were made; seen from within the orientation

of time, its term is the "final judgment" that brings all things to their true conclusion.[2]

God goes forth in all beings and in all beings returns to himself, as even Aquinas (following a long Christian tradition) affirms; but God also does this not as an expression of his dialectical struggle with some recalcitrant exteriority—some external obstacle to be surmounted or some unrealized possibility to be achieved—but rather as the manifestation of an inexhaustible power wholly possessed by the divine in peaceful liberty in eternity. God has no need of the world; he creates it not because he is dependent upon it, but because its dependency on him is a fitting expression of the bounty of his goodness. So all that the doctrine of creation adds to the basic metaphysical picture is the further assurance that in this divine outpouring there is no element of the "irrational": nothing purely spontaneous, or organic, or even mechanical, beyond the power of God's rational freedom. This, however, also means that within the story of creation, viewed from its final cause, there can be no residue of the pardonably tragic, no irrecuperable or irreconcilable remainder left behind at the end of the tale; for, if there were, this irreconcilable excess would also be something God has directly caused, as an entailment freely assumed in his act of creating, and so as an expression of who he freely is. This is no more than the simple logic of the absolute.[3]

Precisely because God does not determine himself in creation—precisely because there is no dialectical necessity binding him to time or chaos, no need to shape his identity in the refining fires of history—in creating he reveals himself truly. Thus every evil that time comprises, natural or moral . . . is an arraignment of God's goodness: every death of a child, every chance calamity, every act of malice; everything diseased, thwarted, pitiless, purposeless, or cruel; and, until the end of all things, no answer has been given. Precisely because creation is not a theogony, all of it is theophany. It would be impious, I suppose, to suggest that, in his final divine judgment on his creatures, God will

---

[2] Ibid., p. 69.
[3] Ibid., p. 71.

judge himself; but one must hold that by that judgment God will truly disclose himself.[1]

Who is the God behind the eschatological curtain? Let's unpack this crucial composite passage.

First, the doctrine of *creatio ex nihilo* asserts the absolute liberty of the Creator in all of his acts. He is not subject to constraints outside of himself. As the infinite plenitude of Being, God did not need to create the cosmos to fill something that was lacking in his life (no passive potency), and having created it, he does not discover that his happiness and bliss have been increased and intensified.

Second, God eternally wills himself as the Good, and his willing of the cosmos is encompassed within this eternal self-willing. He himself is the purpose, telos, and goal of the divine act of creation. The cosmos is created by Love for consummation in Love.

Third, God does not create evil. Only goodness flows from the divine wellspring of being. For this reason, the classical theologians of the Christian tradition have understood evil as a privation of being—a defect, absence, and surd. The presence of evil within God's good creation urgently raises the question of theodicy. Evil will always be the greatest challenge to faith, both intellectually and existentially. It's one thing to acknowledge and suffer evil's destructive presence in the temporal order; it's quite another thing to assert its eschatological perdurance.

The *eschaton*, therefore, necessarily and definitively reveals the character and identity of the Creator. The conclusion of the story can neither surprise nor disappoint him, for it is willed in his eternal creative act. Hence the presence of evil in the *eschaton* is quite impossible, assuming that the Creator is truly good. In Hart's words: "He could not be the creator of anything substantially evil without

---

[1] Ibid., pp. 72-73.

evil also being part of the definition of who he essentially is."[5] If everlasting perdition belongs to the climax of the cosmic narrative, then it was so intended by God from the beginning. Every free act is teleologically directed and therefore defined by its final cause. The inference cannot be avoided. Nothing compelled the Holy Trinity to create this particular universe with this particular eschaton—and the omnipotence/omniscience combo precludes failure. If hell is intended, then God becomes hell.

To summarize: in his goodness the triune God creates the cosmos for consummation in his transcendent goodness. All comes from Love and returns to Love. The Creator is both efficient and final cause. The *eschaton*, therefore, is not simply the climax of a story. It is the apocalypse of the Father, Son, and Holy Spirit in the fullness of their lordship and glory. In the words of the Apostle:

> And, when all things have been subordinated to him, then will the Son himself also be subordinated to the one who has subordinated all things to him, so that God may be all in all. (1 Cor 15:28)

God will be *all in all*. How then hell everlasting?

The Incoherence of Hell

The above reasoning leads Hart to the conclusion that a pernicious incoherence lies deep within the theological tradition. For over a millennium the Church has asserted three claims:

- God freely created the cosmos *ex nihilo*.
- God is the Good and wills only the good.

---

[5] Ibid., pp.70-71.

- God will condemn a portion of his rational creatures to everlasting torment.

Two of these propositions may be rationally held without contradiction, maintains Hart, but not all three simultaneously. If we affirm 1 and 2, we will infer that all will be saved (contra 3). If we affirm 2 and 3, we will infer that God was bound to create this particular world by metaphysical necessity (contra 1). If we affirm 1 and 3, we will infer that God is not perfectly good (contra 2). But to affirm all three propositions only generates nonsense. Yet for well over a millennium the Church has attempted to hold the three together, thereby causing far-reaching mischief and theological confusion:

> This is not a complicated issue, it seems to me: The eternal perdition—the eternal suffering—of any soul would be an abominable tragedy, and therefore a profound natural evil; this much is stated quite clearly by scripture, in asserting that God "intends all human beings to be saved and to come to a full knowledge of truth" (1 Timothy 2:4). A natural evil, however, becomes a moral evil precisely to the degree that it is the positive intention, even if only conditionally, of a rational will. God could not, then, directly intend a soul's ultimate destruction, or even intend that a soul bring about its own destruction, without positively willing the evil end *as* an evil end; such a result could not possibly be comprised within the ends purposed by a truly good will (in any sense of the word "good" intelligible to us). Yet, if both the doctrine of *creatio ex nihilo* and that of eternal damnation are true, that very evil is indeed already comprised within the *positive* intentions and dispositions of God. No refuge is offered here by some specious distinction between God's antecedent and consequent wills—between, that is, his universal

will for creation apart from the fall and his particular will regarding each creature in consequence of the fall. Under the canopy of God's omnipotence and omniscience, the consequent is already wholly virtually present in the antecedent.[6]

Hart is hardly the first person in the history of the Church to see the illogic of the traditional teaching. Back in the seventh century, St Isaac of Nineveh wrote:

> It is not the way of the compassionate Maker to create rational beings in order to deliver them over mercilessly to unending affliction in punishment for things of which He knew even before they were fashioned, aware how they would turn out when He created them—and whom nonetheless He created.[7]

Because the LORD's making of the cosmos is a truly free and unconditioned act (a making that need not have been), it necessarily manifests the intentions, purposes, and identity of the Creator; yet because creation is an unfolding in time, we will only apprehend its meaning in its apocalyptic consummation, when God will be all in all. Who will be revealed when the curtain is pulled back? In faith we confess that the God revealed at the final judgment will be—and is—the God of absolute Love already made known in Jesus Christ, yet the traditional doctrine of hell also declares that this judgment will be a time of final division: the righteous will be rewarded with eternal life and the wicked condemned to everlasting torment and misery. The vision terrifies. Upon hearing it, some may be led to repentance and urgent efforts to attain righteousness. Others may experience the opposite effect, a kind of moral and spiritual

---

[6] Ibid., pp. 81-82. Also see Hart's article "What God Wills and What God Permits," *Public Orthodoxy* (5 May 2020): https://publicorthodoxy.org/2020/05/05/what-god-wills-and-what-god-permits/.
[7] Isaac of Nineveh, *The Second Part* 39.6.

paralysis. Others may rejoice, believing they have already acquired the requisite virtues and good works. And still others may find themselves filled with such deep moral revulsion and loathing that they abandon faith altogether. If God is truly revealed in the final judgment, and if the doctrine of eternal perdition is true, then we must logically posit either a dualistic conflict within the heart of the eternal Creator or deny his goodness altogether. In either case we are no longer talking about the God of the gospel.

> "I think you are a very bad man," said Dorothy.
> "Oh, no, my dear; I'm really a very good man, but I'm a very bad Wizard, I must admit."

At this point, theologians will raise the scholastic distinction between God's *antecedent will* and his *consequent will*. The former refers to God's willing of a good prior to historical and particularist considerations; the latter to his willing of a specific good in concrete circumstances. St Thomas Aquinas explicitly invokes this distinction in his consideration of the question "Whether the will of God is always fulfilled?" It appears, he says, that the divine will is not always fulfilled and cites the classic New Testament statement of God's universal salvific will: "God will have all men to be saved, and to come to the knowledge of the truth" (1 Tim 2:4). In response, Thomas explains that the Apostle's statement refers to God's original intent for humanity before history got messy. God antecedently desires the salvation of all, but given the fall, his salvific will is now refracted through the reality of sin and iniquity:

> To understand this we must consider that everything, in so far as it is good, is willed by God. A thing taken in its primary sense, and absolutely considered, may be good or evil, and yet when some additional circumstances are taken into account, by a consequent consideration may be changed into the contrary. Thus that a man

should live is good; and that a man should be killed is evil, absolutely considered. But if in a particular case we add that a man is a murderer or dangerous to society, to kill him is a good; that he live is an evil. Hence it may be said of a just judge, that antecedently he wills all men to live; but consequently wills the murderer to be hanged. In the same way God antecedently wills all men to be saved, but consequently wills some to be damned, as His justice exacts. Nor do we will simply, what we will antecedently, but rather we will it in a qualified manner; for the will is directed to things as they are in themselves, and in themselves they exist under particular qualifications. Hence we will a thing simply inasmuch as we will it when all particular circumstances are considered; and this is what is meant by willing consequently. Thus it may be said that a just judge wills simply the hanging of a murderer, but in a qualified manner he would will him to live, to wit, inasmuch as he is a man. Such a qualified will may be called a willingness rather than an absolute will. Thus it is clear that whatever God simply wills takes place; although what He wills antecedently may not take place.[8]

Yet does this distinction illuminate the problem of eternal damnation? I think not. It obscures more than it clarifies. The final judgment is not like the judgments a human jurist makes within fallen history. In the *eschaton* God sets the cosmos perfectly to rights, once and for all. That's what *eschatons* are supposed to do. God's antecedent will triumphs. The biblical and cosmic story is brought to eucatastrophic, rapturous, glorious consummation. In the words of the great Origen:

> When, then, the end has been renewed to the beginning and the departure of things joined to their entrance, that condition will be restored which rational beings then had, when they did not need to eat of the tree of the knowledge of good and evil, so that to them, with all perception of wickedness having been removed and having been

---

[8] Thomas Aquinas, *Summa Theologiae* I.19.6.

cleansed, to be sound and pure, he who is alone the one good God himself becomes all, and he himself becomes all not in a few things or in many, but in all, when indeed there is nowhere death, nowhere the sting of death, nowhere any evil, then, truly, God will be all in all.[9]

Yet if we know by divine revelation that God everlastingly punishes the impenitent, how do we reconcile this punishment with God's foundational love? Are we even talking about love? One possible and traditional answer: once evil is brought into the equation, the divine love is eschatologically expressed as retributive justice. This is its inner content, as it were. In the end—and therefore from the beginning—God wills only the damnation, not the salvation, of the obdurately wicked. The apocalyptic curtain is pulled back, and the divine mercy is disclosed as conditional upon repentance. Hence there can be no forgiveness for the impenitent; they get what they deserve. James Brent explains:

> Does God will the salvation of all? Aquinas distinguishes between antecedent and consequent will. To will a good antecedently is to will it prior to considering all particular circumstances. To will a good consequently is to will it given the consideration of all particular circumstances. Aquinas's example is a judge in court. Prior to considering what crimes a certain human being has committed, a judge wills all human beings to live. The judge antecedently wills all human beings to live. But given the consideration that a certain human being has committed a certain crime, say murder, the judge consequently wills him or her to die as punishment. Similarly, God antecedently wills all human beings to be saved. But God does not consequently will the salvation of this or that particular human being. Aquinas is careful to say that "this distinction must not be taken as applying to the divine will itself," as though God's will could change from one moment to the next or as though his knowledge of circumstances could change as his

---

[9] Origen, *On First Principles* 3.6.3.

attention turns from one thing to another. Rather than being a distinction between two acts of will in God, Aquinas says, it is a distinction in "the things willed."[10]

"Do not arouse the wrath of the great and powerful Oz!" In the last judgment, so the Angelic Doctor teaches, absolute love collapses into pitiless hate, at least for the reprobate. The antecedent becomes the consequent; the final will definitively reinterprets the original will. And since the divine essence is immutable and the divine essence is identical to the divine willing, we are forced to conclude that the Creator eternally wills both heaven and hell. We cannot pretend that he wishes otherwise; if he did, he would have created a different world or no world at all. God's end is his beginning; his consequent will is his antecedent will. Such is the logic of *eschaton*.

But surely this God who ordains perdition and hell cannot be the God of absolute love revealed in Jesus Christ. He is not the God whom I worship, the God whom I preach, the God whom I serve. Nor is he the God whom David Hart worships and serves:

> If God is the good creator of all, he must also be the savior of all, without fail, who brings to himself all he has made, including all rational wills, and thus returns to himself in all that goes forth from him. If he is not the savior of all, the Kingdom is only a dream, and creation something considerably worse than a nightmare. But, again, it is not so.[11]

No, it is not so. God will be all in all!

---

[10] James Brent, "God's Knowledge and Will," in *The Oxford Handbook of Aquinas* (2012), ed. Brian Davies and Eleonore Stump, p. 67.
[11] Hart, pp. 90-91.

Chapter Nineteen

Doomed to Happiness

Thirsting for the Living God

David Bentley Hart controversially asserts that human beings are *doomed to everlasting happiness*—yet should the claim be controversial? Christianity has long taught that the human being, created by the divine Word in the image of the Word, exists in dynamic orientation to its transcendent Creator. In all things and at all times, God is the Goodness, Beauty and Truth we desire and seek. As St Augustine memorably states: "Thou hast formed us for Thyself, and our hearts are restless till they find rest in Thee."[1] We cannot help but to crave communion with our Creator. This is how we have been made; this is who we are by nature and grace. We were not created in a neutral state in relation to divinity, as if it were possible for us to generate abiding happiness on our own terms. Our freedom is not a mode of indifference. The human being is nothing less than insatiable thirst for the divine, an inspirited ever-seeking for the One who is our completion and fulfillment. In the words of St Maximus the Confessor: "God, who created all nature with wisdom and secretly planted in each intelligent being knowledge of Himself as its first power, like a munificent Lord gave also to us men a natural desire and longing for Him, combining it in a natural way with the power of our intelligence."[2] God has created humanity for union with himself. Apart from him we cannot find happiness. He is the power and fulfillment of our searchings, the

---

[1] Augustine, *Confessions* I.1.
[2] Maximus, *Various Texts on Theology, the Divine Economy and Virtue and Vice* 5.100.

origin and end of all our desires. Every finite good we seek betokens the transcendent Good to which we are ordered. We desire goodness and beauty because of our desire for God; we seek to know truth because of our appetite for Truth. "Even in desiring to flee God," remarks Hart, "we are desiring God as the 'good end' we seek in godlessness."[3] Simultaneously the plenitude of being and immanent ground of existence, the infinite Creator is our supreme beatitude and therefore our final cause and consummation. Henri de Lubac once asked Maurice Blondel: "How can a conscious spirit be anything other than an absolute desire for God?" Exactly.

Given that we are created by God for union with God, Hart's assertion that humanity is destined to eternal bliss makes perfect sense. God will have his way with us, one way or another, not by force or coercion but by the appetition he has placed in our hearts. The following passage summarizes Hart's fundamental thesis:

> The more one is in one's right mind—the more, that is, that one is conscious of God as the Goodness that fulfills all beings, and the more one recognizes that one's own nature can have its true completion and joy nowhere but in him, and the more one is unfettered by distorting misperceptions, deranged passions, and the encumbrances of past mistakes—the more inevitable is one's surrender to God. Liberated from all ignorance, emancipated from all the adverse conditions of this life, the rational soul could freely will only its own union with God, and thereby its own supreme beatitude. We are, as it were, doomed to happiness, so long as our natures follow their healthiest impulses unhindered; we cannot not will the satisfaction of our beings in our true final end, a transcendent Good lying behind and beyond all the proximate ends we might be moved to pursue. This is no constraint upon the freedom of the will, coherently conceived; it is simply the

---

[3] *Eclectic Orthodoxy* (4 May 2015): https://afkimel.wordpress.com/2015/05/19/david-b-hart-on-universal-salvation-and-human-freedom/.

consequence of possessing a nature produced by and for the transcendent Good: a nature whose proper end has been fashioned in harmony with a supernatural purpose. God has made us for himself, as Augustine would say, and our hearts are restless till they rest in him. A rational nature seeks a rational end: Truth, which is God himself. The irresistibility of God for any soul that has truly been set free is no more a constraint placed upon its liberty than is the irresistible attraction of a flowing spring of fresh water in a desert place to a man who is dying of thirst; to choose not to drink in that circumstance would be not an act of freedom on his part, but only a manifestation of the delusions that enslave him and force him to inflict violence upon himself, contrary to his nature. A woman who chooses to run into a burning building not to save another's life, but only because she can imagine no greater joy than burning to death, may be exercising a kind of "liberty," but in the end she is captive to a far profounder poverty of rational freedom.[1]

The essential point is plain enough. The desire for God is intrinsic to human nature. In our fallen existence, we do not experience this desire in its purity and perfection. It can be temporarily forgotten; it can be perverted and corrupted and twisted from its proper goal; but ultimately it can be neither extinguished nor eradicated. If it could be, we would cease to be human. As theologian Stephen J. Duffy puts it:

> In the concrete nature of fallen humanity there is an interior, absolute desire of the Kingdom that correlates with the universal salvific divine will. This determination is an *existential*. It is prior to all personal options and persists through all possible acceptances or rejections of one's end. Whatever one does, one remains interiorly ordered to absolute communion with God.[2]

---

[1] David Bentley Hart, *That All Shall Be Saved: Heaven, Hell, and Universal Salvation* (2019), pp. 40-41.
[2] Stephen J. Duffy, *The Graced Horizon* (1992), p. 23.

Once we grasp the truth of humanity's primordial desire for the Good, the traditional claim that human beings might freely give themselves over to everlasting misery becomes increasingly problematic. Surely the burden of proof rests upon the defenders of hell.

Wounded by Love

In 2015, David Bentley Hart delivered a now much-discussed lecture at the University of Notre Dame titled "God, Creation, and Evil." When I watched the video of the lecture, this statement jumped out at me:

> No one can freely will the evil as evil; one can take the evil for the good, but that does not alter the prior transcendental orientation that wakens all desire. To see the good truly is to desire it insatiably; not to desire it is not to have known it, and so never to have been free to choose it.[6]

It was a quiet eureka moment. Everything fell into place. Of course, I said to myself, how could it be otherwise? That God is the Good whom all human beings seek I had been taught by my parish priest decades ago. I later came to hope that the grace of God might be *irresistible*. I likened it to falling in love. Does the lover choose to fall in love? Certainly not in the way one chooses to order bacon rather than sausage for breakfast. All lovers know the existential difference. Falling in love comes as astonishment and revelation. "Here is the person I have been looking for. Here is the one who completes me." The choice is embedded in the recognition. To be in the presence of one's beloved is perfect joy; to be joined to him or her in coital union, rapture. Lovers find each other enthralling.

---

[6] David Bentley Hart, "God, Creation, and Evil," *The Hidden and the Manifest* (2017), p. 345.

Destined for Joy

They see each other with the eyes of divinity: "You are altogether beautiful; there is no flaw in you" (Song of Songs 4:7). They are drawn together, as if by some kind of magnetic force. Frequently, they will invoke the language of slavery, even madness, when speaking of their mutual attraction—yet it is a slavery of utter freedom and an insanity of delight and wonder. They are filled with an intensity of life they have never before known. Their one joy is to give themselves to each other and become one flesh, one mind, one soul.

> My bounty is as boundless as the sea,
> My love as deep; the more I give to thee,
> The more I have, for both are infinite.[7]

Beyond all doubt lovers know they will adore and cherish each other forever. They cannot imagine a future apart from their beloved. They exchange solemn vows and promises.

> Ye are Blood of my Blood, and Bone of my Bone.
> I give ye my Body, that we two might be One.
> I give ye my Spirit, `til our Life shall be done.

Their bond transcends the limits and hardships of time.

> Love's not Time's fool, though rosy lips and cheeks
> Within his bending sickle's compass come;
> Love alters not with his brief hours and weeks,
> But bears it out even to the edge of doom.[8]

Surely this must be what it will be like when we see God face to face. All doubts and hesitations will vanish; all obstinacy and egoism forever banished. Here is the true happiness I have been searching

---

[7] Shakespeare, *Romeo and Juliet*, Act II, sc. 2.
[8] William Shakespeare, Sonnet 116.

for all my life, though I knew it not. Here is the abundant life that conquers death. Even the ecstasy of lovers will be infinitely eclipsed.

"Falling in love, being in love"—a door, I propose, through which we might enter to better grasp Hart's vision of apokatastasis and human freedom. The Holy Scriptures, after all, contain the Song of Songs, one of the most beautiful love poems in all of literature. The beloved sings of the wound of love:

> *Bring me into the house of wine,*
> *Set love in order upon me.*
> *Strengthen me with perfumes,*
> *Encompass me with applies,*
> *for I have been wounded by love.*
> *(Song 2:4-5)*

"I have been wounded by love"—all lovers have experienced this rending. The arrow that pierces the heart cannot be removed; the wound it brings cannot be healed. Once struck the beloved cries out for union with her lover. Only through the most profound joining can the pain be assuaged and wholeness restored. As it is between human lovers, so it is between God and the soul, as St Gregory of Nyssa elaborates:

> After she has said these things, she praises the accurate archer because he has directed his arrow straight at her, for she says, I have been wounded by love. By these words she signifies the arrow that lies deep in her heart. But the archer who discharges the arrow is love. From Holy Scripture, however, we have learned that God is love (cf. 1 John 4:8, 16), and he discharges his own chosen arrow (cf. Isa 49:2)—the Only Begotten God—at those who are being saved, having smeared over the triple point of the barb with the Spirit of life (the barb is faith), so that, in the person in whom it is planted, it may introduce the archer together with the arrow, as the Lord says: "I and my Father will come and make our dwelling with him" (John 14:23). See, then, the soul that

has been exalted through the divine ascents sees in herself the sweet arrow of love by which she is wounded and makes boast of such a blow by saying, I have been wounded by love.[9]

Commenting on Song 3:1-8, Gregory writes:

> God comes into the soul, and correspondingly the soul is brought into God. For she says, "My beloved is mine, and I am his. He does his pasturing among the lilies and transfers human life from the realm of shadowy images to the truth of that which is." You see to what a height she has climbed, this soul that, in accordance with the prophetic word, is going "from strength to strength" (Ps 83:8): she seems to attain the hope of the very highest good. For what is higher than to be in the One who is the object of desire and to receive the object of desire within oneself? But in this situation too she bewails the fact that she is needy for the Good. As one who does not yet have what is present to her desire, she is perplexed and dissatisfied, and she broadcasts this perplexity of her soul in her story, describing in her account how she found the one she sought.[10]

Charles Williams speaks of romantic love as a foretaste of heaven: when we fall in love, "a sudden apprehension of the Good takes place."[11] At their best and purest, human lovers mirror our encounter with the divine. To know the Good is to desire the Good; to experience Love is to surrender to Love. The metaphysics of the Good may be difficult to grasp, but we know something about the irresistibility of the One who is Love, if not by direct experience, then through literature and art.

---

[9] Gregory of Nyssa, *Homilies on the Song of Songs, Hom.* 4; trans. Richard A. Norris, Jr. (2013).
[10] Ibid., *Hom.* 6.
[11] Charles Williams, "The Theology of Romantic Love," *Outlines of Romantic Theology* (1990), p. 109.

Doomed to Happiness

We return to the featured sentences. Hart has incorporated them in *That All Shall Be Saved*, with minor changes:

> But to me it seems impossible to speak of freedom in any meaningful sense at all unless one begins from the assumption that, for a rational spirit, to see the good and know it truly is to desire it insatiably and **to obey it unconditionally**, while not to desire it is not to have known it truly, and so never to have been free to choose it.[12]

Note the addition of the response of obedience. The vision of the Good immediately engenders the obedience of love. The will of the lover freely conforms itself to the will of the beloved. But perhaps we need to reverse the roles. In the biblical narrative, God is the Lover who has in Christ made us the objects of his love. By grace he takes the initiative. "In this is love, not that we loved God but that he loved us and sent his Son to be the expiation for our sins" (1 John 4:10). And this love arouses within the soul a reciprocal love for the divine lover. "For when God loves," writes St Bernard of Clairvaux, "he desires only to be loved in return. His love's only purpose is to be loved, as he knows that all who love him are made happy by their love of him."[13]

Sinners most especially know that it is only by the ravishment of God that they may attain the liberty of the blessed. John Donne knew this well:

> Take me to you, imprison me, for I,
> Except you enthrall me, never shall be free,
> Nor ever chaste, except you ravish me.[14]

---

[12] Hart, pp. 79-80; emphasis mine.
[13] Quoted in David Bentley Hart, *The Experience of God* (2014), p. 276.
[14] John Donne, Holy Sonnet 14.

But does this not sound like some kind of determinism? Here is Hart's answer:

> For those who worry that this all amounts to a kind of metaphysical determinism of the will, I may not be able to provide perfect comfort. Of course it is a kind of determinism, but only at the transcendental level, and only because rational volition must be determinate to be anything at all. Rational will is by nature the capacity for intentional action, and so must exist as a clear relation between (in Aristotelian terms) the "origin of motion" within it and the "end" that prompts that motion—between, that is, its efficient and final causes. Freedom is a relation to reality, which means liberty from delusion. This divine determinism toward the transcendent Good, then, is precisely what freedom is for a rational nature. Even God could not create a rational being not oriented toward the Good, any more than he could create a reality in which $2 + 2 = 5$. That is not to deny that, within the embrace of this relation between the will's origin and its end in the Good (what, again, Maximus the Confessor calls our "natural will"), there is considerable room for deliberative liberty with regard to differing finite options (what Maximus calls the "gnomic will"), and considerable room in which to stray from the ideal path. But, even so, if a rational creature—one whose mind is entirely unimpaired and who has the capacity truly to know the substance and the consequences of the choice confronting him or her—is allowed, without coercion from any force extrinsic to his or her nature, to make a choice between a union with God in bliss that will utterly fulfill his or her nature in its deepest yearnings and a separation from God that will result in endless suffering and the total absence of his or her nature's satisfaction, only one truly free choice is possible. A fool might thrust his hand into the flame; only a lunatic would not then immediately withdraw it. To say that the only sane and therefore free natural end of the will is the Good is no more problematic than to say that the only sane and therefore free natural end of the intellect is Truth. Rational spirit could no more will evil on the grounds that it is truly evil than the intellect could believe something on the grounds that it is certainly false. So, yes, there is an

original and ultimate divine determinism of the creature's intellect and will, and for just this reason there is such a thing as true freedom in the created realm. As on the cross (John 12:32), so in the whole of being: God frees souls by dragging them to himself.[15]

Hart bites the bullet. Yes, humanity is *determined* to the Good, but we must not think of this determinism as a form of violence or coercion. It does not constrict our freedom but creates and establishes it. Apart from this innate relation of reason to the Good, the True, and the Beautiful—in other words, God—we would not will anything at all. Volition is intrinsically teleological and intentional. We act to attain a specific end we deem good. Consider how we actually make choices. Invariably we have our reasons:

> At the same time, rationality must by definition be intentionality: the mind's awareness, that is, of a purpose it seeks or an end it wishes to achieve or a meaning it wishes to affirm. Rational freedom, in its every action, must be teleological in structure: one must know the end one is choosing, and why. Any act of the mind or will done without a reason, conversely, would be by definition irrational and therefore a symptom of bondage to something outside of or lower than the rational will. It is not even very sensible to ask, then, whether a free will might not "spontaneously" posit an end for itself out of the sheer exuberance of its power to choose, and then pursue that end out of pure unreasoning perversity. Absolute spontaneity would be an unfree act, a mere brute event beyond the control of mind and desire, while merely partial spontaneity would still be guided by some kind of purpose. If you wish to prove this to yourself, you need only attempt freely to posit an end for yourself without rationale. Then again, do not bother, since you would not actually be acting without rationale; you would instead be pursuing the conscious purpose of following my suggestion that you try to act spontaneously. Anything you might willfully choose to do for the

---

[15] Hart, TASBS, pp. 178-179.

purpose of doing something arbitrary would not, in fact, be arbitrary. And you will find also that even that supposedly arbitrary act, if you conceived of it before doing it, was not really arbitrary after all, but rather corresponded to some concrete intention that you knowingly chose, and for some specific reason, out of a strictly limited range of possible options. This too you can prove to yourself. You would not, for instance, simply in order to try to prove me wrong, leap off the top of a high building. Or, rather, if you did, the rest of us would immediately recognize your action as a feat of lunacy, and therefore not truly free. You cannot actually force yourself to behave "irrationally" except in an ultimately rational way. And to seek to find a first moment of perfect mindless impulse in any free act is to pursue a hopeless descent back along an infinite regress.[16]

All of this is easy enough to grasp upon phenomenological analysis. I eat the apple because I am hungry. I get in the car because I want to go downtown. I study the ant farm because I wish to understand how they organize their society. I give $5 to a homeless person because I wish to assist him in his need.

But what, or who, awakens the will to act in the first place? If we stay within the Christian reading of the Song of Songs, there can be only one answer: Jesus Christ, the eternal Word of God, who has created us in dynamic orientation to the transcendentals of being and thus to himself. He is "the transcendental horizon of reality that animates every single stirring of reason and desire, the always more remote end present within every more immediate end. Insofar as we are able freely to will anything at all, therefore, it is precisely because he is *making* us to do so: as at once the source of all action and intentionality in rational natures and also the transcendental object of rational desire that elicits every act of mind and will toward any purposes whatsoever."[17] In the depths of the human soul, the

---

[16] Ibid., pp. 173-174.
[17] Ibid., p. 184.

incarnate Word acts upon our mind and will as ultimate source and final cause. Because we are enveloped by the Good, we are moved to pursue finite goods for ourselves and the welfare of others; because we are encompassed by the Truth, we desire to understand stars and quasars, molecules and neutrinos, bats and cuttlefish; because we are enfolded in the Beautiful, we seek out the delights of Beethoven's 5th symphony, the starry nights of Vincent Van Gogh, and the poetry of John Keats and William Butler Yeats. In all our actions, we intend the one Lover in whom we live and move and have our being.

I know what many readers are thinking: *I can still say no to God, can't I? I can still choose eternity in hell, right?* But can you, could you, and most importantly, why do you want to? There's something deep in Adamic man that resists the notion that the grace of God is ultimately irresistible. We resist it because it seems to violate human freedom and takes our final destiny out of our hands. Consider Gerhard Forde's answer to the question "But you don't mean that grace is irresistible, do you?"

> Another tricky question. But again the answer can only, in the end, be yes. "Yes, I find it to be so, don't you?" Remember it is grace we are talking about, not force. Absolute and unconditional grace has by very definition to be irresistible, one would think. Did you ever meet someone with irresistible grace? All that means is that you are utterly and completely captivated and so cannot finally "resist." Certainly God's whole purpose in coming was to make grace irresistible, was it not? Do we not hope that in the end all enemies will be overcome, all opposition stilled, grace completely triumphant and God all in all? How can that be if grace is not finally irresistible?[18]

---

[18] Gerhard Forde, *Theology is for Proclamation* (1990), pp. 169-170.

The irresistibility of grace brings us back to Hart's key claim that humanity possesses by its creation a natural desire for God. Every particle of our being cries out for the Good, Beauty, and Truth that is our Creator.

> As a hart longs for flowing streams,
> so longs my soul for thee, O God.
> My soul thirsts for God, for the living God.
> (Ps 42:1-2)

Theosis is Our Freedom

Every human being is divinely ordered to God under the aspects of the transcendentals of Being—the Good, the True, and the Beautiful. We hunger and thirst for union with him, for only in him can we enjoy supreme and overflowing happiness. Divinity is inscribed in the ontological depths of human nature. In the words of Dumitru Staniloae:

> Man, without being himself infinite, not only is fit, but is also thirsty for the infinite and precisely for this reason is also capable of, and longs for, God, the true and only infinite (*homo capax divini*—man capable of the divine). He has a capacity and is thirsty for the infinite not in the sense that he is in a state to win it, to absorb it in his nature—because then human nature itself would become infinite—but in the sense that he can and must be nourished spiritually from the infinite, and infinitely. He seeks and is able to live in a continual communication with it, in a sharing with it.[19]

Created in the image of God, we are incomplete without God. Of course, no one is truly without God. As divine Creator, he acts in the ontological depths of every person. He is more intimate to us

---

[19] Dumitru Staniloae, *Orthodox Spirituality* (2003), p. 78.

than we are to ourselves. Yet we suffer from an existential inquietude that evidences our brokenness and alienation. Despite the counsel of the Church's ascetics and spiritual teachers, we continue to seek our fulfillment in the relative goods and delights of the cosmos, with predictable results. We remain dissatisfied, unsettled, restless and discontent. Once we obtain that which we think will fill the hole in our hearts, we find that we need something else, someone else. And so, the quest continues, *ad infinitum*. We are inescapably drawn to fullness of life. Contrary to the Latin theorists of the *natura pura*, human beings have not been given two ends, natural and supernatural.[20] There is only one *telos* and beatitude for mankind—eternal life in the perichoretic Love that is the Father, Son, and Holy Spirit. The Orthodox Church calls this *theosis*. Hart elaborates:

> Above all, a Christian is more or less obliged to believe that there is such a thing as an intrinsic nature in rational spirits: We are created, that is to say, according to a divine design, after the divine image, oriented toward a divine purpose, and thus are fulfilled in ourselves only insofar as we can achieve the perfection of our natures in union with God. There alone our true happiness lies. This inevitably places Christian thought in the classical moral and metaphysical tradition that assumes that true freedom consists in the realization of a complex nature in its own proper good (the "intellectualist" model of freedom, as I have called it above). Freedom is a being's power to flourish as what it naturally is, to become ever more fully what it is. The freedom

---

[20] For a helpful introduction to the *natura pura* debate in Catholic theology, see Edward T. Oakes, *A Theology of Grace in Six Controversies* (2016), chap. 1. The Thomist notion of a human nature not oriented to *theosis* is alien to Orthodox theology and was rejected by 20th century theologians such as Vladimir Lossky, Sergius Bulgakov, Paul Evdokimov, and John Meyendorff. Hart decidedly rejects the *natura pura* hypothesis both in *TASBS* and in his recently published book *You Are Gods: On Nature and Supernature* (2022).

of an oak seed is its uninterrupted growth into an oak tree. The freedom of a rational spirit is its consummation in union with God.[21]

God, and God alone, is the true happiness of the human being. He is our absolute good and the consummation of all desire. Under the present fallen condition of ignorance, delusion, and disordered passions, we only apprehend the Good partially and defectively through the prism of finite goods. We therefore often find ourselves choosing lesser goods over greater goods, apparent goods instead of real goods—the Church calls this sin—but if we were ever presented with a full and perfect apprehension of the Good, free from ignorance, delusion, and disordered passions, we would necessarily embrace the Good as our own, for we would recognize it as the true and final happiness for which we yearn. Or to put it differently, we would know that the happiness that we will for ourselves and the happiness that God wills for us are identical. Hence the Hartian maxim: *to see the Good is to insatiably desire the Good.* In the unmediated presence of the infinite and transcendent Creator, the will cannot help but to desire and possess him. There is no longer a "choosing" between different possible happinesses: there is only the eternal bliss of the one God who is Holy Trinity. Choosing him is no choice at all. St Thomas Aquinas explains:

> Man does not choose of necessity. And this is because that which is possible not to be, is not of necessity. Now the reason why it is possible not to choose, or to choose, may be gathered from a twofold power in man. For man can will and not will, act and not act; again, he can will this or that, and do this or that. The reason of this is seated in the very power of the reason. For the will can tend to whatever the reason can apprehend as good. Now the reason can apprehend as good, not only this, viz. "to will" or "to act," but also this, viz. "not to will" or "not to

---

[21] *TASBS*, p. 172.

act." Again, in all particular goods, the reason can consider an aspect of some good, and the lack of some good, which has the aspect of evil: and in this respect, it can apprehend any single one of such goods as to be chosen or to be avoided. The perfect good alone, which is Happiness, cannot be apprehended by the reason as an evil, or as lacking in any way. Consequently man wills Happiness of necessity, nor can he will not to be happy, or to be unhappy. Now since choice is not of the end, but of the means . . . ; it is not of the perfect good, which is Happiness, but of other particular goods. Therefore man chooses not of necessity, but freely.[22]

In this sense, but only in this sense, we are eschatologically doomed to happiness. To see God with perfect vision is to will deifying union with him in the necessity of perfect freedom.

If we still balk at our transcendental determination to the Good, perhaps the reason lies in our defective understanding of who and what God is and therefore what authentic freedom must mean. If we think of Deity as a being among beings, then it might appear that we can ultimately choose other gods and other goods instead of him. Why not Baal instead of the LORD? Why not wealth and power instead of the Father of our Lord Jesus Christ? But once God is properly understood as the infinite plenitude and actuality of Being, then he cannot be understood as just one option among many. He is not a discrete object that we can simply choose, as one might choose cake instead of a chocolate sundae. He does not stand alongside other beings and other possible goods. He is Truth itself, Goodness itself, Beauty itself. To be free is to flourish in communion with him. We are not free because we have multiple choices available to us; we become free when we choose well, thereby achieving the happiness for which we are divinely destined. This choosing well in

---

[22] Thomas Aquinas, *Summa Theologiae* I.II.13. On Aquinas' understanding of human freedom and divine agency, see Servais Pinckaers, *The Sources of Christian Ethics*, 3rd ed. (1995), chap. 16, esp. pp. 394-398.

turn requires that we "ever more clearly see the 'sun of the Good' (to employ the lovely Platonic metaphor), and to see more clearly we must continue to choose well; and the more we are emancipated from illusion and caprice, and the more our will is informed by and responds to the Good, the more perfect our vision becomes, and the less there is really to choose."[23] The impossibility of a free and final rejection of God becomes even clearer when we recall the teleological structure of human activity:

> Neither, though, can God be merely one option among others, for the very simple reason that he is not just another object alongside the willing agent or alongside other objects of desire, but is rather the sole ultimate content of all rational longing. Being himself the source and end of the real, God can never be for the will simply one plausible terminus of desire in competition with another; he could never confront the intellect simply as a relative and evaluative good, from which one might *reasonably* turn to some other. He remains forever the encompassing final object that motivates and makes actual every choice, the Good that makes the will free in the first place. Even an act of apostasy, then, traced back to its most primordial impulse, is motivated by the desire for God. Even the satanist can embrace evil only insofar as he thinks it will satisfy a desire for what is most agreeable to his own nature. He is in error in the choice he makes, and is culpable to the degree that he abets the error willingly; but it is also then the case that, to the degree he knows the Good in itself, he cannot but desire it rationally. However the "gnomic" faculty may wander, the "natural" will animating it seeks only one ultimate end. You can reject a glass of wine absolutely; you can even reject evil in its (insubstantial) totality without any remainder of intentionality. Neither of these things possesses more than a finite allure in itself. But you cannot reject God except defectively, by having failed to recognize him as the primordial object of all your deepest longings, the very source of their activity. We

---

[23] Hart, *TASBS*, p. 173.

cannot choose between him and some other end in an absolute sense; we can choose only between better or worse approaches to his transcendence. As I have said, to reject God is still, however obscurely and uncomprehendingly, to seek God.

This means also that God could never be, for the rational will, merely some extrinsic causality intruding upon the will's autonomy, or some irresistible heteronomous power overwhelming the feebler powers of the creature. He is freedom as such, the fiery energy that liberates the flame from the wood. He is the very power of agency. He is the Good that makes the rational will exist. He is the eternal infinite source of all knowledge and all truth, of all love and delight in the object of love, who enlivens and acts within every created act. As an infinite and transcendental end, God's goodness may be indeterminate as regards proximate ends, and that very indeterminacy may be what allows for deliberative determinations. There may be conflicts and confusions, mistakes and perversities in the great middle distance of life; as Duns Scotus says, we frequently must deliberate between which aspect of the Good to pursue, whether to be guided in any moment by our *affectio iustitiae* (our sense of what is just) or the *affectio commodi* (our sense of what is suitable or convenient); but the encircling horizon never alters, and the Sun of the Good never sets. No soul can relent in its deepest motives from the will's constant and consuming preoccupation with God. If this were not so, and if reason had no natural, ontological, and necessary relation to God as the final rationale in all desire and agency, then God would himself be something separate from the Good as such, and from rationality as such, and could attract the rational will merely in the manner of a predilection. But then he would not actually be God in any meaningful sense. In truth, he gives his creatures freedom always by *making* them freely seek him as the ultimate end in all else that intentional consciousness seeks.[24]

---

[24] Ibid., pp. 184-186). For a fuller discussion of divine transcendence and causality, see David Bentley Hart, "Impassibility as Transcendence," *The Hidden and the*

Human beings desire happiness and act toward this end, no matter how perverted and twisted the desire has become. The belief that we may reject God absolutely assumes an absolute—but ontologically impossible—divorce between God and Goodness and therefore between God and happiness. From his very different analytic philosophy perspective, Thomas Talbott has come to a similar conclusion:

> Religious people sometimes speak of God as if he were just another human magistrate who seeks his own glory and requires obedience for its own sake; they speak as if we might reject the Creator and Father of our souls without rejecting ourselves, oppose his will for our lives without opposing, schizophrenically perhaps, our own will for our lives. . . . But if God is our loving Creator, then he wills for us exactly what at the most fundamental level, we want for ourselves; he wills that we should experience supreme happiness, that our deepest yearnings should be satisfied, and that all of our needs should be met.[25]

God wills our good, and our good is God. He has created us with an insatiable hunger for him, to the end that we might become adopted sons of the God and Father of Jesus Christ. This natural desire for communion with the Holy Trinity is the secret of the universalist hope. John Kronen and Eric Reitan state the argument:

> Rational creatures, by definition, can choose based on reasons—that is, they are motivated to act not merely by instinct or appetite, but by the recognition that certain apprehended truths (reason) entail that a course of action is good to do. Saying that *rational* creatures are ordered to the good means two things: first, when they directly and clearly encounter the perfect good in unclouded experience, they will recognize it as the perfect good; and second, the perfect good (which, by definition, is the

---

Manifest, pp. 167-190. This essay is an indispensable companion piece to *That All Shall Be Saved*.
[25] Thomas Talbott, *The Inescapable Love of God* (2014), 2nd ed., p. 172.

standard according to which all other goods are measured) would, under conditions of immediate and unclouded apprehension, present itself as overridingly worthy of love. Creatures' subjective values will thus spontaneously fall into harmony with the objective good, with all choices reflecting this proper valuation.

Put another way, immediate awareness of the perfect good will so sing to the natural inclinations of the soul that love for the good will swamp all potentially contrary affective states. One would have every reason to conform one's will to the perfect good and no reason not to. This latter point gains further strength from the Christian notion that what is prudentially good for rational creatures (what promotes their welfare) does not ultimately conflict with what is morally good—both are realized through union with God. Unclouded apprehension of the perfect good will thus harmonize prudential motives such that every rational creature presented with a clear vision of God would have every reason to love God and no reason to reject Him.

From all of this it follows that God could guarantee uniform salvation-inducing motives in rational creatures simply by presenting an unclouded vision of Himself. God's doing this certainly seems *metaphysically* possible, and hence within God's power; and if (as Aquinas maintained) free acts are not random but motivated, it follows that any rational creature presented with the vision of God will freely but inevitably respond affirmatively to the promise of loving union.[26]

The key to the above argument is the ability of the omnipotent Creator to bring every rational creature to an "unclouded apprehension" of God as perfect goodness. Does God have the power to bring this about? If he does, can he wield it without violating the libertarian freedom of human beings? Exponents of the free will defense of hell seem to think this impossible, even for an omnipotent Deity. Any attempt by God to effect a happy eschatological ending will inevitably violate human free will. We

---

[26] John Kronen and Eric Reitan, *God's Final Victory* (2013), p. 136.

must be free to damn ourselves. Hart finds this a curious line of reasoning that ultimately collapses into a mythological construal of divinity. Properly understood, divine causality does not and cannot compete with creaturely causality. God is not a being among beings. Creator and creature do not operate on the same metaphysical plane:

> The suggestion, then, that God—properly understood—could not assure that a person freely will one thing rather than another is simply false. Inasmuch as he acts upon the mind and will both as their final cause and also as the deepest source of their movements, he is already intrinsic to the very structure of reason and desire within the soul. He is not merely some external agency who would have to exercise coercion or external compulsion of a creature's intentions to bring them to the end he decrees. If he were, then the entire Christian doctrine of providence—the vital teaching that God can so order all conditions, circumstances, and contingencies among created things as to bring about everything he wills for his creatures while still not in any way violating the autonomy of secondary causality—would be a logical contradiction. God, in his omnipotence and omniscience, is wholly capable of determining the result of all secondary causes, including free will, while not acting as yet another discrete cause among them. In one sense, naturally, this is merely a function of the coincidence in his nature of omniscience and omnipotence. Knowing not only all the events that constitute each individual life, but also all of an agent's inner motives and predispositions and desires—all thoughts, impulses, hopes, preferences, yearnings, and aversions—and so knowing what choice any given soul will make when confronted with certain options and situated among certain circumambient forces, God can (if nothing else) so arrange the shape of reality that all beings, one way or another, come at the last upon the right path by way of their own freedom, in this life or the next. . . . God, being infinitely resourceful and infinitely knowledgeable, can weave the whole of time into a perfectly coherent continuity whose ultimate result is that all circumstances and forces

conduce to the union of every creature with himself, and can do this precisely by confronting every rational nature with possibilities he knows they will realize through their own free volitions. It is true that he might accomplish this by imposing limited conditions of choice upon every life; but the conditions of choice are always limited anyway, and deliberative freedom is always capable of only a finite set of possible determinations.[27]

Now we see through a glass darkly; but when we are brought face to face before him and see him in the glory of his Goodness, Beauty, and Truth, how can we not love him?

---

[27] Hart, *TASBS*, pp. 183-184.

Chapter Twenty

The Secret of the Greater Hope

Humanity's Natural Desire for God

"Thou movest us to delight in praising Thee; for Thou hast formed us for Thyself, and our hearts are restless till they find rest in Thee"—perhaps the most famous sentence from one of the most famous prayers in the catholic tradition.[1] St Augustine's words have been quoted by preachers ever since they were penned. They point us to the fundamental truth of our existence: we are made for God and can only find abiding happiness in him. We are divinely ordered to participation and fulfillment in the divine life of the Father, Son, and Holy Spirit. Two hundred years later St Maximus the Confessor would affirm that God has given to humanity "a natural desire and longing for Him."[2] Later still, medieval Latin theologians would affirm we have an innate desire for our supernatural end, the beatific vision. Stephen J. Duffey offers the following commentary on Augustine's prayer:

> Grace is a comprehensive *ambience* for Augustine. No person, event, aspect of his life stood outside the divine intent to bring him to fulfillment. Conversion was not the first entrance of grace into his life, only the compass point from which he could read the presence of grace from the very beginning of his days. Wherever he meets himself, God is there before him. Thus the prayer of gratitude suffuses the Confessions. Grace is inescapable, wholly prevenient. Every movement of his heart, every initiative of his will is preceded by God who calls and

---

[1] Augustine of Hippo, *Confessions* 1.1.
[2] Maximus the Confessor, *Various Texts on Theology, the Divine Economy, and Virtue and Vice* 100, in *The Philokalia* (1984), II:284.

sustains his holy restlessness. The relentless undertow in his life was the emptiness God had set within him, which only God could fill up, and the unfathomable Providence of God, which drew him, yet rescued him from being swallowed by the emptiness. In Augustine's metaphysics of creation the substrate of every creature is the formless void of Genesis. The creature is mutable, defectible, teetering on the brink of nothingness whence it came. In the created spirit, this void is the innate desire for happiness. Attracting us to God yet unable to bring us to God, it leads to dangerous and restless questing. For the created spirit to be complete, this chaos within must be "formed" by the Word and stabilized by the Spirit. Often a dull ache, this inner desire could erupt in sharp pain. It was this experience that grounded Augustine's understanding of grace.[3]

Created in the divine image, we are incomplete without God. Of course, no one is truly without God. As the transcendent Creator, he subsists in the ontological depths of every person. Again Augustine: *Deus interior intimo meo*, "God is more inward than my most inward part."[4] In the deepest depths of our being, there is the living God creating and sustaining us in every moment of our existing. He is more intimate to us than we are to ourselves, always summoning us to the happiness and rest only he can give.

Duffy elaborates a contemporary Catholic understanding of the natural desire for God:

> In the concrete nature of fallen humanity there is an interior, absolute desire of the Kingdom that correlates with the universal salvific divine will. This determination is an existential. It is prior to all personal options and persists through all possible acceptances or rejections of one's end. Whatever one does, one remains interiorly ordered to absolute communion with God. Not that one is in a "state of grace," to

---

[3] Stephen J. Duffy, *The Dynamics of Grace* (2007), p. 82.
[4] Augustine, *Conf.* 3.11.

use the traditional language. But one is always in a graced order and under the influence of the offer of grace. To some degree this existential determination seeps into consciousness. It is an attraction and all attractions are necessarily consciously experienced in some measure. In this case it is perhaps confusedly experienced as an appreciation of the goods of the Kingdom. More often this attraction will be lived rather than reflected upon. But it can rise to the level of reflection and clear articulation, as in the case of Augustine's "You have made us for Yourself, O Lord, and our hearts are restless. . . ."[5]

Humanity is created for communion with the living God. We cannot find happiness apart from him who is the immanent ground of our existence and the consummation of all our searching. God is the origin and end of all human desire.

And here, I suggest, is the secret of the universalist hope. No matter how deeply we sink into our sin and narcissism, no matter how thick the darkness that surrounds and penetrates our hearts becomes, we remain images of the divine Image. We are created for the Holy Trinity and are interiorly ordered to eternal communion with him. The thirst for the beatific vision can never be eradicated from our being. Even the damned continue to thirst for God, even while denying the only One who can slake their thirst. "Those who are tormented in Gehenna are tormented by the invasion of love," declares St. Isaac the Syrian. Constituted by God for *theosis*, we live within his grace and universal salvific will. God yearns for us to repent and enter into deifying communion with him, just as we yearn for rapturous communion with him. This is our fundamental, inescapable truth.

Too often, when reflecting on hell and eternal damnation, we think of human beings as created in a neutral relationship to God, perhaps even in a posture of indifference. We forget that we are

---

[5] Stephen J. Duffy, *The Graced Horizon* (1992), p. 23.

ontologically oriented to God. We may have profoundly enslaved ourselves to our passions and egoism; but we can never obliterate the fundamental desire of our hearts nor definitively cut ourselves off from our Creator. As the psalmist sings:

> Whither shall I go from thy spirit? or whither shall I flee from thy presence? If I ascend up into heaven, thou art there: if I make my bed in hell, behold, thou art there. (Ps 139:7-8)

Thomas Talbott proposes that God can effect the salvation of all people simply by allowing them to suffer the immanent consequences of their rejection of the ultimate Good they desire. Talbott thus sees hell as a mode of purgatory. God does not need to interfere with human freedom; for he has structured human nature in such a way that every departure from the divine will results in interior suffering, dissatisfaction, and misery. All God needs to do is not shield the damned from the terrible consequences of rebellion and disunion. As their misery increases it will become increasingly impossible for them to sustain the illusion that they can find genuine beatitude anywhere but in their Creator.

Alcohol addiction serves as an apt analogy. For an alcoholic to begin the way of recovery, he needs to "hit bottom," as the folks in AA like to say; and he reaches bottom through the process of experiencing the emotional and physical distress caused by his drinking. Eventually he reaches that point where he can no longer convince himself that the benefits of intoxication outweigh the pain and suffering that his drinking has brought upon himself and those he loves.

Those who die enslaved to the passions remain enslaved in the next life. This is their hell. They are sundered from the goods of creation and thus unable to satisfy their disordered desires. Like the addict who is cut off from his drugs when he enters detox, the damned are cut off from anything that might, even momentarily, assuage their cravings. Thus St. John of Damascus:

> The righteous, by desiring and having God, rejoice forever; but the sinners, by desiring sin and not possessing the objects of sin, are tormented as if eaten by the worm and consumed by fire, with no consolation; for what is suffering if not the absence of that which is desired. According to the intensity of desire, those who desire God rejoice, and those who desire sin are tormented.[6]

Talbott advances a similar understanding of damnation, but unlike the Damascene he believes that every person in hell will eventually hit their bottom. Each will reach a point where they can no longer maintain the delusion that selfishness and autonomy will bring happiness. Unbearable suffering breaks us all; it cannot be forever endured. This tiny window is all the God of Love needs:

> Pauline theology provides a clear picture of how the end of reconciliation could be foreordained even though each of us is genuinely free to choose which path we will follow in the present. The picture is this: The more one freely rebels against God in the present, the more miserable and tormented one eventually becomes, and the more miserable and tormented one becomes, the more incentive one has to repent of one's sin and to give up one's rebellious attitudes. But more than that, the consequences of sin are themselves a means of revelation; they reveal the true meaning of separation and enable us to see through the very self-deception that makes evil choices possible in the first place. We may think that we can promote our own interest at the expense of others or that our selfish attitudes are compatible with enduring happiness, but we cannot act upon such an illusion, at least not for a long period of time, without shattering it to pieces. So in that sense, all paths have the same destination, the end of reconciliation, but some are longer and windier than others. Because our choice of paths

---

[6] John of Damascus, *Against the Manicheans* PG 94:1573.

in the present is genuinely free, we are morally responsible for that choice; but because no illusion can endure forever, the end is foreordained. As Paul himself puts it: We are all predestined to be conformed to the image of Christ (see Romans 8:29); that part is a matter of grace, not human will or effort.[7]

Can we imagine any lucid, fully informed person freely embracing eternal misery instead of eternal happiness? Would this not be insanity? If God is our absolute Good, then rejection of the Good is rejection of our own good and thus rejection of ourselves. As Talbott writes:

> Religious people sometimes speak of God as if he were just another human magistrate who seeks his own glory and requires obedience for its own sake; they speak as if we might reject the Creator and Father of our souls without rejecting ourselves, oppose his will for our lives without opposing, schizophrenically perhaps, our own will for our lives. . . . But if God is our loving Creator, then he wills for us exactly what at the most fundamental level, we want for ourselves; he wills that we should experience supreme happiness, that our deepest yearnings should be satisfied, and that all of our needs should be met.[8]

If we hold to a libertarian understanding of human freedom, then, so the free-will model of hell insists, it must be possible for a person to reject God for no good reason at all, even though he or she has every reason to surrender to God and experience the happiness he or she most truly desires. Given that an eternal state of alienation and suffering is infinitely inferior to the state of eternal beatitude, what man or woman (or angel) would rationally choose it? If they should go ahead and choose it anyway, we must conclude that either their decision flows from ignorance, delusion, or pathology, or it is

---

[7] Thomas Talbott, *The Inescapable Love of God*, 2nd. ed. (2014), p. 189.
[8] Ibid., p. 185.

purely random and arbitrary. In either case it is not a truly free decision.

The happiness our heavenly Father everlastingly wills for us and the happiness we truly desire for ourselves are identical. God wills our good, and our good is God. Human personhood and divine personhood thus mysteriously coincide in the depths of the human being. God has created us with an insatiable hunger for union with him and therefore with a deep, incessant longing to become who we were created to be—adopted sons and daughters of the God and Father of Jesus Christ. This innate desire for communion with the Holy Trinity is the secret that underlies the greater hope.

The Mathematics of Salvation

Given humanity's ordination to the Good, what are the chances that all will be saved? Immediately human freedom raises its head. No matter how irrational the choice might be, are we not free to definitively, irrevocably, everlastingly reject the Good we desire? How then can we genuinely hope that all will be saved? Evil lies deep in our hearts. Who can say that in the end there won't be one holdout, ten holdouts or even ten billion holdouts? Hope for the salvation of all? You'll get better odds at the roulette table.

There are, of course, different kinds and degrees of hope. There is the hope that tomorrow will be a bright and sunny day, given that the weatherman says there's only a 5% chance of rain. We might call this an *almost-certain* hope. There is the 3:2 hope that Secretariat will win the 1973 Kentucky Derby. We might call this a *confident* hope. There is the 50–50 hope of the coin-flipper that the quarter will fall heads instead of tails. Let's call this an *even-money* hope. And there is the hope of the Texas Holdem player that he will hit his one-outer on the river and make quads (only a 2%

chance) —a truly *desperate* hope. Our hopes range the gamut of probabilities.

Dare we hope for the salvation of all?—to this question Met Kallistos Ware, following Hans Urs von Balthasar, tenders a cautious yes. God's love for mankind is unshakeable and certain; but human freedom precludes us from affirming anything stronger than an *antinomic* hope:

> If the strongest argument in favor of universal salvation is the appeal to divine love, and if the strongest argument on the opposite side is the appeal to human freedom, then we are brought back to the dilemma with which we started: how are we to bring into concord the two principles "God is love" and "Human beings are free"? For the time being we cannot do more than hold fast with equal firmness to both principles at once, while admitting that the manner of their ultimate harmonization remains a mystery beyond our present comprehension. . . . Our belief in human freedom means that we have no right to categorically affirm, "All *must* be saved." But our faith in God's love makes us dare to hope that all will be saved.[9]

Clearly it is impossible for us to assign a probability to the antinomic possibility of universal salvation. It does not fall into the four categories described above. There are no odds to calculate. What then does it mean to say that we may dare to hope that all will be saved? Is "hope" even the right word?

"Faith," Richard John Neuhaus explains, "is hope anticipated, and hope is faith disposed toward the future."[10] We *hope* God will raise us the dead because we *believe* God has raised Jesus from the dead, and we trust him and his promises. The former enjoys the same level of certainty as the latter. Resurrection is impossible within

---

[9] Kallistos Ware, *The Inner Kingdom* (2000), pp. 214-215.
[10] Richard John Neuhaus, "Will All Be Saved?" *First Things* (August 2001): https://www.firstthings.com/article/2001/08/will-all-be-saved.

the terms of the world as we know it. Even so, our hope possesses an *evangelical* or *de fide certitude*. As Jesus teaches us, "All things are possible with God" (Mark 10:27). The hope of the general resurrection and the eschatological transfiguration of the cosmos transcends antinomies. In his omnipotent love, God will make it so—a 110% guarantee.

But with the universalist theologoumenon, Ware tells us, we face a different situation. Even though God desires the salvation of all (1 Tim 2:4), his desire is apparently constrained by human free will:

> Because humans are free, it is argued, they are at liberty to reject God. His gifts are irrevocable; He will never take away from us our power of voluntary choice, and so we are free to go on saying "No" to Him through all eternity. Such unending rejection of God is precisely the essence of hell. Because free will exists, there must exist also the possibility of hell as a place of everlasting suffering. Take away hell, and you deny freedom. None can be forced to enter heaven against their will. As the Russian theologian Paul Evdokimov observes, God can do anything except compel us to love him; for love is free, and thus where there is no liberty of choice there is no love.[11]

Human freedom excludes divine determination. The Almighty may offer the salvation of the Kingdom, but he neither coerces nor manipulates our free acceptance. Surely at least one person will dig in their heels and definitively and eternally reject God, and if one, then why not a thousand or a million or a billion? How can we speak of hope for universal salvation when our experience of humanity, and of ourselves, leads us to expect the damnation of many?

We would seem to be at an impasse. We may dare to hope that all will be saved; but that hope appears to be a hope beyond hope, a

---

[11] Ware, p. 212.

The Secret of the Greater Hope

hope against hope. Yes, there are many passages in the Scriptures that intimate, even promise, the universality of salvation; but the boundary of human freedom remains—and with it looms the horror of everlasting torment. Ware posits two irreconcilable principles—divine love and human freedom—and declares that "the manner of their ultimate harmonization remains a mystery beyond our present comprehension."[12]

The majority of Christians today—Catholic, Orthodox, and Protestant—affirm what is often called a free-will model of eternal perdition.[13] God does not damn: the wicked damn themselves. Rather than embracing the forgiveness offered by the Father, they instead freely and irrevocably choose separation and autonomy. C. S. Lewis capsulized this model in his oft-quoted statement: "The doors of hell are locked from the inside." The damned are free to make their exit yet inexplicably never turn the key. Underlying the free-will model is a libertarian construal of human freedom: human agents determine their own actions and always remain free *to do otherwise*. Libertarian freedom thus excludes all forms of divine determinism. Thomists and Calvinists will demur, but let us assume that the libertarian account is true and faithfully represents what Christians should believe. Let's also assume that some version of the free-will model of hell is true, that human beings are always free to irrevocably condemn themselves to interminable misery. How might we then understand the possibility and likelihood of universal salvation?

Consider the following five statements, with brief commentary:

---

[12] Ibid.
[13] See Jerry Walls, *Hell: The Logic of Damnation* (1993).

1) *Human beings are created by the Holy Trinity to enjoy eternal fellowship with the Holy Trinity. God is our supreme good, supernatural end, eschatological fulfillment, and true happiness.*

   Humanity is not created in a neutral stance vis-à-vis its Creator. We are created by God and our ultimate desire is always for God.

2) *To turn away from God is to turn away from our supreme good and thus to turn away from true happiness. By our sin we create our own hell and doom ourselves to ever-increasing anguish.*

   Universalists do not deny hell. We know too well its misery. We know, and fear, the possibility that in the end we might choose self over the Good.

3) *God will not permit us to irrevocably decide against union with him based on either insufficient information or disordered desire.*

   Anyone who is ignorant or deceived about the nature of God or the terminal consequences of their choices cannot be said to have freely embraced their destiny. Ditto for anyone who is enslaved to disordered desires and passions. Just as addicts are incapable of making responsible decisions until they have been liberated from addictive substances, so those who are enslaved to disordered desires and passions are incapable of free decisions and actions. They cannot do otherwise.

4) *God never gives up on any sinner; he never withdraws his offer of forgiveness; he never abandons his children to the torment of the outer darkness.*

   God has not set a time limit on the offer of salvation, nor has he configured the afterlife to render it impossible for sinners to repent and turn to him. God loves every human being with an infinite and absolute love. He truly wills the good and salvation of all (1 Tim 2:4). Like the good shepherd, he searches near and far for the one lost sheep; like the woman who loses one of her ten coins, he turns his house upside down until he finds it (Luke 15). Jesus has and will reconcile all to himself. He will not be without his brethren for whom he died and rose again.

5) *When a person surrenders to God in death or in the afterlife, his orientation is definitively stabilized and his eternal bliss confirmed.*

After death the redeemed no longer have the freedom to reject God, for their freedom has been fulfilled in the beatific vision. The blessed cannot sin (*non posse peccare*). Theologians advance various arguments to explain this truth, but all agree upon it. In heaven, once saved, always saved.

The above statements can, I think, be worked into a valid argument for universal salvation. The first premise is uncontroversial and widely accepted in the orthodox tradition. The second premise states the free-will model of hell that has become dominant in ecumenical Christianity. The third premise is rarely discussed in the literature and therefore probably controversial. The fourth is definitely controversial, as it denies a widely held belief, yet the possibility of post-mortem salvation has long been affirmed by many Eastern Christians and is supported by the Orthodox practice of praying for the departed. The final premise is uncontroversial and enjoys ecumenical assent.

Assume, for the moment, that all five statements are true. How confident may we be that God will bring all humanity to salvation? The quick, too quick, answer: we don't know. Every human possesses free will, we continue to insist, and is thus free to make the ultimate Luciferian decision: "Evil, be thou my good." But why would anyone make such a decision if they knew beyond a shadow of a doubt that only God is their true happiness and that rejection of the divine offer of salvation must bring only intolerable misery? Perhaps a person might delude themselves about this truth for a while, but as the agony and despair intensifies, how long can he or she hold out until the truth crashes down upon him? How long before reality shatters all illusions? Satan is ubiquitously invoked at this point. If he can deliberately choose evil for the sake of evil, so can anyone. Herbert McCabe thinks not:

> When we sin it is entirely our choice of something instead of God's friendship. To come to God's friendship in Christ is to choose a good, the greatest good and the greatest good for us; and the creative and gracious power of God is in us as we freely make this choice. It is both our free work and God's work. To do good is to choose the highest good; but to fail to do this, to sin, is not to choose evil. Nobody chooses evil, it cannot be done. When we sin what we do is to choose some trivial good at the expense of choosing God's friendship. Sin is sin not because of the thing we positively choose: the human satisfaction, the pleasure or the power. It is sin because of what we fail to choose, what we sacrifice for the sake of a minor good. Sin is sin because we have opted not to grow up to our flourishing, our happiness which is life in God's love and friendship.[14]

If this is true for ordinary sins committed in this life, how much more must it be true for the eschatological exercise of one's fundamental orientation towards God. Talbott maintains that the proposition that a free rational agent might decisively, definitively, irrevocably reject his supreme good is incoherent: "For no one rational enough to qualify as a free moral agent could possibly prefer an objective horror—the outer darkness, for example—to eternal bliss, nor could any such person both experience the horror of separation from God and continue to regard it as a desirable state."[15] David Bentley Hart concurs:

---

[14] Herbert McCabe, *God Still Matters* (2005), p. 185.
[15] Thomas Talbott, "Towards a Better Understanding of Universalism," in *Universal Salvation?* (2004), p. 5.

> But, on any cogent account, free will is a power inherently purposive, teleological, primordially oriented toward the good, and shaped by that transcendental appetite to the degree that a soul can recognize the good for what it is. No one can freely will the evil as evil; one can take the evil for the good, but that does not alter the prior transcendental orientation that wakens all desire. To see the good truly is to desire it insatiably; not to desire it is not to have known it, and so never to have been free to choose it.[16]

Yet perhaps the libertarian construal of freedom requires the option of choosing alienation from the Creator and the absolute misery it brings. Despite the encounter with absolute Love given in the afterlife and the revelation of the dire consequences of rejection of Love, perhaps a person can still hang on to the delusion that he can bear the isolation and torment. Perhaps, for no good reason whatsoever, a person still chooses an infernal mode of being that contradicts his good and happiness. "Better to reign in Hell, than serve in Heaven!" we cry. As absurd and self-destructive as such a decision must be judged, perhaps we cannot declare it impossible. Let us further stipulate that God will honor the individual's refusal to repent and will allow him or her to endure the terrible consequences of their decision. If this is so, can we still entertain a reasonable and confident hope of universal salvation? Eric Reitan believes that we can, if we affirm that the Father of Jesus never rescinds his offer of salvation.

Like Talbott, Reitan is skeptical of the proposal that a rational agent might voluntarily, freely, and knowingly embrace a final destiny of utter misery. Can we imagine someone choosing an infernal state of being "*knowing* that doing so will doom them to

---

[16] David Bentley Hart, "God, Creation, and Evil," *The Hidden and the Manifest* (2017), p. 245.

eternal alienation from everything of value?"[17] Can we imagine this person enduring the ever-increasing loneliness, despair, and torment for all eternity, never once wondering whether he has chosen wisely? Perhaps he originally chose separation from God under the illusion that it wouldn't be so bad, that he could still might find some measure of happiness; but this is a false belief. There is no happiness divorced from deifying union with God. Is it really possible, asks Reitan, to cling to a false belief *forever* when it produces only ever-increasing misery? Is it not more likely that the punishments of hell will eventually shatter all illusions and bring one to that point where one can only desperately cry out, "Jesus, help me"? Reitan states the matter this way:

> On the progressive view of DH [doctrine of hell], the doors of hell are locked from the inside—that is, God never withdraws the offer of salvation. Hence, if any are damned eternally it is because they eternally reject God's offer. It's not enough to turn God down once. It must be done *forever.*
>
> We are assuming that, to have libertarian freedom on the matter of our eternal destiny, we must be able to reject God's offer of salvation *even when* we know what we are doing and are not in bondage to sin. But this means that it must be possible for us to make a choice that we have no motive to make, and every motive not to make. To say that this is possible is not to say that it is likely. In fact, it seems clear that, however possible it may be for us to act against all our interests, it is very unlikely at any moment that we would actually do so. But in order for someone to be eternally damned, the person must not only make this unlikely choice once. The person must unwaveringly choose to reject God at every moment for the rest of eternity, *even though the person sees absolutely no good reason for doing so, has every reason*

---

[17] Eric Reitan, "Human Freedom and the Impossibility of Eternal Damnation," in *Universal Salvation?*, p. 133.

The Secret of the Greater Hope

not to do so, and has absolutely no compelling desire to do so. Is that really possible?[18]

Reitan advances two objections to the free will justification of hell. First, he asks, is libertarian freedom as valuable as it is often claimed?

> Libertarian freedom as described does not seem worth having. In fact, as described, I sincerely hope that I lack it. The capacity to eternally act against all of my motives would introduce into my life a potential for profound irrationality that I would rather do without. And if I exercise my libertarian freedom as described above, dooming myself to the outer darkness without reason, I sincerely hope that God would act to stop me—just as I hope a friend would stop me if I decided to leap from a rooftop for no reason. I would not regard the actions of that friend as a violation of any valuable freedom, but would see it as a welcome antidote to arbitrary stupidity.[19]

Yet even if extreme libertarian freedom obtains, Reitan believes that we may still have a guarantee, or at least mathematical certainty, of universal salvation. He proposes the following thought experiment:

> Imagine a box of pennies, spread out heads-side up. Suppose that the heads-side of each penny is covered with a thin film of superglue, such that if the penny were to flip over in the box it would stick to the bottom and remain heads-side down from thereon out. Imagine that this box is rattled every few seconds. For the sake of argument, let us suppose that there is no chance of the pennies getting stuck to the walls of the box or anything like that. Let us suppose, furthermore, that for any penny that is heads-side up at the same time that the box is rattled, there is exactly a fifty percent chance that after the box is rattled the penny will land heads-side up, and a fifty percent chance that it will

---

[18] Ibid., p. 136; also see Kronen and Reitan, chap. 8.
[19] Reitan, "Human Freedom," p. 137.

land heads-side down. Once a penny lands heads-side down, however, it sticks to the bottom of the box and remains that way, regardless of how much the box is subsequently rattled. Let us imagine, furthermore, that the box is rattled every five seconds indefinitely, stopping only once all the pennies have landed heads-side down and become stuck that way.

In this situation, we would expect that eventually the rattling would stop, because eventually every single penny in the box would become stuck heads-side down. We expect this outcome even though every penny started out heads-side up, and even though at any given time a heads-side-up penny has a fifty percent chance of staying heads-side up. If the rattling continued forever, we would be inclined to say that this outcome is inevitable.[20]

Reitan argues that, within the context of libertarian freedom, the prospect of universal salvation is analogous to the box of pennies. If we posit both that God never withdraws his forgiveness and that those who have chosen perdition remain free at any point to choose otherwise, then "there must be some possible world in which the person does accept the offer. Thus, the person who has yet to accept the offer of salvation is like the bad penny: While the person has not yet chosen to be saved, at every moment there is some probability that the person will so choose."[21] Remember, the damned have every good reason to change their minds and no good reason not to: the supreme happiness they desire for themselves is identical to the happiness that God wills for them.

Given that the opportunities for repentance are infinite, the probability that any one person will hold out against God approaches zero. This is not to say that the probability ever reaches zero; it still remains theoretically possible for someone to reject God forever. "But," counters Reitan, "the possible world in which this

---

[20] Ibid., p. 138.
[21] Ibid., p. 140.

The Secret of the Greater Hope

occurs is so remote that there seems to be no good reason to think that it is actual."[22] Thus we have a mathematical certainty that all will freely embrace the salvation of God given in Jesus Christ.

Talbott's and Reitan's arguments should encourage us in a *confident* and *robust* hope for the salvation of every human being. God does not need to *force* anyone to repent of his sins and embrace heaven. Precisely because we are created for him, all he needs to do is to allow us to experience the hell that we think we want. Suffering, divine grace, and the prayers of the Church will do the rest.

Yes, Virginia, we may genuinely hope that all will be saved.

---

[22] Ibid.

Chapter Twenty-One

Eternal Damnation and the Solidarity of Love

Hostages to Love

Can you imagine yourself enjoying perfect happiness and bliss in heaven if you *knew* that a beloved spouse, child, or friend was suffering everlasting torment in hell?

In his wonderful parable *The Great Divorce*, C. S. Lewis presents an interaction between an inhabitant of hell, the melodramatic Tragedian, and his redeemed and loving wife, the Lady. The Tragedian tries various ways to evoke pity in his wife, but she steadfastly resists. She will not be held hostage to the unhappiness of her husband.

> "Stop it. Stop it at once," she commands him.
> "Stop what?" he replies.
> "Using pity, other people's pity, in the wrong way. We have all done it a bit on earth, you know. Pity was meant to be a spur that drives joy to help misery. But it can be used the wrong way round. It can be used for a kind of blackmailing. Those who choose misery can hold joy up to ransom, by pity."[1]

This exchange troubles the narrator greatly. He feels that it is wrong that the Lady should be untouched by her husband's misery, and he shares his concern with his guide, George MacDonald.

"Would ye rather he still had the power of tormenting her?"

---

[1] C. S. Lewis, The Great Divorce, chap. 13. All quotations from this book may be found in this chapter.

"Well, no. I suppose I don't want that."

"What then?"

"I hardly know, Sir. What some people say on earth is that the final loss of one soul gives the lie to all the joy of those who are saved."

"Ye see it does not."

"I feel in a way that it ought to."

"That sounds very merciful: but see what lurks behind it."

"What?"

"The demand of the loveless and the self-imprisoned that they should be allowed to blackmail the universe: that till they consent to be happy (on their own terms) no one else shall taste joy: that theirs should be the final power; that Hell should be able to *veto* Heaven."

I long thought that Lewis had given the irrefutable solution to our dilemma: there must be a point where the sufferings of the damned cannot affect the joy of the redeemed; otherwise, hell will hold tyrannical power over heaven for all eternity. But in 2011, I read philosopher Thomas Talbott's book *The Inescapable Love of God*. Talbott raises the question of the damnation of loved ones anew: If we truly love someone, if we truly will their good, if we love them as we love ourselves, how can their interminable misery not affect our enjoyment of heaven? I remember being impressed by the argument. Maybe Lewis was wrong. Hmm, I need to think about this further . . .

On the morning of June 15, 2012, a knock came at our front door. Two police officers informed my wife and me that our son Aaron had committed suicide. At that moment, the question raised by Lewis acquired for me a burning intensity, and I immediately knew the answer: *No!* If we love someone, then of course we will be held hostage to their infernal misery. Their suffering must become ours; otherwise, love is not love. At Aaron's funeral a week later, I cried out from the pulpit with all of my being:

I will not be saved without my Aaron! There can be no heaven for me without my son. My love for him is too great. He is too much a part of my life, my identity. We will be saved together in Christ. God will make it so.

How can I be supremely happy in heaven if I know that my wife, my children, my parents and friends are not sharing with me the rapturous joy of the risen Christ? How can I be supremely happy if they are suffering agony and torment beyond all imagining. In his always dispassionate, quiet manner, Talbott puts it this way:

> Consider first a curiosity about the nature of love. Not only is a disposition to love essential for supreme happiness; it can also be an instrumental evil, making a person more miserable, not less. Indeed, the more one is filled with love for others, the more the unhappiness of others is likely to jeopardize one's own happiness. . . . Curiously, the very thing that makes supreme happiness possible—namely love—also makes us more vulnerable to misery and sorrow. If I truly love my own daughter, for example, and love her even as I love myself, then I simply cannot be happy knowing that she is suffering or that she is otherwise miserable—unless, of course, I can somehow believe that, in the end, all will be well for her. But if I cannot believe this, if I were to believe instead that she has been lost to me forever—even if I were to believe that, *by her own will*, she has made herself intolerably evil—my own happiness could never be complete, not so long as I continued to love her and to yearn for her redemption. For I would always know what *could* have been, and I would always experience that as a terrible tragedy and an unacceptable loss, one for which no compensation is ever conceivable. Is it any wonder, then, that Paul could say concerning his unbelieving kin whom he loved so much: "For I could wish that I myself were accursed and cut off from Christ for the sake of my people" (Romans 9:3)? Nor is there anything irrational about such a wish. From the perspective of Paul's love, his own damnation would be

no worse an evil, and no greater threat to his own happiness, than the damnation of his loved ones would be.[2]

I then went back and looked at the exchange between the Tragedian and his wife and noticed something I had not noticed before: the Lady is able to ignore her husband's misery because in her eyes he is no longer the same man. He has become someone else, something else.

> "Where is Frank," she said. "And who are you, Sir. I never knew you. Perhaps you had better leave me. Or stay, if you prefer. If it would help you and if it were possible I would go down with you into Hell: but you cannot bring Hell into me."
>
> "You do not love me," said the Tragedian in a thin bat-like voice: and he was now very difficult to see.
>
> "I cannot love a lie," said the Lady. "I cannot love the thing which is not. I am in Love, and out of it I will not go."
>
> There was no answer. The Tragedian had vanished. The Lady was alone in that woodland place . . . Presently the Lady got up and began to walk away. The other Bright Spirits came forward to receive her, singing as they came:
>
> "The Happy Trinity is her home: nothing can trouble her joy."

The scene answers to Lewis's conviction that the condition of damnation is eternal and irreversible. Once damnation becomes reality, there can be no other alternative than for the blessed to move into a state of indifference and to see their condemned loved ones as no longer being the persons they once were—perhaps no longer persons at all. At this point, Lewis appears to move very close to annihilationism. May it not then be inferred that the blessed, and presumably also God, have ceased to love the damned, have ceased to desire their eternal happiness? I think the answer must be yes.

---

[2] Thomas Talbott, *The Inescapable Love of God*, 2nd ed. (2014), p. 127.

Destined for Joy

How can one pray for or will the salvation of those who are, by definition, irredeemable? Note the judgment of St Thomas Aquinas:

> Mercy or compassion may be in a person in two ways: first by way of passion, secondly by way of choice. In the blessed there will be no passion in the lower powers except as a result of the reason's choice. Hence compassion or mercy will not be in them, except by the choice of reason. Now mercy or compassion comes of the reason's choice when a person wishes another's evil to be dispelled: wherefore in those things which, in accordance with reason, we do not wish to be dispelled, we have no such compassion. But so long as sinners are in this world they are in such a state that without prejudice to the Divine justice they can be taken away from a state of unhappiness and sin to a state of happiness. Consequently it is possible to have compassion on them both by the choice of the will—in which sense God, the angels and the blessed are said to pity them by desiring their salvation—and by passion, in which way they are pitied by the good men who are in the state of wayfarers. But in the future state it will be impossible for them to be taken away from their unhappiness: and consequently it will not be possible to pity their sufferings according to right reason. Therefore the blessed in glory will have no pity on the damned.[3]

It's a very short step from indifference to the misery of the damned to rejoicing in their misery. The redeemed do not rejoice in their sufferings directly, explains Aquinas—"To rejoice in another's evil as such belongs to hatred"[4]—but they do rejoice in their sufferings indirectly: "in this way the saints will rejoice in the punishment of the wicked, by considering therein the order of Divine justice and their own deliverance, which will fill them with joy."[5]

---

[3] Thomas Aquinas, *Summa Theologiae*, Suppl. q. 94, a. 2.
[4] ST, Suppl. q. 94, a. 3.
[5] ST, Suppl. q. 94, a. 3.

God's Love for the Blessed

The gospel assertion that God eternally wills our supremely worthwhile happiness, therefore, is incompatible with the traditional doctrine of hell. We cannot enjoy the first and best form of eschatological bliss if even one person is condemned to everlasting misery. John Kronen and Eric Reitan have formulated the argument in syllogistic form. They title it "The Argument from God's Love for the Blessed":

1. Anyone in a state of eternal blessedness possesses both perfect bliss and universal love for all persons.
2. Anyone who possesses universal love for all persons and who is aware that some persons are eternally damned cannot possess perfect bliss.
3. Therefore, anyone who is aware that some persons are eternally damned cannot possess eternal blessedness (1, 2).
4. If anyone is eternally damned, anyone who possesses eternal blessedness would be aware of this.
5. Thus, if anyone is eternally damned, then none possess eternal blessedness (3, 4).
6. God, out of benevolent love for His creatures, confers blessedness *at least* on those who earnestly repent and seek communion with Him.
7. Therefore, God does not eternally damn anyone (5, 6).[6]

The first premise is no doubt the most important. Surely, all Christians can agree that God intends human beings to enjoy the most supreme and worthwhile form of happiness and joy in the eternal communion of the Father, Son, and Holy Spirit. The

---

[6] John Kronen and Eric Reitan, *God's Final Victory* (2011), p. 80.

redeemed will, by grace, come to share in God's universal love for humanity, including the reprobate. As Kronen and Reitan note: "The prevailing Christian interpretation of divine love is that it is unconditional, encompassing even the damned."[7] The blessed will love not only each other but also the lost, just as God does. Neither second-best happiness nor defective charity makes the grade. The optimal eschatological condition will thus include "(a) perfect bliss—that is, happiness that is the best *kind* of happiness a person can know, untainted by any dissatisfaction; and (b) moral sanctification, including being perfected in love such that the saved love as God does."[8] To love is to will the good of the other, to identify the good of the other as our own good; but what if that good is no longer possible? Will love then cease? Would we want it to cease?

Perhaps the second premise is the most controversial. Assuming that the redeemed share in God's universal love for all human beings, then their eschatological beatitude will necessarily be reduced if they know that one or more of their brethren are enduring eternal misery. "If we love someone," the authors ask, "how could knowledge of their eternal damnation *not* diminish our happiness?"[9] This must be true even if the condition of perdition is freely chosen. Damnation is, after all, not just a tragic outcome for a human being: it is the ultimate tragedy, the worst possible conclusion of a person's life. How can we not lament those who endure this calamity?

I can imagine myself setting aside the distress caused by the torment of another, *if* I knew that the torment was temporary and reparative; but it is quite another thing to envision my enjoyment of heavenly felicity if I know that the other's torment is interminable:

---

[7] Ibid., p. 81.
[8] Ibid.
[9] Ibid.

There is a difference between temporary and permanent bad states. Perhaps it is possible for happiness to be undiminished by the former—especially if there is an assurance that the bad state will be redeemed. However, it is something else again to suppose that happiness can be undiminished by the latter, especially if there is no hope of redemption. In the former case, the intentional object of one's happiness might be the final state that is ultimately realized. Insofar as this state is worthy of unmitigated approval, supreme happiness might be fitting given even passing evils. What is not compatible with supreme happiness is permanent and ultimate tragedy—for in that case the final state is not one towards which an unmitigated positive judgment is fitting.[10]

Kronen and Reitan have advanced Talbott's argument beyond that particular love of those who are important to us in this life (parent for child, lover for beloved, friend for friend) to reflect the universal intention and character of the divine charity. The blessed have been perfected in love. "The degree to which they love the damned will exceed the degree to which we love even our dearest and closest friends."[11] There are no strangers. No matter how evil and corrupt, no matter how possessed of hatred for God and the company of heaven, the reprobate remain persons made in the image of God and therefore remain objects of love and concern both for God and the saints. The blessed cannot be indifferent to the awful plight of those who inhabit hell, precisely because they love as God loves:

> You have heard that it was said, "You shall love your neighbor and hate your enemy." But I say to you, Love your enemies and pray for those who persecute you, so that you may be sons of your Father who is in heaven. (Matt 5:33-35)

---

[10] Ibid., p. 84.
[11] Ibid., p. 83.

Olivier Clément once asked St Sophrony of Essex what would happen if a person did not open his heart and accept the love of God. The monk answered: "<u>You may be certain that as long as someone is in hell, Christ will remain there with him.</u>" If such is the case for Christ, then surely also for the saints; and if also the saints, then surely we must conclude that God will find a way to restore all humanity to himself in perfect love and beatitude. The vision of the Seer will be fulfilled: "And God shall wipe away all tears from their eyes; and there shall be no more death, neither sorrow, nor crying, neither shall there be any more pain: for the former things are passed away" (Rev 21:4).

Depersonalizing the Saints

When we confront head-on the Argument from God's Love for the Blessed, the impossibility of an everlasting hell becomes increasingly undeniable. Only a person who does not love could find hell for others tolerable—but then that person would himself be in hell. David Bentley Hart vehemently condemns the infernalist insouciance to the plight of the damned:

> It is not merely peculiarity of personal temperament that prompts Tertullian to speak of the saved relishing the delightful spectacle of the destruction of the reprobate, or Peter Lombard and Thomas Aquinas to assert that the vision of the torments of the damned will increase the beatitude of the redeemed (as any trace of pity would darken the joys of heaven), or Luther to insist that the saved will rejoice to see their loved ones roasting in hell. All of them were simply following the only poor thread of logic they had to guide them out of a labyrinth of impossible contradictions; the sheer enormity of the idea of a hell of eternal torment forces the mind toward absurdities and atrocities. Of course, the logical deficiencies of such language are obvious: After all, what is a person other than a whole history of associations, loves, memories, attachments, and affinities? Who are we, other than all the

others who have made us who we are, and to whom we belong as much as they to us? We are those others. To say that the sufferings of the damned will either be clouded from the eyes of the blessed or, worse, increase the pitiless bliss of heaven is also to say that no persons can possibly be saved: for, if the memories of others are removed, or lost, or one's knowledge of their misery is converted into indifference or, God forbid, into greater beatitude, what then remains of one in one's last bliss? Some other being altogether, surely: a spiritual anonymity, a vapid spark of pure intellection, the residue of a soul reduced to no one. But not a person—not the person who was. But the deepest problem is not the logic of such claims; it is their sheer moral hideousness.[12]

Hart's argument, though related to those advanced by Talbott, Kronen, and Reitan, is not identical to them. Given that human beings are constituted *as persons* by their relations to others, what kind of persons must we become in order to enjoy the absolute bliss of the Trinity, all the while remaining impervious to the misery of the lost? Must God make us into different people altogether, substituting other beings in our place, as in *Invasion of the Body Snatchers*? But that would not be the deification of persons, but rather its antithesis. We are shaped into the persons we are by all persons who lived before us, no matter when they lived or where they lived. Perhaps that reciprocal bond even extends to those who will come after us. By the Spirit we exist in solidarity with all as the one Christ.

> Some things are obvious: it is difficult to imagine what becomes of the actual person who was, say, a mother if she enjoys eternal beatitude despite the eternal dereliction of a child whom she loved and who loved her and whose presence in her life (most importantly) constitutes

---

[12] David Bentley Hart, "God, Creation, and Evil," *The Hidden and the Manifest* (2017), p. 344.

an essential part of who she is as a person. In a sense, however, it is no less difficult to understand how, say, a man who never knew that child, and perhaps never even really knew that mother, remains the person he was if he must become indifferent not only to that child's fate, but to her grief as well, in order to enter into the bliss of the Kingdom. The issue here is not merely one of the extrinsic association that exists between persons, but of the very ontology of personhood itself. Our relations to others in fact constitute us as the persons we are, and there is no such thing as a person in perfect isolation. If any person is in hell, so too is some part of every person whose identity was shaped by his or her relation to that damned soul.

But these attachments necessarily belong to a continuum of relations and interrelations that simple logic tells us extends to all persons everywhere. In order to affirm the true beatitude of the saved, one must introduce partitions into that continuum, invariably arbitrary, in order to define areas of morally and emotionally acceptable indifference; but, as soon as one does that, one discovers that that region of indifference is actually limitless, since it must potentially accommodate not only any person who might fail to be saved, however proximate or remote, but also anyone related by bonds of love or fidelity to that person, and so on *ad infinitum*. And this means that one has, morally speaking, proleptically detached one's happiness from the well-being of everyone else, since . . . what one is willing to sacrifice to achieve one's end, even if only as a possibility, is something one has already absolutely surrendered.

At the last, the realm of one's concern must in principle contract until nothing but the isolated self remains; and thus the ethos of heaven proves to be the same as the ethos of hell: every soul for itself. And this remains true—more so, in fact—if one argues that God might spare the redeemed the knowledge of the lost by expunging them from memory (as one especially absurd argument goes). For then, of course, what would then be saved could not really, in any meaningful sense, be a person any longer; it would be only the remnant of a person. In fact, it would be some other creature altogether. In which case, one's "salvation" would really be one's annihilation as a particular person within the community of created persons.[13]

As important and challenging as these philosophical arguments are, though, for me there remains this fundamental existential truth: *Heaven can never be heaven without my son.*

---

[13] David Bentley Hart, "Can Persons Be Saved?" *Public Orthodoxy* (22 May 2020): https://publicorthodoxy.org/2020/05/22/can-persons-be-saved/.

Chapter Twenty-Two

The Roar of Aslan and Afterlife Possibilities

If the greater hope is to be fulfilled, then it must be possible for those who die in a state of mortal sin—and thus outside of Christ Jesus—to repent of their sins and turn to God in faith. Yet how can such be possible? So many die without faith in Christ and his mercy; so many die in sin, evil, and iniquity; so many die with hearts possessed by hatred, greed, pride, and lust; so many die with blasphemy on their lips. Why think everyone would choose God even if given infinite opportunities?[1] The history of human depravity suggests otherwise. We can easily imagine at least one holdout, if not billions. William Lane Craig speaks of *transworld damnation*: in every possible world, hell is populated. How do we know this? Because there is hell!

> Why did God not create a world in which everyone freely receives Christ and so is saved? There is no such world which is feasible for God. He would have actualized such a world were this feasible, but in light of certain true counterfactuals of creaturely freedom every world realizable by God is a world in which some persons are lost.[2]

We may also speak of a given person as possessing the property of transworld damnation: in every feasible world in which that person

---

[1] Andre Buckareff and Allen Plug propose that a God of infinite love would offer to the damned infinite chances to escape their punishment: "Escaping Hell," *Religious Studies* 41 (2005): 39-54.
[2] William Lane Craig, "No Other Name," *Faith and Philosophy*, 6 (1980): 172-188. Cf. Thomas Talbott, "Craig on the Possibility of Eternal Damnation," *Religious Studies*, 28 (1992): 495-510.

exists, he or she always freely chooses to reject God and is therefore always lost. It does not matter how many chances one offers to the transworld damned. They remain obstinate in their rebellion and impenitence. "It is appointed unto men once to die, but after this the judgment" (Heb 9:27).

Multiple Church authorities, Eastern and Western, tell us that repentance is impossible after death: no post-mortem penance, no further opportunities to alter one's orientation toward the Creator. Our final destinies are irrevocably fixed. There is only the waiting for the Last Judgment. Some have speculated that once the soul has been separated from the body, it loses its capacity for new self-determinations. Others propose that personal liberty presupposes the freedom to definitively close oneself to transcendence. If in this life we were on a trajectory toward the light and love of God, so it will be for all eternity; but if toward darkness and self-absorption, so also it must be.

One of the most terrifying scenes in C. S. Lewis's *Chronicles of Narnia* occurs at the end of the *The Last Battle*. Aslan returns to re-create Narnia. But there is a group of dwarfs who seem to be trapped in their own little world:

> "Aslan," said Lucy through her tears, "could you—will you—do something for these poor Dwarfs?"
>
> "Dearest," said Aslan, "I will show you both what I can, and what I cannot, do." He came close to the Dwarfs and gave a low growl: low, but it set all the air shaking. But the Dwarfs said to one another, "Hear that? That's the gang at the other end of the stable. Trying to frighten us. They do it with a machine of some kind. Don't take any notice. They won't take us in again!"
>
> Aslan raised his head and shook his mane. Instantly a glorious feast appeared on the Dwarfs' knees: pies and tongues and pigeons and trifles and ices, and each Dwarf had a goblet of good wine in his right hand. But it wasn't much use. They began eating and drinking greedily

enough, but it was clear that they couldn't taste it properly. They thought they were eating and drinking only the sort of things you might find in a stable. One said he was trying to eat hay and another said he had got a bit of an old turnip and third said he'd found a raw cabbage leaf. And they raised the golden goblets of rich red wine to their lips and said "Ugh! Fancy drinking dirty water out of trough that a donkey's been at! Never thought we'd come to this."

But soon every Dwarf began suspecting that every other Dwarf had found something nicer than he had, and they started grabbing and snatching, and went on to quarreling, till in a few minutes there was a free fight and all the good food was smeared on their faces and clothes or trodden under foot. But when at least they sat down to nurse their black eyes and their bleeding nose, they all said:

"Well, at any rate there's no Humbug here. We haven't let anyone take us in. The Dwarfs are for the Dwarfs."

"You see," said Aslan. "They will not let us help them. They have chosen cunning instead of belief. Their prison is only in their minds, yet they are in that prison; and so afraid of being taken in that they cannot be taken out."

The omnipotence of Aslan has reached its limit. His roar cannot pierce the self-generated deafness of the dwarfs. They have built a wall around themselves through which not even the divine Creator can make his voice heard.

We can all find ourselves in this story. We know the possibility of hell within our souls; we know how easy it is to live in delusion and bitterness and hatred; we know the power of the darkness. Yet is the story of the dwarfs the final word? Do we really have the power to so cordon off ourselves that not even the omnipotent Creator can roar his Word and summon us to himself? Is the crucified and risen Christ so easily defeated?

Harrowing Hell

Scripture provides the crucial hint that matters might be otherwise:

> For Christ also died for sins once for all, the righteous for the unrighteous, that he might bring us to God, being put to death in the flesh but made alive in the spirit; in which he went and preached to the spirits in prison, who formerly did not obey. (1 Peter 3:18-19)
>
> For this is why the gospel was preached even to the dead, that though judged in the flesh like men, they might live in the spirit like God. (1 Peter 4:6)

After his death the eternal Son in his human soul invades Hades and preaches the good news of salvation, not just to the righteous but to the impenitent. The Latin Church has traditionally restricted the rescue mission of the harrowing of Hell to the Old Testament patriarchs and prophets, but not so the ancient Churches of the East.[3] After the Lord destroys the gates of Hades, he preaches the gospel to all the departed—none are excluded—and extends to all his victory over death. St Amphiochius of Iconium (fourth century) is representative of many of the Eastern Fathers:

> When [Christ] appeared to Hades, he destroyed its graves and emptied its tombs. He emptied them not by visibly contesting [Hades], but by invisibly granting resurrection. He did not unloose anybody, but all (*pantes*) were released. He did not talk to anybody, but freedom was announced. He did not call anybody, but all (*pantes*) ran after him. For when he appeared as King, the tyrant was humiliated, the light shone and the darkness faded away. For one could see every (*panta*) prisoner free and every (*panta*) captive rejoicing in the resurrection.[4]

---

[3] See Hilarion Alfeyev's lecture "Christ the Conqueror of Hell": http://orthodoxeurope.org/page/11/1/5.aspx.
[4] Quoted by Hilarion Alfeyev, *Christ the Conqueror of Hell* (2009), pp. 63-64.

St Cyril of Alexandria (fifth century) echoes the teaching of Amphiochius: "For having destroyed hell and opened the impassible gates for the departed spirits, he left the devil there abandoned and lonely."[5]

And in the seventh century, St Maximus Confessor comments on 1 Peter 4:6:

> Some say that Scriptures call "dead" those who died before the coming of Christ, for instance, those who were at the time of the flood, at Babel, in Sodom, in Egypt, as well as others who in various times and in various ways received various punishments and the terrible misfortune of divine damnation. These people were punished not so much for their ignorance of God as for the offences they imposed on one another. It was to them, according to [St Peter] that the great message was preached when they were already damned as men in the flesh, that is, when they received life in the flesh, punishment for crimes against one another, so that they could live according to God by the spirit, that is, being in hell, they accepted the preaching of the knowledge of God, believing in the Saviour who descended into hell to save the dead. So, in order to understand passage in [Holy Scripture] let us take it in this way: The dead, damned in the human flesh, were preached to precisely for the purpose that they may live according to God by the spirit.[6]

Throughout the liturgical year, the Orthodox Church sings:

> Our horrible death has been slain by your resurrection from the dead, for you appeared to those in hell, O Christ, and granted them life.
> Hell was emptied and made helpless by the death of one man.
> Who now is not amazed, O Master, as they see death destroyed through suffering, corruption taking flight through the Cross, and hell emptied of its wealth through death.

---

[5] Quoted by Alfeyev, p. 64.
[6] Quoted by Alfeyev, p. 79.

> Going down to those in hell, Christ proclaimed the good tidings, saying: "Be of good courage, now I have conquered! I am the Resurrection; I will bring you up, abolishing the gates of death."
>
> At present all is filled with light, heaven and earth and the netherworld.; let every creature celebrate the resurrection of Christ.
>
> Those who are held by the bonds of hell, in seeing your bounty, go towards the light, O Christ, on joyous feet, praising the eternal Pascha.
>
> Death gave up the dead it had swallowed, while hell's reign, which brought corruption, was destroyed when you rose from the tomb, O Lord.
>
> Strange is your crucifixion and your descent into Hades, O Lover of mankind; for having despoiled it and gloriously raised with yourself as God those who were prisoners, you opened Paradise and bade it welcome them.[7]

During twenty-five years of preaching as an Episcopal priest, I do not think I preached on our Lord's descent into Hades even once. Years later I read Hilarion Alfeyev's book *Christ the Conqueror of Hell*, and Holy Saturday took on a new meaning for me. Christ's entrance into Hades was no longer a one-time event, with no significance for anyone else. The gates of death have been broken, and Hades is now filled with the vivifying presence of the glorified Son. In the words of St John Chrysostom:

> This place of hades, dark and joyless, had been eternally deprived of light; this is why the gates are called dark and invisible. They were truly dark until the Sun of righteousness descended, illumined it and made hades Heaven. For where Christ is, there also is Heaven.[8]

Christ preached to the sinners of Hades. Death was neither a barrier to their hearing the gospel nor to their repentance. We have no

---

[7] Quoted by Alfeyev, chap. 4. The above is but a small sample of the many hymns cited by Alfeyev.
[8] Sergius Bulgakov, *The Bride of the Lamb* (2001), p. 356.

reason to believe that some, perhaps all, of the impious did not respond to our Lord in conversion and faith. How therefore can we dogmatically teach that there is no repentance after death? How dare we declare the impotence of omnipotent Love!

Sergius Bulgakov on the Afterlife

The great Russian Orthodox theologian Sergius Bulgakov thought deeply on the question of the afterlife. In death, he explains, the soul and spirit of the human person are separated from the body, but the soul remains united to the spirit, thus making possible immortal existence: "The human spirit exists as the hypostatic potency of the integral man, who has a body whose energy is the soul. In death, this energy is paralyzed but not annihilated. It remains a quality of the personal spirit."[9] Life *continues* beyond the grave. Man was intended by God to participate in the corporeal and spiritual realms; but with the aboriginal catastrophe that we call the Fall, he was exiled from the spiritual world, and human consciousness became imprisoned in matter. Death has now imposed a dualism upon man's experience of himself and reality:

> Death divides human life into two halves, as it were: psychic-corporeal being and spiritual-psychic being, before death and after death. The two halves are inseparably linked; they both belong to the life of the same individual, to his unique life that would have been free of this rupture if it had remained apart from this pathological dialectic of life and death, from the schism of the dual-unity. But this is no longer the case: To achieve fullness of humanization, a human being must go to the end of himself, not only in mortal life but also in the afterlife state, in order to attain the ripeness that makes him capable of receiving resurrection to eternal life in the fullness of true humanity. Understood

---

[9] Ibid., pp. 359-360.

this way, as an essentially necessary part of human life, death is actually an act of continuing life, although life that is affected by "dormition."[10]

Man is made in the image of God. He is not made for death. It is alien to his "natural" existence. Yet death pursues him. Death captures him. Death slays him.

What becomes *of* us in death? What happens *to* us? Bulgakov answers:

Truth.

Revelation.

Self-awareness.

Judgment.

"In death and after death," Bulgakov writes, "an individual sees his past early life as a whole, in its synthesis. The latter is, in itself, already a judgment, for it clarifies the general connection, the content and meaning of the life that has passed. Here, there is a clear vision not only of the synthesis but of the truth itself, in the presence of the spiritual world, free of all carnal partiality, in the light of divine justice. This is the self-evidentness of the divine judgment."[11] The judgment of the after-life is self-knowledge and self-verdict, an immanent judgment of conscience. It is not yet a perfect knowledge. That perfect knowledge will only become available to us at the completion of human history and the final judgment. Bulgakov calls it a preliminary judgment: "an afterlife consciousness of self and the existential self-determination that

---

[10] Ibid., pp. 359-60.
[11] Ibid., p. 360.

comes from this consciousness."[12] We are brought into a true knowledge of God, the world, and ourselves. "In the afterlife," he explains, "the false light and shadows of our world have disappeared and all things are illuminated by the sun of justice, fixed in the heavenly heights, with its beams penetrating into the depths of souls and hearts."[13] We will see ourselves as we really are.

Bulgakov rejects the medieval schema of hell—purgatory—heaven and instead proposes that Hades be understood as a form of universal purgatory filled with the uncreated light of the risen Christ:

> One cannot argue against the general idea of a purgatorial state beyond the grave, but is it necessary to schematize it as a third place, alongside paradise and hell? The basic notion here, which is proper to Catholic rigorism and also contaminates Orthodox thought, is that a person is definitively and irrevocably earmarked for one of the two states of the afterlife, paradise or hell, even before the universal judgment. But this assertion does not have a sufficient basis, at least in Orthodoxy, which recognizes the efficacy of the prayer for the deceased, for which no limits are set (this is expressed with particular force in the third prayer of the Pentecost vespers). According to Orthodox doctrine, the state of sinners in the afterlife is that of a temporary purgatory rather than that of an irrevocable hell.[14]

Personal life does not end with death but continues. Self-consciousness and creative self-determination remain proper to the departed human being. Through death the individual is introduced to a new knowledge of God and of the spiritual world:

> This new knowledge consists in communion with the spiritual world of incorporeal beings; first of all, with human souls, communion with whom—in them and through them—is extended to the souls of the

---

[12] Ibid.
[13] Ibid., p. 361.
[14] Ibid.

whole of humankind (for incorporeal souls cannot be confined in isolation cells); as well as with the angelic world and the demonic world. But the supreme spiritual gift acquired in the afterlife state is a new and different knowledge of God, proper to the world of incorporeal spirits. For such spirits, God's being is as clearly visible as the sun in the sky is for us.[15]

Bulgakov criticizes the popular construal that reduces human existence in the afterlife to unchanging passivity. "Such a view," he writes, "contradicts both the nature of the spirit and the data of church tradition and revelation."[16] The human being is the bearer of the divine image. Freedom and creative self-determination constitute his personal existence. He may be deprived of his physical senses and his historical involvement in the world; but he is also granted in the afterlife a dynamic experience of the spiritual realm. In death, says Bulgakov, we are given "new sources and a new knowledge" of life that were inaccessible to us in our mortal existence.[17]

Bulgakov thus sees our afterlife experience as essential to our preparation for our life of resurrection:

> It is also necessary to recognize that this afterlife of an individual in communion with the spiritual world is not less important for his final state than early life and, in every case, is a necessary part of the path that leads to universal resurrection. Every individual must, in his own way, ripen spiritually to this resurrection and determine himself with finality both in good and in evil. One must therefore conclude that, even though in resurrection an individual remains identical to himself in everything he has acquired in earthly life, nevertheless, in the afterlife, he becomes other than he was even in relation to the state in which he found himself at the moment of death. The afterlife is not

---

[15] Ibid., p. 363.
[16] Ibid., p. 362.
[17] Ibid.

> only "reward" and "punishment," and not only a "purgatory," but also a spiritual school, a new experience of life, which does not remain without consequence but enriches and changes each individual's spiritual image. We know nothing about the degree or manner of this process. But it is important to establish that, even in the afterlife, human souls experience and acquire something new, each in its own way, in its freedom.[18]

May the sinner repent of his sins in the afterlife? Absolutely, answers Bulgakov. The departed soul does not lose his freedom and creative energy. He has acquired a new kind of existence that involves an expansion and deepening of spiritual knowledge. Repentance in the afterlife will necessarily be different from repentance in our earthly life: the departed soul no longer acts in the world as he once did; hence the kind of penitence and good works made possible by historical existence are unavailable to him. But still the person may alter his orientation toward God. Still the person may call out to the Lord for mercy and help.

> Of course, here too, the fullness of the life of the living is different from that of the dead, and the measure of their repentance is not the same. Clearly, the repentance of the deceased, as a complex inner process of awakening to spiritual life, differs from what takes place in the living. Earthly life is a foundation for the future life, but it is not the only foundation. Earthly life and the afterlife are connected as different aspects of the one life of one and the same spirit. One usually prefers to conceive the afterlife state of "sinners" (but who is free of sin and therefore does not need to repent?) in the juridical and penitentiary form of a sentence served in an afterlife prison, without possibility of pardon or parole. However, it is completely impossible to allow that the spirit could be in a state so static, so frozen in an unchanging spasm or so immersed in passive contemplation of its past actions and

---

[18] Ibid., p. 363.

deprived of the capacity for future life.... From all this we conclude that the afterlife state is not death, and not even a stupor of the spirit, but a continuation of the life of the spirit begun on earth. Thus, despite the reduced condition for this life which passes outside the body and despite a certain passivity resulting from this, the afterlife state cannot be considered as given once and for all and unchanging, with the total absence of creative freedom. Rather, it is a continuation of spiritual life, which does not end on the other side of death's threshold. The afterlife state is a stage of the path leading to resurrection.[19]

Bulgakov acknowledges that the school theologians "consider death to be the limit that represents the end of the time of deeds and the beginning of the time of retribution, so that, after death, one can neither repent nor correct one's life. Such is the dominant opinion of theologians, which is passed off as the doctrine of the Church."[20] But this view of afterlife paralysis, insists Bulgakov, violates *life*. Life can be neither bottled up nor frozen. The God of Abraham, Isaac, and Jacob is the God of the living, not the dead. Hence we need to understand life after death as a creative dimension of the ascent of the human being into the divine life of God. It brings its own kind of asceticism.

The holy Orthodox Church prays for all the departed, in the confident hope that the God who wills the salvation of every human being will complete his work of salvation in the lives of all. The practice presupposes the synergistic cooperation of the departed with these prayers:

> One of the dogmatic presuppositions of the doctrine of eternal torments understood as unchangeable and infinite is the assertion that repentance is impossible in the afterlife as well as after the Last Judgment. But this impossibility is clearly contradicted by the efficacy

---

[19] Ibid., pp. 365-366.
[20] Ibid., p. 368.

of prayers for the deceased; nor does it have a biblical justification. For the reception of the assistance of prayer presupposes that the souls of the deceased actively receive this prayer in accordance with the general reality of the energy of the spirit, which is characterized by an uninterrupted continuation of life and new self-determinations that rise thence.

It is true that, in the afterlife, human beings lose the capacity for actions of the earthly type, which includes the participation of the soul and the body (*opera meritoria*, according to the Catholic doctrine) and direct participation in the making of history. But the disincarnation in death does not suppress the activity of the spirit. This is clear from the fact that saints participate with their prayers in the life of the world and in human history, as revelation shows (Rev. 7:9-17; 8:1-4; 14:1-4; 15:1-4; 20:4-6) and the Church believes. This activity of the spirit can also be concentrated upon repentance in the afterlife, which is facilitated by the prayers of the Church without the possibility of being concretely realized in earthly life. Nevertheless, the afterlife is a continuation of earthly life.[21]

God does not cease to will the eternal salvation of departed souls, nor does he cease in the afterlife to pursue the impenitent and summon them to himself in mercy and love. God has so ordered reality that the prayers of the Church, in and by the Spirit, gain a powerful salvific efficacy for the inhabitants of Hades. "The boundary between paradise and hell," Bulgakov writes, "is by no means absolute, for it can be overcome by the prayers of the Church."[22] Nor may we entertain the possibility that God does not hear the prayers of the deceased, thus rendering their repentance ineffectual. "To whom is it given," Bulgakov asks, "to measure the

---

[21] Ibid., p. 500.
[22] Ibid., p. 367.

depth of the mercy of God, who 'have concluded them all in unbelief, that he might have mercy upon all' (Rom. 11:32)?"[23]

As long as the rebellious soul continues in his self-chosen defiance and contumacy, his torment continues. He carries his earthly life into the next world. His sins follow him.

Although the terms *retribution* and *reward* are found in Scripture and are uttered by the Lord Himself, we must understand them not as an external juridical law (which would be contrary to the spirit of Christ's gospel) but as an ontological connection, an internal necessity, according to which an individual suffers to the end all that is inappropriate to his vocation but was committed by him in earthly life: "he himself shall be saved; yet so as by fire" (1 Cor. 3:15).[24]

The life of the afterlife is different from earthly life in one other crucial way. The departed no longer fear death, for death is behind them. As an object of hope and fear, death is replaced by the final judgment:

> The face of earthly life is turned toward death. Death is an object of horror, about which people try to forget; terrible is the hour of death and the "preliminary judgment." But despite this and above this, death is a joyous hour of initiation or new revelation, of the fulfillment of the "desire to be delivered and to be with Christ," of communion with the spiritual world. In practical terms, death, as what awaits us on the immediate horizon, blocks for us what is more distant: the resurrection to come, which seems abstract compared with the immediate concreteness of death. But in the afterlife, all this has changed, for the prospect of death and its revelation no longer menaces us: Death has come and its revelation has been accomplished. The place of death is taken by universal resurrection, which naturally becomes an object of fear and trembling for some and of joyous hope for others, while for many, if not for the majority, it becomes an object of fear and hope at

---

[23] Ibid., p. 364.
[24] Ibid., p. 368.

the same time. In any case, in contrast to the world on this side, the spiritual sky in the afterlife shines with the hope of resurrection, and the prayer "even so, come" (Rev. 22:20) has an unfathomable power for us there.[25]

Post Obitum Repentance and the Prayers of the Church

Bulgakov's understanding of the self-determining possibilities for departed souls has been reiterated by Alfeyev:

> Is it at all possible that the fate of a person can be changed after his death? Is death that border beyond which some unchangeable static existence comes? Does the development of the human person not stop after death? It is impossible for one to actively repent in hell; it is impossible to rectify the evil deeds one committed by appropriate good works. It may, however, be possible for one to repent through a "change of heart," a review of one's values. One of the testimonies to this is the rich man of the Gospel. He realized the gravity of his situation as soon as [he] found himself in hell. Indeed, in his lifetime he was focused on earthly pursuits and forgot God, but once in hell he realized that God was his only hope for salvation. Besides, according to the teaching of the Orthodox Church, the fate of a person after death can be changed through the prayer of the church. Thus existence after death has its own dynamics. On the basis of what has been said above, it may be said that after death the development of the human person does not cease, for existence after death is not a transfer from a dynamic into a static being, but rather a continuation on a new level of that road which a person followed in his or her lifetime.[26]

The Church prays for the souls of the departed. In faith and hope the Church prays, and in love and mercy God hears our prayers. Who dares to limit his love and power? Who dares to restrict the

---

[25] Ibid., pp. 375-376.
[26] Alfeyev, pp. 216-217.

universal reach of the incarnate Son who descended into the abyss of death and rose to glory, with the souls of the departed in his train? Who dares to suggest the inefficacy of the intercessions of the Most Holy Mother of God? And so the Churches pray:

> O Christ our God . . . who, also, on this all-perfect and saving Feast, art graciously pleased to accept propitiatory prayers for those who are imprisoned in Hell, promising unto us who are held in bondage great hope of release from the vileness that doth hinder us and did hinder them; and that thou wilt send down thy consolation. Hear us, thy humble ones, who make our supplications unto thee, and give rest to the souls of thy servants who have fallen asleep, in a place of light, a place of verdure, a place of refreshment whence all sickness, sorrow and sighing have fled away: And speedily establish thou their souls in the mansions of the Just; and graciously vouchsafe unto them peace and pardon; for the dead shall not praise thee, neither shall they who are in Hell make bold to offer unto thee confession. But we who are living will bless thee, and will pray, and offer unto thee propitiatory prayers and sacrifices for their souls. (Vespers of Pentecost)
>
> *Domine Jesu Christe, Rex gloriae, libera animas omnium fidelium defunctorum de poenis inferni et de profundo lacu. Libera eas de ore leonis, ne absorbeat eas tartarus, ne cadant in obscurum; sed signifer sanctus Michael repraesentet eas in lucem sanctam, quam olim Abrahae promisisti et semini eius. Amen.* (Requiem Mass)

<blockquote>
Christ is risen from the dead,

trampling down death by death,

and on those in the tombs bestowing life!
</blockquote>

Chapter Twenty-Three

Gehenna as Universal Purgatory

"It is impossible to appear before Christ and to see Him without loving Him."[1]

This statement represents the most striking and provocative claim in the eschatology of Sergius Bulgakov. Upon it rests his confident hope in apokatastasis. In one form or another, we find this claim sprinkled throughout the concluding chapters of *The Bride of the Lamb*. When Christ Jesus returns in glory, he will clothe humanity in himself, and we will see him in his truth, goodness, and beauty; and in seeing we will irresistibly love him, for in him we will discover our authentic selfhood and the fulfillment of our deepest yearnings and desires.[2] "Every human being sees himself in Christ and measures the extent of his difference from this proto-image," Bulgakov explains. "A human being cannot fail to love the Christ who is revealed in him, and he cannot fail to love himself revealed in Christ."[3]

The Sufferings of the Damned

Bulgakov's profound insight regarding eschatological transformation—to truly see the risen and glorified Jesus is to love him—does not lead the Russian theologian to conclude that at the *parousia* all will be instantaneously and magically converted to God.

---

[1] Sergius Bulgakov, *The Bride of the Lamb* (2001), p. 459.
[2] See Rob De La Noval, "We Shall See Him as He is: Bulgakov on Eschatological Conversion," *Eclectic Orthodoxy* (24 October 2021):
https://afkimel.wordpress.com/2021/10/24/we-shall-see-him-as-he-is-bulgakov-on-eschatological-conversion/.
[3] Bulgakov, p. 459.

Gehenna as Universal Purgatory

For some, perhaps many, the return of Christ Jesus in glory will ignite a Gehennic conflagration in the depth of their souls. Imprisoned in their egoism and malice, they will hate the Son and with all their might will seek to extinguish the love born in their hearts. Just so, they will burn. They will know the torment of hell, an agony of love, guilt, self-condemnation, and despair. Guiding Bulgakov's reflections here are the homilies of St Isaac the Syrian, which he knew in Russian translation. He refers to the following passage several times:

> I say that those tormented in Gehenna are struck by the scourge of love. And how bitter and cruel is this agony of love, for, feeling that they have sinned against love, they experience a torment that is greater than any other. The affliction that strikes the heart because of the sin against love is more terrible than any possible punishment. It is wrong to think that Gehenna are deprived of God's love. Love is produced by knowledge of the truth, which (everyone is in agreement about this) is given to all in general. But by its power love affects human beings in a twofold manner: It torments sinners, as even here a friend sometimes causes one to suffer, and it gladdens those who have carried out their duty. **And so, in my opinion, the torment of Gehenna consists in repentance.** Love fills with its joys the souls of the children on high.[4]

This passage is perhaps the most quoted passage from all of St Isaac's writings. But note the bolded sentence: the torment of Gehenna is *repentance* generated by knowledge of the truth. This translation is unfamiliar to those restricted to English translations of Isaac's homilies. The Transfiguration Monastery version, for example, renders the bolded sentence: "Thus I say that this is the torment of Gehenna: bitter regret."[5] There's a world of difference

---

[4] Quoted by Bulgakov, p. 466; emphasis mine.
[5] Isaac, Homily 28, *The Ascetical Homilies of St Isaac the Syrian*, 2nd ed. (2011), p. 266.

379

between repentance and bitter regret. The older translation by A. J. Weinsinck renders the sentence differently still: "I say that the hard tortures are grief for love."[6] I wrote the respected Syriac scholar Sebastian Brock and asked him his opinion about the passage. In his email response, he stated that the Syriac word *twatha* is probably best translated "remorse" and observes that in the original text it is followed by the phrase "which is from love," which Brock interprets as that "remorse that comes from the sudden awareness of God's love: i.e. it is the sudden realisation of how one has sinned against God's love that produces the torment in which Gehenna/Hell consists." This phrase, however, was dropped in the Greek translation, which explains why it is missing from both the Russian and Transfiguration Monastery translations. Weinsinck, working from the Syriac, appears to have captured the meaning of the original better than the others.

> Reading Isaac's homily in the Russian translation, Bulgakov interprets the sufferings of the damned as interior conflict, the painful struggle between their desire to be united to Christ, awakened in their hearts by the parousial manifestation, and their impotence to realize their desire because of the dominating passion to live apart from God. "Hell is love for God," Bulgakov writes, "though it is a love that cannot be satisfied. Hell is a suffering due to emptiness, due to the inability to contain this love of God."[7] Hell is knowing what it means to be made in the image of Christ and being horrified by one's deformity. Hell is the suffering of receiving into oneself the judgment of God, the judgment of divine image upon failed likeness:

> Judgment as separation expresses the relation between image and likeness, which can be in mutual harmony or in antinomic conjugacy. Image corresponds to the heavenly mansions in the Father's house, to

---

[6] Isaac, Chap. XXVII, *Mystic Treatises by Isaac of Nineveh* (1923), p. 136.
[7] Bulgakov, p. 492.

the edenic bliss of "eternal life." Likeness, by contrast, corresponds to that excruciating division within the resurrected human being where he does not yet actually possess what is his potentially; whereas his divine proto-image is in full possession of it. He contemplates this image before himself and in himself as the inner norm of his being, whereas, by reason of his proper self-determination and God's judgment, he cannot encompass this being in himself. He cannot possess part (and this part can be large or small) of that which is given to him and loved by him in God (cf. St Isaac the Syrian); and this failure to possess, this active emptiness at the place of fullness, is experienced as perdition and death, or rather as a perishing and a dying, as "eternal torment," as the fire of hell. This ontological suffering is described only in symbolic images borrowed from the habitual lexicon of apocalyptics. It is clear that these images should not be interpreted literally. Their fundamental significance lies in their description of the torments of unrealized and unrealizable love, the deprivation of the bliss of love, the consciousness of the sin against love.[8]

There can be no easy escape from this suffering, for it is the inevitable consequence of a life lived in passionate attachment to self and the goods of the world. The soul now finds itself naked before fiery Love. The purification of the soul must be lived out to the end. Evil must be expiated; the debt to justice—which is nothing less than personal transformation and restoration of the divine image—must be paid to the last farthing:

> God's love, it must be said, is also His justice. God's love consumes in fire and rejects what is unworthy, while being revealed in this rejection. "For God hath concluded them all in unbelief that he might have mercy upon all. O the depth of the riches both of the wisdom and knowledge of God" (Rom 11:32-33). The one not clothed in a wedding garment is expelled from the wedding feast about which it is said: "If so be that being clothed we shall not be found naked" (2 Cor. 5.3). This

---

[8] Ibid., pp. 474-475.

> *nakedness*, this absence of that which is given and must be present, *stéresis*, as the original definition of evil, is fundamental for the torments of hell. It is the *fire* that burns without consuming. One must reject every pusillanimous, sentimental hope that the evil committed by a human being and therefore present in him can simply be forgiven, as if ignored at the tribunal of justice. God does not tolerate sin, and its simple forgiveness is ontologically impossible. Acceptance of sin would not accord with God's holiness and justice. Once committed, a sin must be lived through to the end, and the entire mercilessness of God's justice must pierce our being when we think of what defense we will offer at Christ's Dread Tribunal.[9]

This passage surprises and confuses. How can Bulgakov declare that sin cannot be absolved, given his emphatic assertion of the love and mercy of the Creator throughout the pages of his Great Trilogy? Surely he is not rescinding what he has so clearly declared. The contradiction can be resolved if we interpret the word "forgiveness" in this passage as "remission." God cannot simply overlook our condition of sinfulness; he cannot receive the unholy into heaven. Every human being must be perfectly conformed to the divine Image and transformed in the Holy Spirit. In this sense, God's forgiveness of sin is nothing less than the regeneration of the sinner through repentance and synergistic cooperation with the Spirit. My interpretation is confirmed, I believe, by Bulgakov's claim that the perditional suffering is redemptive in nature:

> The weeping and gnashing of teeth in the outer darkness nonetheless bears witness to the life of a spirit that has come to know the entire measure of its fall and that is tormented by repentance. But, like all repentance, these torments are *salvific* for the spirit.[10]

---

[9] Ibid., pp. 475-476.
[10] Ibid., p. 499.

Hell must be experienced to the end, *until* it has achieved its divinely-ordained purpose. "The torments of hell, elaborates Bulgakov, "are a longing for God caused by the love for God. This longing is inevitably combined with the desire to leave the darkness, to overcome the alienation from God, to become oneself in conformity with one's revealed protoimage."[11]

Hell as Purgation and Healing

Bulgakov describes Gehenna as "universal purgatory" (*vseobshchee christilishche*), which, as Paul Gavrilyuk notes, "describes the gist of his teaching remarkably well."[12] Rejecting the long-standing retributive construal of eternal punishment, Bulgakov interprets the punishment of Gehenna as a freely accepted purgative condition:

> Hell's torments of love necessarily contain the regenerating power of the expiation of sin by the experiencing of it to the end. However, this creative experiencing is not only a passive state, in chains imposed from outside. It is also an inwardly, synergistically accepted spiritual state (and also a psychic-corporeal state). This state is appropriately perceived not as a juridical punishment but as an effect of God's justice, which is revealed in its inner persuasiveness. And its acceptance as a just judgment corresponds to an inner movement of the spirit, to a creative determination of the life of the spirit. And in its duration ("in the ages of ages"), this life contains the possibility of a creative suffering that heals, of a movement of the spirit from within toward good in its triumphant force and persuasiveness. Therefore, it is necessary to stop thinking of hell in terms of static and inert immobility, but instead to associate it with the dynamics of life, always creative and growing. Even in hell, the nature of the spirit remains unchanging in its creative changeability. Therefore, the state of hell must be understood as an

---

[11] Ibid., p. 492.
[12] Paul Gavrilyuk, "Universal Salvation in the Eschatology of Sergius Bulgakov," *Journal of Theological Studies*, 57 (April 2006): 125.

unceasing creative activity, or more precisely, self-creative activity, of the soul, although this state bears within itself a disastrous split, an alienation from its prototype. All the same, the apostle Paul defines this state as a *salvation*, yet as by fire, after the man's work is burned. It is his nakedness.[13]

The *Purgatorio* by Dante Alighieri immediately comes to mind. Dante envisions purgatory as "the mountain that dis-evils those who climb."[14] Repentant souls ascend the mountain to be cleansed of their sins and made fit for the enjoyment of paradise. The punishments of each terrace are directly correlated to the vice or sin from which the soul needs to be delivered. As Anthony Esolen explains: "In purgatory man is made a 'new creation' by being restored to his original straightness, his original innocence before the fall of Adam."[15] It undoes the damage of sin and is thus best thought of as an infirmary rather than a prison or torture chamber.

In the sixth terrace, for example, souls are cured of their gluttony by deprivation of food and drink. A large tree with "apples sweet to smell and good to eat" stands next to the path, but its branches taper downwards, thus preventing anyone from climbing the tree to reach its fruit. Dante comes across an old friend, Forese, emaciated and gaunt, and inquires about his condition. Forese replies:

> From the eternal providence divine a power descends into the tree and rain back there—a power that makes me lean and fine. And all these people singing in their pain weep for immoderate service of the throat, and thirst and hunger make them pure again. The odor of the fruit and of the spray splashing its fragrant droplets in the green kindle desire in us to eat and drink. And many a time along this turning way we find the

---

[13] Bulgakov, p. 498.
[14] Canto 13, *Purgatorio*, trans. Anthony Esolen (2003).
[15] Ibid., p. xvi.

freshening of our punishment, our punishment—our solace, I should say, For that same will now leads us to the tree as once led the glad Christ to say, "*My God,*" when by His opened veins He set us free.[16]

The gluttons are subjected to the punishment of starvation and thirst, yet instead of raging against the punishment, they embrace it as medicine for the soul that conforms them to the sufferings of Christ. Their desire is purified and reordered to the love of God.

Maurice Francis Egan contrasts the two principal construals of purgatory historically advanced by Roman Catholic theologians—the punishment theory and the purification theory.[17] Proponents of both theories agree that all souls who enter into a condition of purgatorial suffering have been pardoned of their sins and are thus destined for the beatific vision; but they disagree on the purpose of purgatorial suffering.

According to the *punishment theory*, the chastisements of purgatory are strictly retributive. There is a debt of justice (*reatus poenae*) that needs to be satisfied for post-baptismal transgressions for which penance was not made in this life. Cleansing, healing, sanctification are unnecessary, as God accomplishes the perfect regeneration of the elect immediately upon death, "either by infusing the opposite virtues or by withdrawing the '*influxus conservativus*' from the faulty habits, or simply by admitting the soul to glory, in whose light all shadows disappear."[18] Though they still need to expiate their temporal debt, only saints enter into purgatory. For love they must suffer the just punishment which their sins have merited.[19] Those tutored in the 1993 *Catechism of the Catholic Church* are often surprised to learn that this retributive

---

[16] Canto 13.
[17] M. F. Egan, "The Two Theories of Purgatory," *Irish Theologial Review* 17 (1922): 24-34.
[18] Ibid., p. 30.
[19] Martin Jugie, *Purgatory and the Means to Avoid It* (1949), p. 5.

understanding of purgatory was common among Latin theologians right up to the mid-20th century. When Bulgakov describes hell as "universal purgatory," he is not thinking of this punitive view.

According to the *purification theory*, the purpose of the chastisements of purgatory is primarily medicinal, reparative, purgative, transformational. Those who enter purgatory may still retain attachments to the world from which they need liberation and evil inclinations for which they need healing. The theory does not deny, states Egan, the necessity to satisfy the temporal debt incurred by sins; "but it asserts that the payment is the means, the normal though not absolutely necessary means, by which God cleanses their sores and gives them the perfect spiritual health which their future life with Him requires."[20] Dante's vision of purgatory comes under this category, as does St Catherine of Genoa's *Treatise on Purgatory*. Since Vatican II the purification theory has emerged as the dominant interpretation of purgatory in the magisterial teaching of the Catholic Church. Bulgakov's proposal of universal purgatory approximates the purification model, minus the notion of juridical expiation.

The 16th century Reformers rejected purgatory and prayers for the dead as subverting the atoning sufficiency of the death of Christ and justification by faith.[21] But in recent years some Protestant thinkers have proposed therapeutic and transformational models of purgatory, most notably Wesleyan philosopher Jerry Walls. Walls

---

[20] Egan, p. 24. Cf. Neil Judisch, "Sanctification, Satisfaction, and the Purpose of Purgatory," *Faith and Philosophy*, 26 (April 2009): 167-185.

[21] In one of his lectures on Dante, George MacDonald quipped: "When the [Protestant] Church thought that three places for departed spirits was too many, she took away the wrong one. I do indeed believe in a place of punishment, but that longing and pain will bring us back to God." Reported in "George MacDonald on Dante," *Wingfold* 89 (Winter 2015): 34. In the same issue of *Wingfold*, also see Barbara Amell, "600 Years Later: George MacDonald on Purgatory": 38-44.

sees purgatory as a *post obitum* educational process in which justified but imperfect sinners come to a deeper understanding of their vices and sinful dispositions, thus being led by the Spirit into deeper repentance. It is unreasonable, he argues, to think that God would magically transform sinners into saints, without their free cooperation and involvement. Just as sanctification is a synergistic process in our earthly lives, so we may reasonably expect an analogous process to occur in our heavenly lives, until complete deliverance from sin is achieved.

How might we envision the educational process of purgatory? Consider Charles Dickens's classic tale *A Christmas Carol*. Ebenezer Scrooge, whom the narrator describes as "hard and sharp as flint, from which no steel had ever struck out generous fire," is visited on Christmas Eve by three spirits. These spirits disclose to him the truth of his life—past, present, and likely future. The spirits assist Scrooge, Walls explains, "to see others in ways he had not been able to before. By seeing himself rightly in relation to others, he comes not only to see them differently, but himself as well."[22] Scrooge's encounter with reality results in his spiritual awakening and moral conversion. The narrator concludes the story: "And it was always said of him, that he knew how to keep Christmas well, if any man alive possessed the knowledge." Perhaps we may think of purgatory as that eschatological event in which God takes us on a review of our lives, allowing us to "see with full clarity not only how our lives have hurt others, but most importantly, how God sees them. Even more than the visits of the three spirits to Scrooge, such an extended encounter with truth through the Holy Spirit would alter us and heal our disposition to sin."[23]

---

[22] Jerry L. Walls, *Purgatory: The Logic of Total Transformation* (2011), pp. 85-86.
[23] Ibid., p. 85.

In disagreement with Roman Catholic teaching, Walls is willing to entertain the possibility of *post obitum* repentance. Surely the God of infinite love will go to every length to secure the eternal happiness of all human beings. "If we take this picture of God's love as a serious truth claim," he writes, "and not merely a piece of pious rhetoric, we have reason to accept a modified or expanded view of purgatory that grace is further extended not only to the converted who are partially transformed and imperfectly sanctified, but also to those persons who have not yet exercised any sort of saving faith."[24] But the God of love will not coerce. Human beings remain free to choose eternal alienation from the Father of Jesus Christ. Yet Walls is cautiously hopeful: "The fact that we are created in God's image is a much deeper and more resilient truth about us than our sin and whatever damage we have done to ourselves."[25]

Clearly Sergius Bulgakov's understanding of Gehenna as *universal purgatory* can be helpfully supplemented by contemporary discussions of purgatorial sanctification. Those who claim that a person's eternal destiny is definitively determined at death will, of course, disagree. But on the basis of Holy Scripture and Holy Tradition, Bulgakov boldly declares the salvation of all. God will never cease to summon all human beings to himself, until his universal salvific will is sealed on the Day of Judgment.

---

[24] Ibid., p. 150.
[25] Ibid., p. 151.

Chapter Twenty-Four

The Apokatastasis of Judas Iscariot

But what about Judas? The fate of the Iscariot is the challenge most often posed to anyone who dares to proclaim the greater hope. Christians have long debated whether few or many will be saved. St John Chrysostom appears to have been particularly pessimistic: "Among thousands of people there are not a hundred who will arrive at their salvation, and I am not even certain of that number, so much perversity is there among the young and so much negligence among the old."[1] This pessimism characterized the judgment of the Church in most times and places, observes Avery Dulles.[2] In the modern age, Christians have become more hopeful, however. Even a fairly traditional theologian like Pope Benedict XVI has conjectured that "the great majority of people" will be saved, albeit through purgatorial suffering.[3] But on one point eschatological pessimists and optimists agree: there is at least one human being who is damned—Judas, son of Simon, the betrayer of God Incarnate. How could it be otherwise? Not only did he treacherously hand Jesus over to the Sanhedrin, but he compounded the offense by the mortal sin of suicide. The prosecution rests.

In recent centuries, a few brave voices have questioned the finality of this verdict. In the 19th century, for example, the Scottish poet Robert Buchanan sang of the final reconciliation of the apostle

---

[1] John Chystostom, homily 24 in *Act. Apostolorum*, PG 60:189.
[2] Avery Dulles, "The Population of Hell," *First Things* (May 2003).
[3] Pope Benedict XVI, *Spe salvi* (2007), §46.

in his "Ballad of Judas Iscariot."[1] After aeons of wandering in desolate places, the soul of Judas finds Jesus waiting for him at the Wedding Supper of the Lamb:

> The supper wine is poured at last,
> The lights burn bright and fair,
> Iscariot washes the Bridegroom's feet,
> And dries them with his hair.

The great Reformed theologian Karl Barth exhibited a respectful reticence regarding the final destiny of the Iscariot: on the one hand, affirming the election of all human beings in Jesus Christ; on the other hand, declining to proclaim apokatastasis:

> If we follow the Evangelists, then, it would be both hasty and illegitimate to give a final answer one way or the other. In the form, at least, in which we have put it, the question can only be left answered. The better course is clearly to consider the unresolved contrast: Jesus, on the one side, in the full sweep of His absolute care for His Church and therefore for the world, to which He addresses Himself through the service of His Church, in the full sweep of the radical restitution of the basic corruption of the world, and of Israel and of His Church, and therefore of the completion of His own election, His whole mission as the Son of God and Man; and Judas on the other side, for his part only the object of this care, only the bearer and representative of this basic corruption, only the rejected whom God has taken to Himself in the election of Jesus Christ, to whom God has turned Himself in the mission of Jesus Christ. On the one side, Jesus *for*

---

[1] See Addison Hart, "Robert Buchanan and 'The Ballad of Judas Iscariot'": https://afkimel.wordpress.com/2016/09/04/robert-buchanan-and-the-ballad-of-judas-iscariot/.

Judas too, indeed for Judas especially; and on the other side Judas *against* Jesus, against the very Jesus who is for him, who gives Himself wholly and utterly for him, who washes his feet, who offers him His broken body and shed blood, who makes Himself his. The New Testament gives us no direct information about the outcome of this extraordinary "for and against." Really none! It does not describe Judas' repentance in such a way that we may draw an irresistible or even a probable conclusion as to a final and conclusive conversion of Judas in this life. It does not open up for us any prospect of the completion of such a conversion in the hereafter. Nor does it say anything about the inadmissibility of such a conversion. It strikingly fails to make use of the tempting possibility of making Judas a plain and specific example of hopeless rejection and perdition, an embodiment of the temporal and eternal rejection of certain men. It emphasizes the unambiguous contrast on both sides. On the one hand, it places no limits to the grace of Jesus Christ even with regard to Judas. It sets Judas against the brightest radiance of this grace. And on the other hand, it does not use even a single word to suggest that Judas is an example of *apokatastasis*.[5]

The test case of Judas invites us to think more deeply on the mysteries of divine grace, atonement, and the coming kingdom.

How Unconditional is "Unconditional"?

Preachers, theologians, and bloggers, of all denominational stripes and commitments, declare the *unconditional* love of the living God as revealed in Jesus Christ. But the betrayal of Judas pushes this unconditionality to the limit. Just how unconditional is unconditional? The popular view might be described as

---

[5] Karl Barth, *Church Dogmatics*, II/2:476.

"unconditional *but*." God loves us absolutely and completely, not because we have merited this love, not because we have fulfilled a minimal set of obligations and duties, not because any internal force compels him, but because he *is* Love in the utter freedom of his Trinitarian life. The gospel proclaims unbounded grace, without strings and hidden qualifications. "God loves you unconditionally," the preacher tells us—and our hearts rejoice. This is news almost too good to be true. But then there's a pause and a clearing of the throat. "**But** . . . there is one thing you must do." Call it faith, decision, conversion, repentance, confession, commitment, personal response, good works, obedience, asceticism. The *but* is always there. We need to actualize and make real the love of God in our lives; we need to abandon our sins and repent of our selfishness; we need to renounce our attachments; we need to prepare ourselves for *theosis. And if we do not, we, like Judas, will be forever excluded from the beatific vision.* The threat of eternal damnation doesn't even need to be stated. Hidden in the liberating proclamation is the dismaying *but* that throws responsibility for our salvation back upon ourselves. Whatever wonderful things God has done for us, the *but* remains. There just doesn't seem to be any way for the preacher to get around it, at least not without falling into the heresy of antinomianism. There is always the *but*. Our life in time seems to require it. And with that *but* the unconditional love of God is undone—not perhaps from God's point of view (the theologian is quick to point out) but most certainly from ours. It's all quite logical.

- As long as the prodigal son remains in his pigsty, he cannot enjoy the feast his father has prepared for him.
- If the prisoner does not walk through the now-open cell door, he'll never be free.

- If an unknown benefactor deposits $1,000,000 into my checking account yet I do not write any checks, I remain as poor as I ever was.
- If we refuse the summons of Jesus to come out of our tombs, we shall never know the light of day.

The necessity of the *but* seems obvious. The preacher doesn't have to say it to say it, and the hearer will always insert it, even if not spoken.

Preachers need to challenge the synergistic *but* and resist the temptation to fall back into conditional promise. I acknowledge the difficulties. Not only do our bishops and congregations expect the *but,* but so does our common sense. How is it possible for God to fulfill an unconditional promise without violating our autonomy? Philosophy cannot offer a rational account of the eschatological existence bestowed in baptism. Our freedom in Christ is mystery and aporia. Authentic gospel-speaking requires more than acknowledgement of the antinomies of grace. It requires bold proclamation that refuses the *but.* God does not take our *no* as our final answer. In the words of the Apostle: "For all the promises of God find their Yes in Christ. That is why we utter the Amen through him, to the glory of God" (2 Cor 1:20).

Judas Iscariot—Elected Apostle

When we consider the treachery and cowardice of Judas Iscariot, consummated in suicide, we appear to hit a limit to the unconditional love of the Almighty. How can Judas be saved when he rejected incarnate Mercy? "Here is our dilemma," writes Ray Anderson: "if there is no limit to God's grace, then how will God judge those who rebel against him, or who sin against that grace?"[6] In response, Anderson reminds us that Judas, like the other apostles, was an answer to prayer:

> In these days he went out to the mountain to pray; and all night he continued in prayer to God. And when it was day, he called his disciples, and chose from them twelve, whom he named apostles; Simon, whom he named Peter, and Andrew his brother, and James and John, and Philip, and Bartholomew, and Matthew, and Thomas, and James the son of Alphaeus, and Simon who was called the Zealot, and Judas the son of James, and Judas Iscariot, who became a traitor. (Luke 6:12-16)

The Twelve were not chosen by lottery. They were given to Jesus by the election of his Father. We are therefore forced to think through the implications of the calling of Judas. If God makes Judas one of the Twelve, can Judas disqualify himself by betrayal and suicide? If we answer yes, questions arise concerning our own relationship with God. Is our adoption by grace contingent upon our fulfillment of specific requisites and necessities?

Peter denied Jesus three times, but on Easter morning the risen Christ appeared to him in love and mercy. Judas betrayed Jesus and took his own life, and the New Testament offers not a whisper of hope. The divine Son died for the sins of the world, the gospel proclaims, but what of the sins of Judas? By cross and resurrection God destroyed death, yet Judas remains self-damned in death.

> An astounding irony in the biblical story of Judas is the tragic coincidence of his death and the death of Jesus. At the very moment that Judas is enacting the human drama of sin and death, Jesus is enacting the divine drama of redemption and

---

[6] Ray S. Anderson, *The Gospel According to Judas* (1994), p. 59.

atonement. As Judas carries the terrible logic of sin to its ultimate conclusion, as though there were no grace and no forgiveness, Jesus contradicts it by taking sin upon himself and dying the death that will perfect the logic of grace and forgiveness. The first man dies without receiving what the second man is dying to give him.[7]

We confess that the atonement of the Savior applies equally to Judas as it applies to us; but (we add) he cannot *now* be saved, for by his mortal sin he definitively closed himself to grace. As some theologians might say, in his suicide Judas exercised his fundamental option and irrevocably oriented himself in rejection of the Good. Both for Latin and Eastern Christianity (though this is contested in Orthodoxy), death stands as that final point beyond which conversion is impossible. "After death there is for men no repentance," writes St John of Damascus.[8] Mortality conditions both human freedom and divine grace—the grave has the final word. It's as if Pascha had never happened.

In an ancient Irish homily, Judas is said to be the first person to inhabit hell after its harrowing:

> And unhappy Judas, after the betrayal of Christ, fell into despair, and put a noose round his neck, and in desperation hanged himself in his misdeeds, so that his soul was the first on which hell was shut after the Captivity had been rescued from it by Christ."[9]

Bad timing indeed.

---

[7] Ibid., p. 92.
[8] John Damascene, *De fide orthodoxa* II.4.
[9] *The Passions and Homilies of Leabhar Breac*, trans. Robert Atkinson (1887), XVIII, p. 459. Note that this view presupposes that all souls were rescued by Christ at his harrowing of Hell.

Following in the steps of Karl Barth and Thomas F. Torrance, Anderson challenges this disheartening construal of the gospel:

> We know that God loves the world and sent his Son, Jesus Christ, to die so that all may be saved. We know that in dying and being raised again, Jesus is the mediator for all humanity who are under sentence of death. We know that the Spirit of God is the Holy Spirit, the Spirit of Jesus risen from the dead, who has the power to give life where there is death, and to create faith where there is unbelief. This knowledge is sufficient so that we need not speculate about the eternal destiny of those created in the image of God beyond what is revealed to us in Jesus Christ. We know that in Christ, all who are in the world are loved by God.
>
> Our focus should rest not on who of us are God's chosen ones, but on Jesus as the elect one. He is the beloved Son, chosen before the foundation of the world to be the lamb slain for the sins of the world (Rev. 13:8). The radius of the love of God for the world extends to the circumference of all who are in the world. Because all are consigned to death as a consequence of sin, Jesus removed the power of death for all in dying for all. . . . The sin of unbelief has its consequence in death, as does all sin. But if death has been removed from humanity as the final word through the death and resurrection of Jesus Christ, then the sin of unbelief as well is brought within the relation between the Father and the Son.[10]

If Jesus be risen from the dead, then death is defeated and Hades has been emptied.[11] So the Orthodox sing at Pascha:

---

[10] Anderson, pp. 83-85.
[11] See Hilarion Alfeyev, *Christ the Conqueror of Hell* (2009).

The Apokatastasis of Judas Iscariot

> When thou didst descend to death, O Life Immortal, thou didst slay Hell with the splendor of thy Godhead.
>
> Hell has been made empty and helpless through the death of the One.
>
> On this day thou didst rise from the tomb, O merciful One, leading us from the gates of death. On this day Adam exults and Eve rejoices.
>
> Counted among the dead thou didst bind the tyrant, delivering all from the bonds of Hell by thy resurrection.

In light of the Son's victory over death, we must not deny the possibility of the *post-obitum* conversion of Judas Iscariot . . . or Adolph Hitler, Josef Stalin, or that nasty Mary Smith who lives around the block. No matter the heinousness of the crime or the incorrigibility of the sinner,

> death no longer has the power to sever humanity from the bond of God's choice through Christ. The resurrection of Jesus Christ means that he is the "first-born of the dead, and the ruler of kings on earth" (Rev. 1:5). Death no longer determines the fate and final destiny of any human person. Our destiny is finally determined by God, not by our sin nor the consequence of that sin. . . . There are many ways of dying, but only one kind of death. And the power of this death over the fate of humankind has been nullified through the resurrection of Jesus from the dead.[12]

Judas haunts the memory of the Church. We confidently sign his certificate of perdition, yet his ghost walks among us still. The Seer speaks of the twelve foundation stones of the New Jerusalem, upon which are carved the names of the twelve apostles of the Lamb (Rev

---

[12] Anderson, pp. 85-86.

21:14). Will the name Judas be written on one of them? Madeleine L'Engle shares a legend about the salvation of Judas:

> There is an old legend that after his death Judas found himself at the bottom of a deep and slimy pit. For thousands of years he wept his repentance, and when the tears were finally spent he looked up and saw, way, way up, a tiny glimmer of light. After he had contemplated it for another thousand years or so, he began to try to climb up towards it. The walls of the pit were dank and slimy, and he kept slipping back down. Finally, after great effort, he neared the top, and then he slipped and fell all the way back down. It took him many years to recover, all the time weeping bitter tears of grief and repentance, and then he started to climb up again. After many more falls and efforts and failures he reached the top and dragged himself into an upper room with twelve people seated around a table. "We've been waiting for you, Judas," Jesus said. "We couldn't begin till you came."[13]

With all our might we resist the happy ending—hence our preference for generalities. The Barthian assertion that all are elected in Christ or the Byzantine declaration that in the Incarnation human nature has been deified can be just as abstract—and for that reason, evangelically inconsequential—as the liberal claim that generic Divinity loves everyone. The gospel becomes concrete and liberating when we dare to proclaim Pascha to persons with names and faces and histories of deplorable wickedness and crushing failure.

The gospel becomes gospel when we dare to hope for the salvation of Judas.

---

[13] Madeleine L'Engle, *The Rock That is Higher* (2002), p. 26

Chapter Twenty-Five

The Irresistible Truth of Final Judgment

*And he shall come again with glory to judge both
the quick and the dead;
whose kingdom shall have no end.*

The Great Assize—I am brought into the courtroom of the Divine Judge. The prosecutor presents a movie of my life, with infallible commentary. The entirety of my life is presented in exquisite and shameful detail. Nothing is hidden. All of my actions and inactions, with underlying motivations, are revealed. And to make things worse, the movie shows the consequences of my decisions upon the lives of others, rippling down through the centuries. Finally, the prosecution rests its case. No defense is offered, can be offered. With dread I await the verdict.

What's wrong with this scenario?

In the view of Sergius Bulgakov, it fails to grasp the inner connections between creation, incarnation, *parousia*, glorification, and universal resurrection. When the Incarnate Son returns in glory, the dead will be raised and all will be glorified. Every resurrected person will partake of immortality, irrespective of merit. Resurrection is wholly a gift of God, bestowed in the paschal victory of Jesus Christ. Bulgakov quotes the Apostle Paul: "Christ shall change our vile body, that it may be fashioned like unto his glorious body, according to the working whereby he is able even to subdue all things unto himself" (Phil 3:21). He then comments: "This applies, we repeat, to *all* humanity without any exception, for the Lord became the New Adam, assumed humanity in its entirety: 'As we have borne the image of the earthy, we shall also bear the image of the heavenly' (1 Cor. 15:49). The image of the heavenly will shine upon all resurrected bodies, clothed in *glory*."[1]

The joy with which Bulgakov writes of the Second Coming is palpable. One can almost hear in his words the bells of the Paschal Vigil. The Kingdom is so very close. Bulgakov often closed his writings with the acclamation from the Apocalypse: "Even so, come Lord Jesus." The Russian priest eagerly awaits and prays for the return of Christ: the dead will be raised; the world will be made new; all will be transfigured in the Spirit. The *parousia* is the fulfillment of the gospel; but perhaps most surprisingly, the *divine judgment* is the fulfillment of the gospel. "Let the field be joyful, and all that is therein," the Psalmist sings: "then shall all the trees of the wood rejoice before the Lord: for he cometh, for he cometh to judge the earth: he shall judge the world with righteousness, and the people with his truth" (Ps 96:12-13).

Glorification in Christ immediately, simultaneously, inescapably subjects humanity to divine judgment:

> It is necessary to understand that the parousia, the coming of Christ in glory, that is, in the manifestation of the Holy Spirit, is, as such, already the judgment. The parousia cannot be an external and mutually indifferent encounter between God who has come into the world and man who remains in his isolated state of being, as he was before this encounter. On the contrary, man too is clothed in glory and incorruptibility, and the creaturely Sophia becomes transparent for the Divine Sophia. This changes man's very being. This encounter with God, this entering into the realm of the divine fire, is not something optional for human beings. It is inevitable. For some this is the time of liberation ("look up, and lift up your heads" [Luke 21:28]). For others it is a time of fear and horror: "then shall all the tribes of the earth mourn, and they shall see the Son of man coming in the clouds of

---

[1] Sergius Bulgakov, *The Bride of the Lamb* (2001), p. 450.

heaven with power and great glory" (Matt. 24:30). No one can avoid this encounter, for it is not an outward encounter but an inward one. For many this will be an unexpected and undesired transformation of their being, for the transfiguration, the light of glory given to human beings, can do more than illuminate. It can also consume in fire.[2]

The Final Judgment is baptism into glory and light, fire and truth.

The popular image of the courtroom misleads. We think of the divine judgment as an *external* revelation. The book of our life is opened, read, assessed. We stand passively as the verdict is declared and the sentence executed. But this is the wrong way to think of the last judgment. It's not as if we are judged according to a legal standard and then rewarded or punished. Judgment occurs in the event of our baptism in glory, as an encounter with the risen Lord who is not only outside us but within us. "Behold, the kingdom of God is within you" (Luke 17:21). The Final Judgment is both transcendent and immanent. We are judged by the incarnate Son, in whose image we are made, who is the truth of our being:

> The parousia manifestly clothes every human being in Christ by the Holy Spirit. It is precisely in this sense that the parousia is also the judgment. And Christ, as the Judge (John 5:27), judges by the Holy Spirit. Human beings are clothed in Christ, who is the Truth and the Life, by the life-giving Holy Spirit, who is the Spirit of Truth. This means that every human being is inwardly confronted with the truth about himself. Every human being sees in the truth, by a vision that is not abstract but living, like the consuming flame of a fire from whose light one cannot hide, *for* all will become visible. . . .
>
> The manifestation of God's glory in the world is also the manifestation of the truth itself, as well as the abolition of falsehood and the power of the father of lies (John 8:44). No falsehood, no self-deception, no error will have a place in the kingdom of truth, and this

---

[2] Ibid., p. 455.

"exposure" by the Spirit of truth is already the judgment. By virtue of the truth this judgment becomes for everyone a self-judgment, a shedding of the veils of falsehood and self-deception that cover emptiness. The enthronement of Christ in the world, the reign of God come in power, is the Holy Spirit that fully, without any kenosis, pours forth upon all flesh. Christ's revelation in the Holy Spirit has an irresistible force, which is manifested both in the universal resurrection and in the transformation of the world, with a transfiguration and glorification that extend to all flesh. This illuminating and transfiguring power is expressed in the image of *fire*, not natural of course but "spiritual," which will penetrate the "spiritual" body and the spirit itself. The fire of the future age consumes, but it also transfigures, illuminates, gladdens.[3]

Bulgakov speaks here of the Lord's judging word as possessing an "irresistible force." A crucial clarification is needed. Throughout *Bride of the Lamb* the author stresses the importance of human freedom. God works with human beings in synergistic collaboration. "The freedom of the person remains inviolable and impenetrable, even for God"[4] God persuades in love, never by violence. Bulgakov even goes so far to speak of God limiting his omnipotence before the freedom of man. Like Eastern theologians before and after him, he quotes the words of Christ from the Book of Revelation: "I stand at the door and knock: if any man hear my voice, and open the door, I will come into him, and will sup with him, and he with me" (3:20). "This door," he interprets, "is creaturely freedom, the source of the originality and reality of creation in its correlation with the Creator."[5] Freedom is not just an attribute of the human being; it is the foundation of human existence. When Bulgakov speaks of the divine judgment as possessing "irresistible force," therefore, he

---

[3] Ibid., p. 456
[4] Ibid., p. 226.
[5] Ibid., p. 226

cannot mean a divine action that in any way violates human personhood. It must be a word that speaks a truth so compelling and self-evident that it overcomes all delusion and prevarication; it can only be affirmed and appropriated:

> The judgment and separation consist in the fact that every human being will be placed before his own eternal image in Christ, that is, before Christ. And in the light of this image, he will see his own reality, and this comparison will be the judgment. It is this that is the Last Judgment of Christ upon every human being. . . . Just as the Holy Spirit manifests Christ in glory, so it reveals Christ's presence in every human being. The judgment is the theophany to the world of the Son sent by the Father in the Holy Spirit. Resurrection in incorruptibility and glorification is precisely the Last Judgment, in which creation appears before the face of God and sees itself in God. For the image of God, given to man at his creation, is also the judgment upon man in relation to his likeness, which is the realization of this image in creaturely freedom. The "likeness" is the book of life opened at the judgment. God's image will be revealed to every human being by the Holy Spirit as inner justice and judgment for creaturely life. This judgment of Christ is also every human being's own judgment upon himself. It consists in each person seeing himself in the light of his own justice, in the light of his proto-image, which he perceives in his resurrection under illumination by the Holy Spirit. The Judgment is the judgment of every human being in his true image upon himself in his "likeness." As such, the judgment is self-evidently persuasive. This genuine image for every human being is Christ: The judgment consists in the fact that the light has come into the world (see John 3:19). "For judgment I am come into this world" (9:39).
>
> Is it possible to reject this ontological self-judgment upon oneself as inappropriate and unconvincing? No! It is not possible, for one is judged by one's own being, by one's own truth. St Isaac the Syrian says that the torments of hell are the burning of love for God, the burning fire of this love. . . . This idea is also applicable to man's relation to his

divine proto-image: being aware of how distant he is from his proto-image in his given state or likeness, a human being nevertheless recognizes himself in this image as he could and should be according to God's thought. He loves this image of himself, judges himself by it, compares himself to it, does not and cannot retreat from it inwardly.

This proto-image is Christ. Every human being sees himself in Christ and measures the extent of his difference from this proto-image. A human being cannot fail to love the Christ who is revealed in him, and he cannot fail to love himself revealed in Christ. The two things are the same. Such is human ontology. Love is the Holy Spirit, who sets the heart afire with this love. But this love, this blazing up of the Spirit, is also the judgment of the individual upon himself, his vision of himself outside himself, in conflict with himself, that is, outside Christ and far from Christ. And the measure and knowledge of this separation are determined by Love, that is, by the Holy Spirit. The same fire, the same love gladdens and burns, torments and gives joy. The judgment of love is the most terrible judgment, more terrible than that of justice and wrath, than that of the law, for it includes all this but also transcends it. . . . *It is impossible to appear before Christ and to see Him without loving him.*[6]

The divine judgment irresistibly convicts and convinces because it declares the truth that we already know in the depth of conscience: *irresistibly*, because it presents the good that we have always desired; *irresistibly*, because it gives the love for which we have long sought; *irresistibly*, because it discloses our inmost self. Our freedom is not overridden but rather fully engaged. Bulgakov acknowledges that how each person receives the *parousia*, whether in joy or hatred, is conditioned by interior disposition. Resurrection and glory will come as a transcendent reality from which man cannot hide, *ex*

---

[6] Ibid., pp. 457-459; emphasis mine. See especially Roberto De La Noval, "We Shall See Him as He Is: Bulgakov on Eschatological Conversion," *Eclectic Orthodoxy* (24 October 2021): https://afkimel.wordpress.com/2021/10/24/we-shall-see-him-as-he-is-bulgakov-on-eschatological-conversion/

opere operato; yet given free-will the manner of reception remains proper to each person, *ex opere operantis*. But after affirming this synergism, Bulgakov reasserts even more strongly the primacy of grace: "But, to be sure, creaturely limitedness here does not limit the power of divine action in the manifestation of the divine image in man. A human being is saved by this action, though only in connection with what he himself is. These forms of salvation differ depending upon what foundation a human being has built upon. It is possible that he himself will be saved 'yet so by fire' (1 Cor 3:15); and he will be naked, for his work will be consumed."[7]

Surrounded by the light of Christ and penetrated by the fire of his Spirit, we are stripped of our delusions, pretensions, and lies. Denial is impossible. We know ourselves as we are, as we were meant to be, as we shall be. We see ourselves in Christ and Christ in us. In his humanity, we discover our true selves. When Jesus appeared in Galilee, it was possible for men and women to know him and yet not recognize him, possible to know him and crucify him. Such was the kenosis of the Word made flesh. But in the *parousia* Jesus is revealed in glory, and we cannot but acknowledge him as the divine Image in whose image we have been made. "God is so irresistibly persuasive for man because man receives God into himself, in his sophianic proto-image"[8]. All will be immersed in the consuming fire of Christ's judgment. All will know the truth and embrace the truth. All will love the risen and exalted Christ.

Even so, come Lord Jesus.

---

[7] Ibid., p. 457
[8] Ibid., p. 492

Afterword

David Bentley Hart, Ph.D.

In one sense, a book of this kind should not need to be written. Considered purely in rational terms, the traditional story that Christians tell about the destiny of human souls—or, at any rate, what has become the traditional story—is clearly one that cannot be true, in this or any possible world. The notion that a God of perfect love, justice, goodness, and resource could have freely created a reality in which certain rational creatures will spend eternity in conscious misery would seem to be so absurd a contradiction that it scarcely merits the effort required to dismiss it. To believe such a tale is more or less to abandon all the categories of reason and to reduce every concept of justice or mercy to equivocality and meaninglessness. And at no point in the entire history of the faith has a coherent moral justification for the concept or an eternal hell been adduced, or any argument that cannot be taken apart, logically and morally, by any competent logician. As a rule, in fact, the more ardently the believer in eternal suffering strives to justify that belief, the more desperate and absurd his or her arguments tend to become. Moreover, the idea does not even enjoy biblical warrant. Nowhere does Christ speak of eternal torment, even when threatening divine judgment. The Apostle Paul was plainly unacquainted with the very notion. The New Testament abounds both in imagery of the destruction or ruin of the wicked and in imagery of universal redemption, and how the latter should qualify the Christian theological imagination's understanding of the former (or vice-versa) is a perennial question; but Christian scripture

Afterword

nowhere provides a picture of a place of unending suffering for the derelict. That is something we impose upon the text because we have been taught to expect to find it there. The entire doctrine of hell as it came to exist in developed Christian tradition has no real basis in the tradition's sources; its only support is a tenuous thread of suppositions and unfortunate habits of thought. So, as I say, *Destined for Joy* should never have needed to be written.

In another sense, however, the necessity of a book like this cannot be exaggerated. What reason and the evidence dictate is of little avail when the stakes seem so high. It scarcely matters that the doctrine of eternal conscious torment cannot be justified logically; it matters even less that it lacks the scriptural foundations we usually imagine it has. All that really matters is that most Christians have had the idea seared into their minds from childhood through the cauterizing application of that most effective instrument of indoctrination: terror. No one is particularly to blame for this; there is no conspiracy of cognoscenti manipulating the faithful. Believers are their own wardens, their own oppressors; they reinforce each other's faith and each other's fears; whenever one of the faithful begins to waver in his or her faith in the good tidings of God's perpetual torture chamber—or, at any rate, regarding God's willingness to abandon spiritual creatures to such an end—there is an entire community devoted to guiding him or her back into the safety of the fold, with as many soothing or alarming counsels as it takes.

This is a tragedy, of course, not only because of the grim vision of reality the notion of eternal torment cultivates in many souls, but also because of the far richer, far more radiant, far more beautiful vision it has stolen from them. One need only become acquainted with the thought of the greatest of the Christian universalists—Origen, Gregory of Nyssa, Isaac of Nineveh, for instance—to realize how far superior it is to the now standard story of the faith, not only as an interpretation of the testimony of scripture, but as a true entry into the mystery of Christ and of God's love. One need only read Gregory's *On the Soul and Resurrection,* and see the majestic synthesis he works out there (under the guidance of his sister Makrina, it seems) of the whole testimony of scripture, and see also the light his reading casts upon Paul's vision in 1 Corinthians 15—or, alternatively, to read Isaac's treatises or George MacDonald's *Unspoken Sermons,* and so on—to appreciate how much of the glory of Christ has been lost in Christian tradition behind clouds of sulfurous smoke.

The truth is that the negative reactions to this book can be predicted with a fair degree of certainty. No matter how good the arguments it advances, convinced infernalists will dismiss them not only out of hand, without ever having taken the time to absorb them, but will do so belligerently. There is, it seems, a very strict etiquette of hell. I do not mean the manners and mores proper to the establishment itself; I expect those are pretty dreadful, if you are the fastidious sort. Rather, I mean a set of unwritten rules one is supposed to observe when speaking about hell to Christians in a public setting. And these, as far as I can tell, have become ever more restrictive as the centuries have worn on. At one time, for instance, it was still considered to be in good taste, or at least not impolite, to talk about hell in sermons; for the most part today, except in fundamentalist circles (which are by definition somewhat déclassé), most homilists would consider it crass. This is especially true at funerals, for obvious reasons, but no less true at baptisms. For many Christians, hell is the dark family secret, the mad uncle confined overhead whom everyone knows not to mention. And yet, curiously enough, worse than calling the whole dreadful matter to mind is calling it into doubt. While it may be an indiscretion to talk about that poor mad uncle gibbering away in the shadows of the attic,

Afterword

many see it as something close to an abomination to suggest that maybe he is not really there at all, and that his very existence might be just a piece of family lore, originally intended to scare the children into good behavior.

Anyone, that is to say, so tactless as to raise serious questions about the logical and moral coherence of the concept of "just" eternal torment risks the worst sort of censure. But, of course, it's nearly impossible *never* to notice now and again that, soberly considered, the idea of an eternal hell is easily the most horrifying that the religious imagination has ever entertained—one that, taken to heart, can make existence itself seem like a cruel burden visited on us by an unutterably merciless omnipotence. And, having noticed this, one sometimes has to remark upon it. Even then, however, if one *must* call the settled picture into question, the rules of deportment remain inflexible. No matter how distasteful one may personally find the concept that divine justice reveals itself in the eternal torture of the reprobate, one is required to hide that distaste, and even to affect doubt about one's doubts, and to become almost theatrically deferential toward the concept (as a venerable feature of sacred tradition), and to express oneself humbly, hesitantly, demurely, apologetically—even contritely.

In truth, though, all of this really has very little to do with good manners and everything to do with uneasy consciences. It seems clear that below the surface of many believers' seemingly settled convictions regarding the reality an eternal hell, there is a volatile, positively volcanic ferment of doubt seething away that, if not scrupulously repressed, just might erupt into the open and reduce their faith to ashes. Somewhere deep down, even the most convinced defender of the conventional view of hell realizes that there is something morally unintelligible in it, and that this unintelligibility, if frankly confronted, menaces the entire structure of belief. That's why, I suspect, the understanding of hell that Christian culture openly espouses has tended to grow gradually but constantly more emollient over the centuries. At one time, after all, in very late antiquity and the Middle Ages, most Christians could speak with firm if dour certitude of a place of real physical and mental agony to which even babies would be sent forever and ever if they were so thoughtless as to die unbaptized. Today only a tiny remnant of believers still finds that notion tolerable. By the high Middle Ages, it had already been displaced in many minds by the idea of a limbo of infants, a place where unformed souls, though forever denied the vision of God, would nonetheless enjoy a certain natural contentment. But, since then, even in regard to adult sinners who die unrepentant, Christians have grown increasingly uncomfortable with the thought that God himself might actively will their eternal suffering.

This is why reflective believers have more and more over the years come to adopt the notion that, while hell may be eternal, its doors are locked from the inside (to use C.S. Lewis's imagery), and that the damned freely choose their damnation, out of hatred of divine love, while God, out of regard for the dignity of human freedom, leaves them reluctantly to the hell they so jealously crave. In this picture of things the fire and brimstone have been quietly replaced by various states of existential disquiet and jealously guarded self-delusion. That makes the whole issue considerably less troubling, of course, and is psychologically plausible up to a certain point. Past that point, admittedly, there's no way of reconciling the classical and Christian—or, for that matter, merely logical—concept of rational freedom with such a view, as is discussed at length in the above pages. What is most worth noting here is that the need that so many Christians feel to absolve God of any direct responsibility in the imposition of hell's torments—omnipotent and omniscient though he be—is more than enough proof that they know that something is deeply amiss in the doctrine itself.

That is why *Destined for Joy* is necessary. It is well past time that the etiquette of hell be abandoned as nothing more than bad faith masquerading as comity. These rules of good conduct are actually deeply perverse. They are simply conventions for sparing Christians the unpleasant task of confronting the real implications of the things they say they believe. After all, why should anyone feel the need to apologize for denouncing an idea whose principal use down the centuries has arguably been the psychological abuse and terrorization of children, principally, and the emotional control of all believers? The time has come—and has come in every generation of the faith—to confront this bizarre self-contradiction that in an odd sense has survived precisely because of its sheer, immeasurable absurdity. Precisely because it is so grandly false, and so deeply incoherent an instance of cognitive dissonance within the otherwise luminously consistent story that Christianity tells, it has become the great ghastly scandal that we have all collectively agreed not to notice—to bury deep in the dungeons below the level of conscience and then never visit again. But the price is too high, and the consequences have always been too awful. Every time the faith has betrayed itself—say, in the legal murder of "heretics" by means of the "secular arm," of in countless other forms of uncharitable coercion, violence, or neglect—it has justified its actions, explicitly or tacitly, by reference to the far greater—in fact, infinite—coercion, violence, and neglect threatened in the doctrine of eternal torment, all of which it has attributed to God. The one excuse that Christians can always invoke for failing to behave as Christians towards those it deems aberrant in belief or alien in confession is that miserable dogma.

Again, this is a tragedy. The true story is so much more ennobling—and, for that matter, so much more beautiful.

Appendix 1

The Salvation of Lilith

I scrambled to find the right words. How to explain to an old friend the theme of George MacDonald's great fantasy novel *Lilith*? But the words would not come. Well, perhaps that's not quite true. Words came, but they hardly made sense and certainly did not convey the profundity and depth of the story. I read *Lilith* for the first time in the spring of 2015. It did not take me long to realize that this was a story unlike anything I had read before. I decided to just read it through, without pausing to wonder what was going on or what symbolized what. Just enjoy the story. After this initial reading, I knew I was going to have to reread it, but this time more slowly and attentively. A few months later I began my meditative perusal, one or two chapters a day. I think this was a good approach for me. Yet even still, I could not find the words to describe the story to my friend. I finally advised her to read a couple of MacDonald's fairy tales ("The Golden Key," "The Wise Woman," and "Photogen and Nycteris" are three of my favorites) and then, if still interested, to tackle *Lilith*. But be prepared, I warned, for a very different kind of literary experience: in the story of Mr Vane and Lilith, theology becomes mythopoeia; eschatology, a fairy tale.

Lilith is a story of redemption—the redemption of the protagonist Vane but also the redemption of the evil princess Lilith. In some ways she reminds me of the White Witch in *The Lion, the Witch, and the Wardrobe*, desiring power and dominion above all else. Yet there are also differences. Lilith possesses a seductive, erotic attraction that Jadis does not have. She is a succubus who feeds on her victims to maintain her beauty and power. Revisioning Kabbalistic tradition, MacDonald portrays Lilith as an angelic being, given by God to Adam as his first wife. "Her first thought," Adam tells Vane, "was POWER; she counted it slavery to be one with me, and bear children for Him who gave her being." After giving birth to a daughter, she fled Adam and eventually ensnared the heart of the great Shadow, thus becoming the queen of Hell. Since that time she has sought to destroy her daughter, who, it is prophesied, will be her doom. "Vilest of God's creatures, she lives by the blood and lives and souls of men. She consumes and slays, but is powerless to destroy as to create."

Adam offers her the forgiveness of God: "Repent, I beseech thee; repent, and be again an angel of God!" "I will not repent," she retorts. "I will drink the blood of thy child." Her rejection of the Good is firm, obdurate, adamantine. She will not surrender. Can there be redemption for such a creature?

Lilith has a narrative counterpart—Mara, Lady of Sorrow and daughter of Adam and Eve. At one point she is referred to as the Magdalene, yet a strict identification seems inappropriate. Given her love of children and authority over evil, Orthodox and Catholic readers will immediately associate Mara with the Blessed Virgin Mary; but Eve is described in the book as the Mother, so again a strict identification seems incorrect. Perhaps the best we can say is that in the characters of Eve and Mara, MacDonald has incorporated elements of the Theotokos.

Lilith is taken captive by Vane and brought to Mara for final deliverance. "I must do what I can," Mara declares, "to make her repent." Her words suggest a kind of coercion, perhaps even physical violence; yet if what Lilith endures is properly described as violence, it is violence of a special kind, a violence she brings upon herself as she seeks to deny her true self. Mara's role is simply to restrain her while she suffers the revelation of God. Lilith must learn the one necessary truth—she did not create herself and cannot will her nonexistence. As long as she believes that she is an autonomous, self-sufficient being, she remains a slave to the Shadow. The conversation between Lilith and Mara is illuminating:

> "Will you turn away from the wicked things you have been doing so long?" said Mara gently.
> The princess did not answer. Mara put the question again, in the same soft, inviting tone.
> Still there was no sign of hearing. She spoke the words a third time.
> Then the seeming corpse opened its mouth and answered, its words appearing to I cannot shape the thing further: sounds they were not, yet they were words to me.
> "I will not," she said. "I will be myself and not another!"
> "Alas, you are another now, not yourself! Will you not be your real self?"
> "I will be what I mean myself now."
> "If you were restored, would you not make what amends you could for the misery you have caused?"
> "I would do after my nature."
> "You do not know it: your nature is good, and you do evil!"
> "I will do as my Self pleases—as my Self desires."
> "You will do as the Shadow, overshadowing your Self inclines you?"
> "I will do what I will to do."
> "You have killed your daughter, Lilith!"
> "I have killed thousands. She is my own!"
> "She was never yours as you are another's."
> "I am not another's; I am my own, and my daughter is mine."
> "Then, alas, your hour is come!"
> "I care not. I am what I am; no one can take from me myself!"
> "You are not the Self you imagine."
> "So long as I feel myself what it pleases me to think myself, I care not. I am content to be to myself what I would be. What I choose to seem to myself makes me what I am. My own thought makes me me; my own thought of myself is me. Another shall not make me!"
> "But another has made you, and can compel you to see what you have made yourself. You will not be able much longer to look to

The Salvation of Lilith

yourself anything but what he sees you! You will not much longer have satisfaction in the thought of yourself. At this moment you are aware of the coming change!"

We might well describe Lilith as the ultimate libertarian: she is free, so she thinks, as long as she is free to make herself, to assert her independence from absolute reality, to be absolute reality. "What I choose to seem to myself makes me what I am. My own thought makes me me; my own thought of myself is me. Another shall not make me!"

Traditional theology has long believed that God stands impotent before the resolute assertion of the creaturely self. What more can he do than summon to repentance? The Lord knocks at the door, but if the creature refuses to open it, Omnipotence is defeated. For such a being there can only be hell. But MacDonald sees more deeply and hopes more truly.

Lilith speaks again:

"No one ever made me. I defy that Power to unmake me from a free woman! You are his slave, and I defy you! You may be able to torture me—I do not know, but you shall not compel me to anything against my will!"

"Such a compulsion would be without value. But there is a light that goes deeper than the will, a light that lights up the darkness behind it: that light can change your will, can make it truly yours and not another's—not the Shadow's. Into the created can pour itself the creating will, and so redeem it!"

"That light shall not enter me: I hate it!—Begone, slave!"

"I am no slave, for I love that light, and will with the deeper will which created mine. There is no slave but the creature that wills against its creator. Who is a slave but her who cries, 'I am free,' yet cannot cease to exist!"

God is not restricted to being a being external to the creature. His uncreated Fire knows no such boundaries. The Creator wills the salvation of every rational being. As Adam later tells Vane: "Every creature must one night yield himself and lie down: he was made for liberty, and must not be left a slave!" Precisely as the transcendent source of being, God is able to work in the immanent depths of persons for their healing and liberation.

The redemption of Lilith takes place in four stages:

(1) The fire of God enters her. It takes the form of a worm that creeps out of the hearth—"white-hot, vivid as incandescent silver, the live heart of essential fire." Penetrating into her heart and soul, it reveals to Lilith the self she was created to be and the evil she has become. Vane desires to rescue her from her torment but Mara stops him:

> "You cannot go near her," she said. "She is far away from us, afar in the hell of her self-consciousness. The central fire of the universe is radiating into her the knowledge of good and evil, the knowledge of what she is. She sees at last the good she is not, the evil she is. She knows that she is herself the fire in which she is burning, but she does not know that the Light of Life is the heart of that fire. Her torment is that she is what she is. Do not fear for her; she is not forsaken. No gentler way to help her was left. Wait and watch."

Lilith throws herself on the floor, weeping, yet still defiantly resolute in her self-assertion. She now knows that she did not create herself, but blames God for what she has become. She cries out for annihilation. "I will not be made any longer!" she inveighs. "Unmake yourself, then," says Mara. "Alas, I cannot! You know it, and mock me! How often have I not agonised to cease, but the tyrant keeps me being! I curse him!—Now let him kill me!" Lilith has been forced to acknowledge a fundamental truth of her existence:

she is not her own Creator—and this fact has become her torment. Orthodox readers will no doubt be reminded of the famous words of St Isaac the Syrian: "I also maintain that those who are punished in Gehenna are scourged by the scourge of love." Yet Lilith remains firm in her rebellion and hatred of God. The struggle for her salvation must continue.

(2) After further struggle Lilith begins to cry. These are not tears of repentance, Mara explains to Vane, but rather tears of self-loathing. They are helpful only if they lead the sinner to the merciful embrace of the Creator: "Self-loathing is not sorrow. Yet it is good, for it marks a step in the way home, and in the father's arms the prodigal forgets the self he abominates. Once with his father, he is to himself of no more account. It will be so with her." Still Lilith refuses to repent. She will not admit her wickedness.

(3) And now Lilith endures the final consequence of her rebellion. God gives her that which she believes she desires—escape from self, world, God . . . the outer darkness.

> Something was taking place in her which we did not know. We knew we did not feel what she felt, but we knew we felt something of the misery it caused her. The thing itself was in her, not in us; its reflex, her misery, reached us, and was again reflected in us: she was in the outer darkness, we present with her who was in it! We were not in the outer darkness; had we been, we could not have been WITH her; we should have been timelessly, spacelessly, absolutely apart. The darkness knows neither the light nor itself; only the light knows itself and the darkness also. None but God hates evil and understands it.
> Something was gone from her, which then first, by its absence, she knew to have been with her every moment of her wicked years. The source of life had withdrawn itself; all that was left her of conscious being was the dregs of her dead and corrupted life.

Destined for Joy

She stood rigid. Mara buried her head in her hands. I gazed on the face of one who knew existence but not love—knew nor life, nor joy, nor good; with my eyes I saw the face of a live death! She knew life only to know that it was dead, and that, in her, death lived. It was not merely that life had ceased in her, but that she was consciously a dead thing. She had killed her life, and was dead—and knew it. She must DEATH IT for ever and ever! She had tried her hardest to unmake herself, and could not! she was a dead life! she could not cease! she must BE! In her face I saw and read beyond its misery—saw in its dismay that the dismay behind it was more than it could manifest. It sent out a livid gloom; the light that was in her was darkness, and after its kind it shone. She was what God could not have created. She had usurped beyond her share in self-creation, and her part had undone His! She saw now what she had made, and behold, it was not good! She was as a conscious corpse, whose coffin would never come to pieces, never set her free! Her bodily eyes stood wide open, as if gazing into the heart of horror essential—her own indestructible evil. Her right hand also was now clenched—upon existent Nothing—her inheritance!

But with God all things are possible: He can save even the rich!

At that moment, Lilith yields. "I cannot hold out. I am defeated." All of her illusions have been shattered. She is no longer capable of denying the truth.

(4) Yet there remains one final thing that must be done. Lilith's left hand is clenched upon something that does not belong to her. We are not told what this thing is, though we do learn that it becomes the source for the renewal of the world. Perhaps it is not an object at all. Yet try as hard as she might, Lilith finds herself powerless to open her hand. All she can do is acknowledge her impotence: "I have no power over myself; I am a slave! . . . Let me die."

Mara now speaks to her the words of assurance that Lilith could not hear until this point: "A slave thou art that shall one day be a

The Salvation of Lilith

child! Verily, thou shalt die, but not as thou thinkest. Thou shalt die out of death into life. Now is the Life for, that never was against thee!" Mara embraces Lilith and kisses her on the forehead. Misery departs from Lilith's eyes, and she weeps tears of gratitude. Yet her hand remains clenched. She must be taken to the House of Death and given over to the care of Adam.

Lilith lies down on the bed of rebirth, yet she is unable to sleep. "Lilith, you will not sleep, if you lie there a thousand years, until you have opened your hand, and yielded that which is not yours to give or to withhold," Mara tells her. Lilith assures her that she is trying with all of her strength, but to no avail. She begs Adam to cut off her hand with the sword entrusted to him by an angel. "I heard him who bore it say it would divide whatever was not one and indivisible!" Adam consents. He severs the clenched hand from her arm. Lilith gives a single moan and falls fast asleep.

Thus begins Lilith's interior healing and transformation. She must dream . . . and forget . . . and having forgotten remember, as she awaits her awakening "in the morning of the universe."

Appendix 2

Funeral Homily for Aaron Edward Kimel

Aaron Edward Kimel
(1980-2012)
Delivered by Father Alvin F. Kimel, Jr.
22 June 2012

In the Name of the Father and the Son and the Holy Spirit. Amen.

Not once have I ever entertained the possibility that I would ever find myself in this moment, preaching at the funeral of one of my children.

I stand here today not to offer a eulogy for my son, Aaron. There will be other opportunities for such eulogies, as we each seek to find healing for our loss and to understand the tragic decision of Aaron to end his life.

My purpose, rather, is to offer an argument. Aaron was brilliant. He loved a good argument, and he usually won. Aaron and I did not often speak about God. At some point in high school, he moved into a scientific materialism from which he would not be moved. He was not a militant atheist, as he acknowledged that it was possible, however unlikely, that God might exist; but he simply could not, would not, embrace a Christian worldview. Yet for the sake of family, he always said grace with us at dinnertime.

I am not a philosopher. There is no argument I can offer that Aaron could not demolish in five seconds flat. I stand before you as a priest of the Church for over thirty years. But most importantly I stand before you as a bereaved father, who has been utterly devastated by the death of his beloved son.

Aaron's death has been a traumatic—and clarifying—event for me. I see reality more sharply, more clearly than I have ever seen it before. I stand before you, therefore, either as a madman . . . or a prophet of God Almighty. I cannot judge. You must be my judge. God will most certainly be my judge.

Aaron did not believe in God. He did not believe in transcendent reality. He did not believe in a life beyond the grave. Life has no ultimate meaning or significance. After death there is only nothing.

In Aaron's room, I found my old copy of the short stories of Ernest Hemingway. I do not know when he borrowed it. Perhaps he read the story "A Clean, Well-Lighted Place." In this story we read the prayer of nihilism:

> Our nada who art in nada, nada be thy name thy kingdom nada thy will be nada in nada as it is in nada. Give us this nada our daily nada and nada us our nada as we nada our nadas and nada us not into nada but deliver us from nada; pues nada. Hail nothing full of nothing, nothing is with thee.

It is a relentlessly bleak, hopeless view. Despair is its only conclusion.

Aaron was a man who lived in profound interior pain. He had come to the conclusion that nothing in this world, neither medicine nor psychiatry nor career nor even the love of his family could deliver him from the despair and futility that had possessed and paralyzed him. And so, he made what seemed, to him, to be the logical choice.

A logical choice . . . if, and only if, Aaron's worldview is true. If Aaron is right, then he has indeed found relief from his suffering, relief in nothingness, relief in nada, nada, nada. We who have been left behind must now suffer the repercussions of Aaron's decision; but he at least he is at peace . . . if Aaron is right.

But there is an alternative. Consider the possibility that there really is a divine Creator, a transcendent deity of infinite love who has brought the world into being from out of nothing. Consider the possibility that this Creator has made human beings in his image in such a way that we can only find our supreme happiness in communion with him. Consider the possibility that this God has actually entered into his creation, taking upon himself the limitations of humanity, including even suffering and death, precisely to restore us to himself and incorporate us into his divine life. Consider the possibility that for us this God died a cruel and horrific death on Calvary and rose to indestructible life on Easter morning, destroying the power of death once and for all and opening history to the promise of a new heaven and a new earth, a future where "there shall be no more death, neither sorrow, nor crying, neither shall there be any more pain: for the former things are passed away."

God is Love, for he is eternally the Father, Son, and Holy Spirit. The world springs from love and will be consummated in love. In the words of St Isaac the Syrian:

> In love did God bring the world into existence; in love does he guide it during its temporal existence; in love is he going to bring it to that wondrous transformed state, and in love will the world be swallowed up in the great mystery of him who has performed all these things.

This is the Christian faith in which Aaron was raised yet which he eventually found to be unpersuasive. The empiricist worldview which dominates our culture increasingly renders the Christian worldview implausible. The whole world suffers from the despair of nihilism.

Funeral Homily for Aaron Edward Kimel

I cannot, will not acquiesce to Aaron's agnosticism and its resignation to despair. I know something of the darkness that bound Aaron's heart; but this tragedy has quickened my faith, and I pray that it will do so for you also.

One of my favorite books in C. S. Lewis's *Chronicles of Narnia* is *The Silver Chair*. The children, along with the marsh-wiggle Puddleglum, are captured by the Green Lady and taken into her underworld domain. She casts a spell upon them and attempts to persuade them that this dreary underworld is the real world, that everything that they remember about Narnia and the true world is but a dream. But Puddleglum stands fasts; he refuses to disbelieve:

> Suppose we have only dreamed, or made up, all those things—trees and grass and sun and moon and stars and Aslan himself. Suppose we have. Then all I can say is that, in that case, the made-up things seem a good deal more important than the real ones. Suppose this black pit of a kingdom of yours is the only world. Well, it strikes me as a pretty poor one. And that's a funny thing, when you come to think of it. We're just babies making up a game, if you're right. But four babies playing a game can make a play-world which licks your real world hollow. That's why I'm going to stand by the play-world. I'm on Aslan's side even if there isn't any Aslan to lead it. I'm going to live as like a Narnian as I can even if there isn't any Narnia.

The Christian vision of reality is so much more real, more beautiful, more enchanting, and profoundly more true than any vision of reality offered by modern culture and the scientific worldview.

And so here is my first response to my son:

"Aaron, I do not know if you had retained your faith in Christ whether your pain would have been more bearable, but it might have given you grounds for hope, for a supernatural hope that the world cannot give."

But what hope does my son now have? He is dead. He died an unbeliever. He died a suicide. This is the hard, terrible truth. Aaron would not want us to minimize the harshness of any of this. He knew Christine and I would find this impossibly hard. In the old days, some preachers would have declared him damned. He certainly would not have been granted a church burial. Today we know more about depression and mental illness. We know how depression constrains and limits our existential freedom. Aaron did not kill himself with blasphemies on his lips. His suicide was not the culmination of a wicked life. It was an escape from a world that could not heal the sickness of his mind and bring relief from intolerable suffering. Aaron jumped to his death because he had lost all hope, because despair had possessed his being. This I believe to be true. And so, I know that God will be merciful.

But I wish to say something more. Not only will the eternal Father be merciful to my Aaron; but he will most assuredly heal his heart, deliver him from the bonds of darkness, and raise him into glorified life with Jesus Christ the eternal Son, with the Blessed Virgin Mary and with all the saints. Aaron will know the joy and bliss of the kingdom of God.

Despite his suicidal disbelief, Aaron will not be permitted to have the last word. The risen Christ reserves that word to himself, and it is a word of the absolute triumph of love and grace. By the inner promptings of the Holy Spirit, Aaron will open his heart to the mercy and love of God. He will allow the Father to flood him with his holy light and liberate him from darkness. He will allow the Savior to bind his wounds and forgive his sins. He will allow the Spirit to fill his heart with joy and grace. Painful purification may be necessary—it is not easy thing to relinquish our self-will; it is not an easy thing to repent of one's sins—but the grace of God will triumph in the heart of my son. This I declare in the name of Jesus. Amen. Amen.

Funeral Homily for Aaron Edward Kimel

Brought face to face with his Savior, can we entertain, even for one moment, the possibility that Aaron would hold out eternally against that unconditional love and mercy that is the Father, Son, and Holy Spirit? How could he? Did he not love his mother? Did he not love his siblings, Alvin, Bredon, and Taryn? Did he not love his best friends Bryan, Jill, and Laura? Did he not love me, his broken father?

Brothers and sisters, there is no time limit on the unbounded love of God. It does not expire at the moment of death. God has created us for himself. In love Christ searches and searches for that one lost sheep and does not rest until he has found it and restored it to the fold.

Aaron's ultimate salvation is revealed in the love I hold in my heart for my beloved son. In the words of the Scottish preacher George MacDonald:

> Shall a man be more merciful than God? Shall, of all his glories, his mercy alone not be infinite? Shall a brother love a brother more than The Father loves a son?—more than The Brother Christ loves his brother?

God forbid! God's love infinitely surpasses our love for Aaron. God will find a way to awaken faith and repentance in his heart. Divine love will conquer both obstinacy and despair. "God's mercifulness," as St Isaac writes, "is far more extensive than we can conceive."

I will not be saved without my Aaron. There can be no heaven for me without my son. My love for him is too great. He is too much a part of my life, my identity. We will be saved together in Christ. God will make it so.

And so, my brothers and sisters, I bid you to give thanks for the life that was, and is, Aaron Edward Kimel.

Destined for Joy

I bid you to pray for my son. Pray that God will forgive his sins, heal his brokenness, and renew his heart and soul in the life and glory of the Holy Spirit.

And I bid you to hope for Aaron's eternal salvation with confident and indomitable hope. He will be restored to us in the kingdom of Jesus Christ, and we will be restored to him. Our love will not be broken; our love is not broken. The infinite, unfathomable grace of God will triumph.

God is good.
God is merciful.
God is love.

I close with the words of the Lord spoken to Dame Julian of Norwich in the 13th century:

> *All shall be well,*
> *and all shall be well,*
> *and all manner of thing shall be well.*

Amen.

Index

aion 128, 131n3, 133n6, 135-37, 137, 139-40, 140n16, 144, 149n33
   aionios (αιωνιος) xvii, 127, 127n1, 128-29, 131-34, 131n3, 135-37, 137n9, 139-42, 144-50, 149n33
   aeon/aeonian 129
   adialeiptos 138
   aperantos/apeirous 138, 142
   ateleutos 138
   aidios (αιδιος) 136, 137n9, 141, 149, 149n33
   eonios/eonian 128-29, 131n3, 142
Alighieri, Dante 38-39, 383, 385, 385n21
Allin, Thomas xvi, 131n3, 225
Annihilationism 352
Anthony the Great 227
Anthropomorphism 122, 282, 299
Antipatrus of Bostra 234-35
Apollinarius 224
Arius 224
Aquinas, Thomas 119-120, 204, 300, 305, 323, 353
Augustine 47, 92, 208, 227-28, 268-70, 309, 311, 331-32
   on the *misericordes* 153
Balthasar, Hans Urs von 5, 51, 90, 165n14, 174, 263, 297, 338
Barth, Karl 297, 389, 395
Basil the Great 46-47, 143, 226, 289

Bauckham, Richard 153, 159, 162-63, 166
Benedict, Pope 173, 388
Bernard of Clairvaux 47, 316
Brock, Sebastian 178, 379
Bulgakov, Sergius xviii, 51
   on salvation of demons 195-201, *passim*
   his view distinct from that condemned by the Fifth Ecumenical Council 263-65
   view on dogmatic status of universalism 267-69, 273
   on the Afterlife 367-74, *passim*
   on *post obitum* repentance and the prayers of the Church 375-76
   on the sufferings of the damned 377-81, *passim*
   on Hell as purgation 381-87, *passim*
   on the irresistible truth of final judgment 398-404, *passim*
Capon, Robert Farrar xvii, 9, 11, 13, 106-126, *passim*
Casiday, Augustine 257, 260
Chrysostom, John 103, 276, 366, 388
Constantinople I, II 229n6, 242n21, 244-45, 250, 251n33, 252, 257, 299n6
Council of Ephesus (431) 228
Council of Nicaea (I) 226

Nicaea (II) 272
creatio ex nihilo 297-98, 301, 303
Clement of Alexandria 147, 227
Clement, Olivier 357
Craig, William Lane 361
Cyril of Scythopolis 248, 250, 261

Determinism 73, 276, 317-18, 340
   See also Freedom
Didymus the Blind 227, 245n26, 248-52, 254, 254n40, 255-57, 261, 271-72
Diekamp, Franz 241-42, 245, 253
Diodore of Tarsus 183, 226
Donne, John 316
Dostoyevski 171
Duffy, Stephen J. 311, 332-33

Egan, Maurice Francis 384
Eliot, T. S. 118
Epiphanius 156, 225, 227-28
Esolen, Anthony 383
Eucharist 81-82, 92, 124, 154
Eunomius 223
Eusebius of Caesarea 226
Evagrius of Pontus 244, 245n26, 246, 248-51, 254-57, 260-61, 271-72
Evagrius Scholasticus 242. 252-54, 256
Evdokimov, Paul 270, 339

Fifteen Anathemas 223, 237, 242n21, 243, 245-46, 256-57, 259, 262, 271
Fifth Ecumenical Council 223-274
Florovsky, Georges 110n4

Forde, Gerhard xvii, 84-88, 91, 320n18
Foreknowledge 180-81, 207, 294
Freedom
   libertarian 186, 277, 279, 286, 293, 328, 336, 340, 344-47, 408
   free will 38, 71, 101, 158, 205, 227, 276-77, 283-84, 287, 293, 318, 328-29, 336, 339-40, 342, 344, 346, 404
Gavrilyuk, Paul 382
Gehenna 40, 127, 143-44, 148, 150, 169-70, 174, 177, 178-189, *passim*, 377-387, *passim*
   See also Hades, Tartarus
Gregory of Nazianzus xiv, 226, 228
Gregory of Nyssa 141n20, 196n11, 226, 232, 257, 259, 262-63, 265, 268-69, 271, 298, 314
Gregory Thaumaturgus 226
Gregory the Great 223, 240
Gregory the Theologian 226
Grillmeier, Alois
   on the Fifteen Anathemas 241, 242n21
Hades 169, 287, 364, 366, 369, 373, 395
   See also Gehenna, Tartarus
Hanson, James Wesley 140n16, 142, 227, 227n4, 263
Hart, David Bentley 51, 129, 132, 176n14, 263, 265, 297-98, 309, 311-12, 316, 343-44, 357-58, 360
Hell *See* Gehenna, Hades, Tartarus
Heretic(al)

Index

Augustine on heretical status of universalism 158
Canon 11 on various heretical persons and teachings 224
misericordes not found heretical by Augustine 159
on the heretical status of universalism 153, 257, 267
re: Origen 158
said of Origen by Fifth Council 266
said of Origen by Jerome 156n6
Hilarion Alfeyev 1, 2, 5, 188-89, 269-70, 270n58, 364-66, *passim*, 375, 395
Hombergen, Daniel 241, 248-49, 254

Infernalist 44, 51, 226, 357,
Impassible (impassibility) 5, 12, 191-92, 364,
Isaac the Syrian xiv, 1, 7, 35, 45, 51, 220, 262, 272, 333, 378, 380, 402, 410, 415,
on the injustice of grace 23-25
on the scourge of love 168-177, *passim*
on the horror of eternal damnation 178-89, *passim*
on God's love for Satan 191-195, *passim*, 201
Isochristoi 244, 260-61, 265n54

Jenson, Robert xvii, 49-50, 52, 82, 84, 102
on the Gospel as story and promise 56-79, *passim*

on the task of preaching and proclamation 98-100, 104
Jeremias II (Patriarch) 47-49
Jerome 149, 156, 156n6, 159, 161n9, 167, 225, 228,
John of Damascus 50, 173, 335, 394
John Paul II 25-26, 28-29
Julian of Norwich xvii, 51, 171, 419
The Shewings 202-21, *passim*
Justice
compared to grace 20-29, *passim*
relative to wrath and retribution per MacDonald's "Justice" 30-40, *passim*
retributive/punitive vs restorative 33, 37, 184, 385
Justinian 141-42, 223
on Origen and the 543 Synod 229-271, *passim*
Edict of 235

Kalomiros, Alexandre 289-90
Konstan, David 15-16, 134, 135n8, 136, 136n8, 137, 141
Kreeft, Peter 171-72
Kronen, John 327-28, 354-56, 358
Kvanvig, Jonathan 172-73

L'Engle, Madeleine 396
Lewis, C. S. 170-72, 277, 340,
The Great Divorce 349-50, 352
The Problem of Pain 171
Lindbeck, George 105
Luther, Martin 25, 69-70, 77, 106, 116, 357

MacDonald, George xvii, 54, 280-82, 349, 385n21, 405-06, 408, 418
   on the hermeneutics of love 33-35
   on the injustice of retribution 30-32, *passim*
   on the obligations of love 36,
   on the salvation of outer darkness 37-44, 293-94, *passim*
   Robert Falconer 39
   See also MacDonald's "Justice" under Justice
Marcellus of Ancyra 226-27
Macrina the Younger xi, 226
Mark of Ephesus 174
Mary, The Virgin (*theotokos*) 214, 216, 406, 417
Maximus the Confessor 51, 309, 317, 331, 365
McCabe, Herbert 7-8, 11-13, 16-18, 285, 343,
   God, Christ, and Us 13, 16
   God Still Matters 285, 343
McGuckin, John Anthony 343-44
Merton, Thomas 220-21
Metallinos, George 174-75
Methodius of Olympus 226-27
Milton, John 284-86

Nestorius 224, 271
Neuhaus, Richard John 338

olam 133, 133-34n6
   See also aion
Omniscience 176n14, 181, 302, 304, 329,

Origen
   on *aionios* ch 10, *passim*
   on *misericordes* ch 11, *passim*
   on *the salvation of Satan*, ch 14, *passim*
   on The Fifth Ecumenical Council ch 16, *passim*
Oxenham, F. Nutcombe 224, 225n2, 229n6, 232, 233n9, 245n26, 249, 251, 251n33, 253n36, 254n40, 255, 257n44-45, 266n55, 274

Palamas, Gregory 177
Paradise 168-69, 171, 174, 290-91, 367, 370, 374, 384
parousia 116, 197-98, 221, 378, 399-401, 404-05
Parry, Robin 149, 150n34
Participation 332, 374
Patriarch Theophilus 156, 225
Pascha 53, 61, 64, 67-68, 78, 87, 98, 102, 110, 150, 297, 367, 395-96, 398
Passions 95, 311, 324, 335, 342,
Pelagius (Pelagian/ism) 229, 232n8, 235, 240
Pelphrey, Brendan 210-11
Plato 136, 263-65
   Platonic/Neoplatonism 120, 142, 145, 326
Plotinus 265
Price, Richard 231 231n7-8
Purgatory 39, 172, 335, 370, 372, 378-388, *passim*

Ramelli, Ilaria 134-35, 137, 141, 227n4, 260, 261n51, 262-63

Index

Reitan, Eric xviii, 328-29, 345-48, 355-57, 359
Retribution *See* Justice
Robinson, J. A. T. 57, 296

sola fide 25, 86,
sola gratia 47
Synodikon, The 267, 273
Synod of Alexandria 156, 225
Sanders, E. P. 57, 114-115
Satan
  on the salvation of 190-201, *passim*
Sophrony, St. 357
Staniloae, Dumitru 50, 321

Tartarus 38, 142
  See also Hades, Gehenna
Theosis 6, 71, 91-92, 95, 141, 322-23, 324n20, 334, 392

Transworld damnation 362-63
Talbott, Thomas xv, xviii, 145-46, 278-85, 288-96, 328, 335-337, 344-45, 349, 351-352, 357, 359
Tanner, Norman 223
Tarasius (Patriarch) 250-51, 251n33
Theodoret 140n16, 250
Torrance, Thomas xvii, 82, 85, 296-97, 396
Torrance, James 83-84
Turner, Denys 205, 211-12, 218-19
Tzamalikos, Panayiotis 234-236

Walls, Jerry 285, 234, 386-87
Ware, Kallistos 51, 174, 190, 258-59, 263, 339
Weinsinck, A. J. 380
Williams, Charles 316

About the Author

Fr Aidan (Alvin) Kimel is a retired Orthodox priest. Before entering the Orthodox Church, he served for twenty-five years as a parish priest in the Episcopal Church. He has edited two books and has published several essays in various theological journals. He, his beautiful wife Christine, and two Collies live in Roanoke, Virginia. He is also a passionate wearer of fedoras. For the past decade he has blogged regularly on Eclectic Orthodoxy (https://afkimel.wordpress.com/).

Made in United States
North Haven, CT
22 April 2025